MODERN EGYPT

BY

THE EARL OF CROMER

In his first interview with the Governor of St. Helena, Napoleon said emphatically : " Egypt is the most important country in the world."

Rose, *Life of Napoleon*, vol. i. p. 356.

Earum proprie rerum sit historia, quibus rebus gerendis interfuerit is qui narret.

Gellius, *Noctes Atticae*, v. 18.

τὰ δ' ἔργα τῶν πραχθέντων ἐν τῷ πολέμῳ οὐκ ἐκ τοῦ παρατυχόντος πυνθανόμενος ἠξίωσα γράφειν, οὐδ' ὡς ἐμοὶ ἐδόκει, ἀλλ' οἷς τε αὐτὸς παρῆν, καὶ παρὰ τῶν ἄλλων ὅσον δυνατὸν ἀκριβείᾳ περὶ ἑκάστου ἐπεξελθών.

Thucydides, i. 22.

IN TWO VOLUMES

VOL. I

New York

THE MACMILLAN COMPANY

1908

PREFACE

I AM wholly responsible for the contents of this book. It has no official character whatsoever.

CROMER.

London,
December 31, 1907.

EXPLANATORY NOTE

P.T. 1 (Piastre Tariff)   . $= 2\frac{1}{2}$d. $= 26$ centimes.

£E.1 (Egyptian pound)   . $= $ P.T. $100 = £1:0:6 = 25\cdot9$ fr.

1 kantar   .   .   .   . $= 99\cdot05$ lbs. $=$ about 45 kilog.

1 ardeb   .   .   .   . $=$ about $5\frac{1}{2}$ bushels $= 198$ litres.

1 feddan   .   .   .   . $= 1\cdot038$ acres $=$ about $\cdot42$ hectare.

(A feddan and an acre are so nearly equal that in this work the two measures have been considered equivalent.)

CONTENTS

CHAPTER I

INTRODUCTORY

PART I

ISMAIL PASHA

1863-1879

CHAPTER II

THE GOSCHEN MISSION

NOVEMBER 1876

CHAPTER III

THE COMMISSION OF INQUIRY

NOVEMBER 1876-APRIL 1878

ix

CHAPTER IV

THE NUBAR-WILSON MINISTRY

APRIL 1878-NOVEMBER 1878

CHAPTER V

THE FALL OF NUBAR PASHA

NOVEMBER 1878-FEBRUARY 1879

CHAPTER VI

THE COUP D'ÉTAT

APRIL 1879

CONTENTS

CHAPTER VII

THE REPORT OF THE COMMISSION

APRIL 1879

CHAPTER VIII

THE FALL OF ISMAIL PASHA

APRIL–JUNE 1879

CHAPTER XII

THE CHÉRIF MINISTRY

SEPTEMBER–DECEMBER 1881

CHAPTER XIII

THE JOINT NOTE

JANUARY 1882

CHAPTER XIV

THE EFFECTS OF THE JOINT NOTE

JANUARY–FEBRUARY 1882

CONTENTS

PART III

THE SOUDAN

1882–1907

CHAPTER XIX

THE HICKS EXPEDITION

JANUARY–NOVEMBER 1883

CHAPTER XX

THE ABANDONMENT OF THE SOUDAN

NOVEMBER 1883–JANUARY 1884

CONTENTS

PAGE

CHAPTER XXVII

The Relief Expedition

April 21–October 5, 1884

CHAPTER I

Objects of this book—The narrative portion—The effects on Egypt of
the British occupation—Chief point of interest in Egyptian reform
—Difficulty of ascertaining Eastern opinion.

My object in writing this book is twofold.

In the first place, I wish to place on record an
accurate narrative of some of the principal events
which have occurred in Egypt and in the Soudan
since the year 1876.[1]

In the second place, I wish to explain the
results which have accrued to Egypt from the
British occupation of the country in 1882.

The accidents of my public life have afforded
me special opportunities for compiling certain
chapters of Egyptian history. From March 1877
to June 1880, and again from September 1883 up
to the present time (1907), I have been behind the
scenes of Egyptian affairs. Besides those sources
of information which are open to all the world, I
have had access to all the documents in the archives
of the Foreign Offices of both London and Cairo,
and I have been in close communication with, I
think, almost every one who has taken a leading

[1] I have dealt fully and unreservedly with the whole of the principal
historical events which occurred in Egypt from 1876 up to the time
of Tewfik Pasha's death (January 7, 1892); also with Soudan history
up to the end of 1907. It would, in my opinion, be premature to
deal similarly with events in Egypt subsequent to the accession of the
present Khedive.

part in Egyptian affairs during the period the history of which I have attempted to write. Thus, I think I may fairly lay claim to be in a position of exceptional advantage in so far as the attainment of accuracy is concerned.

Now, accuracy of statement is a great merit. Sir Arthur Helps once said that half the evils of the world come from inaccuracy. My personal experience would lead me rather to agree with him. I cannot say that what I have seen and known of contemporaneous events, with which I have been well acquainted, has inspired me with any great degree of confidence in the accuracy of historical writing. The public, indeed, generally end, though sometimes not till after a considerable lapse of time, in getting a correct idea of the general course of events, and of the cause or effect of any special political incident. But, speaking more particularly of the British public, it may be doubted whether even this result is fully achieved, save in respect to questions of internal policy. In such matters, a number of competent and well-informed persons take part in the discussions which arise in Parliament and in the press. Inaccuracy of statement is speedily corrected. Fallacies are exposed. In the heat of party warfare the truth may for a time be obscured, but in the end the public will generally lay hold of a tolerably correct appreciation of the facts.

In dealing with the affairs of a foreign country, more especially if that country be in a semi-civilised condition, these safeguards to historical truth exist in a relatively less degree. English opinion has in such cases to deal with a condition of society with which it is unfamiliar. It is disposed to apply arguments drawn from English, or, it may be, from European experience to a state of things which does not admit of any such arguments being applied without great qualifications. The number of persons who possess sufficiently accurate information to instruct the public is limited, and amongst those persons it not unfrequently happens that many have some particular cause to advance, or some favourite political theory to defend. Those who are most qualified to speak often occupy some official position, which, for the time being, imposes silence upon them. There is, therefore, no certain guarantee that inaccuracies of statement will be corrected, or that fallacies will be adequately exposed. Thus, even if the general conclusion be correct, there is a risk that an erroneous appreciation in respect to important matters of detail will float down the tide of history. The public often seize on some incident which strikes the popular imagination, or idealise the character of some individual whose action excites sympathy or admiration. It would appear, indeed, that democracy tends to develop rather than to discourage hero-worship.

The first stage on the road to historical inaccuracy is that some half-truth is stated, and, in spite of contradiction, obtains a certain amount of credence. It may be, indeed, that the error is corrected; but it sometimes happens that, as time goes on, the measure of fiction increases, whilst that of fact tends to evaporate. A series of myths cluster round the original idea or statement. In India, as Sir Alfred Lyall has shown, the hero passes by easy stages of transition into a demi-god.[1] In sceptical Europe, the process is different. All that happens is that an incorrect fact or a faulty conclusion is graven into the tablets from which future historians must draw their sources of information.

Turning to the second point to which allusion is made above, I wish to explain the results which

[1] *Asiatic Studies.*

accrued to Egypt from the British occupation of
the country in 1882.

On March 23, 1876, Mr. Stephen Cave, who
had been sent to Cairo to report on the financial
condition of Egypt, expressed himself in the following terms :—

Egypt may be said to be in a transition state, and she
suffers from the defects of the system out of which she is
passing, as well as from those of the system into which she
is attempting to enter. She suffers from the ignorance, dishonesty, waste, and extravagance of the East, such as have
brought her suzerain to the verge of ruin, and at the same
time from the vast expense caused by hasty and inconsiderate
endeavours to adopt the civilisation of the West.

An attempt will be made in the following pages
to give some account of the measures adopted since
Mr. Cave wrote his report, to arrest, and, as I hope
and would fain believe, to remedy the disease,
whose main features are described with accuracy
in the passage quoted above.

I trust that such an account will not be devoid
of interest to the general reader, and that it will
be of some special interest to those of my fellow-
countrymen who are, or who at some future time
may be engaged in Oriental administration. It is
to this latter class that I would more especially
address myself, for they can appreciate the nature
of the problems which have presented themselves
for solution, and the difficulty of solving them,
more fully than those who are devoid of special
administrative experience in the East.

I would at the outset state where, as I venture
to think, the chief point of interest lies.

Egypt is not the only country which has been
brought to the verge of ruin by a persistent neglect
of economic laws and by a reckless administration
of the finances of the State. Neither is it the
only country in which undue privileges have been

acquired by the influential classes to the detriment
of the mass of the population. Nor is it the only
country in whose administration the most elementary principles of law and justice have been ignored.
Although the details may differ, there is a great
similarity in the general character of the abuses
which spring up under Eastern Governments where-
soever they may be situated. So also, although
the remedies to be applied must vary according to
local circumstances and according to the character,
institutions, and habits of thought of the European
nation under whose auspices reforms are initiated,
the broad lines which those reforms must take are
traced out by the commonplace requirements of
European civilisation, and must of necessity present
some identity of character, whether the scene of
action be India, Algiers, Egypt, Tunis, or Bosnia.

The history of reform in Egypt, therefore, does
not present any striking feature to which some
analogy might not perhaps be found in other
countries where European civilisation has, in a
greater or less degree, been grafted on a backward
Eastern Government and society.

But, so far as I am aware, no counterpart can
be found to the special circumstances which have
attended the work of Egyptian reform. Those
circumstances have, in truth, been very peculiar.

In the first place, one alien race, the English,
have had to control and guide a second alien race,
the Turks, by whom they are disliked, in the
government of a third race, the Egyptians. To
these latter, both the paramount races are to a
certain extent unsympathetic. In the case of the
Turks, the want of sympathy has been mitigated
by habit, by a common religion, and by the use
of a common language.[1] In the case of the
English, it has been mitigated by the respect

[1] All the Egyptian officials of Turkish origin now speak Arabic.

due to superior talents, and by the benefits which have accrued to the population from British interference.

In the second place, it is to be observed that for diplomatic and other reasons, on which it is unnecessary for the moment to dwell, the Egyptian administration had to be reformed without any organic changes being effected in the conditions under which the government had been conducted prior to the British occupation. Those conditions were of an exceptionally complicated character. A variety of ingenious and elaborate checks had been invented with a view to preventing a bad Government from moving in a vicious direction. These checks, when brought into action under a wholly different condition of affairs, were at times applied, under the baneful impulse of international jealousy, to hamper the movements of an improved Government in the direction of reform. "Je suis sans crédit," said the "plumitif" in Voltaire's *Ingénu*, "pour faire du bien ; mon pouvoir se borne à faire du mal quelquefois." The phrase may rightly be applied to the working of international government in Egypt since 1882. It is, indeed, certain that whatever success has attended the efforts of reformers in Egypt has been attained, not in virtue of the system, but in spite of it. Those who hold, with the English poet, that "Whate'er is best administered is best," may perhaps find some corroboration of their theory in the recent history of Egypt. An experiment under somewhat novel conditions has, in fact, been made in Eastern administration, and, in spite of many shortcomings, this experiment has been crowned with a certain degree of success. It is this which gives to Egyptian reform its chief claim to the interest of the political student.

I have lived too long in the East not to be

aware that it is difficult for any European to
arrive at a true estimate of Oriental wishes, aspirations, and opinions.

Those who have been in the East and have tried to mingle
with the native population know well how utterly impossible
it is for the European to look at the world with the same
eyes as the Oriental. For a while, indeed, the European
may fancy that he and the Oriental understand one another,
but sooner or later a time comes when he is suddenly
awakened from his dream, and finds himself in the presence
of a mind which is as strange to him as would be the mind
of an inhabitant of Saturn.[1]

I was for some while in Egypt before I fully
realised how little I understood my subject; and
I found, to the last day of my residence in the
country, that I was constantly learning something
new. No casual visitor can hope to obtain much
real insight into the true state of native opinion.
Divergence of religion and habits of thought; in
my own case ignorance of the vernacular language;[2]
the reticence of Orientals when speaking to any one
in authority; their tendency to agree with any one
to whom they may be talking; the want of mental
symmetry and precision, which is the chief dis-
tinguishing feature between the illogical and
picturesque East and the logical West, and which
lends such peculiar interest to the study of Eastern
life and politics; the fact that religion enters to a
greater extent than in Europe into the social life
and laws and customs of the people; and the
further fact that the European and the Oriental,
reasoning from the same premises, will often arrive
at diametrically opposite conclusions,—all these
circumstances place the European at a great disadvantage when he attempts to gauge Eastern

---

[1] Professor Sayce, *The Higher Criticism and the Monuments*, p. 558.
[2] I have a fair acquaintance with Turkish, but I do not speak
Arabic.

opinion. Nevertheless, the difficulty of arriving at a true idea of the undercurrents of native opinion is probably less considerable in Egypt than in India. Notably, the absence of the caste system, and the fact that the social and religious fabric of Islamism is more readily comprehensible to the European mind than the comparatively subtle and mystical bases of Hinduism, diminish the gulf which in India separates the European from the native, and which, by placing a check on social intercourse, becomes a fertile source of mutual misunderstanding. On the whole, though I should not like to dogmatise on the subject, I am inclined to think that by constantly seeing people of all classes, and by checking the information received from different sources, a fair idea of native opinion in Egypt may in time be formed.

I would add that it is not possible to live so long as I have lived in Egypt without acquiring a deep sympathy for the Egyptian people. The cause of Egyptian reform is one in which I take the warmest personal interest. A residence of half a lifetime in Eastern countries has made me realise the force of Rudyard Kipling's lines—

If you've heard the East a'calling,
You won't ever heed aught else.

PART I

ISMAIL PASHA

1863-1879

It were good that men in their Innovations would follow the example of Time itself, which, indeed, innovateth greatly, but quietly, and by degrees scarce to be perceived. . . . It is good also not to try experiments in States except the necessity be urgent, or the utility evident ; and well to beware that it be the reformation that draweth on the change, and not the desire of change that pretendeth the reformation.

BACON, *On Innovations.*

It is singular how long the rotten will hold together provided you do not handle it roughly . . . so loth are men to quit their old ways ; and conquering indolence and inertia, venture on new. . . . Rash enthusiast of change, beware !   Hast thou well considered all that Habit does in this life of ours ?

CARLYLE, *French Revolution.*

CHAPTER II

THE GOSCHEN MISSION

NOVEMBER 1876

Financial position in 1863—And in 1876—Suspension of payment of Treasury Bills—Creation of the Commission of the Public Debt—Decree of May 7, 1876—The Goschen Mission—Decree of November 18, 1876—Appointment of Controllers-General—Sir Louis Mallet—I am appointed Commissioner of the Public Debt—Ismail's predecessors—Crisis in the career of Ismail Pasha—Accounts Department.

THE origin of the Egyptian Question in its present phase was financial.

In 1863, when Said Pasha died, the public debt of Egypt amounted to £3,293,000. Said Pasha was succeeded by Ismail Pasha, the son of the celebrated Ibrahim Pasha, and the grandson of the still more celebrated Mehemet Ali.

In 1876, the funded debt of Egypt, including the Daira loans, amounted to £68,110,000. In addition to this, there was a floating debt of about £26,000,000.

Roughly speaking, it may be said that Ismail Pasha added, on an average, about £7,000,000 a year for thirteen years to the debt of Egypt. For all practical purposes it may be said that the whole of the borrowed money, except £16,000,000 spent on the Suez Canal, was squandered.[1]

[1] Mr. Cave, after making out a balance-sheet for the years from 1864 to 1875, adds: "Two striking features stand out in this balance-sheet, namely, that the sum raised by revenue, £94,281,401, is little

11

For some while prior to the general breakdown,
it had been apparent that Ismail Pasha's reckless
administration of the finances of the country must,
sooner or later, bring about a financial collapse.
Towards the latter part of 1875 and the beginning
of 1876, money was raised at ruinous rates of interest by the issue of Treasury bills.   On April 8,
1876, the crash came.   The Khedive suspended
payment of his Treasury bills.

Previous to the suspension of payment, some
discussion had taken place with reference to the
creation of an Egyptian National Bank, which was
to be under the control of three European Commissioners.   France and Italy each agreed to select
a Commissioner, but Lord Derby, who then presided at the Foreign Office, was unwilling to
interfere in the internal affairs of Egypt, and
declined to nominate a British Commissioner.

The project, therefore, dropped, but was shortly
afterwards revived in a different form.   On May 2,
1876, a Khedivial Decree was issued instituting a
Commission of the Public Debt.   Certain specific
duties were assigned to the Commissioners, who
were to act generally as representatives of the
bondholders.   On May 7, a further Decree was
issued consolidating the debt of Egypt, which
then amounted to £91,000,000.

M. de Blignières, Herr von Kremer, a distinguished Orientalist, and M. Baravelli were
nominated to be Commissioners of the Debt at
the instance, respectively, of the French, Austrian,
and Italian Governments.   The British Government declined to select a Commissioner.

less than that spent on administration, tribute to the Porte, works of
unquestionable utility, and certain expenses of questionable utility or
policy, in all amounting to £97,240,966, and that for the present large
amount of indebtedness there is absolutely nothing to show but the
Suez Canal, the whole proceeds of the loans and floating debt having
been absorbed in payment of interest and sinking funds, with the
exception of the sum debited to that great work."

The financial arrangements embodied in the Decree of May 7, 1876, caused much dissatisfaction, especially in England, with the result that Mr. (subsequently Lord) Goschen undertook a mission to Egypt with a view to obtaining some modifications which the bondholders considered necessary.

Lord Goschen, with whom M. Joubert was associated to represent French interests, arrived in Egypt in October 1876.

The arrangement negotiated by Messrs. Goschen and Joubert was embodied in a Decree, dated November 18, 1876. The chief financial features of this arrangement were as follows :—

The loans of 1864, 1865, and 1867, which had been contracted before the financial position of the Khedive had become seriously embarrassed, and the capital of which amounted in all to about £4,293,000, were taken out of the Unified Debt, into which they had been incorporated under the Decree of May 7, and formed the subject of a special arrangement.

A 5 per cent Preference Stock, intended to attract *bona-fide* investors, was created, with a capital of £17,000,000.

The Daira debts, amounting to about £8,815,000, which had, under the Decree of May 7, been included in the Unified Debt, were again deducted, and ultimately formed the subject of a separate arrangement.

The capital of the Unified Debt was thus reduced to £59,000,000. The rate of interest was fixed at 6 per cent, to which a sinking fund of 1 per cent was added.

So far as the effect produced on the future of Egypt was concerned, the purely financial arrangements negotiated by Lord Goschen were less productive of result than the changes which, under his advice, the Khedive introduced into the administration of the country. It was clear that, however rational any Egyptian financial combination might be, it would present but little hope of stability unless the fiscal administration of the country was improved. It was, therefore, decided to appoint two Controllers-General, one of whom was to supervise the revenue, and the other the expenditure. The railways and the port of Alexandria, the revenues of which were to be applied to the payment of interest on the Preference Stock, were to be administered by a Board composed of two Englishmen, a Frenchman, and two Egyptians.

Mr. Romaine was appointed Controller-General of the Revenue and the Baron de Malaret Controller - General of Expenditure. General Marriott was appointed President of the Railway Board. Lord Derby instructed Lord Vivian, who was at this time British representative in Egypt, to inform the Khedive that "Her Majesty's Government could not accept any responsibility for these appointments, to which, however, they had no objection to offer."

About the same time, the Khedive applied to Lord Goschen to nominate an English Commissioner of the Public Debt, the British Government having again declined to assume the responsibility of nomination.

In May 1876, I returned from India, where I had for four years occupied the post of Private Secretary to the Viceroy, Lord Northbrook. I had, in connection with Indian affairs, been brought much in contact with the late Sir Louis Mallet, who was then Under-Secretary of State at the India Office.

I cannot pass by the mention of Sir Louis Mallet's name without paying a tribute of respect to his memory.   To myself his death was an irreparable loss.   Whenever I visited England during the last few years of his life, I always discussed with him the difficulties of the situation in which I was placed in Egypt.   They were at one time very great.   Sir Louis Mallet was not personally acquainted with the details of Egyptian affairs, but, besides the intimate knowledge which he possessed of economic science, of which he had made a special study, his high-minded attachment to principle and his keen insight into the forces in motion in the political world rendered his advice of the utmost value.   He was the best type of the English civil servant; a keen politician but not a political partisan, a trained official without a trace of the bureaucratic element in him, and a man of really liberal aspirations without being carried away by the catchwords which sometimes attach themselves to what, from a party point of view, is called liberal policy in England.

Lord Goschen consulted Sir Louis Mallet as to whom he should nominate as Commissioner of the Debt in Egypt.   Sir Louis Mallet recommended me.   Lord Goschen offered me the post, which I accepted.   I arrived in Egypt on March 2, 1877.

I would here pause in order to make some observations which are suggested by these appointments.

This period constituted the turning-point of Ismail Pasha's career.   The system of government which existed in Egypt during the pre-reforming days was very defective, but it possessed some barbaric virtues, and was perhaps more suited to the country than Europeans, judging from their own standpoint, are often disposed to admit.

The manufacturers of myths have, of course,

been at work at Mehemet Ali's career. They often credit him with ideas and intentions which were absolutely foreign to his nature. Nevertheless, the Egyptians are right to venerate the memory of this rough man of genius, if only for the reason that to him belongs the credit of having amputated their country from the decaying body of the Ottoman Empire, thus giving it a separate administrative existence. Moreover, there was much in Mehemet Ali's character which was really worthy of admiration. He was a brave and capable soldier. He had some statesmanlike instincts, and, though his lights were rude, nevertheless he used them to the best of his ability in furthering the interests of his adopted country, as he understood those interests. He proceeded tentatively along the path of reform. He summoned to Egypt a few Europeans, mostly Frenchmen, of high professional merit.[1] He founded the Polytechnic School, the School of Medicine, and some other similar institutions. Under the direction of M. Jumel, the cotton plant was introduced into the country.

Sir John Bowring, in a report addressed to Lord Palmerston in 1840, said :—[2]

---

[1] One of the predominating ideas in Mehemet Ali's mind was to use French as a counterpoise to British influence in Egypt, not because he had any particular love for the French or dislike of the English, but because, with the instinct of a true statesman, he foresaw that the force of circumstances might, and probably would drive England into an aggressive policy against Egypt. Mr. Cameron (*Egypt in the Nineteenth Century*, p. 105) says that when the celebrated traveller, Burckhardt, visited Egypt in 1814, Mehemet Ali "asked him about England and our plans in the East. He dreaded lest Wellington should invade Egypt with the Peninsular Army. 'The great fish swallow the small,' he said; 'I am afraid of the English, and hope they will not attack Egypt in my absence. . . . England must some day take Egypt as her share of the spoil of the Turkish Empire.'"

[2] The whole of this report, which is but little known, is well worthy of perusal by any one who takes an interest in Egyptian affairs. The history of the early part of Mehemet Ali's reign has been written by a contemporary, Sheikh Abdul-Rahman el-Jabarti. The Sheikh wrote from a strongly Egyptian, that is to say anti-Turkish point of view.

Egypt has, indeed, received immense benefit from the presence of Europeans. They have not only rendered direct services by the knowledge they have communicated, but the circumstance of their having been so much associated with all the improvements which have been introduced has diffused a great respect for their superior acquirements, and a toleration for their opinions, whose influence has been spreading widely among the people.

But, although Mehemet Ali dallied with European civilisation in a manner which was by no means unintelligent and was far less hurtful to his country than that adopted by Said and Ismail, his methods of government were, in reality, wholly Oriental. Those methods may be illustrated by the following anecdote, which I give on the authority of Nubar Pasha.

At the beginning of the war which Mehemet Ali waged against the Porte, the Admiral in command of the Turkish Fleet in Egyptian waters, who was a man of noted courage and ability, was summoned to Constantinople. He probably had more to gain than to lose by deserting the Egyptian cause. He decided, however, to throw in his lot with Mehemet Ali. His decision contributed materially to the eventual victory of Egypt. After the war was over, the Admiral was again summoned to Constantinople. To have obeyed at that time would have meant certain death. The Admiral, therefore, remained at Cairo, and, for four years, enjoyed Mehemet Ali's protection, which he had so well deserved. At the end of that period— whether it was that Mehemet Ali wished to ingratiate himself with the Sultan, who continued to press his request, or whether he had for other

He does justice to Mehemet Ali's military qualities, but he gives an unfavourable account of the condition of the country and of the system of government adopted during Mehemet Ali's time. See also St. John's *Egypt under Mohammed Ali*, published in 1834, and Cameron's *Egypt in the Nineteenth Century*, 1898.

reasons become estranged from the Admiral—he determined to withdraw his protection. He sent one of his confidential agents to visit the Admiral. A short conversation, which it would be difficult to rival in pathos and dramatic effect, ensued. The agent, after the usual Oriental compliments, merely said, 'Life, O Admiral, is uncertain. We must all be prepared to meet our death at any moment." The Admiral at once took the hint. He knew what those fatal words meant. The tenets of his religion had taught him not to resist the decrees of fate. Like many a Stoic philosopher of Ancient Rome, he had probably at times reflected that a self-inflicted death was, as a last resource, a sure refuge from earthly tyranny and injustice, however galling. He merely asked for time to say his prayers, and, when these were completed, drank, without complaint or remonstrance, the poisoned cup of coffee which was offered to him. On the following day, it was announced that he had died suddenly of apoplexy.

Ibrahim, the son and successor of Mehemet Ali, was a distinguished soldier, and a man of great personal courage. It must be added that he was a half-lunatic savage. He it was who commanded the expedition sent to Nejd against the Wahabis. A number of orthodox Mollahs accompanied the expedition. When the military operations had been terminated by the success of the Egyptian arms, Ibrahim arranged that his Mollahs and the religious leaders of the Wahabi sect should meet and discuss the dogmatic and ceremonial points of difference which separated them. After the lapse of three days, Ibrahim inquired what had been the result of their discussions. He was informed that neither party had been able to convert the other to its special views. Ibrahim then said that under the circumstances, although he was no theologian, he must decide the matter for himself. He ordered all the religious leaders of the Wahabi sect to be killed.[1]

Nubar Pasha once related to me an episode in his relations with Ibrahim, which did great credit to his own remarkable conversational powers. He and others were on board a steamer, which was conveying Ibrahim and his suite from Constantinople to Egypt. On nearing Alexandria, Nubar learnt that Ibrahim had suddenly decided that the members of his suite, including Nubar himself, should be thrown overboard. Thereupon, Nubar went to Ibrahim's cabin, entirely ignored the fate which awaited himself and his comrades, and began to talk to Ibrahim of his campaigns. Ibrahim was so much pleased at the flattery which was abundantly administered to him, and also so much interested in all that Nubar said, that for the moment he forgot his recent decision. The conversation continued until the ship arrived at Alexandria. Thus, Nubar and his companions were saved.

Ibrahim died, very shortly after his accession, of pneumonia, brought on, it is said, by drinking two bottles of highly iced champagne at a draught when he was very hot.[2]

Abbas, the next Khedive, was an Oriental despot of the worst type. The stories of his revolting cruelty are endless. There does not appear, as in the case of his predecessors, to have been

---

[1] Palgrave, *Central and Eastern Arabia*, vol. ii. p. 58.

[2] Mr. Pickthall, writing of Ibrahim Pasha's administration of Syria, says: "The radicalism of Ibrahim made his rule offensive to the conservative notables of Syria. Still, he was the kind of tyrant to appeal most strongly to Orientals, heavy-handed but humorous, knowing how to impart to his decisions that quaint proverbial savour which dwells in the mind of the people, and makes good stories; and his fame among the fellaheen is that of a second Solomon."—*Folk-Lore of the Holy Land*, Preface, p. xvi.

My earliest connection with Egyptian affairs was, as a child, being one of a large crowd waiting in St James's Park to see Ibrahim Pasha pass. This must have been in 1846 or 1847. The Londoners called him "Abraham Parker."

any redeeming feature in his character.   It was altogether odious.

The main defects of Said Pasha, who succeeded Abbas, were excessive vanity and hopeless incapacity in the art of government. His follies were duly chronicled by Mr. Senior, who visited Egypt during his reign.   Although less ferocious than his immediate predecessor, he occasionally committed acts which would be considered extremely cruel, had their iniquity not been outrivalled by the deeds of Abbas.

I hesitate to relate the numerous stories which have been handed down to posterity about Abbas and Said.   At this distance of time, it is almost impossible to say how far they are true, and inasmuch as most of them bring out the characters of both of these princes in a highly unpleasant light, it is merely an act of posthumous justice to their memories not to relate them, unless their truth can be substantiated by absolutely trustworthy evidence.   The following, however, supposing it to be true—and it is not at all improbable—is relatively innocuous, and, moreover, is so highly illustrative of the manner in which Oriental despots occasionally jump from an extreme of injustice to a prodigality of generous munificence that I need not refrain from relating it.   On one occasion, Said was coming in a steamer from the Barrage to Cairo.   The Nile was low, and the steamer stuck in the mud.   Said ordered the *reis* (steersman) to receive a hundred blows with the courbash.   These were administered.   The steamer was got off the mud, and proceeded on her journey. Shortly afterwards, she stuck again.   Said roared out: "Give him two hundred," whereupon the unfortunate *reis* made a rush, and jumped overboard.   A boat was put off, and he was brought back to the steamer.   Said asked him why he had jumped overboard. The man explained that he preferred to run the risk of death by drowning to the agony caused by another flogging. "Fool," exclaimed Said, "when I said two hundred, I did not mean lashes, but sovereigns." And, accordingly, the man received a bag containing that amount of money. Eastern history abounds with episodes of this sort. Moreover, the minds of Orientals are so peculiarly constituted that many of them would probably be far more struck with the generosity of the gift than with the cruelty and injustice of the flogging.

Said occasionally indulged in the most insane freaks. Thus, in order to prove his courage, which had been called in question by the European press, it is said that he caused a kilometre of road to be strewn a foot deep with gunpowder. He then walked solemnly along the road smoking a pipe, and accompanied by a numerous suite, all of whom were ordered to smoke,—severe penalties being threatened against any one whose pipe was not found alight at the end of the promenade.

It was Said who first invited European adventurers to prey on Egypt. Nubar Pasha, who could speak with authority on this subject, used to say: "C'est au temps de Said que le commencement de la débâcle a eu lieu." Intelligent observers on the spot were already able to foretell the storm which was eventually to burst over Egypt. In 1855, Mr. Walne, the British Consul at Cairo, said to Mr. Senior:—

Said Pasha is rash and flighty and conceited, and is spoilt by the flattery of the foreigners who surround him. They tell him, and he believes them, that he is a universal genius. He undoes everything, does very little, and, I fear, is preparing for us some great catastrophe.[1]

---

[1] Senior's *Conversations and Journals in Egypt*, vol. i. p. 131. An account of Egypt under Said Pasha is given in Dr. Stacquey's work published in 1865, and entitled *L'Égypte, La Basse Nubie et le Sinai*

These, and many other similar anecdotes which might be related, serve to illustrate the methods of government which prevailed in Egypt immediately prior to the accession of Ismail Pasha. The drastic nature of those methods, and more especially of the punishments which the rulers of Egypt were in the habit of awarding during the first half of the last century, and even at a later period, did not, indeed, differ very materially from those of their Pharaonic predecessors. Herodotus says:—

King Amasis . . . established the law that every Egyptian should appear once a year before the governor of his canton, and show his means of living; or, failing to do so, and to prove that he got an honest livelihood, should be put to death.[1]

If the general principles adopted by Mehemet Ali had continued to be applied, and especially if recourse had not been made to European credit, it is just possible that the Egyptian system of administration would have been gradually reformed in a manner suitable to the requirements of the country. But it is one of the commonplaces of political science that the most dangerous period for a radically bad system of government is the moment when some reformer, himself inexperienced in the art of government, has laid a rash hand on the old fabric, and has shaken it to such an extent as to make it totter to its fall, but when sufficient time has not yet elapsed to admit of an improved system of government taking root.

In the endeavours, possibly well-intentioned,

---

[1] Book ii. p. 177. After remarking that Solon the Athenian borrowed this law from the Egyptians and imposed it on his countrymen—a statement which, according to a note given by Rawlinson, is incorrect—Herodotus naïvely adds, "It is indeed an excellent custom."

but certainly misdirected, that Ismail Pasha made
to introduce European civilisation at a rapid rate
into Egypt, he was necessarily obliged to have
recourse to European assistance. The only chance
of introducing the new wine of European ideas
into the old bottles of Eastern conservatism, without producing a dangerous fermentation, lay in
proceeding with caution, and notably in selecting
with the utmost care the European agents through
whose instrumentality the changes might gradually
have been effected. Unfortunately, no such care was
taken. The Europeans into whose hands Ismail
Pasha threw himself, were but too often drawn from
the very class which he should most of all have
avoided.[1] Many were adventurers of the type
represented in fiction by M. Alphonse Daudet's
"Nabab,"[2] whose sole object was to enrich themselves at the expense of the country. Moreover,
few of those who exercised any influence in matters
connected with the government of Egypt possessed
sufficient experience of the East to enable them
to apply wisely the knowledge, which they had
acquired elsewhere, to the new conditions under
which they were called upon to work.

The result was that Europeans acquired a bad
name in Egypt, from which, after years of patient
labour and instructive example on the part of the
many high-minded Europeans of divers nationalities
who were subsequently engaged in Egyptian work,
they only gradually recovered. It was, moreover,
impossible that constant association with the classes
to which allusion is made above should not have
produced a marked effect on the views of an astute,

---

[1] A highly qualified authority, who wrote under the pseudonym of
"Odysseus," says : "From their first appearance, the Turks displayed
a strange power of collecting together apostates, renegades, and people
who had more ability than moral qualities."—*Turkey in Europe*, p. 62

[2] It is well known that the character of the Nabab was drawn from an
individual who existed in Egypt not many years ago.

but superficial cynic such as Ismail Pasha. **He**
has often been credited with having systematically
based his conduct on the assumption that no
man living was honest,[1] and, looking at the
personal experience through which he passed, it
cannot be a matter for surprise that he should
have entertained such an opinion.

The result of Lord Goschen's mission was that
Ismail Pasha had, for the first time, to deal with a
small body of European officials, who were not only
invested with more ample powers than any which
had previously been conferred on European functionaries in Egypt, but who were also of a different
type from those Europeans with whom he had
heretofore been generally brought in contact. I
do not claim for the European officials who, at or
about this time, came to Egypt any special qualities
which are not to be found in abundance amongst
other members of the civil services of France and
England. We displayed, I conceive, the ordinary
variety of capacity and character which was to be
anticipated from our previous training, and from
the manner in which we had been selected. But
we all possessed some characteristics in common.
We were all honest. We were all capable of
forming and of expressing independent opinions,
and we were all determined to do our duty to the
best of our abilities in the discharge of the functions
which were respectively assigned to us. In one
respect, the position of the British differed from
that of the French officials. The latter had been
selected, and were more or less avowedly supported
by their Government. The British officials could

---

[1] Macaulay says of Charles II. : "According to him, every person
was to be bought; but some people haggled more about their price
than others; and when this haggling was very obstinate and very
skilful, it was called by some fine name. The chief trick by which
clever men kept up the price of their abilities was called 'integrity'"
(*Works*, vol. i. p. 132). This passage probably describes Ismail Pasha's
habit of thought with tolerable accuracy.

not count on any such support. But the distinction was of less practical importance than might at first sight appear. It was well understood that, if the British officials found that their advice was systematically neglected, and that they could not, with a proper sense of what was due to their own self-respect, carry on their duties in a fairly satisfactory manner, they would resign their appointments, a course which would not only have caused a good deal of embarrassment, but would also have strengthened the hostile public opinion then clamouring against the existing régime in Egypt in terms which were daily becoming more menacing.

Ismail Pasha failed to recognise the importance of the changes to which he had assented. Had he succeeded in acquiring the confidence of this small body of European officials, and in enlisting their services on his side, it is not only possible, but even probable, that he would have remained Khedive of Egypt till the day of his death. But, for a variety of reasons, which will appear more fully in the sequel of this narrative, he failed to do so. Perhaps the difficulties of the situation were such that it was impossible for him to do so. The result was that the officials in question were necessarily thrown into an attitude of hostility. And the further result was that a series of events took place which in the end led to the downfall of the Khedive. In fact, an opportunity, such as sometimes presents itself in politics, then occurred, which, had it been skilfully used with a true insight into the main facts of the situation and into the direction to which affairs were drifting, might not impossibly have turned the current of Egyptian history into another channel, and might have saved the Khedive from the disaster which was impending over him. Such opportunities, if they are not grasped at the moment, rarely recur. As it was, the causes which were tending towards the downfall of the Khedive continued to operate unchecked, and the new European element introduced into the administration, far from impeding, hastened the advent of the crisis.

One of the appointments made at this time, namely, that of Sir Gerald Fitzgerald to the head of the Accounts Department, calls for some special remarks.

It is possible for the finances of a country to be badly administered, whilst, at the same time, the accounts may be in good order. On the other hand, it is impossible for the statesman or the financier to commence the work of fiscal and administrative reform seriously until, by the organisation of a proper Department of Accounts, he is placed in possession of the true facts connected with the resources at his disposal and the State expenditure.

In 1876, the Egyptian accounts were in a state of the utmost confusion. The main reason why the financial settlement made in 1876 broke down was that the materials out of which to construct any stable financial edifice were wanting. The Finance Minister, Ismail Pasha Sadik, who was exiled in November 1876, and who, shortly afterwards, met with a tragic death,[1] boasted that in one year he had extracted £15,000,000 from the people of Egypt. The revenue collected in 1875 is said to have amounted to £10,800,000. The financial combination of November 18, 1876, was based on the collection of a revenue amounting to £10,500,000. There can be no doubt that this estimate was excessive. Twenty years later, after a long period of honest and careful administration, the Egyptian revenue was only about £11,000,000.

---

[1] There can be no doubt that Ismail Pasha Sadik was murdered in a boat whilst proceeding up the Nile.

In 1876, it was, indeed, impossible to arrive at a true estimate of the revenue. The inquiries of Messrs. Goschen and Joubert, Lord Vivian reported, "soon disclosed false accounts, glaring discrepancies, and evident suppressions of sources of revenue." It was this which, more than anything else, hampered Lord Goschen's proceedings. He saw that until more light was thrown on the facts connected with Egyptian finance, any arrangement which could be made would have to be of a provisional character.

I give one instance of the difficulties which at that time had to be encountered in arriving at a true estimate of the Egyptian revenue. Relying on the only figures which were at the time available, Lord Goschen took the net railway receipts at £900,000 a year. Some time afterwards, it was discovered that, to the extent of £300,000 a year, these receipts were fictitious. In the first place, a considerable sum was paid every year for the movement of troops, an item which, under a well-regulated system of accounts, would have been shown as an inter-departmental transaction. In the second place, it was discovered that any of the Khedivial family or the friends and boon companions of the Khedive who wished to travel by rail, rarely went by the ordinary trains. They frequently ordered special trains, for which they paid nothing, merely signing a document, termed a "ragaa," intimating that the train had been ordered by the Khedive, and that its cost was to be charged to him. The money was, of course, never paid to the Railway Administration. Nevertheless, these book entries were treated as real receipts in the figures furnished to Lord Goschen.

It was obvious that, under such circumstances as these, the first elementary requirement, which would have to precede any attempt to reform the fiscal

system, was to introduce order into the Accounts
Department. This work was undertaken by Sir
Gerald Fitzgerald, who, by dint of untiring industry
and perseverance, overcame all the very formidable
obstacles which he had to encounter. The Egyptian
Accounts Department is now thoroughly well
organised. It would be difficult to exaggerate
the importance of this achievement. Of the many
Englishmen who, by steady and unostentatious work,
have rendered good service to the cause of Egyptian reform, there is no one to whom greater merit
can be assigned than Sir Gerald Fitzgerald. He
did not take any personal part in the reforms themselves, but he performed work which was indispensable to others if the reforms were to be carried
out. The kind of work which Sir Gerald Fitzgerald
and his successors performed in Egypt does not
attract much public attention, but those who have
themselves filled responsible positions will appreciate its value.

CHAPTER III

THE COMMISSION OF INQUIRY

NOVEMBER 1876–APRIL 1878

Condition of Egypt—The law of the Moukábala—Petty taxes—The
Egyptian public service — The fiscal system — Floating debt—
Efforts to pay interest on the funded debt—Famine—The coupon
of May 1, 1878—The Commissioners of the Debt—The Commission of Inquiry — The Khedive proposes a partial inquiry—
The Commissioners decline to take part in it — The Khedive
accepts a full inquiry.

THE state of Egypt at this time was deplorable.
Estates, representing about one-fifth of the arable
lands of the country, had passed into the hands of
the Khedive; and these estates, instead of being
farmed out to the dispossessed proprietors, were
administered direct by the Khedive and cultivated
to a great extent by forced labour. No single
measure contributed more than this to render the
existing régime as intolerable to the people of
Egypt as it was rapidly becoming to the foreign
creditors.[1]

In 1872, the law of the Moukábala had been
passed. By this law, all landowners could redeem
one-half of the land-tax to which they were liable
by payment of six years' tax, either in one sum or

---

[1] " It is certain, so many overthrown estates, so many votes for
troubles.   Lucan noteth well the state of Rome before the Civil War :
Hinc usura vorax, rapidumque in tempore foenus,
Hinc concussa fides, et multis utile bellum."
Bacon's Essays, " Of Seditions and Troubles."

in instalments spread over a period of twelve years. "The operation of the law of the Moukábala," Mr. Cave said, "is perhaps the most striking instance of the reckless manner in which the means of the future have been sacrificed to meet the pressing needs of the present."

This is quite true, but the explanation is also very simple. There was never the least intention to adhere to the engagements taken towards the land-owners. When the proper time arrived, it was intended to find means for re-imposing taxation in some other form, and thus recoup the loss to the Treasury incurred by the partial redemption of the land-tax.

Besides the land - tax, which was the main resource of the country, a number of petty taxes of the most harassing nature were levied. I gave Lord Vivian a list of thirty-seven of such taxes, and I doubt if the list was complete.

The evil consequences, which would in any case have resulted from a defective fiscal system, were enhanced by the character of the agents through whose instrumentality the taxes were collected. It can be no matter for surprise that they were corrupt and oppressive, and scarcely, indeed, a matter for just blame; for the treatment, which they received at the hands of the Government whom they served, was such as to be almost pro-hibitive of integrity in the performance of official duties. The picture, which Mr. Cave gave of the position held by the Egyptian officials at this time, was certainly not overdrawn. "One of the causes," he said, "which operates most against the honesty and efficiency of native officers is the precarious tenure of office. From the Pasha downwards, every office is a tenancy at will, and experience shows that while dishonesty goes wholly or par-tially unpunished, independence of thought and action, resolution to do one's duty and to resist the peculation and neglect which pervade every department, give rise to intrigues which, sooner or later, bring about the downfall of honest officials; consequently, those who begin with a desire to do their duty give way before the obstructiveness which paralyses every effort.[1]   The public servant of Egypt, like the Roman Proconsul, too often tries to make as much as he can out of his office while it lasts; and the scandal takes place of the retirement, in a few years with a large fortune, of a man whose salary is perhaps £40 a month, and who has plundered the Treasury on the one hand, and the peasant on the other."

In fact, the fiscal system of Egypt at this time violated at every point and in a flagrant degree the four well-known general principles laid down by Adam Smith and adopted by subsequent econo- mists,[2] as those on which a sound fiscal policy should be based.   Glaring inequalities existed in the incidence of taxation.   The sums demanded from the taxpayers were arbitrarily fixed and were

[1] I can give a remarkable illustration, the facts of which are within my personal knowledge, in support of Mr. Cave's statement. Shortly after the Commission of the Debt was established in 1876, it was noticed that the Custom-House receipts at Suez, which were applied to the service of the debt, fell off in a most unaccountable manner ; also, that a new local director had been appointed. Under the Decree signed by the Khedive on November 18, 1876, the whole of the Custom-House revenue was to be paid direct to the Commissioners of the Debt. No other receipt than that signed by one of the Commissioners was legally valid. The suspicions of the Commissioners were aroused. They asked why the director had been changed. They received evasive and very unsatis- factory answers. They insisted, therefore, on the dismissed official being produced, dead or alive. A somewhat acrimonious correspondence took place, with the result that after a delay of several months the official in question made his appearance at the office of the Commissioners of the Debt. It then appeared that he had received an order from the Khedive to pay the Suez Custom-House receipts direct to His Highness. He demurred, on the very legitimate ground that he would thus be com- mitting an illegal act. He was at once arrested and sent to one of the most remote parts of the Soudan, whence he would certainly never have returned, had it not been that the Commissioners took up his case.

[2] Adam Smith, *Wealth of Nations*, bk. v. chap. ii.

uncertain in amount. The taxes were levied without any reference to the time and manner in which it was most convenient for the contributor to pay, and the system of collection, so far from being "contrived so as to keep out of the pockets of the people as little as possible over and above what the tax brings into the public treasury," was such as to ensure results of a diametrically opposite description. Under such circumstances, financial policy, instead of being used as a powerful engine of political and social improvement, had become merely a means for first extorting the maximum amount of revenue from unwilling contributors, and then spending the money on objects from which the contributors themselves derived little or no benefit.

A system such as that described above would at any time have been oppressive. At the particular moment of which this history treats, it weighed on the people of Egypt with exceptional severity.

The interest on the funded debt, heavy as it was, was not the only extraordinary charge which the Khedive had to meet. Large sums of money were due to contractors and others for goods supplied to the Egyptian Government. In default of payment, "orders had been given by all foreign houses trading with Egypt to refuse to furnish the Government with any supplies except for payment in cash on delivery." The claims themselves were "being hawked about for sale at a depreciation of 50 per cent."

In August 1877, Lord Vivian warned the Egyptian Government that the creditors "would certainly fall back upon their indisputable right to attack the Government before the Tribunals." "The Government," he added, "will thus find themselves confronted with a mass of legal sentences against them, which they must either satisfy in full and at once, or it must inevitably attract the serious attention of the Powers who contributed to establish the Courts of the Reform."

But the Egyptian Government had no money with which to settle the claims; neither, in the then exhausted state of their credit, could money be borrowed. Lord Vivian prophesied correctly. The creditors had recourse to the law-courts. Many of them obtained judgments against the Government, and the non-execution of the judgments led to the interference of the Powers under whose auspices the Mixed Courts had but recently been established. Notably, the German Government "considered that the Khedive was acting in a manner which should not be allowed in refusing to pay claims when required to do so by the Courts of Law." The German Ambassador in London informed Lord Derby that "Prince Bismarck wished for united action on the subject by all the Powers, if only to avoid the possibility of separate action on the part of some of them."

In the meanwhile, everything was being sacrificed in the attempt to pay the interest and sinking fund on the funded debt. A sum of £1,579,000 was, in 1877, devoted to the extinction of debt. The nominal capital paid off amounted to £3,110,000, but, as both Lord Vivian and the Commissioners of the Debt pointed out, the operation of the sinking fund was of a delusive character, for a debt, at least equal in amount to that which was extinguished, was being created by the non-payment of the employés and the other creditors, whose claims had not been funded. On January 6, 1877, Lord Vivian wrote: "The Government employés are many months in arrears of pay, so much so that the cashiers of the Caisse are actually being paid out of the private means of the Commissioners (although their own salaries have not been paid), in order not to expose them to the temptation of handling large sums of money whilst actually without the means of subsistence."

While, on the one hand, the employés were unpaid, on the other hand, the taxes were being collected with merciless severity. Lord Vivian, whose despatches throughout this period do credit alike to his humanity and his foresight, felt keenly on this subject. "I hear," he wrote, "reports that the peasantry are cruelly treated to extract the taxes from them, the fact probably being, partly that the taxes are being collected in advance, and partly that, as the date of the coupon falls so soon after the harvest, insufficient time is given to the peasantry to realise fair prices for their grain, and that they are unwilling to make the ruinous sacrifice of forced sales." The Khedive, in conversation with Lord Vivian, "admitted that, in order to pay the coupon, the taxes were being collected for nine months, and in some places for a year in advance."

In spite of the rigour used in collecting taxes, the non-payment of the Government employés, and the neglect of the judgment creditors, it was with the utmost difficulty that sufficient money could be obtained to pay the interest on the funded debt. During the year ending on July 15, 1877, the revenue pledged to the service of the Unified Debt, which had been estimated to yield £4,800,000, only yielded £3,328,000.

It is well-nigh certain that the financial arrangement made in 1876 would, in any case, have broken down. As it was, an exceptionally bad Nile, the Russo-Turkish War with its attendant expenditure, and the depression of trade, hastened the crisis.

Bad as was the state of affairs in 1877, it was worse in 1878, for the full effect of the low Nile of 1877 was only felt in the following year. In Upper Egypt there was a famine. Sir Alexander

Baird, who had been a frequent visitor to Egypt during the winter months, was asked by the Government to assist in the relief of the population. In the report which he subsequently addressed to the Minister of Finance, he said :—

It is almost incredible the distances travelled by women and children, begging from village to village. . . . It is not possible to state how many died from actual starvation, for in no instance does the death-register show a death by starvation, but I am satisfied that the excessive mortality during the period of scarcity was caused by dysentery and other diseases brought on by insufficient and unwholesome food. The poor were in some instances reduced to such extremities of hunger that they were driven to satisfy their cravings with the refuse and garbage of the streets.

The nadir both of financial chaos and of popular misery was reached in the summer and autumn of 1878. On May 1, 1878, a sum of about £2,000,000 was due for interest on the Unified Debt. On March 31, only about £500,000 was in the hands of the Commissioners of the Debt. The balance, amounting to about £1,500,000, had, therefore, to be collected in the space of one month.

The Commissioners of the Debt were of opinion that it would have been better not to pay this coupon. We should have preferred to allow the financial collapse, which was manifestly inevitable, to come at once as a preliminary to the establishment of a better order of things. We were aware that the money could not be paid without taking the taxes in advance, a course to which we were opposed as being oppressive to the peasantry, and also contrary to the true interests of the bondholders. Not only, therefore, did we abstain from putting any pressure on the Khedive to pay, but we even discussed the desirability of protesting against payment.

Unfortunately, the French Government did not share this view. French public opinion held that the Khedive could pay his debts if he chose to do so, that the distress alleged to exist in Egypt was fictitious, and that the arguments based on the impoverishment of the country were fabricated in order to throw dust in the eyes of the public and to excite humanitarian sympathy where no sympathy was deserved. An opinion was also entertained by a large body of the French public that the Khedive had hidden stores of wealth on which he could draw if he thought fit to do so. Subsequent events showed that this story had no foundation in fact. But there were at the time some reasonable grounds for believing it to be true. On December 8, 1876, Lord Vivian reported that "it was impossible to account for the disposal of the very large sums of money over which the Egyptian Government have had control during the last year; £4,000,000 for the Suez Canal shares, £5,000,000 advance from the French, and nearly a year's revenue have disappeared, while the payment of the coupon of the Unified Debt has been deferred, all the public employés are in arrears of pay, and heavy debts remain unsettled." The same idea was developed more fully in a petition presented by the French colony of Alexandria to M. Waddington, who was then Minister for Foreign Affairs. What, they asked, had become of the money which had been of late years poured into Egypt? The Custom-House statistics showed that a great part of it had remained in the country.

Comment alors parler de la détresse du pays, et de l'impuissance de payer ses charges? Que le Gouvernement explique ce qu'est devenu tout cet or! Il est donc bien évident que le Gouvernement Égyptien est inexcusable de ne pas remplir les engagements qu'il a pris solennellement à la face de l'Europe, et c'est sur lui que retombe la lourde responsabilité des ruines qu'il accumule en Égypte et qui frappent pour la plus grande partie la colonie Européenne.

The cause of the bondholders was warmly espoused by the French diplomatic representative at Cairo, Baron des Michels, who turned a deaf ear to all arguments based either on the necessities of the Khedive or the misery of the Egyptian people. The result was that, on April 16, 1878, the French Government, through their Ambassador in London, informed Lord Salisbury, who, on April 2, 1878, succeeded Lord Derby at the Foreign Office, that there was "every reason to believe that the Khedive could pay the coupon, which falls due in May, if he chose to do so." M. Waddington expressed a hope that the British Government would join the French Government in pressing for payment. Lord Vivian was accordingly instructed to act in concert with Baron des Michels on this subject.

The British Government thus became in a certain degree responsible for the oppression which necessarily accompanied the collection of the taxes. Moreover, the step taken at this moment involved a departure both from the local Egyptian policy, which the British Government had hitherto pursued, and also from their general policy in such matters. As regards local policy, the British had never espoused the cause of the bondholders so warmly as the French Government. On the contrary, a just consideration for the interests of the Egyptian people had always tempered any support given to the foreign creditors. As regards general policy, it had for years been the tradition of the London Foreign Office that British subjects, who invested their money in a foreign country, must do so at their own risk. They could not rely on any energetic support in the enforcement of their claims. There was evidently some special reason for so brusque a departure from the principles heretofore adopted. The reason is not far to seek. The Berlin Congress was then about to sit to regulate the situation arising from the recent Russo-Turkish war. Egyptian interests had to give way to broader diplomatic considerations. It was necessary to conciliate the French. The French initiative was, therefore, followed.

Steps were taken to collect the money necessary to pay the coupon. Two of the most iron-fisted Pashas who could be found were sent into the provinces. They were accompanied by a staff of money-lenders who were prepared to buy in advance the crops of the cultivators. Thus, the low Nile having diminished the quantity of the crop, the peasantry of Egypt were deprived of such benefits as some of them, at all events, might have derived from the high prices consequent on the scarcity. "In some cases," Sir Alexander Baird wrote, "perfectly authenticated, corn was sold to the merchants for 50 piastres an ardeb, which was delivered in one month's time when it was worth 120 piastres an ardeb."

The money was, however, obtained. The last instalment was paid to the Commissioners of the Debt a few hours before the coupon fell due. The great diversity of currency, and the fact that many of the coins were strung together to be used as ornaments, bore testimony to the pressure which had been used in the collection of the taxes.

The only result of paying this coupon was that the crisis was delayed for a short time. The sufferings of the people of Egypt were increased, whilst the position of the foreign creditors, so far from being improved, was rendered rather worse than it was before.

Amidst this clash of conflicting interests, the main question which presented itself was, what could be done to place the finances of Egypt on a sound footing. It was clear that the arrangements made in 1876 would have to be modified, but to what extent were they to be modified? By what procedure were the modifications to be introduced? What guarantees could be obtained that any new arrangement would acquire a greater degree of stability than those which had gone before?

The discussion of these questions necessitates some observations on the relations between the Egyptian Government and the Commissioners of the Debt, upon which the main interest of Egyptian affairs centred at this moment.

The position of the Commissioners was one of great difficulty. They were the representatives of the bondholders. An obligation, therefore, rested on them to support the just claims of the bondholders by every legitimate means in their power. Apart, however, from the fact that it was impossible for any one of ordinary humanity and common sense to ignore the pitiable condition in which the people of Egypt were then placed, it was clear that the interests of the bondholders and of the Egyptian taxpayers, if properly understood, were far from being divergent. On the contrary, they were in a great measure identical. Both were interested in being relieved from a system of government which was ruinous to the interests of one class and in the highest degree oppressive to the other. Would it not be possible to use the bondholding interest as a lever to improve the Egyptian administration, and thus both relieve the lot of the peasantry and, at the same time, afford some substantial guarantee to the foreign creditors that whatever fresh financial obligations were taken would be respected? That was the important question of the moment.

In view of the relatively large political and financial interests of France and Great Britain in Egypt, it was natural that the French and British representatives should take the lead in the proceedings of the Commission of the Debt. I was fortunate in being associated with a French colleague who took a broad view of the situation. M. de Blignières was a French official, and the tendencies of most French officials are somewhat more bureaucratic than those of their counterparts in England; but he was a French official of the best type, loyal, straightforward, intelligent, and endowed with a high degree of moral courage. On all essential points, we worked in complete harmony. We were both determined that the petty international rivalries, which had been the bane of Egypt, and which were skilfully used by Ismail Pasha to avert the possibility of common action on the part of France and England, should not be allowed to separate us. That we succeeded in sinking any minor differences of opinion in the pursuit of a common object, was sufficiently proved by the fact that each of us was at times blamed for sacrificing the interests of his own country to that of the other. In later days, when the relations between France and England became unfortunately embittered, I often looked back with regret to the time when I was able to co-operate heartily with a French colleague, such as M. de Blignières, for whom I entertained a sincere respect and a warm personal friendship.[1]

The position of M. de Blignières was in some respects more difficult than my own. I had not been appointed by the British Government, and was, therefore, free to act according to the dictates of my own conscience and to the best of my own

---

[1] M. de Blignières died in 1900. He was a brilliant and also very voluble conversationalist. In 1879, I accompanied him on a visit to Lord Salisbury, who was then residing at Dieppe. In 1887, Lord Salisbury wrote to me : "The other day the gentleman who described himself at my house at Dieppe as a '*personnage muet*'—M. de Blignières —called on me. He had not acquired any fresh claim to that designation But he was very agreeable, and more friendly than I had been led to expect."

judgment. The tendencies and traditions of the British Government, moreover, ran counter to any endeavour to enforce the claims of the foreign creditors at whatsoever cost to the population of Egypt. The personal influence of Lord Vivian was exerted on the side of justice and moderation. The British bondholders were also, as a body, perfectly reasonable. They naturally objected to any arbitrary infringement of their legal rights, but there could be little doubt that if a statement of facts and figures could be put before them, the accuracy of which could be guaranteed by their own trustees, there would not be any insuperable difficulty in obtaining their acquiescence to an equitable settlement of all pending questions. Moreover, the influence of the bondholders in England was limited. A strong body of public opinion existed which was hostile to their presumed interests, and which, in its anxiety to do justice to the people of Egypt, was inclined sometimes even to err on the side of doing less than justice to the foreign creditors. Those who represented this aspect of British public opinion criticised, more frequently than not in a hostile spirit, the action of the European officials who were at that time employed in prominent positions in Egypt. A good deal of this criticism was based on an erroneous appreciation of the facts of the case, but I never regarded it as really hostile. On the contrary, I esteemed it an advantage to be able to strengthen my position in case of need by an appeal to a body of general opinion which, even when misled on points of detail, was pursuing praiseworthy and very legitimate objects.

M. de Blignières, on the other hand, was nominated by the French Government, and the French Government were greatly under the influence of the bondholding interest. The French bondholders were inclined to be far less reasonable than the English, neither did there apparently exist any body of public opinion in France, which could act as a check on any extreme views advanced by the foreign creditors of Egypt.

Both M. de Blignières and myself saw from an early date that the financial arrangements of 1876 would have to be modified, but we also held that an arbitrary reduction in the rate of interest would be unjust to the bondholders and of doubtful benefit to the taxpayers. Before we could approve of any fresh financial combination, it was evident that more light would have to be thrown on the situation. Under these circumstances, the idea of holding a General Inquiry into the financial condition of the country, which was originated about this time, took root, and obtained some support amongst the more moderate of those who were interested in the solvency of the Egyptian Government. "But," Lord Vivian reported, "the bondholders ask that any inquiry into the financial position should be impartial and exhaustive, leaving nothing behind it uninvestigated in the shape of debt, nor any pretext for further resettlement. On these conditions, they are prepared to make such a fair sacrifice of interest as may be found absolutely necessary."

It would have been wise on the part of the Khedive if, at this moment, he had on his own initiative invited a full inquiry into the financial situation of Egypt. But he was not disposed to do so. He hoped to obtain an arbitrary reduction in the rate of interest on the debt without any inquiry. Eventually, the Commissioners of the Debt took the initiative. In a letter addressed to the Minister of Finance on January 9, 1878, they dwelt on the gravity of the situation and suggested an inquiry. The Khedive replied at length, declining to institute a general inquiry into the financial situation, but stating that he was willing to appoint a Commission whose sole duty it would be to ascertain the true amount of the Egyptian revenue. The Commissioners of the Debt were invited to take part in this inquiry.

A partial inquiry of this sort would have been worse than useless. The Commissioners of the Debt, therefore, addressed a further letter to the Egyptian Government, in which they again urged the necessity of a full inquiry, and declined to take part in any inquiry of a partial nature.

No attention was paid to this remonstrance, and, on January 27, 1878, a Khedivial Decree was issued instituting a Commission of Inquiry into the revenue only. A further Decree was to be issued nominating the Commissioners.

The issue of this Decree caused an explosion of European public opinion in Egypt. A meeting was held at Alexandria at which the more extreme of those who advocated the claims of the foreign creditors expressed themselves in terms condemnatory of any inquiry, as they considered that the Egyptian Government could meet all its engagements. A petition was sent to the representatives of the Powers, but it was couched in language so insulting to the Egyptian Government that Lord Vivian refused to notice it.

The Khedive did not, however, immediately abandon the idea of instituting a partial inquiry. The main difficulty was to find any qualified persons to conduct it. General (then Colonel) Gordon was at that time returning from the Soudan. The idea occurred to the Khedive that his services might be utilised. His high character, the weight that his name carried with the British public, and his known sympathy with the sufferings of the Egyptian people, all pointed him out as

a useful instrument; whilst his inexperience in
financial questions would, it was thought, lead him
to accept the accuracy of any facts and figures
which were laid before him by the Egyptian
Government. Lord Vivian pointed out that
"Colonel Gordon, with all his eminent qualities
and abilities, had no experience in finance." The
Khedive, however, held to his idea. General
Gordon was invited to conduct a financial inquiry,
and was at first inclined to accept the invitation.
M. de Lesseps was also asked to serve on the
proposed Commission, and intimated his willingness
to do so. The negotiation with General Gordon,
however, soon broke down, and he left Egypt.[1]

It is unnecessary to describe in detail the
tedious negotiations which then ensued. The
British Government consistently supported "a full
and complete inquiry" into the financial situation
as the only possible solution of existing difficulties.
The German, Austrian, and Italian Governments
also supported the proposal. So also did the
French Government, although as it became daily
more and more clear that the result of any
impartial inquiry must be that the rate of interest
on the debt would be reduced, their support was
rather lukewarm.

After long and wearisome discussions over the
scope of the inquiry and the persons to whom it
should be entrusted, the Khedive eventually yielded.
On March 15, I was able to write to Lord Goschen :
"At last I really think that, after five months of
incessant labour, the inquiry is settled." On

---

[1] These proceedings have formed the subject of much misrepresentation. The account of them given in Sir William Butler's *Charles George Gordon* (pp. 138-139) is incorrect. The sole reason why the negotiation broke down was that it was evident to every one concerned, including General Gordon himself, that he was not fitted to conduct any financial inquiry. He wrote at the time that he felt sure that he "was only to be a figurehead."—*Colonel Gordon in Central Africa*, p. 310.

April 4, 1878, a Khedivial Decree was issued appointing a Commission with the most extended powers of inquiry.   M. Ferdinand de Lesseps lent the weight of his name to the Commission.   He was appointed President, but did not take any active part in the proceedings, and left Egypt on May 9.   Sir Rivers Wilson and Riaz Pasha were named Vice-Presidents.   The four Commissioners of the Debt were appointed members.   A capable Frenchman, M. Liron d'Airolles, was chosen to act as Secretary.

Some opposition had been offered, especially by the French, to the nomination of any Egyptian to be a member of the Commission.   It was feared, with some reason, that no Egyptian would be sufficiently independent to express views which might be displeasing to the Khedive.   These fears proved groundless.   At a time when any show of independent opinion on the part of an Egyptian was accompanied with a good deal of personal risk, Riaz Pasha displayed a high degree of moral courage.   His presence on the Commission was of material help to his colleagues, whose confidence he fully deserved and obtained.

CHAPTER IV

THE NUBAR-WILSON MINISTRY

April 1878–November 1878

Difficulty of the task assigned to the Commission of Inquiry—Chérif Pasha declines to appear as a witness—Defects in the system of administration—The floating debt—The Rouznameh Loan—Loans from the Wakf and Beit-el-Mal Administrations—Ultimate reforms proposed by the Commissioners—Immediate reforms necessary—Enforcement of Ministerial responsibility—The Khedive's Civil List—Cession to the State of the Khedivial properties—The Khedive accepts the proposals of the Commissioners—Nubar Pasha forms a Ministry—Sir Rivers Wilson and M de Blignières named Ministers—Loan authorised on the security of the Khedivial estates.

THE Egyptian Verres[1] was at last, therefore, obliged to render an account of his stewardship to a body of men who were determined to arrive at the truth. The Commissioners, however, soon found that, in the confusion which then existed, the mere discovery of the accurate facts of the situation was a task which presented no inconsiderable difficulties, whilst the abuses which had grown up in the Egyptian administrative system were so general and so deep-rooted as to defy the application of any remedy which would be effectual

---

[1] There is certainly a somewhat close analogy between Verres and Ismail Pasha ; *e.g.* "Hoc praetore Siculi neque suas leges, neque nostra senatusconsulta, neque communia jura tenuerunt . . . Nulla res . . . nisi ad nutum istius judicata est ; nulla res tam patria cujusquam atque avita fuit quae non ab eo imperio istius abjudicaretur. Innumerabiles pecuniae ex aratorum bonis novo nefarioque instituto coactae," etc. — Cicero, *In C. Verrem*, Actio Prima, iv. et v.

and at the same time speedy. We had to deal not with a patient suffering from a single specific malady, but with one whose constitution was shattered and whose every organ was diseased. "Il s'agit, en effet," we said, "de créer tout un système fiscal, et cela avec un personnel très restreint ; à présent presque rien n'existe de ce qui doit exister."

At the outset of the inquiry, a preliminary difficulty of a somewhat serious nature occurred. Chérif Pasha was at that time, next to the Khedive, the leading man in Egypt. No one thought that he was in any degree responsible for the confusion which then existed, but, inasmuch as he was Minister of Justice, it was to him that the Commissioners were obliged to turn for information as to the working of the judicial system in so far as fiscal matters were concerned. Under the Decree instituting the Commission, all Egyptian officials were bound to furnish such information as might be demanded of them. Chérif Pasha, on receiving a summons to attend before the Commission, offered to answer questions in writing, but his proud nature resented — and not unnaturally resented—the idea of appearing in person before the Commissioners. On the other hand, had the latter yielded, all chance of extracting the truth from other witnesses would have been shipwrecked at the outset of the inquiry. The Commissioners, therefore, insisted on Chérif Pasha appearing in person. Under these circumstances, Chérif Pasha could only yield or resign. He chose the latter course.

The first step taken by the Commissioners was to provide for the payment of the arrears due to the Government employés and pensioners. They then set to work to examine into the system of administration of the country, more especially

into the fiscal system. It is unnecessary to give
the results of their inquiries at any length. It was
found that public rumour had not exaggerated the
nature of the prevailing abuses. Certain laws and
regulations existed on paper, but no one ever
thought of obeying them. The principal officials
concerned were, indeed, often ignorant of their
existence. New taxes were levied, old taxes were
increased, and changes introduced without any
formal authority. The village Sheikh executed the
orders of the Moudir, the latter those of the Inspector-General, who, again, acted under " superior
order." This " superior order," in fact, constituted
the law. The officials obeyed it, even though it
were only communicated verbally ; and no taxpayer ever dreamt of challenging it or of protesting
against it. The Inspector-General of Upper Egypt,
on being asked to whom the taxpayer could address
himself if he had any complaint to make, answered,
with a naïveté arising without doubt from long
familiarity with a system which he considered both
just and natural, " Pour les impôts, le fellah ne peut
se plaindre ; il sait qu'on agit par ' ordre supérieur.'
C'est le Gouvernement lui-même qui les réclame ;
à qui voulez-vous qu'il se plaigne ? " [1] The Inspector-General unconsciously indicated the main
difficulty in the path of the Egyptian reformer.
On the one hand, the people had from time
immemorial been accustomed to yield implicit
obedience to the Government. On the other hand,
inasmuch as the Government were themselves the
chief cause of all the mischief in the country, the

---

[1] This answer is alive with the spirit of the ancient Oriental despot-
isms. Thus Buckle (*History of Civilisation*, vol. i. p. 80) records that
the Institutes of Menu laid down that any native of India belonging to
the Sudra caste must always remain a slave for ever, although his master
granted him his freedom. " For," said the lawgiver, " of a state which
is natural to him, by whom can he be divested ? " Paterson (*The
Nemesis of Nations*, p. 60) also alludes to the same point.

direction reform had necessarily to take was that of
putting some restraint on the exercise of arbitrary
power. How were abuses to be reformed without
shaking the props which had so far held Egyptian
society together, and on which the whole edifice
rested? That was a question which, at a later
period, gave cause for much anxiety.

Another characteristic answer was given by a
high Egyptian official who was examined before
the Commission. A professional tax was at that
time levied in Egypt. Nothing, in fact, can be
fairer than that, in an agricultural country such as
Egypt, the non-agricultural classes should bear
their share of taxation. It was, however, perhaps
going rather far to levy the tax on the humblest
of the artisan class. But the Government went
much farther. Agricultural labourers paid the tax;
in fact, it had become a poll-tax, which was paid
by all the poorer classes, whether or not they exercised anything which could be called a profession.
The witness in question was asked whether he did
not think it rather hard that a man who exercised
no profession should be called upon to pay a professional tax. He expressed great and, without
doubt, genuine astonishment. Was it, he said, the
fault of the Government that the man did not
exercise any profession? He could engage in any
profession he chose. The Government did not
prevent him from doing so. But, of course, if he
chose not to engage in any profession, he must
none the less pay the tax; otherwise an injustice
would be done to those who were engaged in professions! Of the many specious arguments which
have been from time to time advanced in Egypt
to make the worse appear the better cause. this is
certainly one of the most remarkable.

The Commissioners did not confine their researches to the methods adopted for the collection

of the revenue. The corvée, they found, was a
"fruitful source of extortion and injustice." It was
ascertained, notwithstanding positive official asser-
tions to the contrary, that the Khedive's private
estates were cultivated by means of forced labour.
The recruitment for the army was managed in an
irregular and very cruel manner.[1] It often happened
that a recruit first paid a heavy sum to obtain exemp-
tion from military service, and was after all obliged
to serve without the money being refunded to him.
In the vital question of the distribution of water
for purposes of irrigation, the interests of the
poorer cultivators were sacrificed to those of the
rich proprietors. No courts of justice, worthy of
the name, existed.

Herr von Kremer and myself were delegated by
our colleagues to inquire into the outstanding claims
against the Egyptian Government. Many a weary
hour did we pass in the broiling heat of an Egyptian
summer afternoon in endeavouring to unravel the
tangled meshes of some of the most astounding
financial operations in which any Government in
the world has ever been engaged. The waste had
been fearful. The head of the Ordnance Department, if he heard that some new description of

---

[1] One of the Inspectors of the Antiquities Department (Mr. Howard
Carter), in the course of some excavations made at Dendera in the
month of August 1904, came across the corpse of a man who had
been tortured and put to death by Daoud Pasha, a former notorious
Moudir of the Province, for trying to evade conscription for the
army. Mr. Carter reported : "The corpse presented a ghastly
sight; the head was turned towards the left, the chin resting on the
shoulder, the features distorted in agony, and the tongue between the
teeth. The body was in a contorted position, with the legs bent and
widely open. The hands were held at the wrists in rough wooden
stocks, made apparently out of two rowlocks from a native boat, fixed
together, extremely tight, by means of two large iron native nails,
which pierced the wrists, and were clamped below. Tied round the
arms, high up near the arm-pits, was a halter, which had evidently
been used to drag the man along, either dead or alive, the back showing distinct signs of laceration. It was even possible to detect that the
hands had been much swollen from the pressure of the stocks."—*Egypt*,
No. 1 of 1905, p. 104.

cannon had been invented, would order, not one as an
experiment, but a couple of dozen, on the ground, as
was explained to us, that Egypt "could not remain
behind other nations in military matters." Names
familiar throughout Europe during the Napoleonic
era turned up as recipients of the Khedivial largesse.
The accounts also showed that the eulogies poured
at one time on Ismail Pasha by a portion of the
European press were not altogether due to dis-
interested motives. Money was due to contractors
and tradesmen of all sorts. An Egyptian princess
had run up an account of £150,000 with a French
dressmaker. Large sums had been spent at Constantinople, as to which it was stated "on n'a pas
pu rendre compte." One financial operation was of
so complicated a nature that it almost defied the
ingenuity of man to get to the bottom of it. It
appeared, however, that the Khedive had been
engaged with his late Finance Minister in an
operation on the Stock Exchange, the basis of
which was that he was to "bear" his own stock.
In some cases, extravagant sums had been paid
for work done or for goods furnished. Thus, the
harbour works at Alexandria cost over £2,500,000.
According to a trustworthy estimate, they should
have cost about £1,400,000. In this case, however, the work was one of real utility, and it was
well executed, although at a high price. In a
number of other cases, large sums were owing
without the Egyptian Government having anything to show for their money. Interest at
exorbitant rates, bonuses on the renewal of bills,
differences between the real and nominal value of
securities, and other financial juggleries, constituted almost the whole of the claim.

There was one series of operations, termed
"opérations d'extourne," which are worth describ-
ing in some detail. The operation was after this

fashion. The Egyptian Government, being in want of ready money, sold to some Levantine firm a quantity of grain which they did not possess, and which, for the most part, they were never likely to possess. The purchase money was paid at once; the grain had to be delivered to the purchasers a few months later. When the time for its delivery arrived, a certain amount was in some cases delivered, as it was then the practice of the Egyptian Government to collect a portion of the taxes in kind. The remainder was bought back by the Government at a price of 25 per cent above that which had been paid by the original purchasers. In other cases, the Government never delivered any grain, neither was any money repaid at the time. The Government, however, still went through the form of repurchase, and the original purchasers received Treasury bills, bearing interest at the rate of 18 or 20 per cent, not for the amount which they had in the first instance advanced, but for the far larger sum for which the Government eventually effected the nominal repurchase of the grain. It is impossible to say what rate of interest the Egyptian Government really paid in the end for money advanced under this system. It must have been something enormous.

Instances might, in fact, be multiplied to show the ruinous nature of the financial operations to which the Government were at that time reduced in order to obtain money. In one case, which may be cited by way of example, the Government, in part payment of a debt due to a local bank, handed over £230,000 worth of Unified Stock at a price of $31\frac{1}{8}$; in other words, in order to pay £72,000, the Government saddled the country permanently with a debt of £230,000, bearing interest at the rate of 6 per cent per annum.

We also found, in the course of our researches, that in 1874 a forced loan, entitled the "Emprunt Rouznameh," had been raised in the provinces. Subscriptions had been invited for a loan of £5,000,000 bearing interest at the rate of 9 per cent. About £1,800,000 was actually paid into the Treasury. We obtained from some of the villages a list of the subscribers to the loan; each list was accompanied by a declaration signed by the Notables of the village stating that the subscriptions were "perfectly voluntary." They were, of course, in no sense voluntary. No bonds were ever delivered to the subscribers and, up to the date of our inquiry, one instalment of interest only had been paid to a few favoured individuals.

We further discovered that the Government had laid their hands upon the money belonging to the Wakfs, that is to say, the Department which deals with Mohammedan religious endowments.

There was also at that time in Egypt an institution termed the Beit-el-Mal,[1] which administered the estates of orphans and minors. The duty of the director of this establishment was to invest the money of which he was trustee in the manner best suited to the interests of the cestuis-que trust. "En vertu d'ordre supérieur," the Director-General lent the money to the Government at 10 per cent interest, but he was never repaid the capital, neither did he receive any interest. The Director-General, on being asked whether the Minister of Finance gave him any security for the trust money which he lent to the Government, replied that, inasmuch as the Khedive had given an order, no security was necessary. "La garantie, c'est l'ordre du Khédive." "Dans le cours de nos recherches," we said, "nous avons été frappés de l'usage presqu'universel qui semble régner chez les fonction-

---

[1] *Lit.* "The House of Property."

naires du Gouvernement Égyptien, et qui consiste dans l'affectation des fonds particuliers qui passent par leurs mains aux besoins du service gouvernemental. Les faits que nous avons racontés à propos de l'administration du Wakf, du Beit-el-Mal, de la Caisse des Orphelins, et des Écoles Nationales, peuvent servir d'exemple du système. Nous pourrions en citer d'autres."

Besides the sums due to bankers and contractors, we found that there were numerous claims from such humble individuals as camel-drivers, barbers, donkey-boys, etc., all of which had to be included in the floating debt.

It is a pity that these claims could not have been submitted to a court of arbitration with full powers to deal with them. The result would probably have been that a few would have been admitted in full; others would have been reduced in various proportions, some very largely; whilst some would perhaps have been rejected altogether. Unfortunately, the Commissioners had no such powers. We could only decide what claims were admissible from a strictly legal point of view, leaving any doubtful cases to be decided by the law-courts. When the list came to be made out, it was found that the outstanding claims amounted to £6,276,000. The deficit for 1878 was estimated at £2,587,000,[1] and that of 1879 at £381,000. In all, therefore, a new floating debt, amounting to £9,244,000, had accrued, which in one form or another had to be added to the funded debt of the country.

It was easy to frame a crushing indictment against the system of government under which Egypt had of late years been administered. It was more difficult to indicate what measures could

---

[1] This was an under-estimate. The actual deficit amounted to £3,440,000.

be taken to ensure any speedy improvement in the system. The Commissioners, however, pointed out the general directions which reforms should take. No tax should be levied save in virtue of a law which should be officially published. The collection of taxes should be really, as well as nominally, under the Minister of Finance. The Accounts Department should be reformed, and a system of annual budgets adopted. A Reserve Fund should be instituted to provide for any extraordinary expenses incurred whenever the Nile was exceptionally high or low. The taxes should no longer be taken in advance. A judicial system should be organised which would protect the people against an arbitrary abuse of authority. A number of small and vexatious taxes should be suppressed. A cadastral survey should be made. Reforms should be introduced into the methods of collecting the salt and tobacco duties. Proper regulations should be made for the distribution of water and the execution of public works. Forced labour should only be employed on public works of acknowledged utility. The terms of military service should be defined and limited, whilst at the same time some equitable system should be adopted for obtaining recruits for the army.

These proposed reforms were excellent in their way. But they all required time to inaugurate; capable administrators to give effect to them; experience to show in what particular form portions of the European system of government could, with advantage, be transplanted to an Eastern country; and above all, a gradual change in the habits of thought, both of the Egyptian officials and of the people themselves, which would enable them in some degree to assimilate a system of administration, based on principles which, since the days of the Pharaohs, had been unfamiliar to the people of Egypt.

In the meanwhile, the pressing questions were,
What could be done at once to enable the machine
of the State to work, however inefficiently ? What
was to be the first step towards the inauguration
of an improved system of government ? How
were the claims which had on all sides surged up
against the Egyptian Treasury to be met ?

There was but little difficulty in stating the
main defect of the existing system, or in indicating
in general terms the nature of the remedy which
ought to be applied. " On ne saurait méconnaître,"
the Commissioners said, " que le Chef de l'État
dispose d'une autorité sans limites." Manifestly,
that was the main blot. The celebrated maxim
attributed to Louis XIV. has never been more
thoroughly carried out in practice than in Egypt
under the reign of Ismail Pasha. He, in his own
person, was the State. He disposed of the lives
and properties of all his subjects. He constituted
the sole and final court of appeal in all affairs,
great or small. He administered in person every
Department of the State. His will was law. His
subordinates obeyed his every word implicitly.
Ancient tradition and personal interest alike forbade an Egyptian official to question the wisdom
of a decision emanating from a ruler, who could at
pleasure dispose of the life and make or mar the
fortune of any one of his subjects. All independence of thought and action was crushed out.
Moreover, Ismail Pasha did more than rule. He
afforded in his own person a striking example of
what may result from concentrating in the hands of
the ruler of the State functions which may more
advantageously be left to private enterprise. He
was the largest landed proprietor in Egypt. He
was the only sugar manufacturer. He was a large
shipowner. In fact, he was omnipresent. The
task which he had undertaken would have taxed

administrative abilities of the highest order. Ismail
Pasha was a man of some natural ability, but he
possessed neither the knowledge, nor the experience,
nor the power of application necessary to govern
successfully on his own principles.[1]

The result was that a state of affairs was produced such as that described in the report of the
Commissioners. At the time they wrote, the
whole machine of government was in danger of
collapsing. It was useless to elaborate any minor
reforms on paper, until steps had been taken to
remedy the main defect of the system. It was
clearly necessary to place some check on the
arbitrary power of the Khedive. The principle
of ministerial responsibility had to be enforced.

Another fundamental reform was also necessary
before the foundations of an improved system of
administration could be laid. So long as the
revenues of the country remained at the disposal
of a despotic and spendthrift ruler, no trustworthy
forecast could be made of the liabilities of the
State, and no reliance could be felt that revenues,
which were intended by the Finance Minister to
defray certain expenses, might not suddenly escape
his grasp and be devoted to some wholly different
object. Neglect to distinguish between the public
revenues of the State and the private income of the
Sovereign is a rock on which the Governments of

[1] Compare Taine, *Ancien Régime*, p. 101. Speaking of the duties
imposed on the King, he says : " En effet, par sa complication, son
irrégularité, et sa grandeur, la machine échappe à ses prises. Un
Frédéric II., levé à quatre heures du matin, un Napoléon qui dicte
une partie de la nuit dans son bain et travaille dix-huit heures par jour,
y suffiraient à peine. Un tel régime ne va point sans une attention
toujours tendue, sans une énergie infatigable, sans un discernement
infaillible, sans une sévérité militaire, sans un génie supérieur, à ces
conditions seulement on peut changer vingt-cinq millions d'hommes en
automates, et substituer sa volonté partout lucide, partout cohérente,
partout présente, à leurs volontés que l'on abolit."
What Louis XVI. was expected to do on a large scale in France,
Ismail Pasha attempted to do on a small scale in Egypt. He naturally
failed.

other countries have foundered before the days of
Ismail Pasha. Such a system must, in fact, lead to
confusion in any country. Under a primitive and
semi-barbarous Government, however, it may continue for a long while without producing a collapse
of the whole machinery of the State. Unless
resort be had to credit, a certain limit is of
necessity imposed on the harm which can be
inflicted by the most capricious despot. He cannot spend more money than he can obtain, and
if he is unable to obtain more than the annual
revenue which his country yields, with perhaps
a certain limited amount taken in advance, the
harm which can be done is not irremediable.
Agriculture is the principal and, indeed, almost
the only resource of most Asiatic States. Neither
the devastation caused by war nor the evils resulting from the most gross forms of misgovernment
can altogether ruin the agriculture of any country.[1]
The *vis medicatrix naturae* soon repairs the harm
which has been done, and leaves a fair field open
for the future labours of some more intelligent
ruler. But the maximum amount of harm is
probably done when an Oriental ruler is for the
first time brought in contact with the European
system of credit. He then finds that he can
obtain large sums of money with the utmost
apparent facility. His personal wishes can thus be
easily gratified. He is dazzled by the ingenious
and often fallacious schemes for developing his
country which European adventurers will not fail
to lay before him in the most attractive light. He
is too wanting in foresight to appreciate the nature
of the future difficulties which he is creating for
himself. The temptation to avail himself to the

---

[1] See Mill's well-known remarks as to why agricultural countries
recover so quickly from the effects of war (*Political Economy*, vol. i.
p. 94).

full of the benefits, which a reckless use of credit seems to offer to him, are too strong to be resisted. He will rush into the gulf which lies open before him, and inflict an injury on his country from which not only his contemporaries but future generations will suffer. This is what Ismail Pasha did. During the early years of his rule, Egypt must have been an earthly paradise for all who had money to lend at usurious rates of interest, or third-rate goods of which they wished to dispose at first-rate prices. I was not acquainted with Egyptian affairs in those halcyon days. I only arrived in Egypt at the moment when the second and inevitable stage on the road to ruin had been reached, and when it was no longer a question of spending money, but of repaying the money already borrowed and spent. Manifestly, the first step to avert further disaster was to prevent more wanton expenditure being incurred, and to obviate fresh abuses accruing from a system which had already inflicted such terrible injury on both the present and future generations of Egyptians. Egypt, it would appear, was to be civilised on a European model. So far, it had assimilated but too often those portions of the European system which were least suitable to an Oriental community, and least worthy of being copied.[1] It was now necessary that at least one cardinal principle of sound European administration should be enforced. The Khedive must accept a Civil List.[2] It should be fixed at a liberal rate,

[1] Mr. Stanley Lane-Poole says with truth, "The Eastern mind has an unequalled aptitude for assimilating the bad and rejecting the good in any system it meets"—*Studies in a Mosque*, p. 106

[2] The acceptance of a Civil List by the Ruler of a misgoverned Oriental State is the first preliminary condition which must precede all other reforms. It would be difficult to insist too strongly on this point. In this connection, I may mention that Sir Edward Malet (*Shifting Scenes*, p. 95) states that, when he was in charge of the British Embassy at Constantinople in 1879, the Sultan had some idea of appointing an Englishman to be his Minister of Finance. Sir Edward

such as would harmonise with the pomp and luxury with which custom has surrounded Oriental rulers; but, when once fixed, it should be unalterable. The residue of the State revenues must for the future be applied by responsible ministers to objects in which the State, as distinguished from the ruler, possessed an evident interest.

As a necessary consequence of the adoption of this system, the estates which had accumulated in the hands of the Khedive had to be handed over to the State. It was an abuse of words to call them private property. They had been bought with public money. It was impossible that any one individual could administer them efficiently. By ceding them, an asset would be obtained to satisfy the outstanding claims of creditors, whilst by the adoption of a system under which the estates could be gradually sold or farmed, great benefit would ultimately accrue to the country.

The Khedive and his family possessed 916,000 acres of land in Egypt. Of these, 485,000 acres were already mortgaged to the Daira creditors. The Khedive, anticipating the demand which was to be made on him, took the initiative during the course of the inquiry, and offered to cede to the State 289,000 acres of the 431,000 which remained to him. The estimated revenue of the lands which he proposed to cede amounted to £167,000

Malet communicated with me. He states, quite accurately, that I sent "a conditional acceptance, which enabled him to go so far as to submit my name to the Sultan." I may now add that the principal of my conditions was that the Sultan should accept a Civil List. I did not for one moment think that this condition would be accepted. My anticipations were realised. I never heard anything more of the matter.

Scarcely less important than the acceptance of a Civil List is the withdrawal of the Crown Domains from the personal administration of a despotic ruler. No one with any knowledge of the government of backward States could have imagined that the system adopted by King Leopold, in connection with the administration of the Congo, would succeed. All the world now knows the results which that system has produced.

a year. That of the 142,000 acres which he proposed to retain amounted to £224,000 a year. The best lands would therefore, under this arrangement, have remained in the hands of the Khedivial family.

The Commissioners were not satisfied with this proposal. They demanded the cession of the whole of the property, rural as well as urban, belonging to the Khedivial family, of which the estimated net revenue was about £423,000 a year.

Such, therefore, were the conclusions to which four months of laborious inquiry had led. The confusion existing in the State accounts was so great, and the system of taxation so irregular, that it was as yet impossible to estimate accurately the resources of Egypt. Neither, indeed, could any general financial arrangement be proposed with advantage until the preliminary questions of principle, to which allusion is made above, were satisfactorily settled. These were, first, the enforcement of the principle of ministerial responsibility; and secondly, the acceptance by the Khedive of a fixed Civil List in lieu of the revenues derived from the properties which, it was demanded, should be yielded to the State.

The Commissioners sent in their report early in August. The Khedive was in doubt as to the line of conduct he should adopt. He was pressed by Nubar Pasha to accept the conclusions of the Commission. After a short period of hesitation, the Khedive yielded. In a speech addressed to Sir Rivers Wilson on August 23, he expressed himself in the following terms: "Quant aux conclusions auxquelles vous êtes arrivé, je les accepte; c'est tout naturel que je le fasse; c'est moi qui ai désiré ce travail pour le bien de mon pays. Il s'agit actuellement pour moi d'appliquer ces conclusions. Je suis résolu de la faire sérieusement, soyez-en convaincu. Mon pays n'est plus en Afrique; nous faisons partie de l'Europe actuellement. Il est donc naturel pour nous d'abandonner les errements anciens pour adopter un système nouveau adapté à notre état social. Je crois que dans un avenir peu éloigné vous verrez des changements considérables. Ils seront amenés plus facilement qu'on ne le croit. Ce n'est au fond qu'une simple question de légalité, de respect à la loi. Il faut surtout ne pas se payer de mots, et pour moi je suis décidé à chercher la réalité des choses. Pour commencer et pour montrer à quel point je suis décidé, j'ai chargé Nubar Pacha de me former un Ministère. Cette innovation peut paraître de peu d'importance; mais de cette innovation, sérieusement conçue, vous verrez sortir l'indépendance ministérielle, et ce n'est pas peu; car cette innovation est le point de départ d'un changement de système, et, d'après moi, la meilleure assurance que je puisse donner du sérieux de mes intentions relativement à l'application de vos conclusions."[1]

A few days later (August 28), the Khedive addressed a letter to Nubar Pasha authorising him to form a Ministry. In this letter, the principle of Ministerial responsibility was reaffirmed. "Doré-navant," the Khedive said, "je veux gouverner avec et par mon Conseil des Ministres. . . . Les membres du Conseil des Ministres devront être tous solidaires les uns des autres; ce point est essentiel." The voice of the majority was to decide upon any question brought before the Council. The chief officials of the State were to be named by the Khedive acting on the advice of his Council of Ministers.

Nubar Pasha undertook the direction of the

[1] This speech had, of course, been prepared by Nubar Pasha for the Khedive.

Departments of Foreign Affairs and of Justice. Riaz Pasha was named Minister of the Interior.

It was, at the same time, decided to introduce an important change into the form in which European agency should be employed in the direction of Egyptian affairs. Only very limited executive functions had been vested in the two Controllers. It was now decided to appoint European Ministers. Thus, the European element was brought into direct contact with the population of the country, instead of acting, as heretofore, through the agency of Egyptian Ministers. Sir Rivers Wilson was named Minister of Finance, and M. de Blignières Minister of Public Works.

On October 29, a Khedivial Decree was issued ceding to the State most of the properties which had heretofore belonged to the Khedivial family, and authorising a loan of £8,500,000 to be raised on the security of those properties. They were to be administered by a Commission composed of an Egyptian, an Englishman, and a Frenchman. The two latter were to be selected by the British and French Governments respectively.

The negotiations which were undertaken with Messrs. Rothschild with a view to the issue of the new loan, delayed the arrival of Sir Rivers Wilson and M. de Blignières in Egypt. It was not till towards the close of November 1878 that they took up their duties.

CHAPTER V

THE FALL OF NUBAR PASHA

NOVEMBER 1878–FEBRUARY 1879

Difficult position of the new Ministry—Support of the British and French Governments—The Khedive declines all responsibility—Convocation of the Chamber of Notables—The principle of Ministerial responsibility—Contest between the Khedive and Nubar Pasha—The Khedive intrigues against the Ministry—Mutiny of the officers—It is quelled by the Khedive—Nubar Pasha resigns—Immediate consequences—Remote consequences—State of discipline of the army—The Khedive's responsibility for the mutiny.

THE new Ministers had undertaken a heavy task. They had to deal not only with difficulties arising from a long course of misgovernment, but also with those due to the special circumstances of the moment. These latter were of a serious nature. The country was staggering under a load of debt which would, under normal circumstances, have taxed its resources to the utmost. Unfortunately, at this particular moment its resources fell below the normal level. The usual Nile flood had failed, and the failure produced the maximum amount of evil consequences, for the system of irrigation was conducted on unscientific principles; neither, although a contingency of this sort was of periodical recurrence, had any preparations been made to meet it. Moreover, the country had been exhausted by the endeavours made to pay the interest on the debt in the previous spring.

64

Further heavy payments were about to fall due. On October 15, 1878, the interest on the Preference Stock, amounting to £443,000, and on November 1, the interest of the Unified Debt, amounting to nearly £2,000,000, had to be paid. To meet these engagements there was, at the end of August, only £442,000 in the hands of the Commissioners of the Debt. The revenue of the first eight months of the year fell short of the receipts during the corresponding period of 1877 by £1,143,000.

The sinking fund of the Unified Debt was, with the consent of the Commissioners of the Debt, temporarily suspended. The relief afforded by this measure was, however, but slight. A sum of £1,260,000 had to be taken from the proceeds of the loan recently negotiated with Messrs. Rothschild in order to pay the interest on the Unified Debt. No sooner had the November coupon been paid, than attention was attracted to the difficulties of meeting the engagements falling due in the following spring. In fact, at this time the Egyptian Government lived from coupon to coupon. Large sums on account of land revenue are generally collected in Egypt during the months of November and December; yet by the end of the year, only £302,000 was in hand to meet a payment of nearly £2,000,000 falling due on May 1, 1879. To meet the coupon on the Preference Stock due on April 15, 1879, and amounting to £443,000, only £117,000 was received from the Railway Administration during the last two and a half months of 1878, although this period embraced the season which was usually the most productive of revenue. Well might Lord Vivian write: "These gloomy returns speak for themselves; they show that the financial position of the country is as bad as it can well be."

From one point of view, however, the new

Ministry began work under auspices which augured well for its success. It was warmly supported by both the British and French Governments. Nevertheless, two points were, from the first, clear. The first was that the new administration could not hope to work successfully unless it were cordially supported by the Khedive. The second was that the Khedive had reluctantly assented to the new order of things, and was inclined to afford a very lukewarm support to his Ministers. It was essential to do all that was possible to ensure his hearty co-operation. The following instructions were, therefore, addressed by Lord Salisbury to Lord Vivian: "In the opinion of Her Majesty's Government a very grave responsibility will rest with His Highness the Khedive for the success or failure of the new régime, especially as regards the collection of taxes. Rumours have already reached Her Majesty's Government which, if well founded, might cause them to apprehend that, under cover of the interference of foreign Governments, attempts will be made in high quarters to throw off all responsibility, a state of things that would soon be understood throughout the country generally. . . .

"Her Majesty's Government have full confidence in the resources of the country, and entertain no doubts as to the result of the new system, if it is only allowed to have a fair trial. But if it be opposed by those in power, or should they even show a disposition to throw discredit upon it, the difficulties of Nubar Pasha and his advisers will be enormously increased, and the responsibility for their failure will involve its promoters in the disastrous consequences that must result."

M. Godeaux, who had taken Baron des Michels' place in Egypt, gave a similar warning to the Khedive on behalf of the French Government.

When these messages were delivered to the
Khedive, he "showed evident signs of great
annoyance, and regretted that Her Majesty's
Government should have thought it necessary
to hold language to him which he thought was
undeserved and unjust." The responsibility which
it was sought to throw on him was, the Khedive
thought, neither just nor logical. What was his
position in Egypt? He had deliberately accepted
the position of a constitutional ruler. A responsible Ministry had been formed to advise him.
"If he rightly understood the first principles of
constitutional government, it was that Ministers,
and not the chief of the State, were made responsible." He must decline to meddle with the
functions of his Ministers. His advice or opinion
was at their disposal if they chose to ask him for
it, but he could not thrust it upon them unasked.
If the Ministers were not responsible for their own
acts, what was the meaning of a responsible
Ministry? Responsibility, he thought, would only
attach to him if he attempted to interfere in the
government of the country. Otherwise, he must
disclaim it.

To all this sophistry Lord Vivian replied, with
obvious good sense, that "His Highness must
remember that, although he had surrendered his
personal power, and a constitutional régime was
established in Egypt, the new order of things was
in its infancy, and it was rather too early for the
strict application of the doctrines of constitutional
government as understood in Europe. His Highness had still all the prestige and influence of the
chief of an Eastern State, combined with greater
knowledge and experience of Egypt than those of
any other person. What Her Majesty's Government desired was that, instead of showing indifference, coldness, or even dislike to the new order of

things, he should place all his knowledge, influence, and experience at the disposal of his Ministers, and loyally and cordially co-operate with them within the proper sphere of his prerogative. A moral responsibility devolved on him for any hostile action that might tend to thwart the new Ministry."

The Khedive's words were ominous. They gave the keynote of what was to follow. The British and French Governments had wished for constitutional government in Egypt. He had complied with their wishes. He would now stand aside whilst the game of constitutional government was being played out. It would soon be found that, without his powerful aid, the country could not be governed at all. If, however, constitutional government was to be tried, he would be thoroughly constitutional. He would leave his Ministers to their own devices, but he could not consent to the imposition of any fresh taxes without ascertaining the will of the people. In 1866, a Chamber of Notables had been created, mainly with a view to throwing dust in the eyes of Europe. The Khedive was fully alive to the fact that, in the then existing condition of affairs in Egypt, the mediæval Italian proverb—*chi dice parlamento, dice guastamento*—applied with full force. He had, therefore, maintained the Chamber in a condition of perfect subserviency to himself. At the time about which I am writing, it had fallen into complete obscurity. It was now to be convoked with a view to the consideration of certain financial proposals, notably the increase in the Ouchouri land-tax,[1] "by which the richer class of proprietors are assessed at rates below the present value of their lands, which have been

[1] The Ouchouri landowners answered, to a great extent, to the Indian jaghirdars. They held fiefs at low rents.

much improved by cultivation." This was constitutionalism with a vengeance, for the Ouchouri
landowners were strongly represented in the
Chamber, and they would not fail to throw on
the new Ministry the odium resulting from an
increase of taxation, which would fall on the class
to which they mainly belonged. Neither would
they be pleased by a measure then under discussion
and subsequently adopted, under which cultivators
residing on Ouchouri lands would no longer, as
heretofore, be exempted from their share of the
corvée.

As has been already explained, the principle
of ministerial responsibility had been accepted by
the Khedive. There were, however, two different
methods of giving effect to that principle.

One was to exclude the Khedive altogether
from the meetings of the Council of Ministers, to
treat him as a cipher, and to endeavour to govern
the country, not only without his co-operation,
but often in a manner which was diametrically
opposed to his personal wishes and opinions. This
system, which involved pushing the principle of
ministerial responsibility to its extreme logical
limit, was advocated by Nubar Pasha, who was
supported by Sir Rivers Wilson. Arguments not
wanting in weight could be advanced in its favour.
The presence of the Khedive at the Council of
Ministers was, it was maintained, incompatible
with free discussion, which often turned either
upon questions affecting His Highness personally,
or upon the errors and abuses of the past, for
which he was principally responsible. Even the
appearance of restoring to him any part of
the power of which he had been shorn would,
it was argued, have a bad effect in the country,
and induce the Egyptians to think that he was
still all-powerful.

This position was perfectly logical; neither, in explaining the causes of Nubar Pasha's attitude, is it necessary to assume that personal ambition and love of power were the motives which prompted him. Without doubt, in attempting to put the Khedive altogether aside, Nubar Pasha thought that he was rendering a real service to his adopted country. Nubar Pasha, although somewhat of a doctrinaire, was an earnest reformer. Moreover, his versatile intellect was capable of grasping a principle. In this case, he had got hold of a principle which was unquestionably sound. His French education, which tended to engender in his mind a somewhat uncompromising attitude on matters of theory, coupled with a certain inaptitude to seize the springs of action which move individuals as well as Governments, conspired to convince him that the principle should be driven home to its logical conclusion. Loyalty to a colleague, personal friendship, respect for Nubar Pasha's abilities, consideration for his superior local knowledge, and a vivid realisation of the harm done by Ismail Pasha's abuse of personal power, all rendered it natural that Sir Rivers Wilson should follow in the same track.

The alternative system, which was supported by Lord Vivian, was less theoretically perfect, but was in a greater degree based on the actual circumstances then existing in Egypt. Lord Vivian thought that Nubar Pasha had overrated his own strength and underrated the power of the Khedive. That power was still an important factor in the government of a country which he and his predecessors had ruled for so long and in so absolute a fashion. The Khedive was the only authority recognised and obeyed by all classes in the land. There was no middle course between deposing him or counting with his power. The only system which presented a chance of success was not to put the Khedive on one side altogether, but to invite his co-operation, whilst at the same time the exercise of his authority would be controlled.

My own views were expressed on February 17, 1879,—the day before the mutiny of the officers to which allusion will presently be made,—in the following terms : "The transition from a purely personal government by the Khedive to a government by an executive council, whose leading members are aliens and Christians, has been too rapid. For some time to come, it will be impossible not to take into account the personal authority of the Khedive as an element in the government of the country ; he will always possess a large influence, which, if it be not used for good, will almost certainly be used for bad ; I therefore think it desirable to consider the best method of giving the Khedive some practical share in the government of the country."

Whatever defects, however, may have existed in the methods of giving effect to a policy of reform, it was certain that the Ministry of Nubar Pasha represented the cause of progress and civilisation. The ultimate consequences of its fall might, and probably would be serious in so far as the Khedive was personally concerned. But the Khedive, true to the traditions of his previous life, took little heed of ultimate consequences. In the meanwhile, the immediate issue of the struggle between the Khedive and Nubar Pasha could scarcely be doubtful. Nubar Pasha was at a great disadvantage. On the one side, was a ruler who was feared and obeyed, who disposed absolutely of the lives and fortunes of his subjects, and who could readily divert the rising tide of popular discontent from his own person and turn it against his Ministers. On the other side, was a Minister who was not only a Christian and associated with other European Christians, but who also belonged to a nationality against which the Mohammedan population of the Ottoman Empire is greatly prejudiced. "When an Armenian rules," says the Turkish proverb, "the State decays."[1] Nubar Pasha carried but little weight with the Egyptian population, with whom, moreover, owing to his ignorance of Arabic, he was unable to communicate in their own language. He could only rely on persuasion and on the support of two foreign Governments. This support, although heartily accorded,[2] did him in some respects more harm than good. Under these circumstances, his eventual fall from power was almost a foregone conclusion.

The crisis did not, however, arise at once. For a few months, the new machine of government worked, although with great friction. The Khedive frequently complained that the anomalous position in which it was sought to place him was daily becoming more and more intolerable, and that, whilst he was not consulted about the measures of his Ministers, at the same time the British and French Governments held him responsible for their result. On the other hand, Nubar Pasha was "evidently discouraged and dissatisfied." "Nous tournons," he said, "dans un cercle vicieux. Nous ne marchons pas."

In the meanwhile, there was good reason for believing that the Khedive was actively intriguing against his Ministers. "There is," Lord Vivian

---

[1] *Ermeni vizir, devlet düsher.* Some of the more superstitious followers of Islam are said to derive a certain amount of consolation from the fact that Armenians have occasionally occupied high posts in the service of their hereditary enemy, Russia.

[2] It has been occasionally stated that if Lord Vivian had supported Nubar Pasha more cordially, he might have been maintained in power. Such is not my opinion. Lord Vivian's instructions were clear, and he acted loyally upon them.

wrote on January 11, "a certain amount of fermentation in the country as evidenced by the arrival of large deputations of Sheikhs from the provinces to protest against any pressure for the payment of taxes at this moment, and I am told that there is a probability of opposition in the Chamber of Delegates to the proposition that is to be submitted to them by the Government for an increase of the Ouchouri tax, which falls especially upon the richer class of proprietors. If this fermentation were natural, it would not be an unhealthy symptom, but I have good reason to suspect that it has been secretly fomented by agents, probably employed by the Khedive; and I hear from a reliable source that the leading men of the Chamber of Notables have been secretly convoked and told that the Khedive would not be displeased to see them oppose the measures of an administration which was imposed upon him, and which was entirely in the hands of Europeans.

"Thus, in addition to their serious financial difficulties, and to the task of attempting to create order out of chaos, the new Ministry have to struggle, not only with open enemies, but with internal treachery of the most dangerous description, carried on in spite of serious warning."

Under circumstances such as these, it only required the occurrence of some adventitious incident to bring about a crisis. No long delay intervened before such an incident occurred. It was, however, unfortunate that it happened in that branch of the State administration which, perhaps less than any other, can be infected with disease without producing after-effects of a serious nature. Hitherto, Egypt had suffered mainly from fiscal misgovernment. The only sound part of the system was that public tranquillity had been preserved, and, whatever may be thought of the methods by which it had been preserved, every one but a devotee of the sacred right of revolution would prefer order of some sort to complete anarchy. The security, which had so far reigned, was now to be disturbed. The financial embarrassments of Egypt were great. To these was now to be superadded the disquietude produced by a mutinous army.

Great discontent had been produced amongst the officers of the army owing to the non-payment of their salaries. The new Ministry decided to pay a portion of the arrears due. At the same time, a large number of officers were placed on half-pay. This measure would, under any circumstances, have been considered harsh, however necessary it might have been in view of the straitened condition of the Egyptian Treasury. It was, however, especially harsh and impolitic to dismiss so large a body of officers without, in the first place, fully liquidating the arrears of pay due to them. The result was that many officers and their families were reduced to a state of complete destitution.

When this measure was adopted, there were about 500 officers in Cairo; but at this moment, Lord Vivian reported, "by an unparalleled act of folly, the Minister of War summoned the remaining 2000 officers up to Cairo from various parts of the country to receive a portion of their arrears of pay and to deposit their arms with the authorities. He thus grouped together a seething mass of 2500 discontented officers, the garrison of Cairo consisting only of 2600 troops, a large proportion of whom had undoubted sympathy with the grievances of the mutineers."

On the morning of February 18, as Nubar Pasha and Sir Rivers Wilson were driving to their

offices, they were mobbed by a crowd of officers
armed with swords, and taken out of their carriages.
After being subjected to some rough treatment,
they were dragged to the Ministry of Finance,
which was close to the scene of the outrage, where
they were shut in by the mutineers, who cut the
telegraph wires.   Means were, however, found to
communicate with Lord Vivian, who at once had
an interview with the Khedive.   What followed
may best be related in Lord Vivian's words.   "The
Khedive," he reported, "drove with me to the
Ministry of Finance, which we found besieged by a
large crowd, who, however, made way respectfully
for the Khedive's carriage, and cheered him.   In a
room on the upper floor, surrounded by the rioters,
we found Nubar Pasha, Sir Rivers Wilson, and
Riaz Pasha, none of them really hurt, although the
two former had received very rough treatment
while they were being forced from the street into
the building.   The Khedive, having assured himself of their safety, turned to the rioters and
ordered them to leave the building on his promise
that their just demands should be satisfied.   'If,'
he said, 'you are my officers, you are bound by
your oath to obey me ; if you refuse, I will have
you swept away.'   They obeyed him, although
reluctantly and with some murmuring, begging
him to leave them to settle their accounts in their
own way.   There were also cries of 'Death to the
dogs of Christians.'   His Highness got them down
the stairs and into and beyond the courtyard,
where they fell back on the larger body who were
besieging the gates.   The Khedive commanded all
of them to disperse and go to their homes, and on
their refusal to do so, he ordered up the troops.
They fired in the air, but a few soldiers were
wounded by the mutineers' revolvers, and a few
of the rioters received bayonet wounds.   The

Khedive's chamberlain was wounded while at His Highness's side by a sabre-cut from one of the mutineers, and the Khedive himself ran considerable risk. The whole affair lasted about half-an-hour, and the Khedive, after providing for the safe escort of the Ministers, returned to the Palace. Sir Rivers Wilson behaved well throughout the affair, which he might have avoided had he not gone to Nubar Pasha's assistance, when he saw him surrounded by the mob."

On the following morning (February 19), a meeting took place at Lord Vivian's house, at which M. Godeaux, Sir Rivers Wilson, M. de Blignières, and myself were present. Lord Vivian stated that the Khedive had on the previous day made a declaration to the Consular body to the effect that his position must be changed, and his proper share of power restored to him, or he would not be answerable for the maintenance of public order. It was decided to ask the Khedive to state in what respects he wished his position to be modified.

We then drove to the Palace. Nubar Pasha, Sir Rivers Wilson, M. de Blignières, and myself remained in a room on the ground floor, while Lord Vivian and M. Godeaux had an interview with the Khedive upstairs. In a short while, they reappeared and communicated the Khedive's reply. His Highness stated "unequivocally that he would not be responsible for public tranquillity unless he were given his proper share in the government of the country, and was allowed either to preside at the Council of Ministers himself, or to select a President in whom he could have confidence. He further required, as a *sine qua non* condition, that Nubar Pasha, whom he accused of sapping and undermining his authority, should immediately retire from the Ministry." Nubar Pasha was asked

whether, in the event of the Consuls-General
insisting on his remaining in office, he would
guarantee the public safety. He naturally declined
to give any such guarantee. "The only course,"
he said, " left open to him under the circumstances
was to tender his resignation, which he begged
Lord Vivian and M. Godeaux as a favour to place
in the Khedive's hands, with a request that he
should be allowed to live unmolested as a private
individual in Egypt." To this request, the Khedive
consented, " on the condition that Nubar Pasha did
not intrigue or meddle in politics."

Thus the struggle between the Khedive and
Nubar Pasha was brought to a close. The attempt
to govern Egypt whilst Ismail Pasha was Khedive,
without allowing him any participation in the
government of the country, had signally failed.
Tried in the manner which has been described
above, the failure of the experiment was certain.
Indeed, looking back on the events of that time
after an interval of many years, my principal
feeling is one of surprise that any one should for
a moment have thought that, under these conditions, the experiment could possibly have succeeded.
Nubar Pasha's fall from power was inevitable.

The circumstances narrated in this chapter
produced important changes, some immediate
and others more remote.

The immediate consequence was that the position of the European Ministers was shaken, and
that before long they were dismissed from office.

The remote consequences were of even greater
importance. The officers of the army had, in the
first instance, been unjustly treated. They were
not paid the money which was due to them. So
long as their complaints were put forward in a
manner to which no exception could be taken,
they remained unheeded. At last, they mutinied.

They then obtained what they wanted.[1] A public
apology was tendered to Sir Rivers Wilson by
Prince Hassan, the Khedive's son and the Commander-in-Chief of the Egyptian army, for the
insults and ill-treatment to which he had been
subjected. But, although the ringleaders of
the mutiny were arrested, and some inquiry
into their conduct was instituted, they were
speedily released. Indeed, under the circumstances which then existed, it would have been
difficult to have subjected them to any punishment without incurring serious risks. It is
impossible to treat any armed body of men after
this fashion with impunity. The discipline of the
Egyptian army was profoundly shaken. The
most humble private soldier discovered, for the
first time, probably to his own exceeding astonishment, that he and his comrades were masters of
the situation, if, with muskets in their hands, they
exerted themselves to coerce the civil elements of
society. History affords abundant proofs of the
ease with which this lesson is learnt. It was not to
be unlearnt until a stronger race of soldiers appeared
on Egyptian soil. The mutiny of 1879 was the
direct precursor of the Arábi revolt. It would be
going too far to say that from this moment a foreign
occupation of Egypt became inevitable, but it is
certainly a fact that the mutiny which led to the

---

[1] At the time of the mutiny, the Treasury chest was empty. It was
imperative to pay the officers, who then held the town of Cairo at
their mercy, but considerable difficulty was experienced in obtaining
the money. I remember being present at an interview between Sir
Rivers Wilson and the representative of a local bank, who offered to
advance money at an exorbitant rate of interest. Sir Rivers Wilson
showed a moral courage after the riot as conspicuous as the physical
courage he had displayed whilst the riot was taking place. He declined
to accept the offer which was made to him, and he also refused to revert
to the pernicious system of taking the taxes in advance, although the
adoption of this measure was pressed upon him. Eventually, Messrs.
Rothschild advanced £400,000, which was repaid from the loan funds,
and the officers were paid.

downfall of Nubar Pasha greatly increased the difficulties of governing the country, and brought the prospects of foreign intervention of a decisive nature appreciably nearer.

There is one further point which calls for remark before leaving the history of this period. An opinion was at the time generally entertained that Ismail Pasha was privy to the mutiny of the officers, and, in fact, that the whole affair was an intrigue got up by the Khedive himself. It is a dangerous thing for a despotic ruler, who depends wholly on force for the maintenance of his power, to encourage a mutiny in his own army, even although he may himself sympathise with the objects of the mutineers. The spirit of mutiny, when once raised, may not improbably turn against the individual who raised it. Nevertheless, unwise though a policy of this sort would have been, there is no inherent improbability in such a dangerous agency as a mutinous soldiery being used by an Eastern ruler, who, in spite of an acute and subtle intellect, was singularly lacking in foresight, who was smarting under the humiliation of a loss of power, and who had unbounded confidence in his ability to rule, by his own drastic methods, the generally docile races who inhabit the valley of the Nile. Any opinion, however, of the degree to which Ismail Pasha was privy to the mutiny must be little more than conjecture. It is impossible to adduce positive proof that he knew anything precise of the intended outrage on Nubar Pasha and Sir Rivers Wilson. The alarm he displayed at the spirit of disorder which had been evoked was perhaps genuine. It is, indeed, more than probable that, when the officers assembled near the Ministry of Finance on the morning of February 18, they had not devised amongst themselves any very definite plan of action. Nevertheless, it

would in any case be incorrect to say that the
responsibility for the outrage does not rest on
Ismail Pasha. On the contrary, he was, without
doubt, morally responsible for it.[1] It does not
require either a very vivid imagination or any
great acquaintance with Eastern politics to form
a fairly accurate idea of what must have taken
place. I can best describe my own conjecture on
the subject by an analogy drawn from a well-
known incident in English history.

When Henry II. wished to get rid of Thomas à
Becket he said, in the presence of his court, "Will
no one rid me of this turbulent priest?" and forth-
with four knights were found who possibly went
beyond their master's wishes, and rid him of the
Archbishop in the rude but effectual manner of
the twelfth century. Ismail Pasha's language and
intentions were, without doubt, more in conformity
with the civilised age in which we live than those
of Henry II., but his procedure was based on the
same principles as those of the English king. He
spoke openly of the dislike which he entertained
towards Nubar Pasha and his European Ministers.
He represented his position as intolerable. In an
Eastern country, this was enough to focus on the
Ministry the responsibility for all the evils which
then afflicted Egypt. The officers of the army
were discontented. They attributed the miserable
condition in which they were placed to the action
of Nubar Pasha and his colleagues, who were
aliens and Christians. They learnt that their ruler,
who was of their own race and faith, and to whom
they had been accustomed to yield implicit
obedience, was as hostile as they were to the new

---

[1] It has been stated on good authority that a few days before the
mutiny, Shahin Pasha spoke to the Khedive about the grievances of
the officers, and that the latter replied: "Pourquoi les officiers
restent-ils tranquilles?" If this be true, it is quite sufficient to
account for the outbreak.

Ministry, and would be pleased if means could be found to bring about its downfall. That was enough. They naturally mutinied, and in doing so they, without doubt, thought that they were not only furthering their own interests, but also that they were acting in a manner which would obtain the commendation of their Sovereign.

This is a sufficient and highly probable explanation of the causes which led to the mutiny. It is scarcely worth while to seek for any other.

CHAPTER VI

THE COUP D'ÉTAT

APRIL 1879

THE Khedive had obtained a considerable triumph. He had got rid of a Minister who was distasteful to him, although the latter had been supported by two powerful foreign Governments. He had shown all the world that, without his co-operation, Egypt could not be governed. The theory of ministerial responsibility might be sound, but the personal power of a despotic ruler in an Oriental State was a practical fact, which had to be taken into account in the application of the best of theories.

If Ismail Pasha had been content with what he had achieved, and had from this time forth worked loyally with his European Ministers, he might possibly have died Khedive of Egypt. But it was one of the characteristics of this singular man that, although he had a quick perception in dealing with points of minor importance, he erred at almost every important crisis of his career. He was unable to frame a correct estimate of the main factors in a general political situation. He was wanting in the power described by the Duke of Wellington, as "guessing at what is going on on the other side of the hill." His political forecasts were singularly faulty. He would frequently show great acuteness in deciding on some matter of detail, but would generally make a mistake on a broad question of principle. Lord Palmerston once said that if a little learning was a dangerous thing, no learning at all was much more dangerous, and so, without doubt, it generally is. But Ismail Pasha was a living proof that there is a good deal of truth in the words of the English poet. He would probably have fared better if he had never made any attempt either to understand European politics or to gauge European public opinion. As it was, he had just sufficient knowledge of these subjects to lead him astray. He knew that Europeans laid much stress on the will of the people. They had large talking assemblies, termed Parliaments, to whose will Kings and Emperors were obliged to conform. Such institutions were, of course, wholly unsuitable to Egypt. Nevertheless, would it not be possible to hoist these Franks with their own petard? It was, indeed, difficult to deal with the French. They scarcely made a pretence of caring for anything but the interests of the French creditors. It was true that, but a short time previously, he had declared that the country was bankrupt, but circumstances altered cases. Egypt had vast resources. Huge sums had before now been screwed out of the unfortunate peasantry. Let him regain his personal power, and adopt his own rude methods for collecting the revenue. A few extra blows of the courbash would produce financial equilibrium. Thus would he conjure French opposition.

The case of the English was different. They cared, or at all events they pretended to care for the welfare of the fellaheen. They disliked to hear of oppression even in the cause of the bondholders. Lectures on this subject had been frequently delivered to him by meddling Consuls-General and by the misguided humanitarian press of England. But the English were an essentially gullible race. They had, at a recent period of their history, got embroiled with the half of Europe because they sympathised with oppressed nationalities, and believed that parliamentary institutions, trial by jury, and the like, were certain remedies for all the maladies with which States, in whatsoever part of the world, were afflicted.[1] They were easily carried away by phrases such as the popular will, constitutional government, and so on. Moreover, the English were a stiff-necked people who would not easily be led by officials. On the contrary, they as often as not thought that, when they had paid their officials high salaries for looking after their interests in a foreign country, they had done enough. They were under no obligation to accept as correct what their representatives said. Indeed, they were at that time rather inclined to disbelieve their officials because they were officials, and, therefore, presumably devoid of popular sympathies.[2] With a people such as this, a great deal might be done. Might not an acute ruler so

[1] "Lord Palmerston, in the most insolent manner, told the Greek Minister that he might tell the King of Greece that he never should have a moment's peace or quiet until he gave his subjects a constitution; that he, Lord Palmerston, would take care that neither he nor any other Sovereign who governed without a constitution should have any peace; that all people so governed had a right to 'insurger,' and he took good care to let them know that such was his opinion" (Sir Robert Peel's *Memoirs*, vol. ii. p. 178). The passage is contained in a letter written in 1839 by "a lady unnamed in the Whig camp."

[2] It must be borne in mind that I am speaking of a period before the birth of modern Imperialism. Since 1876, the general tone of British public opinion has undergone many notable changes.

adapt his language as to suit a foreign public, whilst his acts would be in strict conformity with his own wishes and personal interests? The British Government must not be openly defied. That would be a proceeding both clumsy and attended with some risk. Belial was a wiser councillor than Moloch. But surely if a scheme were devised which would present matters to the British Government and public in a form to which they were accustomed, if their most cherished institutions were apparently copied in Egypt, if the Egyptian people were to express their own views through their own representatives, then the bait would take. An Egyptian Parliament should, therefore, be assembled. The representatives of the Egyptian people should express their devotion to the Khedive, and their satisfaction with his system of government. They would reject as insulting the imputation that the country was bankrupt. They would demur to the changes in the system of taxation proposed by the European advisers of their Sovereign. Those changes were unjust, and, moreover, it was an incidental point of some importance that, under the European proposals, the fresh taxation would fall on the representatives themselves rather than on the people whom, by a bold flight of the imagination, they were presumed to represent. But they would devise another system which would be more equitable. The representatives of the people, who were rich, should preserve their former privileges, but they would make large sacrifices in order to enable Egypt to meet its financial engagements. It was true that those sacrifices would fall, not on themselves, but on their fellow-countrymen in more humble classes of society. But the result would be the same. The interest of the debt would be paid. The members of the Egyptian Parliament must be left to devise their own scheme. That was essential.

Otherwise, constitutional government would be a mere farce. Their patriotism would revolt at the idea of any foreign interference. For the future, it must cease. The European Ministers must be dismissed.

When all this was done, it would not be necessary to talk any more of Parliaments or of popular representation. The necessity for their existence would have passed away. An intelligent despot ruling over a docile people would easily find some means for preventing parliamentary institutions from taking any solid root in the country. The personal rule of the Khedive would be restored. The people, who had before been scourged with rods, would in future be scourged with scorpions. The bondholders would be paid, and no one would be able to complain.

Thus Ismail Pasha pondered over things which were never destined to be accomplished.

The idea was ingenious, but the circumstances under which the experiment was tried were unfavourable to success. Ismail Pasha was too well known in Europe to play the part of an ultra-constitutional monarch. The most ardent partisan of parliamentary institutions, however ill-informed about Eastern politics, whilst yielding a ready assent to the principles involved, would not be able to refrain from some scepticism as regards the intentions of the principal character in the piece. Moreover, there were at the time in Cairo a number of European officials of inconveniently independent characters, who had some knowledge of the country, and who would certainly make their voices heard. They, at least, would be thrown into strong opposition. They knew too much to be taken in by this flimsy travesty of free institutions. Indeed, had not the interests involved, both European and Egyptian, been so serious, they would almost certainly have regarded the whole proceeding not merely as a comedy, but as a screaming farce.   Further, the whole project was tainted by one irremediable defect.   It was based on the assumption that money would be forthcoming to satisfy the claims of the foreign creditors.   Now, in supposing that, by whatsoever means, he could meet all his financial engagements, Ismail Pasha erred.   He forgot to make sure of his foundations before erecting his superstructure.

When Nubar Pasha was forced to resign, Lord Vivian pointed out that "the incident would become still more serious if it were to shake the experiment of reformed government in Egypt, which should certainly be maintained, only with far more consideration than has been shown for the feelings, rights, and prejudices of the natives."

Lord Vivian had indicated the main danger of the moment.   The reformed administration must be supported.   Lord Vivian was, therefore, instructed "to state to the Khedive that the French and British Governments were determined to act in concert in all that concerned Egypt, and that they could not lend themselves to any modification in principle of the political and financial arrangements recently sanctioned by His Highness.   It was to be clearly understood that the resignation of Nubar Pasha had, in the eyes of both Governments, only importance so far as the question of persons was concerned, but that it could not imply a change of system."   Similar instructions were sent by the French Government to their representative in Cairo.

On the Khedive being informed of the tenor of these instructions, he replied "that he would pledge himself to maintain intact the engagements he had taken in August last, and which constituted the charter of the new scheme of administrative

reform.[1] With respect to his financial engagements, he could assure the two Consuls-General
of his sincere desire to observe them, but he could
not prejudice the decisions of his Council of
Ministers on this point."

Nothing could be fairer or more constitutional.
The principles of the reformed administration were
to be maintained. As regards the financial engagements, the Khedive could obviously give no promise.
All the world, in fact, knew by this time that the
arrangements made in November 1876 would have
to be modified. A month previously, Lord Vivian
had reported that "frequent meetings were being
held between Sir Rivers Wilson, M. de Blignières,
and Sir Evelyn Baring, with the object of arriving
at some joint conclusions as to the basis upon which
a general and equitable arrangement, amounting
to a composition of the present financial difficulties
of the Egyptian Government, was possible."

Two important questions then had to be decided.
The first was, who was to be the new Prime
Minister. The second was the nature of the rela-
tions between the Khedive and his new Ministry.

Sir Rivers Wilson pressed for the reinstatement
of Nubar Pasha. He was supported by the British
Government. "Her Majesty's Government," Lord
Salisbury said, "are of opinion that the position
of Sir Rivers Wilson will be extremely difficult,
if not impossible to maintain, unless Nubar Pasha
is readmitted to the Cabinet in some form or
other."

Lord Vivian, however, did not concur in this
opinion. "I desire," he wrote, "to place on record
my strong conviction that Nubar Pasha's idea of
maintaining two distinct and probably antagonistic
powers in the State (the Khedive and the Council
of Ministers) will prove impracticable as long as

[1] Vide ante, pp. 61-63.

the present Khedive remains in power. . . . Any proposal for the re-entry of Nubar Pasha into the Cabinet, after what has happened, would be, I fear, in every respect a serious mistake that might lead to difficulties and complications, which Her Majesty's Government would wish to avoid."

When the Khedive was addressed on the subject, he said that "he could not do otherwise than bow to the will of the English and French Governments, which he had no power to resist, if they persisted in their demand for the re-entry of Nubar Pasha; but he felt bound to warn them beforehand of the consequences, so that they might not blame him hereafter if the new order of things should break down, or if disturbances should again arise."

It was clear that, if Nubar Pasha were forced upon the Khedive, another and perhaps more serious breakdown would ensue. The French Government, therefore, suggested that it might not be advisable to insist on his readmission. The British Government assented, but they "accompanied the concession with a warning to the Khedive that they considered His Highness responsible for the recent difficulties in Egypt, and that if similar difficulties should occur again, the consequences would be very serious to him."

Concurrently with the discussion of the question of Nubar Pasha's readmission to the Cabinet, the relations which were to subsist between the Khedive and his Ministers were considered afresh. The Khedive made certain proposals. The European Ministers made counter-proposals. Eventually, the British and French Governments decided on the following programme:—(1) The Khedive was not in any case to be present at Cabinet Councils. (2) Prince Tewfik, the heir-apparent to the Khedivate, who had been proposed by the Khedive himself, was to be appointed President of the Council. (3) The English and French members of the Cabinet were to have a right of veto over any proposed measure.

On these proposals being laid before the Khedive, he said that "he unreservedly subscribed to all the conditions imposed by the Governments of England and France, more especially as they had listened to his objections against the re-entry of Nubar Pasha into the Cabinet, for which he expressed his gratitude. He fully acknowledged the very serious responsibility that now devolved upon him for the success of the new order of things and for the prevention of disorder, and he pledged his cordial and loyal support to his Ministers if, as he hoped, they would meet him in the same conciliatory spirit."

It appeared, therefore, that the difficulties in the way of the formation of a new Ministry were at an end. On March 10, Prince Tewfik was nominated President of the Council. When, however, the question arose of filling up the remaining places in the Cabinet, fresh dissensions broke out between the Khedive and his European Ministers. Under the Ministry of Nubar Pasha, Riaz Pasha had been in charge of the Department of the Interior. The Khedive now wished to transfer Riaz Pasha to the Ministry of Foreign Affairs and of Justice. The European Ministers objected to this transfer, on the ground that the Khedive's object was to regain his hold over the provinces, which would be impossible so long as a man of such independent character as Riaz Pasha was Minister of the Interior. Lord Vivian and M. Godeaux, on the other hand, considered that it would be inconsistent with the personal responsibility thrown on the Khedive to dictate to him the choice of his Ministers and the posts they should occupy. The British

and French Governments, however, more especially
the former, supported the views of Sir Rivers
Wilson and M. de Blignières. The Khedive was
pressed to maintain Riaz Pasha at the Ministry of
the Interior. He at first declined to do so, but
eventually gave a reluctant assent. On March
22, after the country had remained for a month
without a Ministry, Riaz Pasha was named Minister
of the Interior and of Justice. The remaining
places in the Cabinet were easily filled up.

At the same time, a letter was addressed by the
Khedive to Prince Tewfik, embodying the principles
which were to regulate the relations between the
Khedive and his Ministers. "J'espère," the Khedive
added, "que ces nouveaux arrangements assure-
ront la marche de la nouvelle organisation, dont la
réussite doit amener un grand bien pour l'Égypte.
Le Cabinet peut être assuré qu'en toutes circon-
stances il peut compter de ma part sur le concours
le plus complet et le plus loyal, comme je compte
moi-même sur son dévouement à l'œuvre que nous
poursuivons en commun."

During these discussions, the British and French
Governments had been in a difficult position. The
general political interest of England was clear.
England did not want to possess Egypt, but it was
essential to British interests that the country should
not fall into the hands of any other European
Power. British policy in respect to Egypt had
for years past been based on this principle. In
1857, the Emperor Napoleon III. made overtures
to the British Government with a view to the
partition of the northern portions of Africa.
Morocco was to fall to France, Tunis to Sardinia,
and Egypt to England.[1] On this proposal being

---

[1] The accuracy of this statement is confirmed by M Emile Ollivier,
who speaks with authority on the subject. See his *L'Empire Libéral*,
vol. iii. p. 418.

submitted to Lord Palmerston, he stated his views in a letter to Lord Clarendon. "It is very possible," he said, "that many parts of the world would be better governed by France, England, and Sardinia than they are now. . . . We do not want to have Egypt. What we wish about Egypt is that it should continue to be attached to the Turkish Empire, which is a security against its belonging to any European Power. We want to trade with Egypt, and to travel through Egypt, but we do not want the burthen of governing Egypt. . . . Let us try to improve all those countries by the general influence of our commerce, but let us abstain from a crusade of conquest which would call down upon us the condemnation of all other civilised nations."[1]

The general aims of British policy in 1879 were much the same as they had been when Lord Palmerston wrote these lines twenty - two years previously; but, with a change of circumstances, the method of giving effect to the policy had necessarily to be modified. It was no longer possible to stand aside and neglect the internal affairs of Egypt. The only European Power which was likely to obtain a footing in Egypt was France. The attempt had already been made once, and the misgovernment of Egypt might well lead to its being renewed, more especially as large French financial interests, to which the French Government were prepared to afford support, were concerned. Even admitting, as was without doubt

[1] Ashley's *Life of Lord Palmerston*, vol. ii. p. 125. I cannot refrain from adding the following characteristic passage: "On one occasion to Lord Cowley, he (Lord Palmerston) used a very homely but apt illustration. 'We do not want Egypt,' he said, 'or wish it for ourselves, any more than any rational man with an estate in the north of England and a residence in the south would have wished to possess the inns on the north road All he could want would have been that the inns should be well-kept, always accessible, and furnishing him, when he came, with mutton-chops and post-horses.'"

the case, that the French Government had at that time no designs involving the annexation of Egypt, the pressure of public opinion was so great that it would have been scarcely possible for France to have adopted a policy of complete non-intervention. If the British Government would not act with them, the French Government would have been obliged to act alone.

French policy in respect to Egypt was, in most essential points, the counterpart of the policy of the British Government. It was impossible to adopt a policy of annexation, even had there been any disposition in that direction, without incurring the risk, amounting almost to a certainty, of a serious quarrel with England. But France regarded the exclusive action of England in Egypt with the same jealousy as that with which England would have regarded exclusively French action. Any extension of Turkish influence ran counter to the traditional policy of France. It was clearly in the interests of both Governments to prevent the affairs of Egypt from becoming a cause of serious dissension between them. Both had equal interests in the maintenance of the peace of Europe. It was obviously undesirable that the misgovernment of an Oriental state should threaten a disturbance of the peace. The best way to prevent any risk of dissension was for both Governments to co-operate in Egypt with a view to the establishment in that country of a system of administration, which, although possibly defective, would be sufficient to check the worst of the existing abuses, and thus, by obviating the necessity for further interference, prevent the Egyptian Question from becoming European rather than local.

In the execution of this policy, occasional disagreements occurred. The French Government dwelt strongly on the interests of the foreign creditors. The British Government leant to the cause of the Egyptian peasantry. But in spite of some differences of opinion, the principle of common action was maintained. Moreover, the harmony which existed between London and Paris was reproduced in Cairo. In spite of occasional jars, the local representatives of the two Governments, as also their countrymen who were employed in the Egyptian service, worked fairly well together.

Every one recognised that the anarchical condition of affairs then existing in Egypt was due to the misgovernment of one individual, the Khedive Ismail Pasha. Of that, there could not be any doubt. But, as has been already pointed out, there were two methods of checking the continuance of misgovernment. One was to place Ismail Pasha under such stringent control as to reduce him almost to a cipher. The other was to impose on him a modified form of control, to recognise the impossibility of governing the country without his co-operation so long as he remained Khedive of Egypt, and to endeavour to guide him in the path of reform rather than to exercise extreme compulsion in forcing him along it.

It was a most unfortunate circumstance that at this moment the principal Europeans concerned in the administration of Egypt were not agreed as to which of these two systems should be adopted. The official world was divided into two opposing camps, each honestly believing that its own system was the best. Lord Vivian supported the system which involved counting with Ismail Pasha's personal power. Sir Rivers Wilson supported the rival system, which involved the reduction of the Khedive to a political nullity.

Neither Lord Vivian nor Sir Rivers Wilson had had any previous experience in dealing with Eastern affairs. Sir Rivers Wilson had passed his life in the service of the English Treasury, where he had acquired a sound financial training, which, added to much natural quickness and ability, proved of great service to him in dealing with the technical portions of the Egyptian financial situation.[1] In some respects, however, this training was a disadvantage to him. The fiscal system in an Eastern country differs widely from that which exists in England; neither does the technically sound but somewhat narrow school of the English Treasury afford an ideal training for an Englishman who has to deal with Eastern affairs. It often engenders a somewhat inelastic frame of mind, and a tendency to ignore political considerations which no European financier in the East can afford to neglect.

Lord Vivian, on the other hand, had had no experience in dealing with financial affairs. This was a disadvantage to him at a time when the pecuniary embarrassments of the country, in which he was the British representative, had become the chief subject for diplomatic action. On the other hand, he had been dealing with foreign affairs all his life. He had had a sound diplomatic training. He possessed a calm judgment, great moral courage, and a clear insight into the political forces at work around him.

I was a spectator of these unfortunate dissensions, and was thus in a position to hear both sides of the question. My belief is that, in view of Ismail Pasha's personal character, neither the adoption of the system advocated by Lord Vivian, nor the adoption of that of which Sir Rivers Wilson was the leading representative, would have materially

---

[1] Sir Rivers Wilson was employed in Egypt for a couple of months in 1876, and had thus learnt something of the local financial situation, but the period was too short to enable him to acquire any real experience of Orientals or of Eastern forms of government.

altered the course of Egyptian history. No confidence could be placed in Ismail Pasha's promises. Whatever he might say, he was determined to remain the absolute ruler of Egypt. He might appear to yield for the moment, but he trusted to his resource and to his remarkable power of intrigue to nullify any concessions which might be extorted from him, and thus ultimately regain his previous position. This, however, is mere conjecture. It is possible that I may be doing an injustice to Ismail Pasha, though I do not think that I am. What is more certain is that the system advocated by Lord Vivian gave him a fair chance if he wished to act up to the engagements which he had taken. It presented some hope of success. Sir Rivers Wilson's policy, on the other hand, was foredoomed to failure. It was based on an incorrect appreciation of what was and what was not possible under the political circumstances then existing in Egypt.

In the meantime, the British Government were bewildered by the conflicting accounts which they received from Egypt. One point, however, was clear. The disagreements between Lord Vivian and Sir Rivers Wilson were doing a great deal of harm. Ismail Pasha would gladly play the congenial part of a *tertius gaudens.* He would not be slow to turn the position to his own advantage. On March 15, therefore, Lord Vivian was summoned to London. On March 20, Sir Frank Lascelles arrived to take over Lord Vivian's duties. He was instructed "to give his cordial support to Sir Rivers Wilson in his dealings with the Khedive."

Prince Tewfik, at the time of his assuming the presidency of the Egyptian Council in 1879, was twenty-seven years of age. He was desirous to do all in his power to help in the crisis which then existed in Egyptian affairs. On March 24, he had an interview with Sir Frank Lascelles. The mutinous officers, he said, had been paid. "Tout rentrera dans le calme." The Khedive was determined to act in harmony with his Ministers. "There were, no doubt, great difficulties to be overcome, but with the cordial co-operation of all parties, they might be surmounted."

Nevertheless, the experiment which was made at this time failed. The Khedive had, indeed, got rid of Nubar Pasha, but the principle that he was himself to be reduced to the condition of a political nullity had not undergone any serious modifications. The terms imposed upon him were so onerous and humiliating that, even had he been animated with better intentions than those with which, I fear, he must be credited, it would have been difficult to make the machine of government work smoothly. It was especially a mistake to insist on giving precision in detail to the relations which were to subsist between the Khedive and his Ministers. A man like Ismail Pasha was not to be bound by these ropes of diplomatic sand. Either he meant to act loyally with his European Ministers, or he had no such intention. Either they could acquire a personal influence over him, or they would be unable to do so. In the one case, the machine could have been worked without any very precise definition of the relations which were to exist between the Khedive and his Ministers. In the other case, those definitions were insufficient to prevent a collapse of the system. Under the existing circumstances, personal influence was of greater importance than any powers based on the text of a Khedivial letter or Decree.

Scarcely had the new Ministry been formed, when an incident occurred which gave a correct indication of what was to follow. The interest on

the loan of 1864, which was secured on the
Moukábala tax, fell due on April 1, 1879. It
amounted to £240,000. On March 28, the amount
of money in the hands of the Commissioners of the
Debt fell short of this sum by £196,000. The
Commission of Inquiry was at that time preparing
a project for a settlement of the financial situation.
It was known that the Commissioners contemplated
the repeal of the law of the Moukábala. This proposal was unpopular amongst the wealthier classes
in Egypt. The Ministers, acting in concert with
the Commissioners of Inquiry, considered that the
best plan would be to postpone the payment of the
coupon due on April 1 to May 1. A draft Decree
giving effect to this proposal was submitted to the
Khedive by Sir Rivers Wilson. The Khedive at
first refused to sign it. It was, he said, nothing
less than a declaration of bankruptcy. He did
not consider that the country was bankrupt. He
believed that all the financial engagements of the
Egyptian Government could be met. He could
not sign such a Decree in the face of the political
and financial engagements imposed on him by the
British and French Governments. Ultimately,
some changes were made in the wording of the
preamble, and the Khedive was induced to sign.

Inasmuch as the Khedive had for a long time
past been insisting on his inability to meet all his
financial engagements, it was evident that some
strong motive must have existed to make him
reject a proposal, which was submitted to him
by his European advisers, to postpone payment of
the interest on a portion of the debt. The reason
for this change of policy was abundantly clear.
The Khedive, in spite of his recent promises, was
actively engaged in intrigues having for their
object the overthrow of the Ministry. He was
preparing a financial plan of his own in opposition

to the scheme then being evolved by the Commission of Inquiry. This plan he intended to submit to the Powers.

On April 1, Sir Frank Lascelles reported to Lord Salisbury as follows : "Considerable agitation exists here at the present moment. . . . It appears that the Sheikh-el-Bekri[1] holds meetings with the Notables and Ulemas, with the object of exciting religious animosity against the European Ministers, and that Riaz Pasha has been denounced in the Mosques as a friend of the Christians. There is danger that Riaz Pasha, who has been warned by the Prefect of the Police that his life is in peril, may be forced into resigning."

Three days later (April 4), Sir Frank Lascelles wrote : "It appears that there is no doubt about the meetings having been held, and that there is constant communication between the Khedive and the more influential persons who attended them. Their object, however, is to obtain support to the financial plan, which the Khedive is preparing in opposition to that of Sir Rivers Wilson, and also to get up petitions to His Highness to put into force the Turkish Constitution, which was promulgated here in 1877, but which has hitherto remained a dead letter. . . . I have been told that the arguments addressed to the wealthy portion of the population in order to obtain signatures to the petition were that, if Sir Rivers Wilson's plan were to come into force, the taxes on the Ouchouri lands would be largely increased, and that the benefits conferred by the Moukábala law would be lost, and that the Ulema have been led to believe that it is the intention of the European Ministers to hand over the country entirely to Europeans,

[1] The Sheikh-el-Bekri was the Nekíb-el-Ashraf, or representative of all the descendants of the Prophet in Egypt. He was also the head of the religious Corporations.

and thus seriously jeopardise the Moslem faith, but there can be little doubt that the chief incentive to sign the petition was the knowledge that the signatures would be agreeable to the Khedive.

"Riaz Pasha has informed me that some of the employés of the Ministry of the Interior had been called upon for their signatures, and had not dared to refuse."

On April 6, the European Ministers placed in the hands of the Khedive a formal protest against the line of conduct which he was pursuing, and which, as they rightly pointed out, was in opposition to his former pledges. The Khedive paid no attention to this protest. His plans were now matured. He was ready to strike a decisive blow with a view to regaining his personal power.

On April 9, the Khedive convoked the members of the diplomatic corps and delivered an address to them in the presence of a number of Egyptian Notables, who had been assembled for the occasion. He said that the discontent in the country had reached such a pitch that he felt bound to allay it by adopting radical measures. A financial project, which expressed the true wishes of the country, had been submitted to him signed by all classes of the population. In this project, copies of which would be at once communicated to the representatives of the Powers, "the nation protested against the declaration of bankruptcy, which was contemplated by Sir Rivers Wilson, and demanded the formation of a purely Egyptian Ministry, which would be responsible to the Chamber of Deputies."

Prince Tewfik, "yielding to the will of the nation," had tendered his resignation. He would be replaced by Chérif Pasha. The Khedive would continue to govern in accordance with the Rescript of August 28, which sanctioned the principle of ministerial responsibility. The Decree of November

18, 1876, which had been negotiated by Messrs. Goschen and Joubert, would be strictly observed.

Chérif Pasha then added a few words. "The nation" thought that the Ministers had behaved in a manner which was insulting to its representatives. A declaration of bankruptcy would be dishonourable. The country was determined to make any sacrifices to avoid it. The contemplated repeal of the law of the Moukábala had given rise to great dissatisfaction. "It would have been impossible for the Khedive to have put himself in opposition to the will of the nation, which had been so positively expressed."

The Consuls-General listened to these remarkable declarations "in complete silence." The Austrian Consul-General, however, asked a somewhat pertinent question. Would the persons who had signed the project be prepared to mortgage their own properties as a guarantee for the execution of the financial plan? To this the Khedive replied that there would be no necessity for the adoption of any such course. "It would be impossible to give a stronger guarantee than the determination of the whole country, from the head of the State to the humblest individual, to submit to any sacrifices rather than to the disgrace of national bankruptcy."

Three documents were communicated to the Consuls-General immediately after the meeting.

The first of these was an address from the Chamber of Notables. It stated that the new Ministers had frequently violated the rights of the Chamber. No explanation was, however, given as to the precise nature of these alleged violations. As regards the idea of a declaration of bankruptcy, and the proposed repeal of the law of the Moukábala, the Notables expressed themselves in the following terms: "Tous ces actes sont nuisibles à nos intérêts et contraires à nos droits. Jamais nous n'en accepterons l'exécution." They begged the Khedive, therefore, to take the situation into his consideration, "afin d'éviter les sérieuses difficultés qui pourraient naître à l'avenir si nos droits et ceux de la nation continuaient à être ainsi méconnues ; de graves dangers pourraient même en résulter."

The second document submitted to the Consuls-General was an address presented to the Khedive by a number of delegates chosen from amongst the Ulema, the highest officials of the State, both civil and military, and other Notables. In this address it was stated that the petitioners had examined the financial scheme prepared by Sir Rivers Wilson. They considered that the proposals contained in that scheme were contrary to the interests of the country ; they were of opinion that the revenues of Egypt were sufficient to discharge all the debts due by the State ; they had, therefore, prepared a counter-project, which they asked should be submitted to the Chamber of Notables. They begged that the Khedive would give to the Chamber "les attributions et les pouvoirs dont jouissent les Chambres des Deputés Européennes en ce qui concerne les questions intérieures et financières." The Council of Ministers was to be independent of the Khedive, and was to be responsible to the Chamber.

The third document was a plan for the settlement of the financial situation.

These documents were sent by the Consuls-General to their respective Governments by the mail which was then about to leave for Europe. The same mail should have carried a number of copies of the report, which the Commissioners of Inquiry had just completed. These latter were, however, stopped in the Post-office by order of the

Khedive in the hope that "the plan submitted to the Khedive might be approved of before the report of the Commissioners was generally known."

Letters were written by the Khedive to Sir Rivers Wilson and M. de Blignières stating that "in obedience to the positive wishes of the nation he had entrusted Chérif Pasha with the formation of a new Cabinet, which was to be composed entirely of Egyptians."

When the European Ministers were appointed to the Egyptian Cabinet, the British and French Governments stipulated "that the Commission of Control over the Egyptian finances appointed under the Decree of November 1876, should be *ipso facto* revived in case either the English or French member of the Egyptian Cabinet should be dismissed without the consent of his Government." In order to fulfil the engagement thus taken by the Egyptian Government, Chérif Pasha wrote to M. Bellaigues de Bughas, who had been appointed Commissioner of the Debt in succession to M. de Blignières, and myself, requesting us to assume the offices of Controllers-General of the expenditure and of the receipts. We stated in our reply that we must decline to associate ourselves with a financial plan which in our eyes was impracticable, or with a change of system which was in contradiction to the engagements recently taken by the Khedive towards the British and French Governments. Chérif Pasha thereupon informed Sir Frank Lascelles that he considered our refusal to take office freed the Egyptian Government from any responsibility as regards the immediate re-establishment of the Control. The French and British Governments were, however, asked to name Controllers.

Sir Gerald Fitzgerald, Blum Pasha, the Secretary of the Financial Department, and Sir Auckland

Colvin, who was head of the Cadastral Survey, also resigned their appointments.

A Decree was issued naming Chérif Pasha President of the Council, and charging him with the formation of a Ministry. A letter was at the same time addressed to Chérif Pasha by the Khedive, setting forth the principles which were for the future to guide the Government of the country. This letter began in the following terms: "Comme Chef d'État et comme Égyptien, je considère un devoir sacré, pour moi, de suivre l'opinion de mon pays et de donner une satisfaction entière à ses légitimes aspirations." The Khedive then went on to say that the financial plan prepared by the Minister of Finance, which declared the country in a state of bankruptcy and which violated vested interests, had "achevé de soulever contre le Cabinet le sentiment national." Public opinion had found expression in the address which had been presented to him. Yielding to the wishes expressed in this address, he requested Chérif Pasha to form a Cabinet composed "d'éléments véritablement Égyptiens." As regards the demand for parliamentary institutions, the Khedive said that a Chamber would be formed, "dont les modes d'élection et les droits seront réglés de façon à répondre aux exigeances de la situation intérieure et aux aspirations nationales." The new Cabinet was to prepare electoral laws upon the model of those which existed in Europe, "tout en tenant compte des mœurs et des besoins de la population." The Khedive expressed his approval of the financial plan which had been submitted to him by the Notables. The Cabinet was to carry out that plan in its integrity. The letter concluded in the following terms: "Connaissant votre dévouement au pays, je ne doute pas que Votre Excellence, s'entourant d'hommes jouissant comme Elle

de la confiance et de l'estime publique, ne mène
à bonne fin l'œuvre civilisatrice à laquelle je veux
attacher mon nom."

Immediately afterwards, the other Ministers,
those who were to "enjoy the public confidence
and esteem," were nominated. They were all
men who were under the absolute control of the
Khedive, and who did not in the smallest degree
represent the national party, supposing there to
have been one. Shahin Pasha was named Minister
for War, and Omar Pasha Lutfi Inspector-General
with a seat in the Cabinet. Both had gained unenviable reputations by the unscrupulous methods
which in former capacities they had adopted for
collecting the revenue.

History records several instances of free institutions which have foundered under the influence of
one commanding mind. The Emperors Augustus
and Napoleon were the great high-priests of a
policy having for its object a transfer of power
from the people to their ruler. All students of
history are familiar with the procedures which
they adopted. But, so far as my historical knowledge goes, the clumsy experiment made by Ismail
Pasha was of a somewhat novel character. This
was not a case in which existing free institutions
had, by a combination of force and diplomacy, to
be bent to suit the wishes of a despotic ruler. On
the contrary, the Khedive was already an absolute
ruler. Scarcely a trace of independent thought or
action could be found in the whole body politic of
Egypt. Ismail Pasha endeavoured to call free
institutions temporarily into existence as an instrument through whose agency he might regain his
personal power, which was threatened by foreign
interference. It was a curious sight to see Ismail
Pasha, who was the living embodiment of despotic

government in its most extreme form, posing as an ultra-constitutional ruler who could not conscientiously place himself in opposition to the national will. It was a still more curious sight to see the same man, who had but recently protested that he could not pay his debts, suddenly turn round and reject with disdain the proposals, made to him by those who represented his creditors, that he should declare himself insolvent. But perhaps the highest point of interest in this strange comedy was reached when the unfortunate peasantry of Egypt, who were groaning under Ismail Pasha's rule and who only asked to be relieved of taxation without inquiring into the effect such a relief would exercise on other interests, were represented as being willing to incur any sacrifice rather than submit to the disgrace of national bankruptcy. It may be asserted with absolute confidence that the mass of the Egyptian people understood nothing of what was going on at the time. The Notables, however, understood something. In the first place, they understood that the Khedive, for reasons of his own into which it was no business of theirs to inquire, wished them to say that they ardently desired the establishment of certain institutions of the nature of which they only had a vague idea, but which were said to have produced excellent effects in other countries. Whether or not the same beneficial results would ensue from their adoption in Egypt might be doubtful, but in any case it was clear that the Khedive must be obeyed. In the second place, they understood in a general way that all the difficulties of the moment were due to the fact that large sums of money were owing to Europeans. They had seen the worst side of European interference. That it should be exercised in the true interests of the Egyptian people was not credible. When, therefore, it was represented to them that the last phase of European interference was that the privileges of the classes to which they belonged were threatened, it needed no great amount of persuasion to enlist their sympathies on the side of opposition to the new order of things. Religious antipathy would also drive them in the same direction.

It is, indeed, probable that, from the purely Egyptian point of view, Ismail Pasha's plan would have been more attractive if the proposal to establish an Egyptian Parliament had been dropped out of the programme, and if he had taken his stand on the general feeling of dislike to Europeans, and on religious fanaticism. Appeals to either of these sentiments would have been more comprehensible to his followers, and would have met with a more hearty response, than arguments based on the establishment of institutions which were foreign to the national traditions. Save to a very few, such arguments were probably incomprehensible.

But Ismail Pasha was debarred from using arms of this description, save to a very limited extent. In the first place, he was not a fanatic, and religious fanaticism was a matter of which he had had some experience. He knew its danger, and when it had appeared he had on several occasions adopted summary methods for stamping it out. He did not enjoy the reputation of being a devout Mohammedan, and, had not material interests and the fear of disobedience to a despotic ruler been brought into play, he would have exercised but little influence over those classes who honestly represented Mohammedan devotion. In the second place, it was a necessity of his position that he should not go far in appealing to sentiments of this description. He understood enough of European opinion to appreciate the fact that any such appeals would forfeit the sympathies and evoke the fears of Europe. This might be dangerous. From every point of view it would be safer, and in all probability more productive of result, if the revolution were carried out in the name of civilisation and progress, and under the banner of constitutionalism. His followers could not, indeed, be prevented from acting in some degree according to their own imperfect lights. "Large numbers of the fanatical population" were summoned to Cairo. Sir Frank Lascelles thought they "might become a source of real danger." Provided proceedings of this sort were kept within proper bounds, they might afford powerful aid to the cause. But it would be impolitic if the Khedive were too openly associated with the crude ideas and ill-judged proceedings of his ignorant followers. It would be wiser to pose as an enlightened ruler, following the popular will and, at the same time, standing as a guardian angel between Moslem fanaticism and modern civilisation.

Ismail Pasha was employing dangerous instruments. First, he encouraged mutiny in his own army. Then he played with the uncongenial idea of introducing free institutions into the country. This was perilous work for a despotic ruler. The soldiers had learnt their power, and even amongst the poor ignorant people, who, at their master's behest, asked for things of which the large majority were completely ignorant, there might be some few who would take him at his word. The seed then sown did, in fact, bring forth some fruit at a later period of Egyptian history.

For the moment, however, the success of the manœuvre appeared complete. Europe must surely see that the Egyptian people were singularly unanimous, and that an enlightened ruler was

about to confer on them the blessings of a
constitutional form of government, which they
ardently desired.   The Khedive had defied two
powerful Governments; he had got rid of his
European advisers; and he had appointed in their
places a number of men who would implicitly obey
his orders, and who, albeit free institutions were to
be introduced, would have no scruples in acting on
the most approved principles of personal government.   European Governments might perhaps
lecture him, but international rivalry was so
intense that no common action of a serious nature
was to be feared.   He had, indeed, drawn a heavy
draft on the credulity of Europe.   Even those who
were not conversant with Eastern affairs might not
unnaturally think that when an Oriental Gracchus
complained of sedition his arguments were not
to be accepted without some reserve.   Nevertheless,
the scheme would probably have been successful if
the financial plan, which the Khedive had pledged
himself to carry out, had been based on any solid
foundation.   If he had been able to pay his debts,
no excuse would have existed for further interference from abroad.   Unfortunately for the Khedive,
his financial plan was impossible of execution.
The entire scheme crumbled to the ground and, in
falling, overwhelmed its author.

CHAPTER VII

THE REPORT OF THE COMMISSION

APRIL 1879

Declaration of bankruptcy—Principles of the settlement—The Khedive's Civil List—The Ouchouri land-tax—The Rouznameh loan—The law of the Moukábala—Reductions of taxation—Composition with the creditors—Comments on the report—The Commissioners resign—The Khedive's counter-proposals—Revival of the practices of the old régime—The Commissioners of the Debt institute legal proceedings against the Egyptian Government—My departure from Egypt.

DURING all this period, the Commission of Inquiry had been sitting with a view to the preparation of a plan for the settlement of the financial situation. It is unnecessary to enter into all the complicated details of the questions which came under the consideration of the Commissioners. But it will be desirable to state the main conclusions at which they arrived.

The Commissioners began their report[1] by stating that the Egyptian Government were bankrupt, and, moreover, that the state of bankruptcy had really commenced on April 6, 1876, on which day the Khedive suspended payment of the Treasury bills falling due. It was true that since that date not only had the interest on the debt been paid, but a sum of £2,645,000 had been devoted to sinking

[1] The first draft of this report was prepared by myself. It, of course, underwent a good many modifications before a final text was approved. The French was revised by M. de Blignières.

110

fund. As purchases of stock were made in the market at prices varying from $31\frac{1}{4}$ to 48, nominal capital to the extent of £4,858,000 had been extinguished. On the other hand, the actual deficits of the two years, 1877 and 1878, amounted to no less than £4,822,000. The floating debt had, therefore, been increased by an amount of £2,177,000 in excess of the money applied to sinking fund. "Payer les coupons," the Commissioners said, "dans ces conditions, c'est distribuer des dividendes fictifs, et l'on sait à quels résultats arrivent les sociétés qui persévèrent dans cette voie. Leur situation paraît brillante jusqu'au jour ou la ruine est irrémédiable." In truth, the taxpayers and the creditors had alike suffered from the delay which had occurred in recognising the true facts of the case. The only sound starting-point for the establishment of a better order of things was to be found in facing the facts boldly. "Le pays," M. de Blignières said, "est saigné à blanc." Measures such as those which had been heretofore adopted to produce a fictitious appearance of solvency, must be discarded. The annual expenditure must be brought down to the limits of the annual revenue. It was a great point gained that these preliminary truths should be officially recognised by a trustworthy body of Europeans, amongst whom were included the representatives of the bondholders.

Having ascertained beyond doubt that the Egyptian Government could not meet all their financial engagements, the Commissioners proceeded to lay down the principles which should form the basis of a composition with the creditors of the State. It was impossible to do justice to all the interests involved. "Le système de gouverner le pays," we said, "jusqu'à présent en vigueur a rendu impossible de rendre justice à tous les intérêts engagés. Le seul résultat auquel le nouveau régime pourra aspirer, c'est de partager l'injustice aussi équitablement que possible."

The Commissioners then laid down three principles.

The first of these was that no sacrifice should be demanded from the creditors until every reasonable sacrifice had been made by the debtors. "On n'a pas," the Commissioners said, "à insister sur l'équité de ce principe." It was, in fact, perfectly just and logical. But in its application, a subsidiary question naturally arose. Who in this case were the debtors? Morally speaking, the real debtor was the Khedive. He had for years past disposed absolutely of the revenues of Egypt. He had contracted the debts without reference to the wishes or true interests of the people over whom, by the accident of birth, he had been called to rule. Unfortunately, he had dragged his people along with him. No moral responsibility whatsoever attached to them, for they had never been consulted as regards the measures which had been taken by the Khedive. But, however hard the conclusion might appear, it was inevitable that they should suffer from the faults of their ruler. Considerations of equity and sound financial policy, however, alike dictated moderation in the application of the principle enunciated above. The people of Egypt would have to make certain sacrifices, but, the Commissioners added, "il serait assurément contraire aux intérêts généraux de leur imposer des sacrifices au-dessus de leurs forces. On verra même dans la suite de ce rapport que nous proposons de leur accorder immédiatement des soulagements sensibles."

The second principle laid down by the Commissioners was that, in deciding on the degrees of sacrifice which should be imposed on the different classes of creditors, it was desirable to conform as much as possible to the procedure indicated by the Egyptian code as that which should be followed in dealing with the estate of a private individual who was bankrupt.

In the third place, it was necessary that any general arrangement which might be adopted should be made obligatory on all the persons who were interested. The number of creditors was so large, and their claims were of such various natures, that it was hopeless to expect unanimity in the acceptance of any voluntary arrangement. A small minority might, therefore, prevent the adoption of any general scheme. The only way to avoid this inconvenience was to pass a law, which would have to be accepted by all the Powers, and which would thus become binding on the Mixed Tribunals and on all the parties concerned.

Having laid down these principles, the Commissioners proceeded to deal with the personal position of the Khedive.

His Highness had given up most of the estates of the Khedivial family,[1] upon the security of which a loan had been raised. The proceeds of this loan were about to be applied to the liquidation of the floating debt. It was now necessary to fix the amount of the Khedive's Civil List. "Assurément," the Commissioners said, "au moment de demander de nouveaux sacrifices de la part de ses créanciers, Son Altesse ne voudra pas que ses dotations soient fixées à un chiffre trop élevé." The Civil List was, therefore, fixed at £E.300,000 a year.

The question of the sacrifices to be imposed on the Egyptian taxpayers presented greater difficulties. Three important points had to be

---

[1] The residue which remained over eventually acquired great value. Quite recently, a plot of land in the town of Cairo belonging to some of the Khedivial princes sold for no less than £600,000.

decided. The first was whether the tax on the Ouchouri lands should be increased. The second was whether the Rouznameh loan was to be included amongst the debts of the State. The third was how to deal with the law of the Moukábala. The financial future of the country depended more especially on whether any satisfactory solution could be found to the third of these questions.

Without going into any lengthy description of the system of land-tenure existing in Egypt, it will be sufficient for the purposes of the present argument to state that the land was at that time divided into two main categories, Ouchouri and Kharadji.[1] Ouchouri lands, as their name implies, are supposed to pay a tithe to the State. They were originally, for the most part, fiefs granted by the ruler of the country to his followers. The assessment on the Kharadji was much higher than in the case of the Ouchouri lands, and moreover it was, in theory at all events, variable at the will of the Government. At the time the Commission of Inquiry sat, 1,323,000 acres of land were held under Ouchouri, and 3,487,000 acres under Kharadji tenure. In 1877, the total amount of land-tax paid on Kharadji lands amounted to £E.3,143,000, as against £E.333,000 paid by the Ouchouri landowners. In Lower Egypt, the Kharadji lands were assessed at from P.T. 120 to 170 an acre. In exceptional cases, the tax was as much as, and occasionally even in excess of P.T. 200. The average rate paid on Kharadji lands throughout Egypt was P.T. 116·2. The maximum rate payable on Ouchouri lands was P.T. 83·5 an acre. In many cases, they paid a mere quit-rent. The average rate throughout

[1] "Ouchouri" is derived from the Arabic word "Ushr," meaning the tenth part. "Kharàj" was the word originally applied to the tribute paid, for the most part, by the inhabitants of non-Moslem countries to their Moslem conquerors.

Egypt was P.T. 30·30 an acre. The quality of the Ouchouri lands varied greatly. They included some of the best and also some of the worst land in the country. The best qualities of land were largely held by the Khedivial family. All the Ouchouri lands were in the possession of persons of wealth and importance.

Before the first report of the Commission of Inquiry was sent in, the Khedive had expressed his willingness to raise the tax on the Ouchouri lands. The Commissioners had now to consider in what manner effect should be given to this proposal. They recommended that a cadastral survey should be made with the least possible delay, and that, on reassessing the land-tax, the distinction between Ouchouri and Kharadji lands should disappear. As, however, a cadastral survey would take a long time, they proposed that the Ouchouri land-tax should be at once increased by £E.150,000 a year, to be distributed ratably.

Turning to the question of the Rouznameh loan, the Commissioners pointed out that the Government had considered it as a tax, and that there was manifestly never any intention of paying interest, and still less of repaying the capital to the subscribers. Of the truth of these statements there could be no manner of doubt. In 1877, the Chamber of Notables agreed to a proposal that the payment of interest on the loan should be suspended. At the same time, "il fut ordonné qu'aussitôt que l'intégralité de la Moukábala aurait été perçue, on devrait procéder à la perception des £3,000,000, solde des £5,000,000 originairement fixées comme le montant total de l'emprunt Rouznameh." This decision threw a strong light on the complete subserviency of the Chamber of Notables, as also on the manner in which the Egyptian Government regarded their engagements both towards the

Rouznameh bondholders and towards those who had paid the Moukábala.

There could, of course, be no question of collecting any further sums on account of the Rouznameh loan. The only point to be decided was what was to be done as regards the money already collected. After full consideration, the Commissioners embodied their recommendations in the following words: "Nous croyons devoir proposer, conformément aux intentions primitives du Gouvernement Égyptien, de considérer comme un impôt la somme perçue à valoir sur l'emprunt Rouznameh et de la rayer du montant des dettes de l'État."

This proposal of the Commissioners was based on two grounds.

In the first place, it was thought that the non-recognition by the State of the Rouznameh loan was a fair sacrifice to demand of the debtors, more especially as, in connection with other matters, the Commissioners proposed measures which would afford a sensible relief to the taxpayers of Egypt.

In the second place, if the loan had been recognised as a State debt, great practical difficulties would have arisen in giving effect to the decision. It was clear that no one could be recognised as a State creditor unless he could afford proof of having lent money to the Government. It would have been necessary to insist on this point. Otherwise, fictitious claims would have cropped up on all sides. In the majority of cases, no proofs would have been forthcoming. No bonds or scrip were ever delivered to the subscribers to the loan. Even simple receipts for the money paid into the Treasury had only been given to a few favoured individuals. Under these circumstances, it would have been practically impossible to do justice to all the subscribers, more especially to those in the humblest classes of society who were most deserving of sympathy.

Considering the financial situation which then existed, the decision of the Commissioners on this subject was perfectly justifiable.

The most difficult question of all, however, was how to deal with the Moukábala. It is unnecessary to dwell any further on the ruinous nature of this transaction in so far as the State was concerned. The only procedure which, from a fiscal point of view, could in any way have justified it, would have been to have applied the whole of the money paid in virtue of the law of the Moukábala either to the extinction of debt, or to the execution of public works which would have yielded a direct revenue to the State. Unfortunately, nothing of this sort was done. The financial arrangements of November 1876 did, indeed, contemplate the application of a portion of the Moukábala funds to the extinction of debt, but before that period the money had been applied to current expenditure, and even after November 1876 the greater portion of the Moukábala money was devoted to the payment of interest on the debt.

It was certain that the Egyptian Government never had any intention of respecting the engagements which they had taken towards those who had paid the Moukábala. It was discovered in the course of the inquiries made by the Commissioners that the draft of a law had been prepared, under instructions received from the Egyptian Government, in virtue of which an "impôt sur la propriété" was to be imposed on the expiration of the law of the Moukábala. It was estimated that this new tax would yield £900,000 a year. The intentions, as also the bad faith of the Government were, therefore, sufficiently clear.

It was equally certain that the optional character

of the Moukábala payments was delusive.   "On
ne peut pas douter," the Commissioners said,
"que le caractère facultatif de cette taxe n'existait
pas en réalité.   Les contribuables l'ont toujours
considérée comme aussi obligatoire que toutes les
autres taxes.   Le fait qu'à peine la nouvelle
administration établie, ils refusent de tous les côtés
de continuer le paiement de la Moukábala, en se
référant à son caractère facultatif, prouve l'exactitude de cette assertion."

It was clear that, if the reformed administration
continued to collect the Moukábala, they would
have to do so in a very different spirit from that
which had heretofore animated the Egyptian
Government.   The engagements taken towards the
landowners would have to be respected.   When
once the Moukábala payments had ceased, the land-
tax would have to be reduced to one-half of its
original amount.   No violation of the law or
evasion of its spirit could be permitted.   But, the
Commissioners asked, "la nouvelle administration
peut-elle remplir les engagements pris par ses
prédécesseurs ?"

There could be but one answer to this question.
"Nous n'avons pas," the Commissioners said, "la
moindre hésitation à affirmer que, quel que puisse
être le désir du Gouvernement actuel de remplir
les engagement pris par ses prédécesseurs, les
nécessités impérieuses de la situation ne lui per-
mettront pas de le faire."

Obviously, the only honest course was to state
the truth boldly.   The Commissioners held that
the new Ministry should not render itself responsible for the continuance of a system which
was "radicalement vicieux et d'une application
impossible."   They therefore recommended that
no further collections should be made on account
of the Moukábala.

It remained to be determined what should be done as regards those persons who had already paid the Moukábala in whole or in part. It appeared from the accounts furnished by the Egyptian Government that about £16,000,000 had already been paid on account of Moukábala, but when the figures came to be examined, it was found that the Government had not in reality received nearly so large a sum as this.

In the first place, considerable sums had been paid in "ragaas"; that is to say, certificates acknowledging a debt due by the Government to the taxpayer. "On ne peut guère douter," the Commissioners said, "que l'acceptation de ces 'ragaas' par le Trésor n'ait donné lieu à de nombreux abus; car, par suite de ce système quelques propriétaires puissants ont pu arriver au dégrèvement d'une moitié de leur impôt foncier sans rien payer en espèces." The procedure, in fact, was after this fashion. Some favoured person obtained from the Finance Ministry an acknowledgment of a fictitious debt due to him by the Government. This document was paid into the Treasury in discharge of the sum due by the same person on account of Moukábala. His land-tax was then reduced by one-half, without his having expended a farthing. It was impossible to state with precision the extent to which this practice had been carried on, but there could be no doubt that it had occasioned a heavy loss to the Treasury.

Another point had to be considered. Many of the payments made, even in money, on account of the Moukábala were fictitious. They had only been possible because sums due on account of other taxes were allowed to remain unpaid. A single example will suffice to show how the system worked in practice. The amount of land-tax due by four villages, chosen at hazard in the province of

Galioubieh, was £1640. The amount due on account of Moukábala in these villages was £1472. The total amount due was, therefore, £3112. In the year 1878, £2251 was collected in these four villages. Of this amount, £1472, that is to say the total sum due, was credited to Moukábala, leaving only £779 available for ordinary land-lax. The latter, therefore, remained unpaid to the extent of £861.

When, however, all the deductions based on the above facts were made, there still remained a large sum due by the Government to those persons who had really paid the Moukábala. The most equit- able course to have pursued would have been to have raised a loan and to have repaid this money; but in the then exhausted state of Egyptian credit, the adoption of this course was impossible.

It may be convenient if, passing over the recom- mendations made by the Commissioners of Inquiry, the course eventually pursued as regards those persons who had really paid the Moukábala is here stated. It was found that, when all legitimate deductions had been made, the sum really due was £9,500,000. Under the law of Liquidation of July 17, 1880, an annual sum of £150,000 was allotted for fifty years to those who had paid the Mouká- bala. They are thus now receiving interest at the rate of about $1\frac{1}{2}$ per cent on the capital sums which they paid.

In 1876, the Egyptian Government estimated the annual receipts from the Moukábala at £1,650,000. The amount paid in 1877 was £1,337,000, and in 1878, £1,000,000. For the future, the country was, of course, relieved of these payments. On the other hand, the land-tax was raised by £1,130,000.

The results of this change affected the Ouchouri and Kharadji proprietors in different proportions.

Out of 3,487,000 acres of Kharadji land, only 240,000 acres had paid the Moukábala in full. For the most part, therefore, the Kharadji landowners were slightly relieved of taxation.

The case of the Ouchouri landowners was different. There were 1,323,000 acres of Ouchouri land in Egypt. On about 480,000 acres, the Moukábala had been paid in full, but most of the payments had been made in "ragaas," and were, therefore, fictitious. The changes in the law fell most severely on this class. Not only did they have to pay the amount of land-tax, as it stood previous to the enactment of the law of the Moukábala, but they also had to bear their share of the increase of £150,000 which was placed on the Ouchouri lands. Even, then, however, they paid much less than the Kharadji landowners.

The Moukábala had been paid in part on 725,000 acres of Ouchouri land. On these lands, the immediate increase of taxation, if any, was slight.

Finally, no Moukábala payments had been made on 118,000 acres of Ouchouri land. The owners of these lands were not, of course, affected by the repeal of the law of the Moukábala, but they had to pay their share of the £150,000 increase on all Ouchouri lands.

In order to compensate for the withdrawal of the privileges accorded by the law of the Moukábala, the Commissioners proposed several measures, from the adoption of which great benefits, it was rightly thought, would accrue to the population. The arrears due for land-tax prior to January 1, 1876, and amounting to about £30,000, were to be remitted. All agriculturists were to be relieved from payment of the professional tax. It was estimated that the adoption of this measure would involve a relief of taxation amounting to £80,000

a year. The poll-tax, yielding £205,000 a year,
was to be abolished; so also were the octroi dues
in the villages, yielding £21,000 a year; the "droits
de voirie" in the villages, yielding £8000 a year;
the market dues in the villages, yielding £10,000
a year; the weighing dues in the villages, yielding
£17,000 a year; the dues on stamping mats and
tissues, yielding £23,000 a year; the dues on the
sale of cattle, yielding £1500 a year; and some
other minor taxes. In all, a remission of taxation
to the extent of about £400,000 a year was
proposed.[1]

On the whole, although it is, in my opinion, to
be regretted that no higher rate of interest was
allowed to those to whom money was really
due on account of Moukábala, it may be said
that the proposals of the Commissioners were as
just to the people of Egypt as the very difficult
circumstances of the case admitted.

It is unnecessary to dwell at any length on
the proposals made by the Commissioners in
respect to the creditors of the Egyptian Government. Those proposals underwent considerable
modifications before a final settlement was eventually made in July 1880. It will be sufficient
to say that the general principle on which the
Commissioners based their recommendations was
that the special security held by each class of
creditor was to be respected as far as possible.
No change was proposed in the position of the
Preference bondholders. The Commissioners were
of opinion that for the moment it was impossible
to state definitely what should be the rate of
interest on the Unified Stock. They proposed,
therefore, that the rate should be temporarily

---

[1] The relief was in reality much greater, for it cannot be doubted
that far larger sums were collected than were paid into the Government
Treasury.

reduced from 6 to 5 per cent. The rate of interest on the Daira Sanieh and Daira Khassa loans was also reduced to 5 per cent. As regards the creditors who held no special securities, a sum of about £6,801,000 was available to liquidate claims amounting to about £8,210,000. After discharging certain debts which had to be paid in full, the Commissioners recommended that the balance left over should be distributed ratably amongst the creditors. It was estimated that sufficient money would be available to pay the creditors 52 per cent of their claims.

Finally, the Commissioners prepared a Budget for the year 1879. The revenue was estimated at £9,067,000, and the expenditure at £8,803,000, thus leaving a surplus of £264,000. A sum of £3,130,000 was included in the estimates for administrative expenditure.

Such, therefore, were the general conclusions at which the Commissioners arrived. Fifteen months were to elapse before their recommendations, in a modified shape, took the form of law. Subsequently, important political events ensued. The work of fiscal reform had to be recommenced under different auspices from those which existed in 1879. Many years were to pass before the crisis in Egyptian financial affairs could be said to have terminated. Some errors were, without doubt, made by the Commissioners. Nevertheless, the work performed by the Commission of Inquiry has stood the test of time as well as could be expected, looking to the difficult circumstances of the situation with which they had to deal. It afforded a sound starting-point for further reforms. For the first time, an earnest effort had been made to grapple with the difficulties of the Egyptian financial situation. The inquiries of the Commissioners threw a flood of light on the extent of

Egyptian liabilities, the resources available to meet those liabilities, and the system under which the Government had heretofore been conducted. *Ad consilium de republicâ dandum, caput est, nosse rempublicam.* This elementary truth had been too much forgotten in dealing with Egyptian affairs. Now that the true facts of the situation were more accurately known, although mistakes might be made in subsidiary matters, it was no longer possible to draw erroneous conclusions as to the main questions at issue. The Egyptian Treasury was insolvent. The system of government had been as bad as possible. Both the people of Egypt and the creditors of the Egyptian Government were alike interested in the adoption of an improved system. It was futile to attempt to impose fresh burthens on the country. On the contrary, certain taxes should be abolished.

Even if the Commissioners had done nothing more than bring home the main facts of the situation to all concerned, they would have deserved well both of the Egyptian people and of all who were interested in the prosperity of Egypt.

The report of the Commission of Inquiry was signed on April 8. On the previous day, the Khedive dismissed his European Ministers, and charged Chérif Pasha with the formation of a new Ministry. The situation was thus completely changed. All hopes of introducing a reformed system of administration had for the time to be abandoned ; and, without reforms, the scheme proposed by the Commission of Inquiry was incapable of execution. The Commissioners, therefore, tendered their resignations to the Khedive. They were, of course, accepted.

The counter project which[1] was prepared by the Khedive in concert with the Chamber of Notables

---

[1] *Vide ante,* p. 102.

was published on April 23. Little need be said of this plan. It was open to the most serious objections.

In the first place, it was impossible of execution. The revenue for 1879 was estimated at £9,837,000. This was nearly £800,000 in excess of the estimate made by the Commissioners of Inquiry, which was £9,067,000. Even this latter estimate erred on the side of optimism, and it was certain that the collection of such a sum as that named in the scheme of the Chamber of Notables was impossible without resorting to the oppressive methods of the past, and without again sacrificing the future to the present.

In the second place, although both the Khedive and his advisers had rejected the idea of national bankruptcy as dishonourable, the settlement which they proposed did, as a matter of fact, constitute an act of bankruptcy. The interest on the Unified Debt was to be reduced from 6 to 5 per cent, although hopes were held out that payment of interest at a higher rate would be resumed at some later period. In fact, as the Commissioners of Inquiry pointed out in a letter addressed to the Khedive, the scheme "protestait contre toute déclaration de faillite, mais en consacrait la réalité."

These objections would alone have been fatal to the scheme. Moreover, there was one very significant omission in the project. There could be no hope for reforms in Egypt unless a fixed sum were assigned for the private expenditure of the Khedive and his family. The scheme of the Chamber of Notables made no mention of any Civil List. In fact, the basis of the plan was that the Khedive should regain his personal power, and that the upper classes should preserve their privileges intact.

The effect of the change of policy inaugurated

by the Khedive made itself immediately felt. On April 19, Sir Frank Lascelles reported that "Shahin Pasha, the Minister of War, had gone to Behera, probably for the purpose of collecting money; his former position as Inspector-General in Lower Egypt having secured for him an unenviable notoriety as one of the harshest and most successful tax-gatherers in the country."

A few days later, the British Vice-Consul at Zagazig wrote: "You ask how is the new régime working? Worse than before. Three-fourths of the taxes and one-half of the Moukábala are now exacted by means of the usual oppressions. The fellah, having no crop of cotton or grain to realise, is obliged to have recourse to usurers for money, which he gets at some 4 to 5 per cent per month. He has no alternative if he would avoid the 'courbash.' The 'Zawats' (aristocracy), meanwhile, only pay the 'Mal' (land-tax proper) at their pleasure, and, therefore, see everything *couleur de rose.* . . . Omar Pasha Lutfi, Inspector-General of Lower Egypt, has been here of late, and has given stringent orders for the collection of money by all possible means."

In a word, all the abuses of the old régime returned immediately the new Ministry came into power.

In the meanwhile, the Commissioners of the Debt were considering what action they should take. Under the changed circumstances of the situation, there was but one course left for them to pursue. They commenced a lawsuit against the Government in the Mixed Tribunals.

For some while previous to these events, I had been wishing to leave Egypt. I had, however, become interested in the work. So long as there appeared any hope of placing Egyptian financial affairs on a sound footing, I hesitated whether to go or to remain. All hopes of this sort seemed, however, to be dashed to the ground. Under the circumstances, I did not care to remain any longer in the country. I therefore resigned my appointment and left Egypt on May 24, 1879. From that date until I returned as Controller-General after the abdication of Ismail Pasha, I cannot speak from personal experience of what occurred in Egypt. Sir Auckland Colvin was appointed to be Commissioner of the Debt in my place.

CHAPTER VIII

THE FALL OF ISMAIL PASHA

April–June 1879

Embarrassment of the European Powers—Turkey—England—France
—Italy—Russia—Germany and Austria—The French and British
Governments demand the reinstatement of the European Ministers—The Khedive declines to reinstate them—Question of re-
establishing the Control—The German Government protest against
the proceedings of the Khedive—The British and French Governments advise abdication—The Khedive appeals to the Sultan—
The Sultan deposes the Khedive—Inauguration of Prince Tewfik
—Ismail Pasha leaves Egypt—Remarks on his reign.

THE action taken by the Khedive in dismissing his
European Ministers embarrassed the various Powers
who were interested in the affairs of Egypt. Moreover, all the most important Governments in Europe
claimed a right to make their voices heard in any
general settlement of Egyptian questions. The
local difficulties of the situation were great. They
were rendered greater by the fact that no serious
step could be taken without producing a clash of
conflicting international interests.

The Sultan was concerned lest his suzerain
rights should be endangered. Turkish policy was,
as usual, vacillating and inconsistent. Should not
the Khedive be deposed? Nay, did not an opportunity now present itself to realise the pernicious
dream which had haunted the minds of Turkish
statesmen since the days when Mehemet Ali won
by the power of the sword a quasi-independent

position for himself and his dynasty? His descendant had shamefully abused his power. The people of Egypt were groaning under his yoke. Europe was dissatisfied with him. Could not all this be rectified by cancelling the Firmans and by the despatch of a Turkish Governor, with a few sturdy Ottoman battalions at his back, to rule the country? Truly, whispered interested diplomacy in the garb of a candid friend, but is not all this European interference somewhat dangerous? Might not the principle of deposition by reason of misgovernment be applied elsewhere? Was it not possible that public opinion, which was now so powerful, might apply the Horatian maxim and contend that many of those things, which inquisitive Commissioners of Inquiry had said of Egypt, might, with a change of name, be applied to other parts of the Ottoman dominions? This argument was not without its weight. From this point of view, perhaps it would be better to congratulate the Khedive on his defiant attitude, and to encourage him in his opposition to the appointment of European Ministers. But then came rival diplomatic mutterings. What would be the position of the Sultan if the two Western Powers, with a mere appearance of consultation with Constantinople, deposed the Khedive on their own initiative? If that were to happen, the world would see that Turkish suzerainty over Egypt was nothing more than a mere diplomatic expression. Would it not, therefore, be better to act at once so as to prevent others from taking action? Under all these circumstances, perhaps the best plan of all for a bewildered ruler, who was, perforce, obliged to speak the language of civilisation, but whose principles of civil government were very similar to those of his warlike ancestors, when they planted their horse-tails on the banks of the Bosphorus, was to fall back on the reflection that the times were out of joint, to await events, and to take no decisive action of any kind.

The difficulties of the British Government were also great. Their political interests in Egypt were of a nature which precluded total inaction. Indeed, there was manifestly a danger that a policy would be forced upon them which it had always been one of the objects of British statesmanship to avoid. "The Englishman," a man of literary genius had said some thirty years previously, "straining far over to hold his loved India, will plant a firm foot on the banks of the Nile and sit in the seats of the faithful."[1] Unless care were taken, the prophecy might be on the point of fulfilment, and the Anglo-Saxon race, in addition to responsibilities which were already world-wide, would have thrust upon it the burthen of governing Egypt.

British diplomacy, which may at times have been mistaken, but which was certainly honest, did its best to throw off the Egyptian burden. But circumstances were too strong to be arrested by diplomatic action. Egypt was to fall to Kinglake's Englishman. Moreover, it was to fall to him, although some were opposed to his going there, others were indifferent as to whether he went or not, none much wished him to go, and, not only did he not want to go there himself, but he struggled strenuously and honestly not to be obliged to go. The Moslem eventually accepted the accomplished fact, and muttered "Kismet"; but the European, blinded by international jealousy, not unfrequently attributed the whole affair to a deep-laid plot, and found in British policy as regards Egypt another convincing proof of the perfidy of Albion.

French diplomacy, on the other hand, was mainly interested in preventing the Englishman

[1] Kinglake's *Eothen*, p. 288.

from planting his foot firmly on the banks of the Nile, and was, moreover, hampered by the financial necessities of "Great Paris Syndicates," and the like. A Turkish occupation was undesirable, the remedy being, in French opinion, worse than the disease, whilst the French Government of the day had the wisdom to see that a joint Anglo-French occupation would probably become a fertile source of disagreement between France and England. Had not Prince Bismarck been credited with the blunt epigrammatic saying that Egypt would be to France and England even as Schleswig-Holstein to Prussia and Austria?

Italy hovered around, clamorous to satisfy the restless ambition, which might perhaps have better been employed in improving the lot of the Tuscan or Neapolitan peasant, by obtaining some share of government on the cosmopolitan soil of Egypt.

Russia had no local interests to serve, and stood aloof. Possibly, however, as events developed, something might occur which could be turned to the advantage of Muscovite interests. It was to be observed, moreover, that the shipwreck of a Mohammedan Government afforded an additional proof that Orientals could not manage their own affairs. It behoved, therefore, any one who claimed to be heir-apparent to any part of the Ottoman dominions to be on the watch. In the meanwhile, perhaps a little diplomatic capital might be made out of the affair by posing as the protector of Turkey against foreign encroachments. "Nous avons," said a well-known Russian diplomatist, "tellement écorché ces pauvres Turcs au nord, c'est bien le moins que nous pourrons faire de les protéger un peu au sud."

Germany, which connoted Austria, had so far interfered but little in Egyptian affairs. Never-

theless, the co-operation of France and England
in the execution of a common policy was perhaps
regarded with no very friendly eye at Berlin.
There were, moreover, certain German creditors
of the Egyptian Government who had obtained
judgments in the Mixed Courts. Were they not
to be paid? Prince Bismarck would shortly ask
that question, and when the master of many
legions asked a question, it was understood that
he expected some satisfactory reply.

The responsibility of taking the initiative devolved on the British and French Governments.
It was evidently desirable, if possible, to avoid
the extreme step of deposing Ismail Pasha.
Supposing he refused to abdicate, it might become
necessary to use force. In that case, both Governments might be obliged to adopt the policy which
each honestly wished to avoid. Moreover, the
summary dismissal of the European Ministers,
though an unwise act, and one which constituted a
grave discourtesy to both the British and French
Governments, was not a violation of any positive
engagement taken by the Khedive. On every
ground, therefore, it was desirable to see what
could be done by remonstrance before resorting to
extreme measures. After the matter had been
discussed in London and Paris, the two Governments agreed on a common line of action. In a
despatch addressed to Sir Frank Lascelles on
April 25, Lord Salisbury expressed himself in the
following terms :—

"The Khedive is well aware that the considerations which compel Her Majesty's Government to take an interest in the destinies of Egypt
have led them to pursue no other policy than that
of developing the resources and securing the good
government of the country. They have hitherto
considered the independence of the Khedive

and the maintenance of his dynasty as important conditions for the attainment of these ends; and the same sentiments have, they are well assured, animated the Government of France. . . . We would rather assume that the decision thus hastily taken by His Highness, both with respect to the future conduct of the reform and the attitude he proposes to maintain towards the two Governments, is not final. We prefer to look to his future action for a favourable interpretation of the conduct he has lately pursued. But if he continues to ignore the obligations imposed upon him by his past acts and assurances, and persists in declining the assistance of European Ministers whom the two Powers may place at his disposal, we must conclude that the disregard of engagements which has marked his recent action was the result of a settled plan, and that he deliberately renounces all pretension to their friendship. In such a case, it will only remain for the two Cabinets to reserve to themselves an entire liberty of appreciation and action in defending their interests in Egypt, and in seeking the arrangements best calculated to secure the good government and prosperity of the country."

When the Khedive dismissed his European Ministers, he was well aware of the serious nature of the step which he had taken. His first intention was to adopt a defiant attitude. An oath was administered to the superior officers of the army pledging them "to bear true allegiance to the Khedive, and to resist all the enemies of the country, of himself, and of his family." The strength of the army was at the same time increased. A few days, however, sufficed to show that the Khedive could not count on the loyalty of his own troops. Writing on April 26, Sir Frank Lascelles, after dwelling on the misery and discontent caused

by the harsh measures of the new Ministry, added:
"The discontent caused by such a state of things
exists, I am informed, to a large extent in the
army, and has given rise to a feeling of hostility
against the Khedive, not only among the private
soldiers, who are recruited from among the suffering classes of the population, but also among
the officers, who, although they may be strongly
opposed to European interference, regard the
Khedive as being responsible for the disasters that
have fallen upon the country."

When the British and French Consuls-General
communicated to the Khedive the views expressed
in Lord Salisbury's despatch of April 25, he deprecated any idea that he should have been guilty
of intentional discourtesy towards the British and
French Governments, but he declined to reinstate
the European Ministers. It was, indeed, obvious
to every one in Egypt that their reinstatement was
undesirable, even if it had been possible.

Some discussion then took place as to the form
in which Europeans should be associated with the
government of Egypt. There could be but little
hope that the revival of the Control would lead to
any satisfactory results. With whatever nominal
authority the Controllers might have been invested,
they would have had no real power. They would
not have been supported by any external force, or
by the willing assistance of the Khedive, or by the
sympathy of the people. They would have been
associated with Ministers belonging to the retro-
grade Turkish party, with whose ideas they would
have been unable to sympathise. Under such circumstances, their control would have been illusory,
whilst, had they been nominated, the Governments
of England and France would, at least in appearance, have assumed some responsibility for the
financial catastrophe which was evidently impending.

The idea of reviving the Control was, therefore, wisely set aside.

In truth, every day it was becoming more apparent that no satisfactory solution of Egyptian difficulties was possible so long as Ismail Pasha remained at the head of affairs. The action of the German Government hastened the decision which would probably in any case have been taken, though perhaps somewhat later. The German Consul-General in Cairo was instructed to declare to the Khedive "that the Imperial Government looks upon the Decree of April 22, by which the Egyptian Government at their own will regulate the matters relating to the debt, thereby abolishing existing and recognised rights, as an open and direct violation of the international engagements contracted at the institution of the judicial reform; that it must declare the Decree to be devoid of any legally binding effect in regard to the competency of the Mixed Courts of Justice and the rights of the subjects of the Empire, and must hold the Viceroy responsible for all the consequences of his unlawful proceedings." The other Great Powers of Europe joined in this protest, although the form of communication to the Khedive underwent some modifications.

The end was evidently approaching. On June 19, Sir Frank Lascelles, acting under Lord Salisbury's instructions, made the following communication to the Khedive :—

"The French and English Governments are agreed to advise your Highness officially[1] to abdicate and to leave Egypt. Should Your Highness follow this advice, our Governments will act in concert in order that a suitable Civil List should be assigned to you, and that the order

[1] A private communication to the same effect had been made some days previously.

of succession, in virtue of which Prince Tewfik will succeed Your Highness, should not be disturbed. We must not conceal from Your Highness that if you refuse to abdicate, and if you compel the Cabinets of London and Paris to address themselves directly to the Sultan, you will not be able to count either upon obtaining the Civil List or upon the maintenance of the succession in favour of Prince Tewfik." It was necessary to give a warning as to the possibility of the succession passing away from Prince Tewfik. According to Mohammedan law, Prince Abdul Halim was the rightful heir, but the Firman of June 8, 1873, laid down that the succession was to proceed by right of primogeniture. The Khedive had obtained this concession from the Sultan by the expenditure of large sums of money. There was now some danger that his efforts to keep the succession for his children would have been made in vain. It was known that the candidature of Prince Halim found favour at Constantinople.

Simultaneously with the transmission of orders to Sir Frank Lascelles that he should, in conjunction with his French colleague, advise the Khedive to abdicate, a despatch was written by Lord Salisbury stating the reasons why the British Government had been led to take this decision. "It is not possible," Lord Salisbury said, "to review the events which ended in the dismissal of the European Ministers without the conviction that the Khedive never sincerely accepted the limitations of his power proposed by the Commission, and was quite resolved to resume his full prerogative as soon as the immediate purposes of his apparent concession should have been answered.

"The two Powers have given to His Highness ample time to recall any hasty step, and to re-

enter, if he had been willing to do so, upon the
path of reform marked out by the International
Commission. He has refused to avail himself of
any such opportunity, and has only employed the
interval of delay in renewing the extortion and
cruelty by which his Treasury had formerly been
filled. It therefore remains for the two Governments, in accordance with the warning addressed
to His Highness by them in their despatches of
the 25th of April, to consider the course which
is necessary for defending their interests in Egypt,
and securing the good government of the country.

" It is evident that the remedies for misgovernment hitherto proposed have been tried and have
wholly failed. . . . Any further attempt on the
part of the Powers to assist the Khedive in avert-
ing the consequences of his own misgovernment
can have no other effect than to make them
responsible for it in the future. His power to
frustrate all projects of reform, and his resolve to
use it, have been sufficiently demonstrated by events.

" If Egypt were a country in whose past history
the Powers had no share, and to whose future
destiny it was possible for them to be indifferent,
their wisest course would be to renounce at this
point all further concern with the relations between
the Egyptian Ruler and his subjects. But, to
England at least, this policy is impossible. The
geographical situation of Egypt, as well as the
responsibility which the English Government have
in past times incurred for the actual conditions
under which it exists as a State, make it impossible
to leave it to its fate. They are bound, both by
duty and interest, to do all that lies in their power
to arrest misgovernment, before it results in the
material ruin and almost incurable disorder to
which it is evident by other Oriental examples
that such misgovernment will necessarily lead.

"In the case of Egypt, the evil has not yet gone so far but that it may be arrested by changes of small scope and immediate operation. The sole obstacle to reform appears to lie in the character of its Ruler. His financial embarrassments lead almost inevitably to oppression, and his bad faith frustrates all friendly efforts to apply a remedy. There seems to be no doubt that a change of policy can only be obtained by a change of Ruler.

"It may be the duty of the Western Powers to submit these considerations to the Sultan, to whose Firman the Khedive owes his power. But before taking a step so grave, and which, in its results, may possibly be disastrous not only to the Khedive but to his family, it is right, in the first instance, to intimate to the Khedive the conclusion at which the two Powers have arrived, and to give him the opportunity of withdrawing, under favourable and honourable conditions, from a position which his character and his past career have unfitted him to fill."

When the British and French Consuls-General communicated to the Khedive the views entertained by their Governments, he asked that time should be given to him to consider the matter. On June 21, he informed them that he had referred the question to the Sultan. There was, in fact, some hope of support from Constantinople. The Khedive had sent a special agent to the Sultan. Money had been spent in bribes. Moreover, the jealousy of the Sultan had been excited by representations that the two Western Powers intended to disregard his sovereign rights. The Khedive, therefore, felt confident of support, and for a moment it appeared probable that support would be accorded to him. The European Powers were, however, now all combined. Germany, Austria, Russia, and finally Italy, advised the Khedive to abdicate. Italian adhesion was, however, somewhat tardily given. Italy had throughout shown some disposition to support Ismail Pasha.

It required some strong remonstrances on the part of the Ambassadors at Constantinople to prevent encouragement being given to the Khedive by the Sultan. If, however, the Khedive were to be deposed, the Sultan preferred that the act of deposition should emanate from himself, rather than that it should result from any independent action taken by the two Western Powers. On the night of June 24, M. Tricou, the French Consul-General, received information from Constantinople to the effect that the Porte had decided upon the deposition of the Khedive and the appointment of Halim Pasha as his successor. Although it was past midnight, Sir Frank Lascelles, M. Tricou, and Baron de Saurma, the German Consul-General, went at once to the Khedive's palace. "I have been informed," Sir Frank Lascelles wrote, "that when it was known in the harem that the Europeans demanded to see the Khedive at that hour of the night, there was a scene of indescribable confusion. The Princess Mother, fearing the existence of a plot to assassinate her son, implored His Highness not to receive us, but on hearing that the Europeans consisted of the representatives of Germany, France, and England, and were accompanied by Chérif Pasha, the Khedive himself pointed out that there could be no danger for his life, and consented to receive us. His Highness, who was evidently in a state of great excitement, gave me the impression of scarcely knowing what was passing. He, however, remained perfectly firm in his intention not to abdicate."

On the morrow, June 25, there was a last flicker of resistance. A Khedivial Decree was prepared under which the army was to be increased to 150,000 men. Some wild proposals, having for their object the inundation of the country round Alexandria, were also discussed. But the Khedive was conscious that the game was played out. Many of his valuables had already been embarked on board his yacht at Alexandria.

In the meanwhile, the diplomatic pressure brought to bear at Constantinople had produced its effect. The Powers of Europe were evidently determined that Prince Tewfik, and not Prince Halim, should be Khedive of Egypt. On June 26, the Sultan sent a telegram to Cairo addressed "to the ex-Khedive Ismail Pasha," in which the following passage occurred :—

"Il est prouvé que votre maintien au poste de Khédive ne pouvait avoir d'autre résultat que de multiplier et d'aggraver les difficultés présentes. Par conséquent, Sa Majesté Impériale le Sultan, à la suite de la décision de son Conseil des Ministres, a décidé de nommer au poste de Khédive Son Excellence Mehemet Tewfik Pacha, et l'Iradé Impérial concernant ce sujet vient d'être promulgué. Cette haute décision est communiquée à Son Excellence par une autre dépêche, et je vous invite à vous retirer des affaires gouvernementales, conformément à l'ordre de sa Majesté Impériale le Sultan."

At the same time, another telegram was sent to Prince Tewfik nominating him Khedive of Egypt.

It was clear that further resistance was useless. The last hope of support had disappeared. The Khedive sent for Prince Tewfik, and, in the presence of his Ministers, made over his power to him. The scene is said to have been affecting. Both father and son showed signs of emotion.

It was desirable that there should be no delay

in the inauguration of the new Khedive. It took place at once. At 6.30 P.M., on June 26, 1879, Sir Frank Lascelles telegraphed to Lord Salisbury: —"A royal salute on Prince Tewfik's accession was fired this evening from the citadel, where His Highness held an official reception, which was attended by the whole diplomatic and consular corps, the Ministers, and Government officials, and a large number of people." A crowd had collected in the streets of Cairo, but the whole transaction had been so expeditiously concluded that the mass of the population were unaware of the deposition of Ismail Pasha until they heard the guns of the citadel thundering in honour of his successor.

One further scene remained to be enacted. It was undesirable that the ex-Khedive should remain in Egypt. There was some question of his going to Constantinople, and also to Smyrna. He eventually decided to seek an asylum at Naples, where the King of Italy had placed a residence at his disposal.[1] At 11.30 A.M. on June 30, Ismail Pasha left Cairo for Alexandria. He gave it to be understood that he did not wish any official notice to be taken of his departure. None of the foreign representatives were, therefore, present at the railway station. A large crowd, however, assembled to witness his departure. The ladies of the harem, dressed in black, were present in carriages outside the station and were loud in their lamentations. Before entering his carriage, Ismail Pasha addressed a few words to the people who were present, telling them that on leaving Egypt he confided his son, the Khedive, to their care. The latter then took leave of his father and of his brothers, who accompanied Ismail Pasha.

---

[1] At a later period, Ismail Pasha went to Constantinople. He died on March 2, 1895.

An eye-witness stated that "the scene was so affecting that there were few among the spectators who were able to refrain from tears."

On arrival at Alexandria, Ismail Pasha embarked on board his yacht, the *Mahroussa*. Mr. Calvert, the British Vice-Consul at Alexandria, reported that "the deck of the *Mahroussa* was crowded with officials and European residents who had come to take leave of Ismail Pasha. His Highness met everywhere, both on shore and on board, with marked respect and consideration. Though his features bore the traces of strong recent emotion, he bore up manfully, and was quite cheerful, addressing a pleasant word and thanks to every one who took leave of him, and shaking hands."

If Ismail Pasha's rule had been bad, his fall was at least dignified. His worst enemies must have pitied a man in the hour of his distress who had stood so high and who had fallen so low. "Who," says Bacon, "can see worse days than he that, yet living, doth follow at the funeral of his own reputation?" Any chance moralist who may have watched the *Mahroussa* steaming out of Alexandria harbour on that summer afternoon must perforce have heaved a sigh over one of the most striking instances that the world has ever known of golden opportunities lost.

It may be that the events of Ismail Pasha's reign in Egypt are too recent for an impartial verdict to be passed upon them. Neither perhaps do I possess all the qualifications necessary to strict impartiality. At the same time, I am quite unconscious of any bias in the matter. In the course of this narrative, I have criticised Ismail Pasha's conduct, but I never felt any personal dislike to the man. My feelings throughout all these struggles were inspired by pity rather than by anger. I always felt that if Ismail Pasha had fallen into better hands in the early part of his career, the recent history of Egypt might have been changed. Probably few individuals ever experienced more fully than Ismail what has aptly been termed "the lonely friendlessness of selfish power."[1] The conduct of those who flattered him, and then preyed upon him, cannot be too strongly condemned. But as regards himself, however severe may be the censure inflicted on him, it must be admitted that there are some extenuating circumstances. He wished to introduce European civilisation into Egypt at a rapid rate, but he had little idea of how to set about the work. He had neither the knowledge nor the experience necessary to carry out the task. It should be remarked that Ismail was utterly uneducated. When Mr. Nassau Senior was returning to Europe in 1855, he found that an English coachman, who had been in Ismail's service, was his fellow-passenger. The man's account of Ismail's private life is worth quoting. There can be little doubt of its accuracy. "Ismail," he said, "and his brother Mustapha, when they were in Paris, used to buy whatever they saw; they were like children, nothing was fine enough for them; they bought carriages and horses like those of Queen Victoria or the Emperor, and let them spoil for want of shelter and cleaning. . . . The people he liked best to talk to were his servants, the lads who brought him his pipes and stood before him with their arms crossed. He sometimes sat on his sofa and smoked, and talked to them for hours, all about women and such things. . . . I have known him sometimes try to read a French novel, but he would be two hours getting through a page.

[1] Dill's *Roman Society from Nero to Marcus Aurelius*, p. 379.

Once or twice, I saw him attempt to write. His letters were half an inch high, like those of a child's copybook. I don't think that he ever finished a sentence."[1]

My personal relations with Ismail Pasha were of a friendly nature, a fact which redounds to his credit, for if there was one person in Egypt against whom he had a right to bear a grudge, it was myself. I took a prominent part in the events which brought about his deposition, and especially in the nomination of the Commission of Inquiry, a blow from which he never recovered. Ismail Pasha was not a man who bore malice.

Whenever and by whomsoever the verdict on his rule in Egypt is passed, it can scarcely be anything but unfavourable. Few people have enjoyed a more enviable position than that of Ismail Pasha when he became Khedive of Egypt. He was absolute ruler over a docile people, inhabiting one of the most fertile spots in the world. He had power, rank, and a degree of wealth such as has been given to few individuals. With reasonable prudence he could have satisfied every legitimate ambition, and left a name which posterity would have revered. All this he threw away. He fell a victim to ὕβρις, the insolent abuse of power. A great Nemesis fell upon the Egyptian Crœsus. He squandered his wealth, and when, finally, he was deposed at the behests of the Powers of Europe, there were not a dozen of his own countrymen, albeit they disliked the interference of the foreigner, who did not think that he had merited his fate.

It is frequently the habit of deposed Sovereigns to think that their former subjects long for their return to power. I do not know if Ismail Pasha

---

[1] *Conversations, etc.,* vol. ii. p. 228.

ever cherished thoughts of this description. If so, he was wrong. From the date of his deposition, he was politically defunct, and his former subjects would now regard his reign as a bad dream were it not that they still suffer, and that their children's children must continue to suffer, from the effects of his misrule.

The centenary of Mehemet Ali's birth has recently been celebrated in Egypt. National *fêtes* are reasonable enough when they call to mind the occurrence of some event for which the gratitude of posterity is due. Thus, it is not unnatural that the French, forgetful of the horrors which accompanied the fall of the Bastille, should recognise that event as symbolical of the dawn of a new era, and should, therefore, have raised the date on which it occurred to the dignity of a national anniversary. It is also perfectly natural that the Egyptians should commemorate the birth of the remarkable man who gave their country a separate administrative existence. Nevertheless, another very suitable anniversary for the modern Egyptians to celebrate would be the day on which Ismail Pasha, under pressure from the Powers of Europe, abdicated. That day marked the advent of a new era. It should be borne in grateful remembrance by the present and future generations of Egyptians. Ismail Pasha's abdication sounded the death-knell of arbitrary personal rule in Egypt. It may be hoped and believed that that rule can never be revived; but in spite of the strongest guarantees which can be recorded on paper, there would unquestionably be a considerable risk of its revival in some form or another if the British occupation of the country were allowed to terminate prematurely. When it is quite clear that this risk has ceased to exist, the question of the cessation of the occupation

will assume a new aspect. In the minds of all
well-informed and calm observers it seems, however, probable that some long while must elapse
before they can feel assured that this political
transformation has really taken place.

PART II

THE ARÁBI REVOLT

August 1879–August 1883

The daughter of Egypt shall be confounded; she shall be delivered into the hands of the people of the north.

JEREMIAH xlvi. 24.

CHAPTER IX

THE INAUGURATION OF TEWFIK

August–November 1879

State of the country—Chérif Pasha's Ministry—The Khedive assumes the Presidency of the Council—Ministry of Riaz Pasha—Relations between the Khedive and his Ministers—The Sultan cancels the Firman of 1873—Objections of France and England—The Mohammedan law of succession—The right to make Commercial Conventions, and to contract loans—The Army—The Khedive's investiture—Appointment of Controllers—Relations between the Government and the Controllers—Division of work between the Controllers—The Commission of Liquidation.

WITH the deposition of Ismail Pasha, the main obstacle which had heretofore stood in the way of Egyptian reform was removed. His sinister influence was, however, felt for long after his abdication. He had, indeed, left a *damnosa hereditas* to his successor. The Treasury was bankrupt. The discipline of the army had been shaken. Every class of Egyptian society was discontented; the poor by reason of the oppressive measures of their ruler; the rich because the privileges which they enjoyed were threatened; the Europeans because the money owing to them was not paid, and because, in the general confusion which existed, trade was naturally depressed. The Powers of Europe had, for a while, combined in the presence of a common danger, but the ceaseless jar of petty international rivalries was sure to make itself felt whenever any question of local interest was discussed. The Arab hated and mistrusted the Turk. The Turk hated and mistrusted the European. European assistance was necessary, but it was difficult to decide in what form it should be given. Reforms dictated in the best interests of the country would be misunderstood and misrepresented. It was well-nigh impossible that they should bear immediate fruit, whilst any temporary unpopularity which might arise from their adoption would of necessity devolve mainly on the alien and Christian elements in the Government. Time would have to elapse before the sorely-tried people of Egypt would begin to see dimly, through a thick mist of ignorance and misrepresentation, that some material benefits might accrue to them from foreign interference. At the head of affairs was a young Prince animated with the best intentions, but wanting in experience. His own predisposition, as well as the censures which his father's oppressive system of government had evoked, alike led him to favour a reign of law and order. But the proper administration of justice was impossible until law-courts had been established and qualified judges appointed. The period of transition from an arbitrary to a legal system of government was to be not only painful but dangerous. The minds of the people had been unsettled by frequent discussions about organic changes. "It is unwise," said one of England's greatest political thinkers, "to make the extreme medicine of the constitution its daily bread."[1] The habits of obedience, which the Egyptians had inherited from their forefathers, had been rudely shaken. All this ferment was not to settle down at once. A more serious collapse of the State machinery than any which had yet taken place was to occur before the calm waters of peaceful progress could be reached. A well-known

---

[1] Burke, *Reflections on the French Revolution.*

Conservative statesman in conversation with me once gave utterance to an opinion which involves the *ne plus ultra* of anti-conservative principles. "The East," he said, "is languishing for want of a Revolution." This statement is true; for the violent changes from one Amurath to another, which Oriental history has frequently recorded, have generally been the result, not of revolution, but of palace intrigue. The Egyptians were now to try whether their lot could be improved by a movement, whose leading feature was that it combined some vague national aspirations, which were incapable of realisation, with the time-honoured tactics of a mutinous prætorian guard. In the meanwhile, the machine of State worked laboriously, but apparently with some fair prospect of success. It was not till the Egyptian Sisyphus had got his stone some little way up the hill that it escaped from his grasp and rolled back again into the slough of anarchy. Then all the work had to be begun again, but under new conditions which augured better for the final result.

Before the new State machine could be got to work, the various parts of the machinery had to be adjusted. A Ministry had to be formed. The degree to which the Khedive was to take an active part in the administration had to be settled. The relations between the Sultan and the Khedive had to be regulated. The form in which Europeans should be associated with the government of the country had to be decided. It was also essential to adopt measures which should place the new relations between the Egyptian Government and their creditors on a legal footing.

The Khedive charged Chérif Pasha with the formation of a Ministry. He at once submitted to the Khedive a project for a constitution of which His Highness disapproved. On August 18, therefore, he tendered his resignation, which was accepted. The Khedive resolved to retain the Presidency of the Council of Ministers in his own hands for the present. His Highness explained to Sir Frank Lascelles the reasons why he had disapproved of Chérif Pasha's proposals. " He was aware," Sir Frank Lascelles wrote, " that it would be said that his action was an attempt to return to the old system of personal government. He could assure me that he had no wish to do so ; but that at present liberal institutions were utterly unsuited to the country, and the constitution which had been submitted to him was nothing more than a *décor de théâtre.* . . . He was himself responsible for the government of the country, and had determined to take his share of the labour, and not to shelter himself behind an unreal and illusory constitution." Chérif Pasha, on the other hand, told Sir Frank Lascelles that, though he was personally glad to be relieved of his duties, " as an Egyptian, he regretted the return to personal power. There were many persons both in and outside the palace who would be glad, for their own ends, to see the absolute power of the Khedive re-established, but it was a real misfortune for the country if it should again fall under the rule of an absolute Sovereign."

There can be little doubt that the Khedive acted wisely in declining the proposals submitted to him by Chérif Pasha. Any Egyptian constitution must of necessity at that time have been a mere *décor de théâtre.*[1] The only form of government suitable to

[1] The methods of government which found favour about this time amongst many of those who favoured, or pretended to favour constitutional government, may be judged from a statement made in 1903 by Sheikh Mohammed Abdou to Mr. Wilfrid Blunt (*Secret History*, etc., p. 493). Sultan Pasha, the Sheikh said, " had promised to bring petitions from every Notable in Egypt in favour of the Constitution. This was true, for all the Omdehs were angry with Riaz for having put down their habit of employing forced labour." In other words, Riaz Pasha, who was supposed to be a somewhat extreme representative of personal

Egypt was a despotism, but it would have to be a
benevolent despotism, which would be under some
effective control. The control was to be sought
more in the careful selection of the individuals to
whom power was confided than in any endeavour to
copy European institutions, which were uncongenial
to the manners and customs of the people and to the
condition of society which then existed in Egypt.
Nevertheless, the attitude assumed at this moment
by Chérif Pasha merits a word of sympathy. He
was a perfectly honest man. He was convinced
of the harm done by the absolute rule of the
ex-Khedive. He was slow to believe that, with
a change of despot, the character of the despotism
would undergo any material alteration. Although,
therefore, his views as to the best system of governing the country appear to have been unsuited to
the circumstances of the time, both his proposals
and his resignation did him credit personally.

The arrangement under which the Khedive was
to be his own Prime Minister was of doubtful
wisdom. Fortunately, it did not last long. Riaz
Pasha was summoned to Egypt, and on September
22 was charged with the formation of a Ministry.
The principles of Ismail Pasha's Rescript of August
28, 1878, were maintained. Riaz Pasha was named
President of the Council, but the Khedive reserved
to himself the right to preside at the meetings of
the Council whenever he thought it desirable to
do so.

The duration of the new Ministry was much
longer than that of its predecessors. One of the
reasons why it acquired a certain character of
stability was that the relations between the Khedive
and his Ministers were at last placed on a footing

government, was endeavouring to abolish the iniquitous corvée system,
whilst the constitutionalists hoped that, through the introduction of
free institutions, it would be found possible to ensure its continuance.

which was adapted to the actual requirements of
the country. A compromise was effected between
the system of excluding the Khedive altogether
from the exercise of any real power and that under
which his authority would be absolute. It was
essential to associate the Khedive with the government of the country. This was secured by according to him the right to preside at the Council
whenever he thought fit to do so. On the other
hand, it was undesirable that the Khedive should
be his own Prime Minister. Apart from the risk
of a return to the old régime, which the adoption
of this system would have involved, there was the
further objection that the ruler of the State would
have become personally responsible for every act of
the administration. The natural remedy for any
serious defect in the government of a State is a
change of Ministry. If the Khedive had become
his own Prime Minister, this safety-valve would
have been removed. A case might have arisen in
which a change of policy would have been well-
nigh impossible without a change of Khedive. Of
course, much depended upon the spirit in which
the compromise was to be worked. Had the
Khedive meant to evade the spirit of the Rescript
of August 1878 he might have done so. On the
contrary, however, he loyally accepted the principle
of ministerial responsibility. The system worked
well, and although many difficulties of a different
nature were in store for Egypt, the question of the
part which Tewfik Pasha was to take in the government of the country was finally set at rest by the
arrangement made in September 1879.

The settlement of the relations between Turkey
and Egypt gave rise to considerable difficulties,
which were only arranged after a somewhat stormy
diplomatic negotiation. The Porte made a determined effort to tighten its hold on Egypt.

Simultaneously with the issue of the order deposing Ismail Pasha, an Imperial Iradé was signed repealing the Firman of 1873. The issue of a new Firman was necessary in consequence of this action of the Sultan. The Porte showed great disinclination to submit the terms of the Firman before issue to the British and French Governments. The result was that peremptory orders had to be sent to the Ambassadors at Constantinople. The Sultan and his advisers were made to understand that, in their endeavour to tighten their hold on Egypt, they ran a risk that the country would escape from their grasp altogether. They therefore yielded. The principle that the terms of the Firman must be discussed with the French and British Governments was accepted. A discussion then commenced as to the stipulations which were to be incorporated into the new Firman.

In 1873, Ismail Pasha, in return for large sums of money lavished at Constantinople, had obtained four concessions from the Sultan. In the first place, the Mohammedan law of succession was set aside. Primogeniture was for the future to be the principle under which succession to the Khedivate was to be regulated. In the second place, the right to conclude Commercial Conventions with other Powers was conceded to Egypt. In the third place, full power was given to the Khedive to contract foreign loans. In the fourth place, the Khedive obtained the right to fix the strength of the Egyptian army at any figure he might consider necessary without reference to Constantinople. The Sultan now wished to cancel these concessions.

The views entertained by the British and French Governments upon the points at issue were not altogether identical. The traditional policy of

France favoured, if not an independent Egypt, at all events the relaxation of the bonds which united the suzerain and his feudatory. The French Government were, therefore, opposed to the restrictive measures which the Sultan wished to adopt. More especially M. Fournier, who was then French Ambassador at Constantinople, insisted strongly upon opposition being offered to them. Successive British Governments, on the other hand, had for a long time past been averse to any measures which tended towards the dismemberment of the Ottoman Empire. Except in the matter of the succession, Lord Salisbury did not consider the proposals made by the Sultan as open to any great objections on their own merits. Moreover, the spokesman of the British Government at Constantinople was Sir Austen Layard, a strong Turcophile.

On the question of the succession, however, the two Governments were agreed. Under the Mohammedan law of succession the eldest member of the family is Heir-Apparent. This practice has, during the whole course of Ottoman history, been a fertile source of intrigue, and has often led to much bloodshed. The maxim of Bajazet I.—"Better the death of a Prince than the loss of a province"—is still inscribed over one of the inner gates of the old Imperial Palace at Constantinople. The slaughter of collateral branches of the family is, in fact, a means of protection against conspiracy which the rulers of Oriental States have not unfrequently adopted.[1]

---

[1] It cannot be doubted that the practice of murdering or keeping in confinement the heir to the throne, more especially if he showed any signs of ability, has been one of the many causes of Ottoman decay. For instance, Sultan Ibrahim (1640-48) was the sole surviving brother of Amurath IV, the remainder having been put to death at the time of the latter's succession. On his deathbed, Amurath ordered Ibrahim, who had been kept for eight years in prison, to be killed, but the order

The British and French Governments, therefore, insisted that the principle of primogeniture should be ratified in the new Firman. On this point, the Porte yielded.

"With regard," Lord Salisbury wrote, "to the limit to be assigned to the military and naval forces which the Khedive may maintain, and his power to negotiate Commercial Conventions, Her Majesty's Government will not object." The French Government, on the other hand, attached great importance to the question of the right to make Commercial Conventions, with the result that the Porte yielded. The new Firman was on this point substantially a reproduction of the Firman of 1873.

The Porte, however, gained its point as regards the restrictions which it wished to place on the strength of the Egyptian army. The new Firman laid down that in time of peace the army was not to exceed 18,000 men.

As regards the power of borrowing money, Lord Salisbury wrote: "The power to contract loans has been so grievously abused, and with such disastrous results to the prosperity of Egypt, that it might advantageously be withdrawn altogether, for it is quite clear that the country can bear no further attempts to bolster up its credit by such means." The French Government would have been glad to preserve the Firman of 1873 intact, but seeing that the British Government were lukewarm on the subject, and that they had already achieved a diplomatic victory on the two

---

was not executed. When Amurath died, Creasy says (*Ottoman Turks*, p. 259), "Ibrahim came forth and mounted the Turkish throne, which received in him a selfish voluptuary, in whom long imprisonment and protracted terror had debased whatever spirit nature might have originally bestowed, and who was as rapacious and bloodthirsty as he was cowardly and mean."

The practice is of very ancient date. Jehu, on obtaining possession of the throne, killed the seventy sons of Ahab. — 2 Kings x. 1-11.

important questions of the succession and the right
to make Commercial Conventions, they agreed to
the withdrawal from the Khedive of the right to
contract loans.

It is difficult to prophesy, especially in politics.
No one could foresee that, a few years later, the
British Government would find the work of reform
in Egypt to some extent hindered by the restrictions which, in 1879, were considered un-
objectionable and even beneficial. That, however,
is what actually happened. French diplomacy had,
in fact, unconsciously worked to facilitate the
future task of the British Government, whilst the
latter, with equal unconsciousness, had used their
influence to place obstacles in their own path.

On August 14, the ceremony of reading the
Firman of Investiture took place in Cairo.

The next question which had to be decided was
the form in which Europeans should be associated
with the government of Egypt. Immediately
after the Khedive's accession, a letter was addressed
by Chérif Pasha to the representatives of England
and France in Egypt, expressing a hope that, if
Controllers were nominated under the Decree of
November 18, 1876, their functions would be
limited to investigation and verification, and that
they would not be invested with any administrative
or executive powers. In reply to this communication, the Consuls-General were authorised to state
that "the two Governments accepted in principle His
Highness's offer to re-establish the office of Controllers-General, and that the details respecting their
powers and functions would form the subject of a
further communication."

Three questions had then to be decided. In the
first place, who were to be the Controllers ? In
the second place, what were to be the relations
between them and the Egyptian Government ? In

the third place, how was the work to be divided
between them ?

Perhaps the first of these questions was the
most important of the three. More depended on
the character and personal influence of the individuals who were chosen than on the special
functions which might be assigned to them by a
Khedivial Decree. The situation of the European
advisers of the Khedive would, necessarily, be one
of great difficulty. They would have to guide with
as little appearance of guiding as possible. They
could not hope to succeed unless two conditions
were fulfilled. The first was that they should
be to some extent in sympathy with the Egyptian
Government. The second was that they should be
in sympathy with each other. If the more distasteful aspects of European interference were
constantly being presented to the Egyptian
Ministers without any compensatory advantages
being derived from European assistance in the
defence of Egyptian interests, another breakdown
was sure to ensue before long. Further, the
selection of a Gallophobe Englishman, or of an
Anglophobe Frenchman, would have ensured the
failure of the experiment which was about to be
made.

The choice of the French Government fell on
M. de Blignières. Lord Salisbury offered the post
of English Controller to me. After some hesitation,[1] I accepted the offer.

As regards the relations which were to exist
between the Egyptian Government and the Con-

---

[1] My intention at this time had been to stand for East Norfolk at
the next General Election. The acceptance of Lord Salisbury's offer
made me abandon the idea of entering Parliament. I think that it
was in 1880 that, happening to meet Mr. Gladstone at Sandringham,
I spoke to him on this subject. He told me that he thought I was
quite right not to enter Parliament as all the principal questions which
interested Liberals had been solved. Very shortly afterwards, the
Home Rule project was launched on an astonished world.

trollers, there was no difficulty in meeting the
Khedive's wishes. M. de Blignières and myself,
who were consulted on the subject, were of opinion
that the system of direct government by Europeans
was unsuitable to the circumstances which then
existed in Egypt, and that it would be preferable
to give us general powers of supervision and
inspection, trusting to the exercise of personal
influence to do the rest. The Decree, which was
eventually issued, laid down that the most ample
powers of investigation were to be conferred on
the Controllers, but that they were not to be invested with any administrative functions. They
could only make suggestions. They were to have
seats in the Council of Ministers, with *voix con-
sultatives* ; that is to say, they might give their
opinions, but they had no right to vote.

It was further provided that the Controllers
could not be dismissed without the consent of
their respective Governments. When, three years
later, Egypt was occupied by British troops, a discussion took place as to whether the Liberal or the
Conservative Government was responsible for the
events which led up to the occupation. The point
is now one of purely historical interest, and at
no time was it of much interest save to party
politicians. It may, however, be observed that,
in the discussions which took place in 1882, the
politicians on the Liberal side of the House of
Commons maintained that the necessity for British
interference was mainly due to the fact that in 1879
the Control, which was formerly financial, became
political. Mr. Gladstone, speaking on July 27,
1882, said : " What is a political control ? I assert
that this was not a political control then (*i.e.* prior
to 1879) because the Government were not concerned in it. The fact that the Egyptians chose
to establish foreign Controllers, an arrangement

attended with great benefits to the people of England (? Egypt), was not necessarily an arrangement entailing foreign interference, because they retained the right to dismiss the Controllers, but in the year 1879, in depriving them of that right, you brought foreign intervention into the heart of the country, and established, in the strictest sense of the phrase, a 'political control.'" There is some force in this argument.   Nevertheless, as will appear at a later portion of this narrative, the main responsibility for the British occupation, in so far as it was due to events which were in any way capable of control, would appear to lie with the Government of Mr. Gladstone rather than with that of Lord Salisbury which preceded him.

A further question, which had to be decided, was how the work was to be divided between the two Controllers.

Under the Decree of November 18, 1876, the Englishman was Controller-General of Receipts, and the Frenchman Controller-General of Expenditure.   Subsequently, when European Ministers were appointed, the Englishman was placed in charge of the Ministry of Finance, and the Frenchman of the Ministry of Public Works.   Under both these arrangements, the preponderating influence was in the hands of the Englishman.   The French chafed at their position of inferiority, and it appeared both unwise and unnecessary to insist upon a position of marked superiority being given to the Englishman.   Either M. de Blignières and I could, or could not work together.   If we could do so, any distinction between us was unnecessary, and would only serve to wound the *amour propre* of the French without producing any useful result. If we could not do so, the collapse of the system was inevitable, and could not be averted by any definition of our respective functions.   Various

M

proposals were made with a view to precise definition, such as that one Controller should deal with
Upper and the other with Lower Egypt.   But
in the end it was wisely decided to leave the
matter to the discretion of the Controllers themselves.

The last point which had to be settled was the
method under which legal effect should be given
to the relations about to be established between
the Egyptian Government and their creditors.   In
other words, the bankruptcy of Egypt had to be
sanctioned by law.   The two reports of the Commission of Inquiry had prepared the way for a
settlement, but it was essential that it should be
made binding on all the parties concerned.   On
April 2, 1880, after some long and tedious discussions, a Khedivial Decree was issued instituting
a Commission of Liquidation with full powers to
regulate the financial situation.   The Great Powers
bound themselves by anticipation to accept the
conclusions at which the Commissioners might
arrive.   Sir Rivers Wilson was named President
of the Commission.   The four Commissioners of
the Debt were named members.   An additional
French member (M. Liron d'Airolles) was named
so as to give France the same degree of representation as England.   Germany was represented by
M. de Trescow.   The new Commission of Liquidation was, in fact, the old Commission of Inquiry
"writ large"—that is to say, with extended powers
and with the addition of a German representative.   The Controllers were not appointed members
of the Commission.   The interests of the creditors
were strongly represented, and it was thought both
just and politic that the Controllers should stand
outside and represent the interests of the Egyptian
Government and people, rather than those of
the creditors.   Without European assistance, the

Egyptian Ministers would scarcely be able to resist the pressure which the Commission was almost certain to bring to bear on them in the bondholding interest.

The various essential parts of the State machine were thus adjusted. A new Khedive ruled. The relations between the Khedive and his Ministers were placed on a satisfactory footing. A Prime Minister had been nominated who had taken an active part in opposing the abuses prevalent during the reign of Ismail Pasha. The relations between the Sultan and the Khedive had been regulated in such a way as to ensure the latter against any excessive degree of Turkish interference. The system which had been devised for associating Europeans with the Government held out good promise of success, inasmuch as it was in accordance with the Khedive's own views. Lastly, an International Commission had been created with full powers to arrange matters between the Egyptian Government and their creditors.

It now remained to be seen how the machine would work. There were great difficulties still to be overcome, but on the whole the prospect was brighter than at any previous moment during recent times.

CHAPTER X

THE DUAL CONTROL

NOVEMBER 1879–DECEMBER 1880

Working of the Control—Relations between the two Controllers—And between the Controllers and the Egyptian Government—Delay in paying the Tribute—Interest on the Unified Debt paid at 4 per cent—Financial scheme proposed by the Controllers—The Budget for 1880—Reforms in the fiscal system—Confidence inspired by the Control—Reports on the state of the country—The Law of Liquidation—The military danger.

On November 30, 1879, I wrote to Sir Edward Malet, who had been appointed Consul-General in Egypt: "On the whole, I think the start has been favourable. If we can only sit tight for six months, I believe we may pull the thing through. But I devoutly hope that there will be no change of Ministry, or any unexpected event, such as often happens in the East, to upset everything and to oblige a new beginning to be made." Time, and a stable political situation,—these were the two principal conditions which were essential to success. Only the first of these conditions was, to a very limited extent, fulfilled.

The Ministry of Riaz Pasha lasted for nearly two years, and an acute observer who was on the spot subsequently wrote that "with all its faults it was the best administration which Egypt has enjoyed before or since." [1]

---

[1] *Khedives and Pashas*, p. 134. This was written in 1884, that is to say, before the reforms introduced subsequent to the British occupation had produced much result.

164

The main reasons why the machine of Government worked fairly well for a time were twofold.

In the first place, the best relations existed between the two Controllers. In the second place, a *modus vivendi* was found between the Controllers and the Egyptian Government.

It has been mentioned in the previous chapter that before the Controllers-General were appointed, some discussion took place as to how the work should be divided between them. Eventually, M. de Blignières and I were left to settle the matter between ourselves. The solution which we adopted was a simple one. We never attempted to solve the question at all. We were in constant communication with each other, and we worked in common. Any precise definition of our respective functions would have been difficult, and was quite unnecessary.

It was a more difficult matter to establish friendly relations with the Egyptian Government. Riaz Pasha was thoroughly honest and well-intentioned, but he was incapable of dealing unaided with the perplexing financial questions which at that time presented themselves for solution. He saw the necessity for European assistance, but, at the same time, in whatever form it was given, it was distasteful to him. He was himself a reformer, and had courageously protested against the abuses of Ismail Pasha's time, but he was slow to accept the inevitable conclusion that no reforms were possible without European guidance and assistance. *Qui veut la fin veut les moyens*, formed no part of Riaz Pasha's political creed. It was clear that, under these circumstances, the best hope of success lay in the Controllers submitting themselves to a self-denying ordinance. They would have to pull the strings behind the scenes, but appear on the stage as little as possible.

Another essential requisite to success was that both the Egyptian Ministers and the Egyptian people should see that the Controllers were of some use to them. Duty and justice alike pointed to the necessity of standing as a buffer between the Egyptian Government and their creditors. The Ministers had neither the strength to oppose the pressure which, in European interests, was brought to bear on them, nor the knowledge requisite to resist it with effect. The policy adopted by M. de Blignières and myself was to associate ourselves, as much as possible, with the Egyptian Government, and to defend them against any excessive demands and encroachments on their rights. By adopting this line of conduct, we hoped soon to inspire confidence, and gradually to disabuse the minds both of the Ministers and of the Egyptian people of the prejudices which were entertained against Europeans. If once we could inspire confidence, our advice, we thought, would generally be followed, and our influence could be used to the benefit both of the country and of the creditors.

Opportunities for giving effect to these principles were not slow to present themselves. Heavy instalments of the Tribute, as also the half-yearly interest on the Unified Debt, had to be paid. Money was not forthcoming to meet these engagements. M. de Blignières and I had not yet arrived in Egypt. Our advice was requested by telegraph. The Egyptian Government flinched at the responsibility of committing an act of insolvency. They asked us whether they ought to borrow money in order to meet their engagements. The reply could not be doubtful. If the Tribute could not be paid, so much the worse for the Tribute. The same was to be said as regards the interest on the Unified Debt. The main thing was, once and for all, to abandon the ruinous expedients of the past. The employés of the Government must, in the first instance, be paid; then the Tribute, whenever there was money enough to pay it. As for the Unified Debt, the taxes should on no account be taken in advance. If, when the interest fell due, the revenues pledged to the service of the debt were insufficient to meet the whole charge, a dividend should be distributed.

The letter which we wrote from Paris on this subject was published. One result of our advice was that the Tribute due to the Porte remained unpaid for some little while. A further result was that the full interest on the Unified Debt was never paid. The amount due on November 1 was £1,989,000. The rate of interest fixed by the Decree of November 18, 1876, viz. 6 per cent, had not as yet been legally changed. When the 1st of November arrived, only £1,147,000 was in the hands of the Commissioners of the Debt. Interest at the rate of 4 per cent was distributed to the bondholders.

Directly after we arrived in Egypt, another step of importance was taken. Difficulties were being encountered in arranging for a Commission of Liquidation to make a final settlement of Egyptian financial affairs. In the meanwhile, both the country and the creditors were suffering. We therefore recommended the Egyptian Government to cut the diplomatic knot by preparing their own scheme, which could be submitted to the Commission of Liquidation, if one were appointed, and which could be put into operation without the sanction of any law, in the event of no agreement being arrived at as regards a Commission. The suggestion was accepted, and, in concert with the Egyptian authorities, we proceeded to prepare a scheme.

On January 1, 1880, we submitted our report

to the Khedive. "Experience," we said, "has shown that the main defect of all former attempts to regulate the Egyptian financial situation has been that they have been too optimistic." It was essential to steer clear of that danger. The Commission of Inquiry had recommended that the interest on the Unified Debt should be fixed at 5 per cent. M. de Blignières and I thought that rate too high. We recommended that only 4 per cent interest should be guaranteed. The public had become accustomed to the idea that the rate of interest would have to be reduced to 4 per cent. When our proposals were made known, so far from producing a bad effect, Unified Stock rose from 51 to 56. A sum of £1,684,000 was due to the bond-holders for back interest on coupons which had only been partially paid. "We cannot," we said, "hold out the least hope that these sums will ever be paid."

The next thing was to frame a Budget for the year 1880. The Commission of Inquiry had estimated the Egyptian revenue at £9,067,000. We considered this estimate too high. We reduced it to £8,562,000. A sum of £4,323,000 was required to pay the Tribute and to carry on the administration of the country, thus leaving £4,239,000 available for the creditors of the Egyptian Government.

The reforms proposed by the Commission of Inquiry were at the same time taken in hand. On January 6, 1880, the law of the Moukábala was repealed. On the 18th, an additional tax of £E.150,000 a year was placed on the Ouchouri lands. On January 17, the poll-tax was abolished. It yielded a revenue of £205,000 a year. Persons whose sole employment was agriculture were, at the same time, relieved from the payment of the professional tax. Octroi duties, highway,

market, and weighing dues were suppressed in
the villages, while in the towns, octroi duties were
abolished on 105 articles, mostly agricultural produce. Twenty-four petty taxes of a vexatious
nature were abolished by a stroke of the pen.

An important reform was also made in the
method of levying the salt tax. Under a law
passed in 1873, every individual in Egypt was
supposed to consume a certain amount of salt a
year. The population of each village was roughly
calculated at the time the law was passed, and the
tax divided amongst the villagers. The salt tax
had, in fact, become a poll-tax, which was paid
equally by those who consumed a great deal of
salt, and by those who consumed little or none.
No account was taken of changes, which might
have occurred since 1873, in the population of
each village. The defects of this system were
obvious. It was abolished, and, in substitution for
it, salt was constituted a Government monopoly.

The system of paying the land-tax in kind,
which had hitherto existed in some parts of Upper
Egypt, had given rise to numerous abuses. It
was suppressed. For the future, only payment in
money was allowed.

The dates at which the instalments of land-tax
were to fall due were fixed in a manner which was
convenient to the cultivators. At the same time,
the names of the taxpayers belonging to each
village were inscribed in one register. An extract
from this register was given to each taxpayer,
showing the total of the sums which were due
from him under the several heads of account, and
the dates on which he would be called upon to
pay. Of all the reforms which were introduced,
this was perhaps the most important and the
most beneficial. It was not so much the amount
of the land-tax which had heretofore weighed

heavily on the country, as the fact that the
dates of collection had been regulated without
any reference to the convenience of the taxpayers.
Further, inasmuch as none of the taxpayers knew
with any degree of certainty how much they had
to pay, a wide door was opened for extortion and
illegal taxation.

At the same time, an improved system was introduced for the payment of the village accountants.
Hitherto they had received no fixed salaries, but
were allowed to retain a certain proportion of the
sums which they collected.

The main reason why these and other reforms
were carried into execution was that the Controllers and the Egyptian Ministers worked
cordially together. The Control had, in fact,
inspired confidence.

I remember one incident which contributed in
no small degree to the establishment of this confidence. A British syndicate, on the list of which
some influential names figured, was formed with a
view to the purchase of the Egyptian Railways.
The representatives of the syndicate laid their
proposals before the Egyptian Government. The
Ministers were anxious as to the attitude which
the Controllers, and particularly the British Controller, would take up on this subject. It scarcely
occurred to them that any foreigner would do
otherwise than push the presumed interests of his
own countrymen. Great, therefore, was their surprise when, directly the question was mooted in
the Council, I said that I considered that it was
for the Ministers to decide whether they would
entertain any proposal to purchase the railways;
that if they wished to reject the offer which had
been made to them, I had no wish to press them to
accept it; but that if, on the other hand, they chose
to accept the principle, I was ready to go into

the details and see that they obtained reasonable terms. They at once decided not to sell the railways. I had anticipated this decision. From that time forth, I never had any serious difficulty in getting my advice accepted. Shortly after the occurrence of this incident, I was asked to see if terms could be arranged with Messrs. Greenfield, the contractors for the construction of the harbour works at Alexandria, to whom a large sum of money was due. The subject was full of difficulties. However, in forty-eight hours I had made an arrangement which seemed reasonable. The contract had to be signed by Riaz Pasha. It was prepared by about three o'clock one afternoon. Messrs. Greenfield's representatives wished to leave Cairo by a train at five o'clock the same afternoon in order to catch a steamer at Alexandria. I thought this difficult, as Riaz Pasha had not yet had the matter explained to him. But I said that I would do my best. I took the contract to Riaz Pasha and explained its provisions to him. He said that if I was satisfied he was ready to accept my conclusions, and accordingly signed the contract without reading it.

On April 30, Sir Edward Malet wrote to the Foreign Office that the Controllers had never been obliged to apply for diplomatic support.

In the course of the summer of 1880, Sir Edward Malet asked the British Consular officers in Egypt to report on the condition of the country. All the Consuls told the same tale. A "general feeling of satisfaction" prevailed. The taxes were being regularly collected. The rate of interest charged by the village money-lenders had fallen by 50 per cent. The value of land had risen, in some cases as much as 100 per cent. The use of the courbash was greatly diminished.

Whilst these reforms were in progress, the

difficulties connected with the appointment of a
Commission of Liquidation had been overcome.
After discussions which lasted some three months,
the Commissioners agreed on a law which was
submitted to the Khedive and signed by him on
July 17, 1880. The Commissioners never sent in
any report explanatory of the provisions of the
law. In a letter addressed by Sir Rivers Wilson
to Lord Granville, who succeeded Lord Salisbury
at the Foreign Office on April 28, 1880, it was
stated that there "was an apprehension lest the
divergencies of opinion which manifested themselves on certain points among the Commissioners
should render impossible a unanimous report, and
lead to reservations or even protests detracting
from the authority of the official decisions of the
Commission."

It is unnecessary to allude at any length to
these differences of opinion. It will be sufficient
to say that some members of the Commission, who
were supported by the Controllers, were in favour
of a cautious estimate of revenue, and an estimate
of administrative expenditure which would have
left a margin to be applied to the benefit of the
country, whilst others took a more optimistic view
of the revenue and endeavoured, in the bondholding
interest, to keep the administrative expenditure
down to the lowest possible figure. Eventually,
a compromise was effected. The revenue was
taken at £E.8,362,000 for 1880 and 1881, and at
£E.8,412,000 for subsequent years. The administrative expenditure was fixed at £E.4,520,000.
The rate of interest on the Unified Debt was
fixed at 4 per cent. The outstanding portions
of the short loans were absorbed into the Unified
Debt. A fresh issue of Preference Stock to the
extent of £E.5,600,000 was made in order to
assist in paying the Floating Debt. The Floating

Debt creditors were divided into three categories, viz. privileged creditors, creditors holding special securities, and ordinary creditors. The privileged creditors were paid in full. Special arrangements were made with the creditors holding special securities. Their claims were reduced by about $7\frac{1}{2}$ per cent. The ordinary creditors received 30 per cent in cash and 70 per cent in Preference Stock. At the price then current, they lost $8\frac{1}{2}$ per cent on the capital of their claims. On the whole, it may be said that the arrangement was a fair one. Its main defect was that too large a proportion of revenue (66 per cent) was mortgaged to the bondholders, whilst the balance left at the disposal of the Government was insufficient.

Thus, matters were improving in Egypt. Several beneficial reforms had been carried out. Some of the worst features of the old oppressive system of government had disappeared. The relations between the Government and their creditors were established on a legal basis, and the charge on account of debt, although still very heavy, had been brought more into conformity than heretofore with the resources of the country. There were, however, some dark specks on the horizon. For instance, a petition was circulated amongst the officers of the army, couched in language which was intended to incite the Moslem population against the European Control. It concluded with a threat that the petitioners might have recourse to the sword to attain their ends.

In June 1880, I was appointed Financial Member of the Governor-General's Council in India. Sir Auckland Colvin succeeded me as Controller-General in Egypt.

In December 1880, I visited Cairo on my way to India. At that time, it was manifest that the only serious danger which threatened Egypt arose from the fact that the discipline of the army had been profoundly shaken by the events of 1878. I warned Riaz Pasha of this danger, and urged him to remedy any grievances of which the army could justly complain, but at the same time to treat severely any signs of insubordination. Riaz Pasha said that my warning was unnecessary, for that not the smallest danger was to be apprehended from the army.

For the moment, therefore, it appeared that Egypt had at last fairly entered the path of reform, and that all that was required was time to complete the superstructure of which the foundations had been so laboriously laid.

CHAPTER XI

THE MUTINY OF THE EGYPTIAN ARMY

JANUARY–SEPTEMBER 1881

Discontent amongst the officers—They petition Riaz Pasha—Mutiny of
February 1—Dismissal of the Minister of War—Imprudent con-
duct of the Khedive—Conduct of the French Consul-General—
Increase of discontent in the army — Mutiny of September 9—
Sir Auckland Colvin—Demands of the mutineers—Dismissal of
the Ministers — Reluctance of Chérif Pasha to accept office—
Nomination of the Chérif Ministry—Chérif Pasha supports the
European Control—Arábi is the real ruler of Egypt—His conduct
due to fear—Situation created by the mutiny.

SIR JOHN BOWRING wrote in 1840 : "The situation of the Osmanlis in Egypt is remarkable ; they
exercise an extraordinary influence, possess most
of the high offices of state, and, indeed, are the
depositories of power throughout the country. . . .
They are few, but they tyrannise ; the Arabs are
many, but obey."

After Sir John Bowring wrote these lines, the
Egyptians, properly so called, gradually acquired a
greater share in the administration of the country,
but in 1881, as in 1840, the Turks were the " paramount rulers."   In the army, however, the number
and influence of the Turks sensibly diminished as
time went on.   During the reigns of Abbas, Said,
and Ismail, the Egyptian element amongst the
officers had increased to such an extent as to
jeopardise the little that remained of the still
dominant Turco-Circassian element.

The large number of officers who were placed
on half-pay in 1878 were, for the most part,
Egyptians. The discontent due to this cause was
increased by the fact that, whilst great and in some
degree successful efforts were made to improve the
civil administration of the country, nothing was
done to improve the condition of the army. The
prevailing discontent eventually found expression
in a petition addressed by certain officers of the
army to Riaz Pasha on January 15, 1881.

Ahmed Arábi, an Egyptian of fellah origin,
who was colonel of the 4th Regiment, soon took
the lead in the movement which was thus begun.
But the prime mover in the preparation of the
petition was Colonel Ali Bey Fehmi, who commanded the 1st Regiment. His regiment had
been the object of special attention on the part of
the Khedive. It guarded the palace. For some
time previously, however, there had been a marked
cessation of friendly relations between the Khedive
and Ali Bey Fehmi. In the East, to be in disgrace
is to be in danger. Ali Bey Fehmi determined
to strengthen his position by showing that the
Egyptian portion of the army could no longer
be treated with neglect, and that he himself could
not with impunity be dismissed or exiled.

The petition set forth that the Minister of War,
Osman Pasha Rifki, had treated the Egyptian
officers of the army unjustly in the matter of
promotions. He had behaved " as if they were his
enemies, or as if God had sent him to venge His
wrath on the Egyptians." Officers had been dismissed from the service without any legal inquiry.
The petitioners, therefore, made two demands.
The first was that the Minister of War should be
removed, "as he was incompetent to hold such a
high position." The second was that an inquiry
should be held into the qualifications of those who

had been promoted. "Nothing," it was said, "but merit and knowledge should entitle an officer to promotion, and in these respects we are far superior to those who have been promoted."

This petition was presented by the two Colonels in person to Riaz Pasha. Riaz Pasha was ignorant of military affairs, and had never interfered with the administration of the army, which he considered to be a prerogative of the Khedive. He endeavoured unsuccessfully to induce the Colonels to withdraw their petition, promising at the same time that inquiry should be made into their grievances. A fortnight was allowed to elapse, during which time further unsuccessful efforts were made in the same direction. In the meanwhile, the Colonels had learnt that their petition was viewed with disfavour by the Khedive and his Turkish surroundings. Riaz Pasha received a hint from the palace that the dilatory manner in which he was treating the question was calculated to throw some doubts on his loyalty. He determined, therefore, to provoke an immediate decision. The matter was discussed at a meeting of the Council of Ministers held under the presidency of the Khedive on January 30, from which Sir Auckland Colvin and M. de Blignières were most unwisely excluded. All idea of compromise was rejected. It was resolved to arrest the Colonels, and to try them by Court-martial. Subsequently, an inquiry would be made into their grievances. An order was drawn up and countersigned by the Khedive, summoning the Colonels to the Ministry of War on February 1.

One peculiarity of Egyptian official life is that no secrets are ever kept. The Colonels were immediately informed of the decision at which the Council of Ministers had arrived. Everything was, therefore, arranged for the action which followed. It was settled that, in the event of the

Colonels not returning in two hours, the officers and men of their regiments should go to the Ministry of War and deliver them if they were under arrest. At the same time, a message was sent to Toura, about ten miles distant from Cairo, with a view to securing concerted action on the part of the regiment quartered there. This programme was faithfully executed. The Colonels were summoned to the Ministry of War on the pretext that certain arrangements had to be made for a procession which was to accompany one of the princesses on the occasion of her marriage. They obeyed the summons. On their arrival at the Ministry of War, they were arrested and placed on their trial. Whilst the trial was proceeding, the officers and men of their regiments arrived, and broke into the room where the Court was sitting. They treated the Minister of War roughly, destroyed the furniture, and delivered the Colonels, who then marched with their troops to the Khedive's palace, and demanded the dismissal of the Minister of War. The Ministers and other high functionaries soon gathered round the Khedive. Some counselled resistance, but the practical difficulty presented itself that no force was available with which to resist. The only sign of fidelity given by any of the troops belonging to the Cairo garrison was that the regiment quartered at Abbassieh, two miles distant from the town, refused to join the mutineers, but the most their Turkish officers could do was to keep them where they were. They would not have defended the Khedive against the mutinous regiments. The regiment stationed at Toura marched to Cairo, according to previous arrangement, and insisted on continuing its march, although messengers were sent to dissuade the men from advancing after the obnoxious Minister had been dismissed.

Under these circumstances, resistance was impossible. After some hesitation, the Khedive sent for the Colonels and informed them that Osman Pasha Rifki was dismissed and Mahmoud Pasha Baroudi[1] named Minister of War in his place. This announcement was received with cheers. The troops dispersed and tranquillity was for the time being restored. The mutinous Colonels were allowed to remain in command of their regiments. They waited on the Khedive, asked his pardon for their past misconduct, and gave assurances of unalterable fidelity and loyalty to his person.

This was the second mutiny of the Egyptian Army. It had followed the same course as the first. It originated with legitimate grievances to which no attention was paid. The next stage was mutiny. The final result was complete submission to the will of the mutineers. The whole affair was mismanaged, and for this mismanagement the Khedive appears to have been largely responsible. Two courses were from the first open to the Khedive. Either he should have endeavoured to rally to his side a sufficient force to crush the mutineers, or, if that was impossible, he should have made terms with the officers before discontent developed into mutiny. Unfortunately, he adopted neither of these courses. The attempt to decoy the Colonels away from their troops and to punish them without any trustworthy force behind him to ensure effect being given to the decisions of the Court-martial, was probably the most unwise course which could have been adopted. Sir Edward Malet expressed his opinion that the officers were treated "in the way best calculated to destroy all confidence in the Khedive and his Government,

---

[1] Baroudi was the family name. He was also frequently called Mahmoud Pasha Sami.

although it was in harmony with the traditions of Oriental statesmanship."

The Egyptian officers and soldiers now learnt for the second time that they had only to assert themselves in order to obtain all they required. With this encouragement, they would not be slow to mutiny a third time, should the necessity for doing so arise.

For the moment, however, a truce was established between the Khedive and his mutinous officers; but suspicions and fears were rife on both sides. The Khedive and his Ministers were afraid to disband the disaffected regiments, or even to remove them from Cairo. The officers, on the other hand, although their victory had been complete, were fearful of the consequences of their own action. They mistrusted the Khedive and thought that, should an opportunity occur, the reluctant pardon which they had received would be cancelled, and that they would be visited with condign punishment. They felt even greater resentment against Riaz Pasha than against the Khedive, and began a series of intrigues with a view to bringing about a change of Ministry.

These intrigues were encouraged by Baron de Ring, the French Consul-General, who had frequent interviews with the mutinous Colonels. The action of Baron de Ring increased the difficulties of the situation. If, in addition to financial embarrassments, defective administration, and a mutinous army, there was to be superadded hostile intrigue on the part of the representative of the French Government, the position of the Egyptian Ministry would clearly become untenable. Riaz Pasha wished to resign, but was dissuaded from doing so. The Khedive eventually wrote to the President of the French Republic to complain of Baron de Ring's conduct. The result was that

he was recalled.   He left Egypt on February 28.
The Khedive then summoned the principal officers
of the army to the palace, and expressed the
confidence he entertained in Riaz Pasha, of
whom he spoke in eulogistic terms.   Already
the pay of the unemployed Egyptian officers
had been increased, and a public declaration had
been made by the Khedive to the effect that for
the future every class of officer, whether Turk,
Circassian, or Egyptian, would be treated on the
same footing.   These measures somewhat improved
the position of the Ministry.   When Sir Edward
Malet left in May on a short leave, he "had reason
to believe that confidence was being restored; that
the officers had, in fact, nothing to fear from intrigue; that they were gradually relaxing measures
for their own protection, and beginning to feel that
the Khedive and the Ministers no longer aimed at
their lives."

It is unnecessary to give the detailed history of
the next few months.   The officers still entertained
a deep-rooted mistrust of the intentions of the
Khedive and his Ministers.   "The traditions of
the days of Ismail Pasha," Sir Edward Malet
wrote, "stalked like spectres across their paths."
They thought that their lives were in danger.   Insubordination increased daily.   A Commission was
appointed to inquire into the grievances of the
army.   Arábi Bey was one of its members.   His
language to the Minister of War was very dis-
respectful.   In the month of July, an artilleryman
was run over by a cart and killed in the streets of
Alexandria.   His comrades bore his dead body to
the palace, and forced an entrance in defiance of
the orders of their officers.   They were tried and
the ringleaders condemned to punishment.   About
the same time, nineteen officers brought charges
against their Colonel (Abdul-Al).   These charges

formed the subject of inquiry. They were found to be groundless. The officers were in consequence dismissed from the active list of the army, but were shortly afterwards restored to their former positions by the Khedive. The Colonels were greatly offended. They believed that the Khedive's action had been taken with the intention of encouraging the insubordination of their junior officers towards them. About the same time, Mahmoud Pasha Baroudi, the Minister of War, who sympathised with the officers concerned in the mutiny of February 1, was dismissed, and the Khedive's brother-in-law, Daoud Pasha, was appointed in his place. This measure also caused great dissatisfaction.

Within the Ministerial circle, a good deal of dissension reigned. The relations between Riaz Pasha and M. de Blignières became strained. The Khedive's confidence in Riaz Pasha was impaired. It was whispered that His Highness favoured the return to power of Chérif Pasha.

It was clear that another crisis was not far off, but at the moment it was about to occur, the Government were hopeful that their main difficulties had been overcome. "At no period," Sir Edward Malet wrote, "since February 1 had the confidence of the Khedive and his Government been so complete as immediately before the outbreak of September 9. On the very eve, and on the morning itself of that day, Riaz Pasha assured those with whom he conversed that the Government were masters of the situation, and that the danger of a military movement had passed away. But, in fact, all the terrors of the Colonels for their personal safety had been again aroused. A story had got abroad that the Khedive had obtained a secret Fetwa, or decree from the Sheikh-ul-Islam, condemning them to death for high treason. There was absolutely no foundation for this story, but it is currently believed, and at this moment the position of the Sheikh-ul-Islam is precarious in consequence of it. Spies were continually hovering about the residences of the Colonels, and on the night of the 8th September a man presented himself at the house of Arábi Bey, was refused admittance, and was afterwards followed and seen to return to the Prefecture of Police. There was no doubt in the mind of Arábi Bey that he was to be murdered; he left his house and went to that of the other Colonels, to whom a similar incident had just occurred. It is my belief that then only were measures taken for immediate action, that it was concerted and planned that night, as it was executed on the following day."

On September 9, the 3rd Regiment of Infantry, which was stationed at Cairo, was ordered to Alexandria. This order produced a mutiny. Arábi Bey, with 2500 men and 18 guns, marched to the square in front of the Abdin Palace. The Khedive was at the Ismailia Palace, distant about a quarter of a mile from Abdin. He did the wisest thing possible under the circumstances. He sent for Sir Auckland Colvin.

Sir Auckland Colvin was a member of the Indian Civil Service. In the hour of trial he did not belie the proud motto, *Mens aequa in arduis*, inscribed under the picture of Warren Hastings which hangs in the Calcutta Council Chamber. It is one which might fitly apply to the whole of that splendid body of Englishmen who compose the Indian Civil Service. The spirit of the Englishman rose high in the presence of danger. It was not the first time he had heard of mutiny. He knew how his own countrymen had met dangers of this sort. The example of Lawrence and Outram, of Nicholson and Edwards, pointed the way to the

Indian Civilian. His duty was clear. He must endeavour at the risk of his own life to impart to the Khedive some portion of the spirit which animated his own imperial race. He spoke in no uncertain terms. "The Viceroy," he subsequently wrote, "asked my opinion on what should be done. I advised him to take the initiative. Two regiments in Cairo were said by Riaz Pasha to be faithful. I advised him to summon them to the Abdin Square, with all the military police available, to put himself at their head, and, when Arábi Bey arrived, personally to arrest him. He replied that Arábi Bey had with him the artillery and cavalry, and that they might fire. I said that they would not dare to, and that if he had the courage to take the initiative, and to expose himself personally, he might succeed in overcoming the mutineers. Otherwise, he was lost. Stone Pasha[1] warmly supported me. . . . While his carriage was coming Sir Charles Cookson[2] arrived, expressed to the Viceroy his concurrence in my views, and returned to the Agency to telegraph to his Government."

What followed may best be told in Sir Auckland Colvin's words. "I accompanied the Viceroy," he wrote, "in a separate carriage; the Ministers also, and some five or six native officers of rank, with Stone Pasha. We went first to the Abdin barracks, where the regiment of the guard turned out, and with the warmest protestations swore loyalty. Thence we drove to the Citadel, where the same occurred; but we learnt that this regiment, previous to our arrival, had been signalling to the regiment (Arábi Bey's) in the Abbassieh barrack. The Viceroy then announced his intention of going to the Abbassieh barrack. It was already 3.30; I

---

[1] An American officer in the Egyptian army.
[2] Sir Charles Cookson was acting as Consul-General during the temporary absence of Sir Edward Malet.

urged him to return to the Abdin Square taking
with him the Citadel Regiment, and when he
arrived at the square to put himself at the head
of that regiment, the regiment of the guard and
the military police.   He drove off, however, to
Abbassieh.   It was a long drive, and when we got
there about 4 (the Ministers having left us at the
Citadel and returned direct) we found Arábi Bey
had marched with the regiment to Cairo.   We
followed, and on entering the town the Viceroy
took a long *détour*, and arrived at the Abdin
Palace by a side door.   I jumped out of my
carriage, and urged him on no account to remain
in the palace, but to come into the square.   He
agreed at once, and we went together, followed at
a considerable distance by four or five of his native
officers, Stone Pasha, and one or two other European officers.   The square was entirely occupied
by soldiers drawn up round it, and keeping all
spectators at a distance.   The Viceroy advanced
firmly into the square towards a little group of
officers and men (some mounted) in the centre.   I
said to him, 'When Arábi Bey presents himself, tell
him to give you his sword, and to give them the order
to disperse.   Then go the round of the square and
address each regiment separately, and give them the
order to disperse.'   Arábi Bey approached on horse-
back; the Viceroy called out to him to dismount.
He did so, and came forward on foot, with several
others and a guard with fixed bayonets, and saluted.
I said to the Viceroy, 'Now is your moment.'
He replied, 'We are between four fires.'   I said,
'Have courage.'   He took counsel of a native
officer on his left, and repeated to me: 'What can
I do?   We are between four fires.   We shall be
killed.'   He then told Arábi Bey to sheathe his
sword.   The order was obeyed; and he then asked
Arábi Bey what all this meant; Arábi Bey replied

by enumerating three points, adding that the army had come there on the part of the Egyptian people to enforce them, and would not retire till they were conceded. The Viceroy turned to me and said, 'You hear what he says.' I replied that it was not fitting for the Viceroy to discuss questions of this kind with Colonels, and suggested to him to retire into the Palace of Abdin, leaving me to speak to the Colonels. He did so, and I remained for about an hour till the arrival of Sir Charles Cookson, explaining to them the gravity of the situation for themselves, and urging them to retire the troops while there was yet time."

The three points to which Sir Auckland Colvin alluded as constituting the demands of Arábi were : (1) that all the Ministers should be dismissed ; (2) that a Parliament should be convoked ; and, (3), that the strength of the army should be raised to 18,000 men.

Sir Charles Cookson then entered into negotiations with the mutineers. The Khedive consented to dismiss his Ministers on the understanding that the other points demanded by the officers should be left in suspense until reference could be made to the Porte. Arábi agreed to these terms. The question then arose of who should be President of the Council. One or two names were put forward by the Khedive, and rejected by Arábi and his followers. The Khedive then intimated that he would be prepared to nominate Chérif Pasha. This announcement "was received with loud and universal shouts of 'Long live the Khedive !' . . . Arábi Bey then asked to be allowed to see the Khedive and make his submission. This favour was granted to him and the other Colonels, and then the troops were drawn off in perfect quietness to their respective barracks."

Some difficulty was encountered in inducing

Chérif Pasha to accept office. He objected to becoming Prime Minister as the nominee of a mutinous army. Sir Charles Cookson, M. Sienkiewicz (the French Consul-General), and Sir Auckland Colvin endeavoured to overcome this reluctance, which was in no degree feigned. They so far succeeded that Chérif Pasha consented to enter into negotiations with the leaders of the military movement. At first, there appeared but little prospect of an arrangement. Chérif Pasha asked that, on condition of his undertaking the government, and guaranteeing the personal safety of the leaders of the movement, the mutinous regiments should withdraw to the posts assigned to them. The more violent amongst the officers had, however, got the upper hand. They did not fear Turkish intervention, the probability of which now began to be discussed. Indeed, there was some reason to suppose that the mutineers had received encouragement from Constantinople. Chérif Pasha's terms were rejected, and he declared that he would not undertake to form a Ministry.

Under these circumstances, the Khedive intimated that he was "ready to yield everything in order to save public security." Suddenly, however, on September 13, things took a turn for the better. The relief came from an unexpected quarter. Arábi had summoned to Cairo the members of the Chamber of Notables. When they arrived, "they proved more capable of appreciating the true situation than their military allies. Informed of the negotiations going on with Chérif Pasha, they in a body went to him, and entreated him to agree to form a Ministry, offering him their personal guarantee that, if he consented, the army should engage to absolute submission to his orders. The military leaders seem to have been more struck by this conduct than by all the previous representations made to them." Seeing that public opinion was not altogether with them, Arábi and his followers modified their tone. They tendered their "absolute submission to the authority of Chérif Pasha as the Khedive's Minister." They only made two conditions. One was that Mahmoud Pasha Sami should be reinstated in office. The second was that the Military Law recommended by the Commission, which had been recently sitting, should be put into immediate execution. "To both of these demands," Sir Charles Cookson wrote, "Chérif Pasha, most reluctantly, was compelled to yield, but as to the latter, he expressly reserved to himself the liberty of omitting the most important article, which proposed to raise the army to 18,000 men."

This incident was significant. It showed that there were two parties in opposition to the Khedive. These were, first, a mutinous army half-mad with fear of punishment, and secondly, a party, the offspring of Ismail Pasha's dalliance with constitutionalism, who had some vague national aspirations, and who, as representing the civil elements of society, shunned the idea of absolute military government. Under statesmanlike guidance, this tendency to separation between the two parties might perhaps have been turned to account. The main thing was to prevent amalgamation. If the national party were once made to believe that the only hope of realising its aspirations lay in seeking the aid of the soldiers, not only would the authority of the Khedive disappear altogether, but all hope of establishing a régime under which the army would be subordinate to the civil Government would have to be abandoned.

One of the many political apophthegms attributed to Prince Bismarck is the following:

"La politique est l'art de s'accommoder aux circon-
stances et de tirer parti de tout, même de ce qui
déplaît." It would have been wise for the Khedive
at this moment to have acted on the principle set
forth in this maxim. The military party and the
national party were alike distasteful to him. The
interests both of his dynasty and of his country
pointed, however, to the necessity of conciliating
the latter in order to keep in check the former of
these two parties. Unfortunately, the Khedive
did not possess sufficient political insight to
grasp whatever opportunities the situation offered
to him.

The new Ministry was nominated on September
14. Chérif Pasha was assured of the support of
the British and French Governments. At his own
request, he was further assured that "in case the
army should show itself submissive and obedient,
the Governments of England and France would
interpose their good offices with the Sublime Porte
in order to avert from Egypt an occupation by an
Ottoman army." The usual exchange of letters
took place between the Khedive and his Prime
Minister setting forth the principles which were to
guide the new Ministry. These letters contained
only one remark which is noteworthy. Chérif
Pasha was no friend to European interference in
Egypt. But he had learnt that it might be
productive of some good. His letter to the
Khedive, therefore, contained the following
passage : "The institution of the Control, at first
criticised from different points of view, has greatly
assisted towards the re-establishment of the
finances, at the same time that it has been a real
support for the Government of Your Highness.
In this twofold capacity, it is important to maintain it as instituted by the Decree of November
15, 1879." To this, the Khedive replied as

follows: "A perfect understanding between the
Control and my Government is necessary; it must
be maintained and strengthened."

The new Ministry, therefore, began work with
such props from without as were possible under the
circumstances. But for all that, it was clear that
the real masters of the situation were the leaders
of the mutinous army. Arábi had already treated
on equal terms with the representatives of the
Powers. He had issued a Circular on September 9 signed "Colonel Ahmed Arábi, representing the Egyptian army," in which he assured
the Consuls-General that he and those acting in
concert with him "would continue to protect the
interests of all the subjects of friendly Powers."
There could be no mistaking this language. It
was that of a ruler who disposed of power to assert
his will, and who intended to use his power with
that object.

Yet, whilst Arábi was heading a mutiny against
his Sovereign, and employing language which could
only lawfully proceed from the Khedive or from
one of his Ministers, there can be little doubt that
his conduct was mainly guided by fear of the
Khedive's resentment and vengeance. Sir Charles
Cookson thought that the officers had "exclusively
regarded their own safety and interest throughout
the agitation." Sir Edward Malet entertained a
similar opinion. Every word and deed of the
mutineers showed, indeed, that fear was the predominating influence at work amongst them. In
the Circular which Arábi addressed to the representatives of the Powers, he said: "Since the
Khedive's return to Cairo, intrigues have been on
the increase, while we have been threatened both
openly and secretly; and they have culminated in
an attempt to create disunion among the military,
in order to facilitate the object in view, namely,

to destroy and avenge themselves upon us. In this state of things, we consider it our duty to protect our lives and interests." Sir Edward Malet was informed by "a Musulman gentleman, who had had long and frequent conversations" with Arábi, that the latter thought that action had become absolutely necessary in self-defence. At a later period, Arábi said that he believed that a party of Circassians agreed together to kill him, as well as every native Egyptian holding a high appointment, on October 1, 1881. "We heard," he said, "that three iron boxes had been prepared into which to put us, so that we might be dropped into the Nile."[1] Men in this frame of mind would probably not, at an early stage of the proceedings, have been uncontrollable. But, in order to control them, one condition was essential. They might have been treated with severity, or, if that was impossible or undesirable, with leniency, but in either case it was essential that they should be treated in a manner which would leave no doubt in their minds as to the good faith of their rulers. Moreover, the practices which until a recent period had existed in Egypt, notably the fate of Ismail Pasha's Finance Minister,[2] the naturally suspicious character of Orientals, and their belief, which is often well founded, that some intrigue lies at the bottom of every action of the Government, should have rendered it clear to the Khedive that the slightest whisper imputing bad faith would be fatal to his reputation for loyalty. The utmost caution was, in fact, necessary. A bold, straightforward conduct, and a stern repression of all palace intrigues, might perhaps have quieted the fears of the officers. Riaz Pasha, although he may not have grasped the whole

---

[1] "Instructions to my Counsel," *Nineteenth Century*, December 1882.
[2] *Vide ante*, p. 26.

situation, had sufficiently statesmanlike instincts to appreciate the true nature of the danger. He warned the Khedive frequently not to do or say anything which could give rise to the least suspicion as to his intentions. It is improbable that the Khedive had any deliberate plan for wreaking vengeance on the mutineers. It is certain that his humane nature would have revolted at any idea of assassination, such as was attributed to him. At the same time, if he had considered himself sufficiently powerful to act, he would not improbably have made his displeasure felt in one form or another, in spite of the pardon which had been reluctantly wrung from him. Like Macbeth, he would not play false, but yet would wrongly win. It would be in harmony with the inconsistency even of an honest Oriental to pardon fully, and at the same time to make a mental reserve, which would enable him at some future time to act as though the pardon had only been partial. He allowed his surroundings, which almost always exercise a baneful influence in an Oriental court, to intrigue and to talk in a manner which was calculated to excite the fears and suspicions of the mutineers. Arábi, in his Circular to the Consuls-General, made special allusion to the intrigues of Yousuf Pasha Kemal, the Khedive's agent, and Ibrahim Aga, the Khedive's Tutunji (Pipe-bearer), who, he said, "had been sowing discord." National proclivities and foreign intrigue may, therefore, have had something to do with the mutiny of September 9, but there can be little doubt that the main cause was truly stated by Arábi. It was fear.

This was the third mutiny of the Egyptian army. On each occasion, the mutineers gained confidence in their strength. On each occasion, the submission of the Government was more complete

than previously. The first mutiny was quelled
by the sacrifice of an unpopular Minister (Nubar
Pasha), whom the ruling Khedive did not wish to
maintain in office.   On the second occasion, the
War Minister (Osman Pasha Rifki) was offered up
to appease the mutineers.   On the third occasion,
the mutineers dictated their own terms at the point
of the bayonet; they did not rest satisfied without
a complete change of Ministry.   " Things bad
begun make strong themselves by ill."   No remnant of military discipline was now left.   The
Khedive was shorn of all real authority.   The
smallest incident would suffice to show that the
Ministers only held office on sufferance from
the mutineers.   No long time was to elapse before
such an incident occurred.

CHAPTER XII

THE CHÉRIF MINISTRY

SEPTEMBER–DECEMBER 1881

The Porte wishes to interfere—Objections of France and England—
Despatch of Turkish Commissioners to Cairo — Effect of their
mission — British and French ships sent to Alexandria — Arábi
leaves Cairo with his regiment—Remarks on Turkish interference
—Divergent views of France and England—Despondency of the
Khedive—Chérif Pasha's policy—Sir Auckland Colvin's views—
Arábi's policy — Insubordination in the army—Violence of the
local press—Attitude of the civil population—Summary of the
situation at the end of 1881.

ONE of the first results of the events related in
the last chapter was to stimulate the ambition
of the Sultan, who saw, in the confusion with which
Egypt was threatened, another opportunity for
reasserting Turkish supremacy over the country.

There was, indeed, a good deal to cause anxiety
to a ruler whose own tenure of power was so far
precarious in that it was, and still is mainly based
on the jealousies of the different heirs to his
succession. Arábi had sent a petition to Constantinople stating that Egypt was falling into the
hands of foreigners and being Christianised, and
that, unless the Sultan intervened, the country
would soon share the fate of Tunis. From the
Sultan's point of view, it was not desirable to
discourage Arábi too much, and accordingly some
slight encouragement was given to him. But,
whilst running with the hare, it was also necessary

to hunt with the hounds. Heterodox political
views were in the air. There was some vague talk
of an Egyptian constitution. Now, the Sultan
objected strongly to the introduction of constitutional government into any part of the Ottoman
dominions. Then, again, there had been whispers
of a secret movement which was on foot with a
view to the establishment of an Arab kingdom in
Egypt and Syria. If this were done, what would
become of the homogeneity of the Ottoman
Empire, and, indeed, of the House of Osman itself?
From the days when Sobieski repulsed the Turks
from the walls of Vienna, the Ottoman Empire
had been steadily declining. One province after
another had been torn from its flank. For the
moment, the onward march of European civilisation
took no very militant form; but it was probable
that the combat, which had been going on for a
couple of centuries or more, would sooner or later
be renewed, and, if it were renewed, it might well
be that, although the Christian Powers might
quarrel over the heritage, the fate of the rightful
heir would be sealed. The House of Osman might
have to abandon its European possessions. In
that case, the only refuge left would be to establish
the Khalifate somewhere on the other side of the
Bosphorus, notably at Baghdad, which, according
to ancient tradition, was to be the Dar-el-Selam
(the House of Peace) of the dynasty of Osman.
The establishment of an Arab kingdom, more
especially if it was to be encumbered with new-
fangled ideas of constitutions and the like, would
materially interfere with the execution of a policy
of this sort. Any such proposal was, therefore, to
be resisted as strongly as possible.

The first idea of the Sultan was to occupy the
country with Turkish troops. Early in September
1881, preparations were made to transport an

Ottoman force to Egypt. The French Government, however, true to their traditional policy, entertained strong objections to any Turkish interference in Egypt. The British Government were also of opinion that "it would not be desirable that any active measures of repression should be taken by the Sultan until, at all events, the necessity for them had been clearly demonstrated, and the method to be adopted had been discussed and agreed upon. But they saw no objection to the Sultan, if His Majesty should be so disposed, sending, with the consent of England and France, a Turkish General to Egypt to support the Khedive's authority, and aid His Highness with his advice."

The French Government, however, thought that "even the despatch of a Turkish General to Egypt might lead to further steps, resulting, perhaps, in a permanent occupation of the country by Turkish troops." The British Government yielded to the French representations on this subject, and on September 18, Lord Dufferin, who was at the time Ambassador at Constantinople, was instructed, in the event of the Sultan proposing to send a Turkish General to Cairo, "to endeavour to dissuade His Majesty from adopting this course." The French Ambassador at Constantinople had already received instructions "to protest against any sort of intervention on the part of Turkey in Egyptian affairs."

If, however, Turkish troops could not be sent to Egypt; if the deposition of Tewfik Pasha in favour of Halim Pasha, which was also contemplated, was impossible by reason of British opposition; if, moreover, the idea of despatching a Turkish General to Egypt had to be abandoned, at all events a sort of shadowy supremacy would be asserted if a Turkish official were sent in some kind of capacity to Egypt, even although neither

the envoy nor the Sultan had any very clear idea of
what functions he would perform on arrival. The
Sultan, therefore, informed the French Ambassador
"that he considered, in view of Turkey's enormous
interests both in Egypt and the Hedjaz, that he
had a perfect right to despatch an emissary with
his compliments and advice to the Khedive, and
this he intended to do, though the person would
not have the character of a Commissioner." Ali
Fuad Bey and Ali Nizami Pasha were, therefore,
sent to Egypt, and arrived at Alexandria on
October 6.

The effect of the despatch of these envoys
was instantaneous on all the parties concerned.
Every one recognised that the Sultan had some sort
of technical right to interfere. Some recognised
that, in an extreme case, his interference would be
the least of many evils. Others were anxious to play
with Turkish suzerain rights in order to subserve
their own interests. But there was one point on
which Lord Granville,[1] M. Barthélemy St. Hilaire,
Chérif Pasha, Arábi, the Egyptian military party, the
Egyptian national party, the bondholding interest,
and the public opinion of Europe, appeared to be
agreed. It was that Turkish interference in Egypt
would do a great deal of harm, and was to be
avoided if possible.

The British and French Governments informed
the Sultan that they had "learnt with surprise and
regret" of the decision to send envoys. Sir Edward
Malet and M. Sienkiewicz were instructed "to
receive the Turkish envoys with all the honours
due to their rank, but to firmly oppose any interference on their part in the internal administration
of Egypt." Moreover, both the British and French
Governments suddenly found out that, "with a

[1] Lord Granville assumed charge of the Foreign Office on April
28, 1880.

view to diminishing the danger of a panic amongst the foreign population in Cairo and Alexandria, which the absence of a place of refuge might occasion amongst them in the event of disturbances," it would be desirable to send a couple of ships to Alexandria, a measure which gave considerable umbrage at Constantinople. It was calculated, the Sultan thought, "to cause agitation and disturbance among the whole Arab population, and it was not improbable that it might lead to a general revolution."

To the Khedive, the intelligence that two Turkish envoys were to come to Cairo was "altogether unexpected," and he asked Sir Edward Malet and M. Sienkiewicz whether they "could throw any light upon it"; to which question, Sir Edward Malet reported, "we replied in the negative." As regards Chérif Pasha, he was of opinion that, as two Turkish envoys were to come, the main thing was to get rid of them as soon as possible. Accordingly, at the request of the Egyptian Government, the British and French Ambassadors at Constantinople were instructed to "urge upon the Porte that they should shorten as much as possible the stay of the Turkish envoys in Egypt."

A considerable effect was also produced on Arábi. He was willing enough to strengthen his own cause against Circassians and Europeans by an appeal to the Sultan, but he never intended that the appeal should be taken seriously. There was, indeed, something strangely inconsistent, not to say comical, in asking the Sultan to countenance a movement which was avowedly directed against Turkish supremacy in Egypt. Arábi, therefore, made no further difficulties about moving his mutinous regiment from Cairo to Suez. "He had always said," Sir Edward Malet reported, "that he was ready to go, but no date had been fixed for his departure, and he himself had spoken about leaving perhaps in three weeks, but I have little doubt that there would have been considerable difficulty in inducing him to fix a day had it not been for the unexpected announcement of the advent of the envoys."

Under all these circumstances, it was clear that the Turkish mission could not be productive of much practical result. As a matter of fact, all that the Turkish envoys did was to inspect the troops at Cairo. After the inspection, Ali Nizami Pasha harangued the officers. He reminded them that the Khedive was the representative of the Sultan, and that therefore disobedience to the Khedive was disobedience to the Sultan. After that, nothing more was done. The pressure exerted from all sides on the Turkish envoys with a view to getting them out of the country was too great to be resisted. The question, however, arose as to which were to leave first, the British and French ships, or the Turkish envoys. Musurus Pasha, the Turkish Ambassador in London, told Lord Granville "that it would be impossible for the Sultan to withdraw his mission until after the departure of the ships." Lord Granville, on the other hand, said that the ships had already left Malta for Alexandria, but would not arrive till October 19, "by which time it was to be presumed that the Turkish Commissioners would be taking their departure." Lord Dufferin was instructed to tell the Sultan that the ships would leave on the same day that the Turkish Commissioners embarked. M. Barthélemy St. Hilaire also told Lord Lyons that when once the Turkish envoys had gone, both ships might quit Alexandria without delay, and simultaneously. Both Governments were of opinion that, after the departure of the envoys, there was no longer any necessity to provide a place of refuge for Europeans in the event of disturbance. The result of all this diplomatic skirmishing was that H.M.S. *Invincible* arrived at Alexandria on October 19. Twenty-four hours before her arrival, the Turkish envoys had left Cairo for Alexandria with a view to embarkation at that port, and twenty-four hours after her arrival both the British and French ships left Alexandria harbour.

This episode has been narrated at some length, because an important principle was involved in the discussion connected with the mission of the Turkish envoys. Who, as a last resort, was to be responsible for the maintenance of order in Egypt?

It is a most unfortunate thing that at no stage of the Egyptian Question has it been possible to make any suggestion against which valid objections might not be urged. Turkish intervention in Egypt was open to obvious objections; but could any alternative and less objectionable policy be suggested? The British Government thought not; they, therefore, from the first leant towards the idea that, as a last resort, the Sultan should be used as the *Deus ex machina*, who should restore order. They were, however, so hampered by their partnership with the French as to be unable to give effect to their own views.

Both the British and French Governments were honestly desirous of acting together. M. Barthélemy St. Hilaire said that "his policy with reference to Egypt was well known, and never varied; it was summed up in the absolute necessity, as in the past, so in the future, of perfect frankness between the two Governments, and joint action on every occasion." There cannot be the least doubt that these words honestly represented the views of the French Government at this time, and that the desire to co-operate was as honestly reciprocated by the British Government. Unfortunately, the views of the British and French Governments were divergent on one important point of principle. The French Government regarded Turkish intervention in Egypt as the worst possible solution of the Egyptian Question. M. Barthélemy St. Hilaire told the British Chargé d'Affaires that he would prefer an Anglo-French to a Turkish occupation of Egypt. Moreover, the French Government feared that, if Turkish intervention were allowed, the pretensions of the Sultan would be raised and his prestige increased amongst the Mohammedan population of Northern Africa. Thus, a spirit of fanaticism might be aroused in Tunis.

The objections of the British Government to Turkish intervention, on the other hand, were far less strong than those of the French. This was evidenced by their willingness to allow the Sultan to send a Turkish General to Egypt, although, at the instance of the French Government, they ultimately withdrew their support to this measure. If any armed occupation became necessary, the British Government preferred that it should be Turkish rather than Anglo-French. But they allowed French diplomacy to take the lead, and the main end of French diplomacy was to prevent any Turkish interference in Egypt.

When the Egyptian Question was subsequently (July 24, 1882) discussed in Parliament, Lord Salisbury said: "There were two modes of going to work with the Government of Egypt. You might have used moral force as you have made use of material force.[1] Your only mode of acting by moral force is by means of the hearty co-operation of the Sultan of Turkey. But you took the best

---

[1] This was in allusion to the bombardment of Alexandria, which, when Lord Salisbury spoke, had recently taken place.

means of alienating that hearty co-operation. If
you had gone to him from the first, taken him into
your counsels, and made him the instrument of
what you desired, and indicated from the first that
you wished to take no steps without his concurrence
and co-operation, there might have been objections
to such a plan ; but, at least, you would have had
him heartily with you." Lord Salisbury then indicated various steps which had been taken, and
which, in his opinion, must "in themselves have
resulted in setting any Sultan of Turkey in
opposition."

There was much force in Lord Salisbury's criticism. In October 1881, the necessity for armed
foreign intervention of any kind had not yet arisen.
Lord Granville was, without doubt, acting wisely in
deprecating measures of repression on the part of the
Sultan until their necessity had been clearly demonstrated. On the other hand, it was apparent that
Egypt was threatened with a degree of confusion
against which moral force, persuasion, or even
threats would be employed in vain. It was, therefore, necessary at the outset to have a clear idea as
to the method by which physical force was to be
employed in case of need. There were but two
alternative courses possible. One was an Anglo-
French occupation, for at that time no one thought
of an occupation by France or by England alone.
The other was a Turkish occupation. The French
preferred an Anglo - French occupation as the
lesser evil of the two. Their views were perfectly
logical and consistent, and, for a time at all events,
the French Government acted upon them. Whether
the policy they advocated was the best in the true
interests of France or England is a matter of
opinion.

The British Government, on the other hand,
contemplated the possibility of a Turkish occupa-

tion, and preferred this solution to any other. In
a despatch addressed to Sir Edward Malet on
November 4, 1881, Lord Granville laid down the
general lines of British policy in connection with
Egyptian affairs. He deprecated the idea that
either the French or the British Government
entertained any "self - aggrandising designs" as
regards Egypt. "The Khedive and his Ministers,"
he added, "may feel secure that Her Majesty's
Government contemplate no such deviation from
the policy which they have traced for themselves."
He set forth the British view of the Turkish connection with Egypt. It was that the *status quo*
should be maintained. The tie with Turkey should
not be severed. At the same time, Lord Granville
pointed out that the British Government "desired
to maintain Egypt in the enjoyment of the measure
of administrative independence which has been
secured to her by the Sultan's Firmans. The
Government of England would run counter to the
most cherished traditions of national history were
it to entertain a desire to diminish that liberty or
tamper with the institutions to which it has given
birth." Lord Granville then went on to say that
"the only circumstance which would force Her
Majesty's Government to depart from the course
of conduct which he had mentioned would be the
occurrence in Egypt of a state of anarchy." These
were wise words. They indicated that Turkish
intervention was undesirable, but that, if material
force had to be employed, a Turkish was to be
preferred to an Anglo-French occupation.

Unfortunately, while the British Government
contemplated using the Turk, with all his obvious
defects, as the instrument by which order was as a
last resort to be maintained in Egypt, they allowed
themselves to be led away by the objections
which could be urged against Turkish intervention

considered exclusively on its own merits. They followed the French Government in a line of conduct which irritated and discouraged the Sultan. As the Sultan's military forces might eventually have to be used for the preservation of order, it would have been wise to have encouraged the exercise of his authority by viewing with a friendly eye the despatch of a Turkish mission to Egypt, in spite of the objections urged from Cairo in deprecation of the mission. But this was not done. The Sultan was discouraged and opposed in the exercise of his authority. The British Government thus entered a groove hostile to Turkish intervention, with the result that British intervention became eventually a necessity.

It is, of course, true that this subject presents another aspect. So far as the welfare of the Egyptian people and of all Europeans interested in the affairs of Egypt is concerned, European intervention, whether British, French, or Anglo-French, was to be preferred to Turkish intervention. But, on the assumption that it was desirable to avoid the occupation of Egypt by British or French troops, it would appear that Turkish intervention, in spite of its acknowledged drawbacks, should, from the first, have been less totally discouraged.

It is curious, in reading over the correspondence after a lapse of many years, to observe how heartily the French Government worked to bring about the solution which eventually occurred, and which was probably more distasteful to them than any other, namely, a British occupation of Egypt. The British Government, on the other hand, acted throughout on the principle of *Video meliora, proboque, deteriora sequor.* They saw the objections to any European occupation. They preferred a Turkish occupation. Yet, although they appear to have shown greater political foresight than the

French, they failed to act in a manner which would have enabled effect to be given to their own principles. The more unreasonable amongst the French eventually said that England, with her habitual perfidy, was merely playing a part with a view ultimately to bring about a British occupation. They were quite wrong. The British Government acted, as they always act, with perfect honesty, but, at the same time, with so little consistency in the pursuit of political aims, that it can be no matter for surprise that their motives should have been subsequently misrepresented. Their vacillation was, without doubt, due to a desire to ensure French co-operation, and also probably in part to an excessive deference to English public opinion. The idea of handing over Egypt, even temporarily, to the rule of the Sultan would unquestionably have met with much hostile criticism in England, probably from the same classes who were eventually most strongly opposed to a British occupation. But it can scarcely be held that this argument constituted a sufficient plea for discarding the policy. No one would have been able to propose any alternative policy which would have been preferable. The duty of a Government is to take the lead, especially as regards foreign affairs, and to stand criticism even, when matters of the first importance are concerned, at the risk of bringing about its own downfall.

Shortly after the mutiny of September 9, Sir Edward Malet reported that the "general tone of the Khedive with regard to the future was despondent. His Highness said that he could no longer believe in any professions of fidelity made by the officers of the army." These observations gave the keynote to the Khedive's conduct during the next few months. He resented the humiliation to which he had been subjected by the

mutinous conduct of his officers. It rankled in
his mind, and led him to nurture schemes for
revenge. He constantly expressed his opinion that
there could be no tranquillity in the country until
the army was mastered. It can be no matter for
surprise that the Khedive entertained views of this
description, but it would have been wiser and more
statesmanlike if he had sunk all personal feelings
of resentment against the army. As it was, the
breach between the Khedive on the one hand, and
the army and the national party on the other hand,
continued to widen every day.

Chérif Pasha took a broader view of the situation. He appreciated the desirability of separating
the national party from the army. He told Sir
Edward Malet on September 21 "that it was his
intention later on to convoke the Chamber of
Notables, which he hoped would by degrees
become the legitimate exponent of the internal
wants of the country, and by this means deprive
the army of the character which it had arrogated
to itself in the late movement. . . . The Notables
would be a representative body on which the
Khedive and his Government would be able to
lean for popular support against military dictation."
On October 8, a Decree was issued convoking the
Chamber of Notables for December 23. The
functions and composition of the Chamber were
regulated by Ismail Pasha's law of 1866. Arábi
pressed for the adoption of a law giving greater
power to the Chamber, but eventually yielded.
Sir Edward Malet reported on October 2 that
Arábi once more "professed confidence in Chérif
Pasha, and stated his intention of leaving the
matter entirely in his hands."

The situation at this time was well described in
a Memorandum written by Sir Auckland Colvin
on September 19. "As to the position," he said,

"my view of it is that it is essentially an armistice. The arrangement we have been able to come to gives us a little breathing-time, during which we can take count of the forces that are at work around us, and endeavour to guide or repress them. There should be no illusions on this point. That we are entering on a fresh period of order and regularity, there seem to be no grounds for believing. The army is elated by what it has achieved, and its leaders are penetrated with the conviction that their mission is to give Egypt liberty. The Notables, who are now in large numbers in Cairo, though they have taken into their own hands the right to ask for an extension of civil liberties, and deny the officers any right of petition or of interference in the matter, are at one with them in the desire to obtain some solid concessions. All is being done in an orderly and even exemplary manner : but the chance of any final settlement depends :—

"(1) On the army dispersing to the several quarters assigned to it.

"(2) On the moderation shown by the Notables in their demands.

"(3) On the tact and firmness of the Ministers in dealing with the army and the Notables. . . .

"I do not think it is at all my duty to oppose myself to the popular movement, but to try rather to guide and to give it definite shape. So long as the financial position of the country, or the influence of the Control, is not likely to be affected by concessions made to the Notables, I believe I should be very foolish to express any hostility to their wishes. It is in this sense that I propose to act, and to advise Chérif Pasha when the matter is ripe for discussion. It is, to sum up, by advising promptness in carrying out the necessary measures with the army, and, in the second place, by reasonable discussion of any petitions presented by the Notables, that we can alone hope to assist in converting the armistice into a peace."

Sir Auckland Colvin rightly judged the situation. Chérif Pasha was the nominal Prime Minister but Arábi, as Sir Edward Malet said, was the "arbiter of the destinies of the country." A local newspaper, *El Hedjaz*, which was the organ of the Arábist party, spoke of "the illustrious and magnanimous Emir, His Excellency Ahmed Bey Arábi." When Arábi received orders to leave Cairo with his regiment, he did not take his departure as a simple Colonel in command of a battalion. He made a sort of royal progress through the streets of Cairo, which were crowded with spectators on the occasion. He was received with enthusiasm, and, on arrival at the railway station, he harangued the troops. "Une ère nouvelle," he said, "vient de s'ouvrir pour l'Égypte, et grâce aux hommes placés à la tête des affaires, en qui nous devons avoir toute confiance, l'heure du développement et de la prospérité vient de sonner pour nous. Rendons hommage aux qualités et mérites qui distinguent les membres du nouveau Cabinet; et en particulier à Mahmoud Pacha Sami, notre Ministre de la Guerre . . . Je voudrais que vous puissiez comprendre tous, quelle glorieuse mission est réservée à une armée bien unie, bien commandée, bien disciplinée, et ne marchant que vers un but unique, le bien de la patrie. Vous avez une force entre les mains, et tous réunis vous en représentez une invincible."[1] A little later, a fête was given at Zagazig in honour of Arábi. About 1000 people were present, "all patriots" having been invited to attend. Arábi was received with

---

[1] This speech was, of course, delivered in Arabic. The French translation, quoted above, was subsequently published in the local newspapers.

enthusiasm.   He made a speech in which he insisted
on the necessity of reforms, inveighed against the
employment of Europeans in Egypt, and said that
he had three regiments in Cairo on whom he
could rely to carry out his behests.

Whilst, however, in public Arábi incited hatred
to Europeans, in private he used a different
language.   On November 1, Arábi, Ali Bey Fehmi,
and Toulba Bey Ismet had an interview with Sir
Auckland Colvin.   Arábi "described the Government of the Mamelukes and that of the present
dynasty as being equally oppressive to the Arab
population.   His point was to show that up to the
present the Egyptians have had no security for life or
property.   They were imprisoned, exiled, strangled,
thrown into the Nile, starved, and robbed according to the will of their masters.   A liberated slave
was a freer man than a freeborn Arab.   The most
ignorant Turk was preferred and honoured before
the best of the Egyptians.   He illustrated his
statement by the case of the Mufettish.[1]   He then
went on at great length to explain that men came
of one common stock and had equal rights of
personal liberty and security.   The development
of this theme took some considerable time, and
was curious in its naïve treatment, but it evidently
was the general outcome of the speaker's laboured
thoughts, and was the expression, not of rhetorical
periods, but of conviction.   Passing on to the
bearing of his reasoning on facts, he said that on
the 1st February the Circassian rule (by which he
meant the arbitrary Turkish régime) had fallen in
Egypt; on the 9th September, the necessity of
substituting for it the era of law and justice had
been recognised and established.   It was for law
and justice that he and the army contended.   He
disclaimed in the plainest words the desire to get

[1] Ismail Pasha's Finance Minister, who was assassinated in 1876.

rid of Europeans, whether as employés or residents ;
he spoke of them as the necessary instructors of
the people. He himself and the two officers
(pointing to them) had never been to school.
Intercourse with Europeans had been their school.
He and all felt the need of it ; they had no wish to
question the need of Europeans in the administration ; on the contrary, if more were required let
them come. . . . The impression left on my mind
was that Arábi, who spoke with great moderation,
calmness, and conciliation, is sincere and resolute,
but is not a practical man. The exposition, not
the execution of ideas, is his strength. The other
two Colonels are clearly more practical men, and
act, I should say, as a sedative on Arábi, when his
views excite and stimulate him too dangerously."

Whilst the leading officers of the army were
thus assuming the rôle of demagogues, the discipline of the men became daily more and more
shaken. Early in November, a couple of soldiers,
who had been arrested by the police for brawling,
were forcibly released by their comrades from the
guard-house to which they had been conveyed. A
little later, the Government decided to change the
Colonel of the artillery quartered in Cairo, but the
soldiers of the regiment opposed the change, and
declared that they would not obey any new Colonel
who might be appointed. Their opposition was
overcome, but not without considerable concessions having been made to them. About the
same time, the band of a regiment quartered at
Cairo refused to obey an order to play at the
theatre. The troops at Suez also showed signs
of insubordination, due to a soldier having been
murdered by an Italian. These symptoms were
sufficient to indicate that there was no public
force in Egypt on whom reliance could be placed
to maintain order.

In the meanwhile, the minds of the civil population were excited by the vernacular press, which attacked Europeans and their systems of government with virulence and appealed to Mohammedan fanaticism. "We are the prey," wrote one of these newspapers, "of two lions, England and France, who are watching for the favourable moment to realise their designs, hidden under a deceptive policy. . . . One day we hope to see our administrations cleared of all Europeans, and on that day we can say that England and France have rendered us a great service, for which we shall really thank them." "Some people," another newspaper wrote, "pretend that fanaticism is ruinous to progress, yet our best days were those in which we conquered the Universe by devotion to our faith. To-day we have neglected it, and we and our country are in the hands of strangers, but our misfortunes are a just punishment for our sins. O ye Ulema of El-Azhar! whose sacred duty it should be to combat this religious decadence, what will be your answer at the Day of Judgment to Him who can read the secrets of your hearts ?"

Writings of this sort naturally led to retorts from the local European press. A French paper, *L'Égypte*, described Osman, the third of the Khalifs, as "le fanatique héritier d'un faux prophète." The editor's life was threatened, and he left the country. His newspaper was suppressed, as also was *El Hedjaz*, a newspaper which had specially distinguished itself by the violence of its language in support of Pan-Islamic views. "The suppression of this newspaper," Sir Edward Malet wrote, "especially while Arábi Bey was still at Cairo, was regarded as a sign of returning authority to the Government ; and consequently had the effect of, to some degree, restoring confidence."

In spite of all this inflammatory literature, the mass of the people remained for some time indifferent to all that was passing. Eventually, however, the insubordination, which had shown itself in the army, began to spread to the civil population. This it was sure to do, for the reason given by Sir Auckland Colvin in a Memorandum dated September 24. "What," he said, "gives a show of justification to the recent conduct of the army and gives them support among great numbers of the respectable Egyptians, is that there is a great deal of truth in their complaints. They are sure of sympathy when they ask for justice, and protest against acts of arbitrary violence. The only way in which the Government can deprive them of the influence which they acquire by their appeal is by taking the game out of their hands."

When the year 1881 closed, therefore, the condition of affairs was as follows. The Khedive was brooding over the humiliation inflicted on him by his mutinous army, and was desirous of an opportunity to reassert his authority. Chérif Pasha was inspired by some statesmanlike principles, and was endeavouring to regain the legitimate authority of the Government, but he was wanting in the energy and strength of character necessary to control the turbulent elements which had been let loose. He was ably seconded by Sir Edward Malet and by Sir Auckland Colvin. Arábi was the real ruler of the country. He had the army at his back. Early in January 1882, he was appointed Under-Secretary of State for War, as "it was thought better that he should belong to the Government than be outside it." The population of Egypt was discontented, but the junction between the national party and the mutinous army was not complete. The civil element still looked askance at the soldiers. The native press was appealing to Mohammedan fanaticism, and inciting hatred against Europeans.

Under circumstances such as these, the utmost care was necessary. In the general ferment which then existed, a false step would be fatal. The British and French Governments were about to take a step which was to be well-nigh destructive of all hope of guiding the movement, and was to render foreign interference of some sort, whether Turkish or European, an almost unavoidable necessity.

CHAPTER XIII

THE JOINT NOTE

JANUARY 1882

Proposal to establish an Anglo-French Military Control—Change of
Ministry in France—M. Gambetta proposes joint action—Lord
Granville agrees—Sir Edward Malet consulted—Sir Auckland
Colvin's recommendations—M. Gambetta prepares a draft note
—Lord Granville agrees—Instructions sent to Cairo—Proposed
increase in the army—Reorganisation of the Chamber of Notables
—Effect produced by the Note—Remarks on the Note.

IMMEDIATELY after the mutiny of September 9,
M. Barthélemy St. Hilaire proposed to Lord
Granville that a joint Military Control should be
established in Egypt. A British and a French
General were to be sent to Cairo. These officers,
the French Minister thought, "would be able to
introduce order and discipline into the Egyptian
army." The British Government asked "what
consequences would ensue supposing these Generals
were set at nought by the Egyptian army." To
this question, "M. Barthélemy St. Hilaire answered
that in such a case it might be necessary to make
it unmistakably manifest that the Generals had the
support of England and France. He spoke in very
general terms of a naval demonstration, of the
despatch of English and French ships of war to
Alexandria, but he did not make any definite proposal or suggestion on the subject." The proposal
was referred to Cairo, where it was scouted by

Chérif Pasha and by Sir Auckland Colvin.   The
fact that it should have been made showed how
little the French Government realised the true
nature of the local situation.   At a moment when
every endeavour was being made to incite the
population against European interference of any
kind, it was absurd to suppose that two European
Generals could, by mere force of character, have
obtained any control over the mutinous army.
The only result of sending them would have been
to cause another and probably more serious mutiny.
This proposal was, therefore, allowed to drop.

No further proposal for joint action on the part
of England and France was put forward until the
middle of December, by which time a change
of Ministry had taken place in France.   M.
Gambetta assumed the direction of affairs.   His
masterful spirit soon imparted a fresh impulse to
Egyptian policy, in which he took a lively personal
interest.

On December 15, M. Gambetta told Lord
Lyons that "he considered it to be extremely
important to strengthen the authority of Tewfik
Pasha.   On the one hand, every endeavour should
be made to inspire Tewfik himself with confidence
in the support of France and England, and to
infuse into him firmness and energy.   On the
other hand, the enemies of the present system,
the adherents of Ismail Pasha and Halim Pasha,
and the Egyptians generally should be made to
understand that France and England, by whose
influence Tewfik has been placed on the throne,
would not acquiesce in his being deposed from
it. . . . Any interposition on the part of the
Porte, M. Gambetta declared emphatically to be,
in his opinion, wholly inadmissible. . . . He
thought the time was come when the two Governments should consider the matter in common in

order to be prepared for united and immediate action in case of need."

To this communication, Lord Granville replied on December 19: "Her Majesty's Government quite agree in thinking that the time has come when the two Governments should consider what course had better be adopted by both Governments. Her Majesty's Government also think that it is desirable that some evidence should be given of their cordial understanding; but that it requires careful consideration what steps should be taken in case of disorder again reappearing."

To any one who can read between the lines, this correspondence is instructive. It gives a correct indication of what was to follow. Both Governments were in a frame of mind which is dangerous in politics. They both thought that, in ordinary conversational language, "something must be done." The action of the French Government was directed by a fiery and energetic Minister who could not brook inaction. M. Gambetta thoroughly understood what he wanted. He wished to bring Egypt under Anglo-French control without an armed occupation, if that were possible; but if it were impossible, then he would accept the occupation as the best solution of the question.

On the other side of the Channel, affairs were directed by a Minister with a far calmer judgment than M. Gambetta, but who was wanting in initiative. It is a dangerous thing in politics for a responsible Minister to accept vaguely the principle that "something must be done," when he has not a clear idea of what should be done. The acceptation of the principle will not improbably lead him into doing things which he will subsequently wish had been left undone. At a later period, Lord Granville was to see that, though there "were objections to every possible course," at the same time, the main question was, "which of them offered the least inconvenience." But he discovered this too late. For the moment, he allowed his headstrong French associate to drag him in a direction opposed to that which, as a choice of evils, he most approved, namely, a Turkish occupation. He was eventually to drift into a solution to which he was much opposed, namely, a British occupation, and it was only by the accident of a change of Ministry in France that he was prevented from drifting into what was probably the worst solution possible, namely, an Anglo-French occupation.

On December 24, M. Gambetta developed somewhat more fully the nature of the steps which he thought might advantageously be taken by the British and French Governments. The Chamber of Notables was about to assemble at Cairo. Their meeting would, M. Gambetta thought, "produce a considerable change in the political situation of Egypt." He proposed, therefore, that "the two Governments should instruct their representatives at Cairo to convey collectively to Tewfik Pasha assurances of the sympathy and support of France and England, and to encourage His Highness to maintain and assert his proper authority. . . . This seemed to him a simple and practical measure, to be adopted without delay, and the two Governments might make it a starting-point for considering in concert what further steps they should be ready to take in case of need."

Lord Granville communicated M. Gambetta's proposal to Sir Edward Malet, and, on December 26, asked him whether he saw any objection to it. On the following day, Sir Edward Malet replied: "I see no objection to M. Gambetta's proposal. The support that the Khedive is most likely to require is towards the maintenance of the independence of the Chamber against the jealousies and suspicions of the Porte." Thereupon, Lord Granville instructed Lord Lyons to inform M. Gambetta that the British Government agreed to his proposal. When this message was communicated to M. Gambetta, he said that he would prepare a draft of an instruction to the British and French representatives at Cairo for submission to the British Government.

On December 30, Sir Edward Malet telegraphed to Lord Granville stating that it would be desirable to await the arrival of a despatch then on its way from Cairo before deciding on the terms of the communication which was to be addressed to the Egyptian Government. "It would be unadvisable," Sir Edward Malet added, "that the Khedive should be encouraged to hope that we would support him in maintaining an attitude of reserve towards the Chamber. It has been convoked with the full approval of Chérif Pasha, who looks to it for success and support. To discountenance it would be to play into the hands of the Porte, increase the influence of the military, and diminish that which we are now obtaining as befriending moderate reform. The reply of the Chamber to the Khedive's speech is stated to be extremely moderate and satisfactory."

The despatch to which Sir Edward Malet alluded in this telegram was dated December 26. It enclosed a remarkable Memorandum prepared by Sir Auckland Colvin, who wrote as follows :—

"The events of the last three months, and the movement still going on in Egypt, must necessarily make itself felt in the relations of Egypt with the two Powers. It will be well to describe briefly what the present movement seems to be, and in what direction it threatens to encroach on the ground held by England and France.

"In its origin, the movement is, I think, unquestionably an Egyptian movement against Turkish arbitrary rule. The rebound from Ismail Pasha's tyranny, the growing emancipation of the Egyptian mind owing to its close contact with Europeans, and the opportunity given by the anomalous position in which Egypt finds herself in relation severally to Turkey and the two Powers, have immediately led to the events we are now witnessing. Chérif Pasha, having been placed at the head of the movement, partly from conviction but more by weakness, is allowing himself to be carried forward on it, and will, I think, be eventually swept away by it. He is quite incompetent to control, and little able to guide it.

" The movement, though in its origin anti-Turk, is in itself an Egyptian national movement. For the moment, it is careful in its attitude towards Europeans because it has need of them in its duel with its immediate opponents, but it cannot look on them with favour, or be animated, *au fond*, by any other desire than that of eventually getting rid of them."

" So much for the nature of the movement; next, as to the direction in which it threatens to encroach upon the ground now occupied by England and France.

" There will be, I think, a twofold danger : first, a disposition to ignore or modify the engagements by which Egypt is bound ; secondly, to get rid of foreign interference in branches of the administration in regard to which there exists no direct engagement.

" With regard to the first point, . . . if the right of voting the Budget, in other words, control over the finances, is given to the Chamber, the position of the Anglo-French Control will be profoundly modified. At present, it is effective because the Council governs the country, and in the Council the Control has a seat and an effective voice, whilst it is in constant and intimate relations with the different individuals composing the Cabinet. But it can have no relations, except of the most indirect character, with the Chamber, nor any confidence in the decisions of that irresponsible and ill-instructed body. How, if the Chamber is to vote the Budget, can the Control exercise any useful check on the finances? The Chamber, doubtless, in voting the Budget, can only do so within the conditions allowed by the Law of Liquidation; but those conditions are sufficiently elastic to allow of the finances being misapplied in a degree which would endanger financial equilibrium.

"We have caused this to be pointed out to Chérif Pasha, who is said to be prepared to modify his projects in accordance with our views. But whether the Chamber will accept his modification is another matter."

As regards the second point, that is to say, the desire to get rid of foreign interference in those branches of the administration in respect to which the Egyptian Government were under no distinct international engagement, Sir Auckland Colvin said that "successful attacks on one or more of those administrations would sap the moral influence of the Control, as well as destroy, proportionately as such attacks are successful, the material hold acquired by the Powers in the country."

Under these circumstances, Sir Auckland Colvin thought that for the guidance of himself and the other high British and French officials in Egypt, the "wishes of the two Cabinets should be expressed as to the attitude that they were to assume."

He then proceeded to lay the following recommendations before the British Government. "The liberal movement," he said, "now going on should, I think, in no wise be discouraged. It has many enemies, no less among Europeans than amongst Turks. But I believe it is essentially the growth of the popular spirit, and is directed to the good of the country, and that it would be most impolitic to thwart it. But precisely because I wish it to succeed, it seems to me essential that it should learn from the first within what limits it must confine itself. Otherwise, expectations may be formed and hopes raised, the failure of which may lead to its entire discomfiture. In all that is doing or to be done, neither the Government nor the Chamber should be allowed to forget that the Powers have assumed a direct financial control over the country and intend to maintain it. The Powers should not, in my opinion, accept any proposed measures which jeopardise this control, which is essential at present to the well-being of the country, and is, therefore, the main safeguard against the recurrence of an 'Egyptian Question.' All that is guaranteed by the Law of Liquidation and preceding Decrees should also be authoritatively placed beyond the pale of discussion. All that is designed to transfer the centre of financial authority from the Control to the Chamber should be especially discountenanced and, if need be, negatived, as neutralising and nullifying the agency through which the Powers assure themselves of the efficient conduct of financial affairs, for which they have made themselves responsible in Egypt.

"At the same time, I should give Chérif Pasha, or whoever may represent the Government, to understand that he is expected to discourage and oppose popular attacks on European administrations, and that the Powers will by no means look with indifference on the success of any such attacks. Each of these administrations is in itself, though doubtless with many imperfections, a centre of reform. They are the spokes of the wheel representing the Control. . . . The line, it will be thus seen, that I advocate, is the open and firm recognition by the Powers, through their diplomatic agents, at this critical juncture when Egypt is remoulding her internal reorganisation, of the material interest they possess and intend to maintain in the administration, leaving full liberty to the Egyptians to frame what measures they please for their internal government, so far as they are not inconsistent with the status acquired by the Powers. In fact, the Egyptian administration is a partnership of three. Unless the Powers are prepared to modify their share, they must secure and strengthen it, now that the Egyptians are in a state of movement and change. They cannot look on with indifference, and allow matters to be discussed and settled here without some intimation of their views. If a clear understanding is not imposed from the first, much misunderstanding will arise, embittering more, as I think, the relations between us and the Egyptians than would the authoritative declaration, now when the Chamber is about to meet, of the intentions of the Powers."

Sir Auckland Colvin's Memorandum has been quoted at length because it is important to ascertain what information as regards the situation in Egypt was before the British Government when it was decided to agree to M. Gambetta's proposal. The Memorandum was received at the Foreign Office on January 2. On the same day, the draft note prepared by M. Gambetta, which was to be sent to the British and French Consuls-General at Cairo, reached London. It was couched in the following terms :—

"You have already been instructed on several
occasions to inform the Khedive and his Government of the determination of England and France
to afford them support against the difficulties of
various kinds which might interfere with the
course of public affairs in Egypt. The two
Powers are entirely agreed on this subject, and
recent circumstances, especially the meeting of the
Chamber of Notables convoked by the Khedive,
have given them the opportunity for a further
exchange of views. I have accordingly to instruct
you to declare to the Khedive that the English
and French Governments consider the maintenance
of His Highness on the throne, on the terms laid
down by the Sultan's Firmans, and officially
recognised by the two Governments, as alone able
to guarantee, for the present and future, the good
order and development of general prosperity in
Egypt, in which France and Great Britain are
equally interested. The two Governments being
closely associated in the resolve to guard by their
united efforts against all cause of complication,
internal or external, which might menace the order
of things established in Egypt, do not doubt
that the assurance publicly given of their formal
intentions in this respect will tend to avert the
dangers to which the Government of the Khedive
might be exposed, and which would certainly find
England and France united to oppose them. They
are convinced that His Highness will draw from
this assurance the confidence and strength which
he requires to direct the destinies of Egypt and
his people."

On January 6, the British Government agreed
to M. Gambetta's draft, with the reservation
"that they must not be considered as committing
themselves thereby to any particular mode of
action, if action should be found necessary." On

January 7, M. Gambetta wrote to Lord Lyons: "We observe with pleasure that the only reservation of the Government of the Queen is as to the mode of action to be employed by the two countries when action is considered necessary; and this is a reservation in which we participate."

It was, therefore, four days after the arrival in London of Sir Auckland Colvin's Memorandum, which is quoted above, that the British Government intimated their acceptance of M. Gambetta's proposals. On January 6, the instructions were telegraphed to Sir Edward Malet. Identic instructions were at the same time sent by the French Government to M. Sienkiewicz.

When these instructions reached Cairo, the local situation was as follows. The Chamber of Notables had been opened by the Khedive on December 26. Sultan Pasha, the President of the Chamber, and Suleiman Pasha Abaza, one of the leading members, replied to the Khedive's opening address in terms expressive of their loyalty and devotion to the public interests. On January 2, Sir Edward Malet reported: "At an interview which I had with the Khedive on the 31st ultimo I found His Highness, for the first time since my return in September, cheerful in mood and taking a hopeful view of the situation. He spoke with much satisfaction of the apparently moderate tendencies of the Delegates, and he expressed his belief that the country would now progress. The change was very noticeable, because His Highness had, up to the time of the opening of the Chamber, been full of misgiving, and I feared that this feeling was prompted not only by a mistrust of what the Delegates might do, but also by a dislike of the Chamber as an institution."

Two difficulties, however, lay ahead. In the first place, the military party wished the army to be increased to 18,000 men, the maximum figure allowed by the Firman of 1879. The Controllers were prepared to grant a certain increase, but they declined, on financial grounds, to give all that the military party desired, and in this matter they were supported by the British Government. Chérif Pasha was at first inclined to go farther than the Controllers approved in the direction of increasing the army. At last, however, " he sided entirely with the Control, and was equally resolved not to give way." On the eve of the meeting of the Chamber, it was decided to fix the Military Budget for 1882 at £E.522,000, an increase of £E.154,000 over the Budget for the previous year. The Minister of War, however, was not satisfied. He wished for a further increase of about £E.126,000, which would have enabled the army to be brought up to 18,000 men.

The other difficulty was of a different character. The Chamber was convoked under Ismail Pasha's law of 1866. It was known that, when the Chamber met, it would demand larger powers than those conferred by this law. In anticipation of such demands, the Egyptian Ministry had prepared new regulations, which were submitted to the Chamber on January 2. In sending these proposals to Lord Granville, Sir Edward Malet remarked : " Your Lordship will observe that guarantees are given in these regulations for the observance of the duties of Egypt towards foreign Powers. With the exception of these restrictions, the constitution of the Chamber is extremely liberal, and there is little doubt that, as time goes on, further changes in a liberal direction will be made." It remained to be seen whether the Chamber would be satisfied with the proposals of the Government.

The situation was evidently critical. Still, there was hope that, with very careful guidance, the difficulties of the moment might be overcome, and a complete upset of the State machinery obviated.

One main point should surely have been borne in mind before the Joint Note was delivered. It was that a National Party existed in Egypt. On this subject, the British Government appear to have been under a delusion from the first. They thought that the movement was wholly military, and, therefore, undeserving of sympathy. At a later period (July 22, 1882), when British military intervention had become necessary, Mr. Gladstone, speaking in the House of Commons, said : "There have been periods in this history at which it has been charitably believed, even in this country, that the military party was the popular party, and was struggling for the liberties of Egypt. There is not the smallest rag or shred of evidence to support that contention. . . . Military violence and the regimen established by military violence are absolutely incompatible with the growth and the existence of freedom. . . . The reign of Cromwell was a great reign, but it did nothing for English freedom. . . . The reign of Napoleon was a splendid reign, but, founded on military power, it did nothing for freedom in France."

However true these general principles may be, nothing can be more certain than that at that time there existed in Egypt a national party who were working more or less in co-operation with the military party. Chérif Pasha, who was, as Sir Auckland Colvin said, an Egyptian *grand seigneur*, and who was one of the dominant race, recognised its existence, and wisely recommended a policy which would encourage the development of the national, at the expense of the military elements in the movement. Sir Edward Malet also[1] had distinctly warned the Government of the unwisdom of taking any step which would be construed as one of hostility to the national movement. One of the most able Europeans in Egypt at that time was Sir Auckland Colvin. He was a trained Anglo-Indian official, and was certainly not carried away by any Utopian ideas as to the possibility or desirability of rapidly developing free institutions amongst a backward Oriental people. His official position obliged him to look after the interests of the Egyptian Treasury, but his political insight was too keen to allow of his being deceived as to the true nature of the movement which was in course of progress. He had warned the British Government that "the liberal movement then going on should in no wise be discouraged. Though in its origin anti-Turk, it was in itself an Egyptian national movement."

Such, therefore, was the situation in Egypt when the British and French Governments communicated the Joint Note to their diplomatic representatives in Cairo.

The instructions were received at Cairo on the night of January 6. At 5.30 P.M. on the 8th Sir Edward Malet telegraphed to Lord Granville: "My French colleague and I communicated the dual note to the Khedive to-day." "His Highness," he added, "requested us to express to our respective Governments his sincere gratitude for the solicitude which it showed for his own welfare and that of his people."

In an article written by Mr. John Morley in the *Fortnightly Review* (July 1882), the effect of the Note is described in the following words: "At

[1] *Vide ante,* p 218.

Cairo, the Note fell like a bombshell. Nobody had
expected such a declaration, and nobody there was
aware of any reason why it should have been
launched. What was felt was that so serious a
step on such delicate ground could not have been
taken without deliberate calculation nor without
some grave intention. The Note was, therefore,
taken to mean that the Sultan was to be thrust
still farther in the background; that the Khedive
was to become more plainly the puppet of England
and France; and that Egypt would, sooner or
later, in some shape or other, be made to share the
disastrous fate of Tunis. The general effect was,
therefore, mischievous in the highest degree. The
Khedive was encouraged in his opposition to the
sentiments of the Chamber. The military, national,
or popular party was alarmed. The Sultan was
irritated. The other European Powers were made
uneasy. Every element of disturbance was roused
into activity."

Chérif Pasha called on Sir Edward Malet and
M. Sienkiewicz on January 10, and said that the
"message was regarded, first, as encouraging the
Khedive to place himself in antagonism to reform;
secondly, that the wording which connected, as it
were, the events of September with the opening of
the Chamber, showed a spirit unfavourable to the
latter; thirdly, that it indicated a desire to loosen
the tie to the Porte; fourthly, that it contained a
menace of intervention, which nothing in the state
of the country at present justified."

Sir Edward Malet's personal testimony was no
less conclusive. On January 9, he telegraphed to
Lord Granville: "The communication has, at all
events temporarily, alienated from us all confidence.
Everything was progressing capitally, and England
was looked on as the sincere wellwisher and protector of the country. Now, it is considered that

England has definitely thrown in her lot with France, and that France, from motives in connection with her Tunisian campaign, is determined ultimately to intervene here." "It is too soon," Sir Edward Malet wrote on January 10, "to judge at present of the ultimate result of what has taken place; but for the moment it has had the effect to cause a more complete union of the national party, the military, and the Chamber, to unite these three in a common bond of opposition to England and France, and to make them feel more forcibly than they did before that the tie which unites Egypt to the Ottoman Empire is a guarantee to which they must strongly adhere to save themselves from aggression. The military, who had fallen into the background on the convocation of the Chamber, are again in everybody's mouth, and Arábi Bey is said to be foremost in protesting against what he is represented to consider as unjust interference."

The greatest General, it has been said, is he who makes the fewest mistakes. The same may be said of politicians and diplomatists. A remark made to me in this connection many years ago by Sir Francis Baring, the first Lord Northbrook, has sunk into my memory. I was staying at his country-house in 1864, having just returned from America, where I had been present as a spectator with the Northern army. I discussed the prospects of the war which was then going on, and expressed my opinions with all the confidence of youth. After listening for a while, Sir Francis said to me : "Now that you are a young man, you should write down not what has happened but what you think is going to happen. You will be surprised to find how wrong you are." Nearly half a century of official life, during which time I have been behind the scenes whilst events of some

interest and importance were passing, has convinced me of the justice of the remark made by
my shrewd old relative. I have myself made too
many erroneous political forecasts to be inclined
to criticise severely the mistakes of others. It
must, however, be admitted that, in agreeing to
the Joint Note, Lord Granville made a serious
mistake. It is clear that the British and French
Governments were aiming at different objects.
The French Government, whilst admitting the
partnership with England as an unavoidable, though
perhaps unpleasant, necessity, wished to tighten the
hold of France over Egypt. The British Government, on the other hand, wished above all things
to avoid the necessity of serious interference in
Egypt. When, on January 6, Lord Granville
made a reservation in agreeing to the Joint Note
to the effect that he was not committed "to any
particular mode of action," and when, on January 7,
M. Gambetta replied "c'est une réserve qui nous
est commune," they were in reality far from being
agreed. Each interpreted his reservation in a different manner. Lord Granville meant that, as a last
resource, he would fall back on Turkish armed
intervention. M. Gambetta, on the other hand,
was "emphatically of opinion that any intervention of the Porte was wholly inadmissible." On
January 14, the *République Française*, which was
the recognised organ of M. Gambetta, declared
that "it would be a grave error to imagine that the
two Powers were not firmly resolved to follow up
their platonic demonstration in a suitable manner if
order should be disturbed, or if the authority of the
Khedive should again be placed in jeopardy." In
other words, M. Gambetta contemplated an Anglo-
French occupation.

Another consideration should have made Lord
Granville pause. Before he agreed to the Joint

Note, he was in possession of Sir Auckland Colvin's Memorandum of December 26. Sir Edward Malet drew his special attention to this memorandum, and urged that it should be considered before any decision was taken. It is an extremely able paper. It gave a very clear description of the local situation. Sir Auckland Colvin pointed out that it would be most "impolitic to thwart" the movement then going on in Egypt, the national character of which he fully recognised. His principal business, however, was to look after the finances of Egypt. He was aware that without European assistance it was hopeless to expect that the finances could be brought into good order. He deprecated anything which would jeopardise the financial control exerted by France and England. He advocated "the open and firm recognition by the Powers . . . of the material interest they possess and intend to maintain in the administration." In point of fact, the Egyptian administration was "a partnership of three," and he advocated the principle that no change could be made in the terms of association without the consent of all the partners.

All this was perfectly true. Moreover, it was natural that, holding the position which he held, Sir Auckland Colvin should have advocated views of this nature. They were views to which the French Government would readily have assented, for French policy in Egypt had, for a long time past, been guided to a great extent by the interests of individual Frenchmen in the solvency of the Egyptian Treasury. But the case of the British Government was somewhat different. They had, indeed, agreed to the appointment of Controllers. They had been parties to the Law of Liquidation. But it was going a distinct step farther to give a solemn pledge that they would interfere seriously if any complication arose, whether "internal or external, which might menace the order of things established in Egypt." If this pledge meant anything, it meant that the British Government would give material support to the Controllers ; and, indeed, when the matter came to be discussed at a later period in Parliament, the case of the Government rested upon the alleged obligation to support the Control. An obligation, indeed, existed, but it did not extend nearly so far as the French Government, with the British Government following in their train, implied. The British Government might perfectly well have accepted as correct Sir Auckland Colvin's description of the facts of the situation, without adopting to the full his recommendations. They were in a position to take a more unbiassed view than Sir Auckland Colvin of the extent to which it was wise to go in the direction of interference in Egypt on purely financial grounds. There was no reason why, at this moment, the Controllers should not have been informed that they could rely on nothing but moral support, and that they must do the best they could, in the difficult circumstances in which they were placed, by persuasion and force of character. At the same time, the Egyptian Government and the Arábists might have been told that the British and French Governments had no wish to check any reasonable development of the national movement. The Khedive might have been encouraged to come to terms with his people rather than to resist their wishes. Attention might have been drawn to the views of the Controllers, on the ground that their financial knowledge and experience would be of great use to the Egyptian people, and that, in the event of their advice being systematically neglected, financial disorder would almost inevitably ensue. At the same time, it might have been hinted that no armed intervention was to be feared in respect to a mere financial question,

however much the two Governments might regret
to see financial disorder prevail.   Armed intervention would be reserved for the time when life and
property were no longer secure.   It cannot, indeed,
be stated with any degree of confidence that, if
language of this sort had been held, the occupation of Egypt by foreign troops would have been
avoided.   The financial interests concerned were
so great, and the risk that financial disorder would
eventually have led to anarchy was so considerable,
that it may well be that armed intervention of
some sort would ultimately have become an unavoidable necessity.   This, however, is mere conjecture.   What is more certain is that, by following
M. Gambetta's lead, the British Government
pledged themselves to a greater degree of interference in Egyptian internal affairs, and especially
financial affairs, than the actual circumstances of
the case appear to have necessitated.

There can be little doubt that Lord Granville
associated himself with M. Gambetta's Note because
he failed to appreciate the effect which the Note
would produce.   In the debate which subsequently
took place in the House of Lords, Lord Granville
alluded to his despatch of November 4, 1881, which
set forth the policy of the British Government.[1]
That despatch, he said, "had the singular good
fortune of being generally approved both at home
and abroad."   This statement was quite correct.
When the despatch in question was communicated
to Chérif Pasha by Sir Edward Malet, he "expressed
great satisfaction at it, and stated that he should
have it translated for insertion in the local press,
as it ought to have an excellent effect."   Lord
Granville then went on to say: "At the end of
December, M. Gambetta proposed that we should
join with France in a Dual Note on the same lines

---

[1] *Vide ante,* p. 203.

as my despatch of November, but possibly accentuated as to its terms by the fact of its being drafted by a more eloquent pen." There was, however, a wide difference between both the tone and the substance of Lord Granville's despatch of November 4, and the Joint Note of January 8. The former was friendly and sympathetic. The latter was menacing. The former indicated that nothing but "the occurrence in Egypt of a state of anarchy" would be likely to lead to foreign intervention of a serious description in Egypt. The latter stated in somewhat harsh terms that the British and French Governments were determined to maintain "the order of things established in Egypt," an expression which might be held to cover a very wide field. Moreover, it was to be inferred from the despatch of November 4 that, if any foreign intervention were found necessary, the military forces of the Sultan would be employed. The British and French Governments deprecated the idea that they entertained "any self-aggrandising designs." On the other hand, the studied silence of the Joint Note in respect to the contingency of Turkish intervention naturally led to the supposition that, in an extreme case, Anglo-French and not Turkish intervention was contemplated. Neither, in so far as M. Gambetta was concerned, was the inference incorrect.

When carburetted hydrogen and air in certain proportions exist in a mine, no great harm is done so long as they are left alone. But if a miner enters with a lighted candle, an explosion at once takes place. This is what the French and British Governments did in Egypt when they issued the Joint Note. Previous to the issue of the Note, the National Party and the Military Party existed side by side. Chérif Pasha, aided by Sir Edward Malet and Sir Auckland Colvin, was laboriously and wisely endeavouring to keep the two parties separate. There was some hope that their united efforts would be successful, and that the National Party, which constituted the more healthy of the two elements, would eventually predominate over the Military Party, which constituted an element of obvious danger. At this moment, the British and French Governments appeared, without any sufficient reason, on the scene. They applied a lighted candle to the inflammable material. In an instant, the two elements combined with an explosion. The French Government possibly wished for an explosion. They were, at all events, callous as to whether an explosion occurred or not. But Lord Granville's action can only be explained on the assumption, either that, in his desire to act with the French Government, he momentarily forgot the safety-lamp of diplomatic prudence and reserve, or else that he did not sufficiently appreciate the fact that the mine was full of fire-damp.[1]

From the moment the Joint Note was issued, foreign intervention became an almost unavoidable necessity.

[1] It has been occasionally stated,—apparently on the authority of Mr. Wilfrid Blunt (*Secret History*, etc., pp. 159 and 182),—that, in following the French lead during these negotiations, the British Government were influenced by their desire to conclude a Commercial Treaty with France. I believe this statement to be wholly devoid of foundation. Sir Charles Dilke, who was at the time Under-Secretary of State at the Foreign Office, and whose evidence on this point seems to me conclusive, wrote, on June 27, 1907, to the *Manchester Guardian*: "At no time was the Egyptian policy of either Cabinet allowed to have a bearing upon the commercial relations of the Powers."

Whilst the proofs of this work were passing through the press, a second edition of Mr. Blunt's book was published. In the Appendix, a correspondence is given between Sir Charles Dilke and Mr. Wilfrid Blunt, which is confirmatory of the opinion that there was no connection whatever between the policy set forth in the Joint Note and the commercial relations between France and England.

CHAPTER XIV

THE EFFECTS OF THE JOINT NOTE

JANUARY–FEBRUARY 1882

The British Government wish to explain the Joint Note—The French Government object—The Chamber of Notables claims the right to vote the Budget—Proposals of the British Government—Objections of the French Government—The Consuls-General instructed to oppose the Chamber—The Chamber demands a change of Ministry —Appointment of a National Ministry—The French Government press for an Anglo-French occupation—The British Government favour a Turkish occupation—Resignation of M. Gambetta— Remarks on his policy.

WHEN Lord Granville agreed to the Joint Note he possibly thought that the best method to obviate the necessity of armed intervention in Egypt, whether Turkish or Anglo-French, was to threaten to intervene. The Note itself, indeed, almost expressed this view in plain words. It appeared, however, that the Note had produced an effect opposite to that which was intended. It had increased the chances that armed intervention would be necessary. Lord Granville recognised that he had made a mistake. He accordingly applied himself to the task of rectifying his error. His French partner, on the other hand, was far from being convinced that any mistake had been made. On the contrary, he adhered strongly to the policy indicated in the Joint Note.

On January 10, Chérif Pasha expressed a hope that the two Powers would make some further communication which would tend to remove the bad impression caused by the Joint Note. On the same day, Lord Granville instructed Lord Lyons to consult the French Government on the desirability of sending "an explanatory telegram to Sir Edward Malet to the effect that the character of the dual communication had been misunderstood."

On January 11, Lord Lyons reported the result of his consultation with M. Gambetta. M. Gambetta "was, of course, ready to study attentively any proposal of Her Majesty's Government, but he was himself decidedly of opinion that it might be extremely unadvisable to send any explanation at all of the dual communication."

Chérif Pasha further suggested that the Khedive might reply to the Note in a sense which would perhaps mitigate its bad effects. Sir Edward Malet (January 11) "did not see any particular objection" to this proposal, but his French colleague would not hear of it. He thought that the Egyptian Government "had only to listen to the advice of the two Powers and be silent."

In the meanwhile, the immediate effect of the Joint Note was to bring to a head the quarrel between the Ministry, backed up by the Controllers, and the Chamber of Notables. The Egyptian Budget was at that time divided into two parts. The first part dealt with the revenues which were assigned to the payment of the interest on the Debt. The second part dealt with the remainder of the revenues, which was left at the disposal of the Government. The Chamber of Notables claimed the right of voting the second part of the Budget. The Controllers and Chérif Pasha objected to this proposal, on the ground that, if the right claimed by the Chamber were accorded to them, the Council of Ministers and, therefore, the Controllers, would lose their hold over the finances of the country. "There was a chance," Sir Edward Malet telegraphed on January 10, "of arriving at an understanding, but this is apparently now passed. The Chamber may exercise its right with moderation and good sense, but it is a sanguine presumption. On the other hand, it is impossible now to suppress the Chamber except by intervention, which I earnestly deprecate. In fact, intervention could only be justified on the violation of the Law of Liquidation, not on the apprehension of its violation, and it is right to say that as yet I have heard of no intention on the part of any one to infringe it."

When this message reached Lord Granville, he made an effort to release himself from French guidance. As an English Liberal, he could not do otherwise than sympathise to some extent with the development of free institutions in Egypt. He appears also to have seen that he was being hurried rapidly along the road which led to increased intervention in the internal affairs of Egypt. Moreover, the somewhat overbearing conduct of the French was distasteful to the more fair-minded English statesman, whose character and training alike led him to favour compromise and to reject extreme measures. Lord Granville, therefore, telegraphed to Sir Edward Malet : "Her Majesty's Government do not wish to commit themselves to a total or permanent exclusion of the Chamber of Notables from handling the Budget. Caution, however, will be required in dealing with it, regard being had to the pecuniary interests on behalf of which Her Majesty's Government have been acting." The French Government, however, speedily placed a check on any idea of making concessions to the Chamber. Lord Lyons reported that M. Gambetta "expressed a very strong objection to any interference at all by the Egyptian Chamber with the Budget. He said that it behoved France and

England to be very firm, lest any appearance of
vacillation on their part should encourage the pretensions of the Notables to lay their hands on the
Budget ; and he argued that their touching the
Budget must inevitably lead to the overthrow of
the arrangement made by the Liquidation Commission, to the subversion of the French and
English Control, and to the ruin of the Egyptian
finances. Finally, M. Gambetta expressed his conviction that any explanation of the joint communication of the two Governments would serve
to swell the arrogance of the opponents of France
and England, and encourage them in their designs
upon the Budget."

Lord Granville yielded to French pressure.
" The proposal of the Notables," he wrote to Lord
Lyons, " at all events in its present shape, cannot be
agreed to, although there may be points worthy
of consideration hereafter. Sir Edward Malet has,
therefore, been instructed to join his French
colleague in supporting Chérif Pasha in his opposition to the demand of the Chamber in this
respect." When this message was communicated
to M. Gambetta, it became at once apparent that
he had no intention of leaving the door open to
future concessions. He seized at once on that
portion of Lord Granville's message which was
favourable to his own views, and rejected the rest.
" A very strong instruction " had, he said, been
already sent to the French representative at Cairo,
" directing him to concert with Sir Edward Malet,
and to insist upon Chérif Pasha absolutely rejecting the demands of the Notables, on the ground
that they were incompatible with the state of things
established in Egypt by international engagements
with France and England." A compromise had
been suggested at Cairo to the effect that the
rejection of the demands should be accompanied

by an assurance that they would be favourably considered at some later period. M. Gambetta, however, told Lord Lyons that he had "especially instructed M. Sienkiewicz not to listen for a moment to anything of the kind."

In spite of the support given by the two Powers to Chérif Pasha and the Controllers, it became clearer every day that the Chamber of Notables would not yield. On January 20, Sir Edward Malet telegraphed : " The Chamber will almost certainly vote the counter-project of Law, which places the administrative and financial power in its hands, and amounts to Government by Convention. . . . Armed intervention will become a necessity if we adhere to the refusal to allow the Budget to be voted by the Chamber."

Two days later (January 22), Sir Edward Malet asked Lord Granville whether "he might consider proposals which had been made to him unofficially by the President of the Chamber, with a view to coming to an arrangement which would accord to delegates from the Chamber the right to co-operate with the Ministers in the vote and examination of the Budget." Sir Auckland Colvin thought "that the negotiation might possibly result in a reasonable arrangement," but his French colleague, M. de Blignières, "was strongly opposed to receding in any way from an absolute refusal to allow the Chamber to participate in framing the Budget."

No answer appears to have been sent to this proposal, but a plan was elaborated in London under which some control over the public revenues would have been given to the Chamber of Notables. In sending this scheme to Lord Lyons, on January 25, Lord Granville said : " It seems clear that the claim of the Notables, in the form in which it is presented, is unacceptable, if not impracticable. . . . At the same time, it would be consistent with the desire which Her Majesty's Government and that of France entertain to encourage the judicious development of the institutions of Egypt, and for this purpose, as well as for the practical advantage that would be derived from it, it would seem advisable and probably would not be difficult to find matters confined to the expenditure side of the Budget in which the local knowledge of the Notables could be profitably employed."

When M. Gambetta received this communication, he replied (January 29) that the French Government agreed in principle to Lord Granville's proposals. Agreement in principle to the proposals made by a foreign Government is not unfrequently a diplomatic euphemism for total rejection. Such it was in the present case. M. Gambetta made so many objections in detail to Lord Granville's proposals as to render the concessions to the popular party in Egypt of little value. More especially, he was of opinion that the Budget of the Police and of the Administration of the Wakfs (religious endowments) should not be under the control of the Chamber of Notables.

Lord Granville's reply, which is dated February 2, brings out clearly the different spirits which animated the French and the British Governments. "Her Majesty's Government," Lord Granville wrote, "are unable, without further information, to offer an opinion upon the classification of the Egyptian Police, nor does it appear to them that the Governments of England and France are called upon to interfere in the question of Musulman religious foundations, in which they do not see that their interests are affected, and which would appear at first sight to be a matter with which the Chamber of Notables would be peculiarly competent to deal. . . . Her Majesty's Government apprehend that neither of these are questions upon which it rests with the Governments of England and France to give or withhold privileges, but if the Egyptian authorities are disposed to concede them, they do not think that it is for them to object."

It is clear from this correspondence that M. Gambetta wished to interfere in every detail of the Egyptian administration, even although no semblance of international right could be invoked to justify such interference. Lord Granville, on the other hand, wished to keep within the strict limits of international right, and to deal in a fair spirit of compromise with the national movement in Egypt.

Whilst these negotiations were going on in London and Paris, Sir Edward Malet and M. Sienkiewicz made a written communication to Chérif Pasha setting forth the attitude which the British and French Governments intended to adopt towards the Chamber of Notables. They explained "that the Chamber could not vote the Budget without infringing the Decrees establishing the Control, and that an innovation of the nature proposed by the Chamber could not be introduced without the assent of the English and French Governments." In order, however, not to close the door to a possible understanding, the two Consuls-General added that "if the Government of the Khedive deemed fit to open negotiations on the subject, they were prepared to transmit its proposals to their respective Governments, but they considered that such a negotiation should be on the understanding that the Government and the Chamber were agreed with regard to the rest of the proposed Organic Law." When Chérif Pasha received this communication, he wrote (February 1) to the Chamber explaining the situation, and requesting them "to formulate a basis of negotiation with the Powers."

This communication brought matters to a head. On February 2, a deputation from the Chamber waited on the Khedive and requested him to change his Ministers. "His Highness asked on what law of the Chamber they founded their right to make the request. This they could not answer, but insisted on a change. They also presented a copy of the draft Organic Law of the Chamber, and requested His Highness to sign, saying that the right to vote the Budget was not one for discussion with foreign Powers. His Highness dismissed them, saying that he would consider their request."

It was clear that a change of Ministry was inevitable. The Khedive was obliged to yield because, as he told Sir Edward Malet, "he had no force to resist." Later on the same day, the Khedive received the deputation again and asked them to "name the persons whom they desired as Ministers. This they at first declined to do on the ground that the selection was the prerogative of His Highness." On the following day, however, a further deputation from the Chamber waited on the Khedive, and stated that they wanted Mahmoud Pasha Sami, who was then Minister of War, to be appointed President of the Council. He was accordingly appointed on February 5. Arábi Bey was, at the same time, named Minister of War. The other members of the Cabinet, except Mustapha Pasha Fehmi, who assumed the direction of Foreign Affairs, were members of the National or Military parties, terms which had now become wholly synonymous.

The effect produced by the change of Ministry on the views of the Khedivial party in Egypt was marked. Until then, Chérif Pasha had entertained hopes of guiding the movement, and had stood out against any idea of armed Turkish intervention. He now informed Sir Edward Malet that "the only issue from the situation was the immediate despatch to Egypt of a Commissioner from the Porte, to be followed as soon as possible by a Turkish force. . . . He thought that by acting with tact, and accepting any Ministry the Chamber asked for, the moment could be tided over without public disturbance; but he was of opinion that, as the army had again exercised dictatorship, there was no hope for the future unless it were rendered powerless by force." The Khedive shared Chérif Pasha's views.

As events developed, it became more and more clear that M. Gambetta wished to force on an Anglo-French occupation of Egypt. On January 25, Lord Granville wrote to Lord Lyons in the following terms :—

"The French Ambassador told me yesterday evening that M. Gambetta had written to him expressing his opinion that it was desirable, in view of the probable crisis in Egypt, that the English and French Governments should come to an understanding as to the course which they should pursue. M. Gambetta, it appeared, had not in his letter given his opinion as to what steps should be taken, but he was desirous to know the views of Her Majesty's Government. Any Turkish intervention was, in M. Gambetta's opinion, the worst possible solution. M. Gambetta's attention had been called to a plan, which had appeared in the press, of calling in the co-operation of Europe. M. Gambetta remarked that the position of England in Egypt, in consequence of her Indian possessions, was unique. That of France, owing to her being a great African Power, and to other circumstances, was of the greatest importance.

Besides this normal position of the two Powers, arrangements had been entered into by Egypt, which had been acquiesced in by the European Powers generally. It would, in M. Gambetta's opinion, be most disadvantageous to Egypt and to the two Powers that these arrangements should be in any way weakened."

When Lord Granville received this communication, it was impossible to ignore any longer the radical difference of opinion which existed between the British and French Governments. In a despatch to Lord Lyons, dated January 30, he laid down the policy of the British Government: "Her Majesty's Government," he said, "desire to maintain the rights of the sovereign and vassal as now established between the Sultan and the Khedive, to secure the fulfilment of international engagements, and to protect the development of institutions within this limit. They believe that the French Government share these views. The question remains—If in Egypt a state of disorder should occur which would be incompatible with this policy, what measures should be taken to meet the difficulty? . . . It is to be regretted, but it appears to Her Majesty's Government apparent, that if such a contingency unfortunately occurred, there are objections to every possible course. The question remains — which of them offers the least inconvenience? . . . Her Majesty's Government have a strong objection to the occupation by themselves of Egypt. It would create opposition in Egypt and in Turkey; it would excite the suspicion and jealousy of other European Powers, who would, Her Majesty's Government have reason to believe, make counter-demonstrations on their own part, which might possibly lead to very serious complications, and it would throw upon them the responsibility of governing a country inhabited by Orientals under very adverse circumstances.

"They believe that such an occupation would be as distasteful to the French nation as the sole occupation of Egypt by the French would be to this country.

"They have carefully considered the question of a joint occupation by England and France, and they have come to the conclusion that, although some of the objections above stated might be lessened, others would be very seriously aggravated by such a course.

"With regard to Turkish occupation, Her Majesty's Government agree that it would be a great evil, but they are not convinced that it would entail political dangers so great as those attending the other alternatives which have been mentioned above. . . . The most important point is that the union of the two countries should be both real and apparent.

"M. Gambetta entertains objections to any further admission of the other European Powers to interference in Egyptian affairs. Her Majesty's Government agree that England and France have an exceptional position in that country owing to actual circumstances and to international agreements, and they also believe that inconvenience might arise from many Powers being called upon to join in any administrative functions; but they would submit for the consideration of the French Government whether it would not be desirable to enter into some communication with the other Powers as to the most desirable mode of dealing with a state of things which appears likely to interfere with the Firmans of the Sultan and the international engagements of Egypt."

The day after this despatch was written (January 31), M. Gambetta resigned office. He was succeeded by M. de Freycinet, under whose auspices a complete change took place in the Egyptian policy of the French Government.

During the short time M. Gambetta was in office, he exercised a decisive and permanent influence on the future course of Egyptian history. Lord Granville, M. de Freycinet, and others might do their best to put back the hands of the clock, but it was impossible that they should ever restore the *status quo ante Gambetta.* When he assumed office, the Egyptians entertained confidence in the intentions of England and France, especially in those of England. The amalgamation of the military and national parties in Egypt was not complete. The Egyptian movement was not altogether beyond control. When he left office, England and France were alike mistrusted by the Egyptians. The ascendency of the military over the national party was complete. Any hope of controlling the Egyptian movement, save by the exercise of material force, had well-nigh disappeared. Possibly, the movement was incapable of being controlled, but an *ex post facto* conjecture of this sort hardly appears a sufficient answer to the plea that, before reverting to extreme measures, every possible endeavour should have been made to control it.

In the opinion of many competent authorities, M. Gambetta adopted a mistaken policy. But there are always at least two sides to every question. It will be as well, therefore, to examine the case from M. Gambetta's point of view. It was stated by his friend and political supporter, M. Joseph Reinach, in an article, published in the *Nineteenth Century* of December 1882.

One portion of M. Reinach's argument may be very briefly treated. He complained that there was

a want of "sincerity and cordiality" in the dealings
of the British Foreign Office with France. Also
he thought that public opinion in England "experienced the influence of certain Tories, who
believed that it would be best to slacken proceedings as much as possible, in the hope of finding some opportunity for entering the Nile valley
without France." As to this argument, all I have
to say is that I believe I have seen every official
document, whether published or unpublished, which
is in the possession of the British Foreign Office,
bearing upon the questions now under discussion.
I have also had ample opportunities of ascertaining,
by personal and verbal communications, the views
of the principal actors on the scene. These events
are now matters of past history. Many of the
principal persons concerned are dead. Had there
been any design of outwitting France, such as
M. Reinach insinuated, I certainly should not be de-
terred by any false spirit of patriotism from stating
the true facts of the case. I am, however, able to
state with the utmost confidence that the insinua-
tions of M. Reinach are without a shadow of
foundation. The policy of the British Government
at the time may or may not have been mistaken,
but it was certainly sincere. When Lord Granville deprecated a British or Anglo-French armed
intervention in Egypt, there can be no doubt that
he meant what he said, and, moreover, that he had
behind him the preponderating weight of British
public opinion.

Leaving aside this collateral issue, I proceed to
state M. Reinach's main argument. He thought
that "grave mistakes" were committed by the
British Government. The British Foreign Office
failed to understand how dangerous the situation
in Egypt had become when the Chamber of
Notables met. Neither Mr. Gladstone nor Lord

Granville saw that "the Chamber of Notables was a sham assembly, Arábi an ambitious intriguer, encouraged and suborned by the fanatic Council of Constantinople, and the national party a ludicrous invention of some badly informed or too well paid journalist." M. Gambetta, on the other hand, "simply made use of his eyes and ears." He saw all these things plainly enough. "The hesitation of the English Government," M. Reinach continued, "to suppress the first acts of the insurrection plotted by the military *camarilla* at Cairo was much more than a lack of cordiality towards us (the French) and our alliance; it was, as far as Egyptian matters are concerned, pernicious and deplorable to the highest degree. It encouraged the spirit of rebellion among Arábi's partisans. It helped to kindle and rouse a fire, which a bucket of water shed at the proper time would have extinguished, into a conflagration where lives and treasures have been uselessly destroyed."

In other words, to put the matter plainly, M. Gambetta was convinced, as early as December 1881, that armed intervention of some sort in Egypt would, sooner or later, become necessary. Therefore, he did not hesitate to take steps which he knew might and probably would precipitate the final and, as he thought, inevitable conclusion.

It is impossible to prove that M. Gambetta was wrong. It is equally impossible to prove that he was right. There can be no doubt that the Arábi movement was in some respects a *bona fide* national movement. There can be equally little doubt that, if Arábi and his followers had been left at the head of affairs without any control, a state of the utmost confusion would have been produced in Egypt, and that eventually armed foreign intervention of some sort might have become necessary. In December 1881, however, the only practical question was, would it be possible to control and guide the movement? It is not certain that it would have been impossible to do so. A few able Europeans, like Sir Auckland Colvin, by the exercise of tact and judgment, by encouraging the civil elements of Egyptian society, and by the exhibition of some sympathy with reasonable native aspirations, might possibly in time have acquired a sufficient degree of moral control over the movement to have obviated the necessity for armed intervention. In any case, on the assumption that armed intervention was a solution to be avoided, save as a last resource, the experiment was worth trying. It is impossible, however, to read the correspondence on this subject without seeing that M. Gambetta did not regard armed intervention, provided it was Anglo-French and not Turkish intervention, in this light. On the contrary, he wished to bring about a state of things which would render it necessary. Obviously, therefore, from his point of view, the experiment was not worth trying. But his conclusion cannot command assent unless his premises be accepted, and there are strong grounds for holding that his premises were wrong. The essential point, at all events from the British point of view, was to avoid any armed intervention.

Mr. John Morley summed up the case in the following words, which appear to be correct. " It is impossible," he said, "to conceive a situation that more imperatively called for caution, circumspection, and deference to the knowledge of observers on the scene, or one that was actually handled with greater rashness. and hurry. M. Gambetta had made up his mind that the military movement was leading to the abyss, and that it must be peremptorily arrested. It may be that he was right in supposing that the army, which had first found its power in the time of Ismail, would

go from bad to worse. But everything turned upon
the possibility of pulling up the army, without
arousing other elements more dangerous still. M.
Gambetta's impatient policy was worked out in his
own head without reference to the conditions on the
scene, and the result was what might have been
expected."[1]

It may be conceded to M. Reinach that at this
time "grave mistakes" were committed by the
British Government in respect to Egypt. An
Englishman who holds, as Lord Granville held, that
a British or Anglo-French occupation of Egypt was
above all things to be avoided, may with perfect consistency indicate those mistakes. But a Frenchman,
more especially a partisan of M. Gambetta, has no
right to criticise them. His mouth should be closed,
for "the hesitations, indecisions, perplexities, half-
measures, and delays which characterised English
tactics," and of which M. Reinach complained, were
due to the strong desire of the British Government
to co-operate with the French. Lord Granville
honestly wished to avoid any armed intervention in
Egypt, and as honestly wished, if any intervention
eventually became necessary, that the arms employed should be those of the legitimate Suzerain of
Egypt, and not those of France or England. Had
he been left from the first to act according to the
dictates of his own judgment, it is possible that no
foreign occupation would have been necessary, and
it is more than probable that no British occupation
would have taken place. But he allowed himself
to be influenced by his French colleague, whose
strong will and rash policy dragged him to such an
extent along a road which he had no wish to
follow, that eventually retreat became impossible.
Englishmen may criticise Lord Granville for yielding too much to France. French criticism can only

[1] *Fortnightly Review*, July 1882.

be based either on the assumption that M. Gambetta's action was best calculated to prevent a foreign
occupation, or on the allegation that an Anglo-
French occupation of Egypt was in itself to be
desired as a preventive against evils which might
arise, rather than as a cure for evils which had
already arisen. The verdict of subsequent events
has disproved the assumption. The allegation is a
matter of opinion. M. Gambetta and M. Reinach
held one opinion on this point. Lord Granville
held another, and, as I venture to think, a wiser
opinion.

During the parliamentary discussions which
took place in England, a great deal of ingenious
special pleading was devoted to showing that the
occupation of Egypt was due, not to any action
taken in 1881 and 1882, but to the appointment
of European Controllers in 1879.[1] The facts connected with this subject may be explained by a
metaphor. Suppose a man to be suffering from a
severe but not necessarily fatal disease. He calls
in a doctor who prescribes some mild remedies, and
warns him that, unless he be careful, the disease
will increase in virulence. He fails to profit by
the advice which he has received, and in consequence gets worse. He then calls in another
doctor, who abandons the mild treatment of his
predecessor, and applies some more drastic remedy.
The remedy, far from producing any good effect,
aggravates the disease, and the patient dies. Under
these circumstances, the friends of the patient, provided they be impartially minded, will not inquire
carefully into the suitability or otherwise of the
remedies applied by the first doctor. They will
hold with reason that the patient's death was
hastened, if indeed it was not caused, by the heroic
but mistaken treatment of the second medical

[1] *Vide ante*, p. 160.

adviser. In the case of Egypt, Lord Salisbury stood in the place of the first doctor. Lord Granville, acting under the advice of his impetuous French colleague, stood in the place of the second.

Similarly, in France the mistakes made by M. Gambetta were forgotten, and the British occupation of Egypt was subsequently attributed by M. Joseph Reinach and other Gambettists to the fact that "the demeanour of the Freycinet Ministry was unworthy of France and of the Republic." Whether this accusation is true or the reverse is a matter for Frenchmen to decide. To an Englishman it would appear that the fact of M. de Freycinet's having been opposed to an Anglo-French occupation of Egypt does not relieve M. Gambetta from the responsibility of having largely contributed to create a situation from which it was well-nigh impossible to escape except by means of armed intervention of one sort or another.

The atmosphere of party politics, whether in France or England, is not congenial to the formation of an impartial judgment. A Minister, who is in the thick of a tough parliamentary struggle, must use whatever arguments he can to defend his cause without inquiring too closely whether they are good, bad, or indifferent. However good they may be, they will probably not convince his political opponents, and they can scarcely be so bad as not to carry some sort of conviction to the minds of those who are predisposed to support him. Politicians who are not bound by any strong party ties can weigh the arguments in a somewhat more judicial spirit. The conclusions stated in this chapter will, it is hoped, commend themselves to those who stand outside the immediate sphere of political partisanship.

CHAPTER XV

THE ARÁBI MINISTRY

FEBRUARY–MAY 1882

Proposal to revise the Organic Law—Mr. Wilfrid Blunt—M. de
Blignières resigns—Concessions made to the army—Disorganisation in the provinces — The Porte protests against the Joint
Note—The Powers are invited to an exchange of views—M. de
Freycinet wishes to depose the Khedive—Lord Granville proposes
to send Financial Commissioners to Egypt—Alleged conspiracy to
murder Arábi—The Ministers resign, but resume office—M. de
Freycinet assents to Turkish intervention — Arábi requested to
leave Egypt—He refuses to do so—The Ministers again resign—
The Khedive reinstates Arábi—And asks for a Turkish Commissioner.

THE official transactions of the next four months
are recorded in several ponderous volumes, but
the main facts admit of being very briefly stated.

The Chamber of Notables, whose powers were
at once increased by the new Ministry, was, Sir
Auckland Colvin wrote on February 13, "wholly
under the influence of a mutinous and successful
army." Some well-meaning proposals were put
forward by the British Government with a view
to revising the Organic Law in a sense which
would be liberal but, at the same time, would not
give excessive powers to the Chamber. A few
months earlier, a suggestion of this sort might
perhaps have led to some useful result. But the
propitious moment had been allowed to pass,
and it was now too late to stem the Egyptian
Revolution, for such it really was, by redrafting

an article in a Khedivial Decree. "It would be childish," M. de Freycinet thought (April 20), "to be discussing the pattern of a carpet when the house in which it was laid down was in flames." Sir Auckland Colvin's opinion was no less decisive and his metaphor no less apt. "The house," he said, "is tumbling about our ears, and the moment is not propitious for debating whether we would like another storey added to it. Until civil authority is reassured and the military despotism destroyed, discussion of the Organic Law seems premature and useless."

The civil elements of the national party still made some slight show of independence, but the tendencies which were at work to ensure the predominance of the mutinous army were too strong to be resisted. Not only did Arábi receive encouragement from the Sultan, but the advice of English sympathisers with the nationalist cause tended to consolidate the union between the military and civil elements of the movement.

Of these sympathisers, the most prominent was Mr. Wilfrid Blunt. Mr. Blunt had lived a good deal with Mohammedans, and took a warm interest in all that related to themselves and their religion. He appears to have believed in the possibility of a regeneration of Islam on Islamic principles. It chanced that he was in Egypt during the winter of 1881-82. He threw himself, with all the enthusiasm of a poetic nature, into the Arábist cause, and became the guide, philosopher, and friend of Arábi and his coadjutors. Mr. Blunt saw that he had to do with a movement which was in some degree unquestionably national. He failed to appreciate sufficiently the fact that the predominance of the military party would be fatal to the national character of the movement. At one period of the proceedings, his services

were utilised as an intermediary between Sir
Edward Malet and the nationalists.   The selection was unfortunate, for it is abundantly clear
from the account which Mr. Blunt has given
of his own proceedings[1] that, with the exception
of some knowledge of the Arabic language, he
possessed none of the qualifications necessary to
ensure success in the execution of so difficult and
delicate a mission.   He advised the nationalists to
hold to the army or they would be "annexed to
Europe."[2]   The advice was, without doubt, well-
meant, but it was certainly inopportune and mischievous.   Whatever danger of "annexation to
Europe" existed lay rather in the direction of the
consolidation of the national and military parties
than in that of their separation.   A trained
politician would have seen this.   Mr. Blunt had
had no political training of any value.   He was
an enthusiast who dreamt dreams of an Arab
Utopia.   He, therefore, failed to see what Chérif
Pasha and others on the spot saw.   He worked
earnestly and to the best of his abilities to prevent
a foreign occupation of Egypt.   But the impartial
historian must perforce record his name amongst
those who, by ill-advised action at a critical moment,
unwittingly contributed to bring about the solution
which they most of all deplored.

Terrorised by a mutinous army on the one side,
urged, on the other side, by their English advisers,
whose weight with the British public they greatly

[1] Blunt's *Secret History of the British Occupation of Egypt.*
[2] A letter from Dr. Schweinfurth, the well-known botanist, was
published in the *Times* of June 21, 1882.   He related an interview
he had had with some members of the Chamber.   He commended their
moderation and good sense, and then went on to say: "From England
they expect more for their cause than from France.   They imagine
that in England you are all of the same complexion as Mr. Blunt,
or at least, as Sir William Gregory.   At Ghirgeh, they showed me
with much satisfaction Mr. Blunt's telegram addressed to all the
members of the Egyptian Chamber: 'Si vous allez vous désunir de
l'armée, l'Europe vous annexera.'"   See also *Secret History, etc.*, p. 271.

overrated,[1] to seek salvation in submitting to military dictation, it can be no matter for surprise that the ignorant and inexperienced men who feebly represented genuine constitutionalism sank into insignificance and ranged themselves on the side of the mutineers.

The power of the Controllers disappeared. Sir Edward Malet wrote to Lord Granville (February 20) that he thought it had "become a question whether the Control should be maintained, now that it existed only in name." M. de Blignières resigned his appointment.

Mahmoud Pasha Sami, the new President of the Egyptian Council, shared the usual fate of revolutionary leaders. He was violently attacked because he failed to carry out his engagement that all Europeans should be turned out of Egyptian employment. Arábi, Sir Auckland Colvin wrote (February 27), warned him that "he was like a man trying to balance himself on a plank." Every effort was made to keep the army in a good humour. Fresh battalions were raised. The pay of the officers and men was increased without reference to the sufficiency of the revenue to meet the fresh expenditure thus incurred. Hundreds of officers were promoted. The Khedive pointed out that "the law required the previous examination of officers under the rank of full Colonel," but Arábi was ready with an explanation. The officers, he said, "were of such well-known capacity that examination was unnecessary. Moreover"—and this was perhaps more to the point—"they refused to be examined, and were supported in their refusal by the rest of the army." The Khedive was obliged to yield. Clearly, as Sir Charles Cookson wrote, "all the pretended aspirations for legality and constitutional liberty had ended in substituting

[1] See Appendix to this chapter.

the indisputable will of the army for all lawful authority."

In the provinces, complete disorganisation prevailed. The Moudirs had lost all authority. At Mansourah and elsewhere, Mr. Rowsell, the English administrator of the State Domains, found that "all power was paralysed." In the neighbourhood of Zagazig, the British Vice - Consul reported, "armed bands continue to attack and pillage villages." An active trade was carried on in fire-arms. At Damietta, the black soldiers of Abdul-Al's regiment robbed and ill-treated the inhabitants with impunity. An unwise attempt was made by the Government to deprive the Bedouins of the privileges which they had enjoyed since the days of Mehemet Ali, but the heads of the various tribes met on April 8, and declared that they would allow no interference in their affairs. The banks would no longer lend large sums of money ; petty usurers asked as much as 6 per cent monthly interest on small loans. Land was everywhere losing in value. Sir Edward Malet quoted one example of land, bought a few months previously for £60, being sold at £28 an acre. An officer of the army told the peasants at Zagazig that the acres belong-ing to their landlords "were theirs by right." In a word, all the usual symptoms of revolution were prevalent in Egypt. The moderate men became alarmed. "The disorganised and uneasy state of the provinces," Sir Charles Cookson wrote, "has caused many of the Notables and others who have a stake in the country to draw back from the hastily formed alliance with the military party, and seek for other means of escaping from its domination."

It is now time to return to the history of diplo-matic action. The Porte protested against the Joint Note. The answer of the four Powers

(Russia, Austria, Germany, and Italy) was to the effect that they "desired the maintenance of the *status quo* in Egypt on the basis of the European arrangements and of the Sultan's Firmans, and that they were of opinion that this *status quo* could not be modified except by an understanding between the Great Powers and the Suzerain Power." This reply did not answer the expectations of the Sultan. He was irritated by the use of the word "Suzerain" instead of "Sovereign."[1] Moreover, his design of acquiring a more absolute control over Egyptian affairs was in no way advanced by the opinion expressed by the Powers that any change in the Egyptian *status quo* was a matter of general European interest.

The protest of the Porte, however, stimulated the British and French Governments to place themselves in communication with the other Powers. The British Government took the initiative. The French Government were invited to join Her Majesty's Government in addressing the Powers. M. de Freycinet agreed "with the reservation that it be well understood that the French Government reserve their adhesion to any military intervention in Egypt, and that they will examine that question when the necessity for any intervention shall have arisen." Accordingly, on February 11, a Circular was addressed by the British and French Governments to the Cabinets of Berlin, Vienna, Rome, and St. Petersburg, asking them whether they would be prepared to enter into an exchange of views on the affairs of Egypt. "The

---

[1] The Sultan is Suzerain of Bulgaria. Article 1 of the Berlin Treaty says : "Bulgaria is constituted an autonomous and tributary Principality under the Suzerainty of His Imperial Majesty the Sultan." In so far as Egypt is concerned, the word "Sovereign" is technically more correct. The Firman of 1841 granted to Mehemet Ali uses the expression "Ma connaissance Souveraine." The Sultan cannot depose the Prince of Bulgaria. Technically speaking, he can depose the Khedive, and, in fact, in 1879 he deposed Ismail Pasha.

Governments of England and France," it was said, "do not consider that a case for discussing the expediency of an intervention has at present arisen. . . . But, should the case arise, they would wish that any such eventual intervention should represent the united action and authority of Europe. In that event, it would also, in their opinion, be right that the Sultan should be a party to any proceeding or discussion that might ensue."

The proposal to treat Egyptian affairs as an international, rather than as an exclusively Anglo-French question, was well received. All the Powers expressed their willingness to enter into an exchange of views. No progress had, however, so far been made as to the nature of the views which were to be exchanged. Until the British and French Governments could agree as to the proposals they were to submit to the other Powers, it was hopeless to expect any general agreement.

Both Governments were, however, daily becoming more convinced that some action was necessary. "The Egyptian question," M. de Freycinet said to Lord Lyons (April 3), "was like a bill of exchange. The exact day at which the bill would be presented for payment was not known, but it was quite certain that the presentation would not be long delayed, and it would be only prudent to provide means of meeting the liability before the constable was upon us." The remedy he proposed was to depose the Khedive, and to substitute Halim Pasha in his place. The authority of the Sultan would, without doubt, have to be brought into play, but M. de Freycinet thought that "the great object was to ward off a military intervention of whatever kind it might be, and he would rather the Sultan should depose twenty Khedives than send one soldier to Egypt." Lord Granville rejected this proposal. He did not see that it would do any good, and, moreover, he pointed out "that after the declarations of support so recently given to the Khedive, in the name of the British and French Governments, it would be an act questionable in point of good faith if we were now not only to abandon him, but to combine for his removal without any new or more apparent cause than can at present be shown to exist."

The Khedive also found a warm defender in Sir Edward Malet, who expressed himself in the following terms: "When I hear him (the Khedive) abused for lack of energy and capacity, I doubt whether there be many men who would have been able to extricate themselves from the difficulties in which he has been involved." In the place of so drastic a remedy as the deposition of the Khedive, Lord Granville put forward a characteristic proposal of his own. The idea of sending special Commissioners to report on the situation in Egypt appears, during a considerable period, to have presented some strong attractions to the British Government. Lord Granville now fell back on a proposal of this sort. He suggested to the French Government that "the British and French Representatives at Cairo might each for the moment be advantageously supported by having at their side an adviser possessed of the necessary technical experience, who had been in the habit of considering economical reforms, and to whom they might have recourse for an independent and impartial opinion upon any points which seemed to them doubtful or complicated." Lord Granville wished this proposal to be considered by the French Government, but he "had no wish to press the suggestion if M. de Freycinet saw decided objections to it." M. de Freycinet saw some obvious objections to the proposal; amongst others, it would, he thought, "be difficult to prevent the

Controllers from supposing that it was with a view to controlling them that the agents were to be furnished with special Financial Advisers. They would, in fact, suppose that they would sink from the position of 'Contrôleurs' into that of 'Contrôlés.'" This proposal was, therefore, allowed to drop. A more strange idea than that of sending two gentlemen, "who had been in the habit of considering economical reforms," in order to control a mutinous army certainly never entered into the head of a responsible statesman.[1]

Whilst these barren diplomatic negotiations were going on in Europe, another incident occurred in Cairo of a nature to precipitate the crisis, which had now become inevitable. A large number of Egyptian officers had, as has been already mentioned, been promoted. This caused great discontent amongst the Turkish and Circassian officers who had been passed over. Arábi and his colleagues feared their resentment. A story was, therefore, got up that the leaders of the military and nationalist party were to be murdered. On April 12, nineteen officers and soldiers were arrested on a charge of conspiracy to murder Arábi. By April 22, as many as forty-eight persons had been arrested. Amongst these, was Osman Pasha Rifki, the late Minister of War. They were tried by a Court-martial, whose proceedings were secret. They were undefended by counsel. Forty officers, including Osman Pasha Rifki, were condemned to exile for life to the farthest limits of the Soudan.

Arábi's account of this affair is given in a document entitled " Instructions to my Counsel," which was subsequently published. " A Mameluke slave

---

[1] This proposal, though in a somewhat different form, appears to have emanated from Mr. Wilfrid Blunt. On March 20, 1882, he wrote to Lord Granville suggesting that "something in the nature of a commission of inquiry" should be sent to Egypt.—*Secret History, etc.*, p. 232.

of the Khedive's," he said, "and a Circassian, made
a plot to administer arsenic to Abdul-Al Pasha at
the Koubbeh school. The Circassian succeeded
in putting some of the poison into the Pasha's
milk, which he took nightly, but fortunately the
servant found it out in time to save his life. . . .
This plan having failed, another was set on foot
to get rid of me. A party of Circassians agreed
together to kill me as well as every native Egyptian
holding high appointments." There does not,
however, appear to have been a shadow of trustworthy evidence to show that the charge of conspiracy was true. The verdict of the Court-martial
is a wild rambling document, bearing the character
of a political manifesto rather than that of a judicial
decision. Like most ignorant men, Arábi was very
suspicious. The conspiracy to murder him merely
existed in his own imagination.

The Khedive was now placed in a position of
great difficulty. The sentence of the Court-
martial was manifestly unjust, but it was questionable whether he would be able to resist the pressure
brought to bear on him by his Ministers, who were,
of course, in favour of its being confirmed. The
Porte interfered. Osman Pasha Rifki bore the
title of Ferik, or General, which was conferred by
the Sultan and could only be taken away by His
Imperial Majesty. The Sultan, therefore, desired
that the matter should be referred to him. The
Khedive answered that he would comply with this
request. By doing so, he threw himself into the
arms of the Porte, and assumed an attitude of
direct hostility to his Ministers, but he explained
to Sir Edward Malet (May 6) that he thought
it better that Egypt should lose some of its
privileges at the hands of the Porte, and that
proper authority should be re-established, rather
than that the existing misgovernment should

continue. The Ministers were much incensed. The President of the Council told Sir Edward Malet "that if the Porte should send an order to cancel the sentence of the Court-martial on the Circassian prisoners, the order would not be obeyed, and that if the Porte sent Commissioners, they would not be allowed to land, but would be repulsed by force, if necessary."

The defiant attitude adopted by the Egyptian Ministers towards the Porte was, without doubt, in a measure due to the belief that, in resisting Turkish interference, they could count on French support. As a matter of fact, directly it was suggested that, by reason of Osman Pasha Rifki's rank, Turkish interference was necessary, M. de Freycinet stated that "he was strongly of opinion that the Khedive should himself grant the pardon immediately by virtue of his own prerogative without waiting for action on the part of the Porte." Lord Granville agreed. Identic instructions to advise the Khedive in this sense were, therefore, sent to the British and French representatives at Cairo. The Khedive acted on this advice. On May 9, he signed a Decree commuting the sentence of the Court-martial on the forty officers into exile from Egypt, but not to the Soudan. The commutation of this sentence widened the breach between the Khedive and his Ministers. On May 18, Sir Edward Malet reported that "relations had been broken off between the Khedive and his Ministers," and that "the situation had become most serious." The representatives of the great Powers, with unconscious humour, requested the President of the Council "to describe the situation." The latter replied that, as the Khedive and his Ministers could not agree, the Chamber had been convoked without the authority of the Khedive having been requested. "The complaint against His Highness was that he had acted in a way to diminish the autonomy of Egypt, and on many occasions without consulting his Ministers." There appears to be little doubt that the intention of the military party at this time was to depose the Khedive, to exile the family of Mehemet Ali, and to appoint Mahmoud Pasha Sami Governor-General by the national will.

By this time, the civil elements in the national movement had again become alive to the folly of their conduct in allying themselves with the mutineers. Sultan Pasha, the President of the Chamber, told Sir Edward Malet that "in overthrowing Chérif Pasha the Chamber had acted under pressure from Arábi, and that the very deputies who had then insisted on the course taken, finding that they had been deceived, were now anxious to overthrow the Ministry." On May 13, Sir Edward Malet wrote: "The President of the Chamber and the deputies ostensibly take the part of the Khedive, but they have requested His Highness to pardon and to be reconciled with his Ministers. The Khedive has refused. His Highness remains firm, and will not be reconciled to a Ministry which has defied him openly, threatened himself and his family, and, by the convocation of the Chamber without his sanction, has violated the law. At Cairo, there is considerable uneasiness, and many persons are leaving."

The President of the Council then tendered his resignation to the Khedive. The British and French Consuls-General proposed that Mustapha Pasha Fehmi should be appointed President. "We agree," Sir Edward Malet said, "to the nomination of any one, except Arábi Pasha." The leaders of the military party had stated that, if the Ministry were changed, they would not be responsible for the maintenance of order. The British and French Governments, however, would not accept this denial of responsibility. Their representatives in Cairo were authorised "to send for Arábi and inform him that if there is a disturbance of order, he will find Europe and Turkey, as well as England and France, against him, and will be held responsible."

When Mustapha Pasha Fehmi was offered the Presidency of the Council, he declined to accept the post. The Ministers also said that "they would only resign if the Chamber of Notables desired it." The President of the Chamber "declared that it would be impossible to change the Ministry so long as the military power continued to be vested in Arábi Pasha." Under these circumstances, the British and French Consuls - General informed the Khedive that "personal questions must be set aside." As His Highness was unable to form a new Ministry, he was "requested to enter into relations with the present one."

It was by this time evident that some decisive intervention in Egypt was inevitable, but the question of whether that intervention should be Turkish or Anglo-French still remained undecided. On May 21, however, M. de Freycinet took a great step in advance. He recognised the possibility of Turkish armed intervention. The following proposals were submitted to the British Government :—

1. An Anglo-French squadron was to be sent to Alexandria.

2. The British and French Governments were to "request the Porte to abstain for the present from all intervention or interference in Egypt."

3. The Cabinets of Germany, Austria, Russia, and Italy were to be informed of the despatch of

an Anglo-French squadron to Alexandria, and they were to be asked to send to their representatives at Constantinople similar instructions to those sent to the British and French Ambassadors.

4. The French Government agreed to abandon the idea of deposing the Khedive, "a plan which, if adopted in time, might, in their opinion, have prevented serious complications."

5. As regards the important question of Turkish intervention, M. de Freycinet expressed himself in the following terms: "The French Government continue to be opposed to Turkish intervention, but they would not regard as intervention a case in which Turkish forces were summoned to Egypt by England and France, and operated there under English and French control, for an object, and on conditions which France and England should have themselves defined. If, after the arrival of their ships at Alexandria, the French and English Governments should consider it advisable that troops should be landed, they should have recourse neither to English nor to French troops, but should call for Turkish troops, on the conditions above specified."

6. The Consuls-General were to be instructed "to recognise as legal no other authority than that of Tewfik Pasha, and not to enter into relations with any other *de facto* Government, except for the purpose of securing the safety of their countrymen."

Lord Granville at once acceded to these proposals. He thought, however, that in requesting the Sultan to abstain for the present from all interference in Egypt, it would be "desirable to intimate in guarded language that it was not improbable that further propositions might be made hereafter to the Porte." Moreover, Lord Granville suggested "in view of the very large

force which it is proposed should be despatched
to Alexandria by England and France, that it
might be as well, if not inconsistent with the
other objects which M. de Freycinet has in view,
that the other Powers, including Turkey, should
be invited to have their flags represented." In
other words, the British Government wished for
Turkish executive action under international
sanction. Both the Turkish action and the
international sanction were, on the other hand,
distasteful to the French. M. de Freycinet,
however, agreed to Lord Granville's first proposal
so far as to instruct the French Ambassador at
Constantinople that he might "hint to the Sultan,
in very moderate terms, that it was not improbable
that further proposals might be made to the Porte
hereafter." As regards the international sanction,
M. de Freycinet would make no concession. "I
am not of opinion," he said, "that we should at
present invite the other Powers to send ships by
the side of ours. It is not, in my judgment, for
our own interest that we should in this way take
an initiative which would deprive the Anglo-
French action of the directive character, which
Europe herself assigns to it, and appears desirous to
leave to it in Egypt." When M. de Freycinet's
reply was communicated to Lord Granville, he
"told the French Ambassador that Mr. Gladstone
agreed with him in regretting that the other
Powers had not been invited to co-operate. Her
Majesty's Government thought this a mistake, but
as the French Government had gone so far to
meet the views of Her Majesty's Government,
they have concurred in the course taken."

The weak part of this scheme was that the
intention to invite Turkish co-operation was not
publicly announced. Sir Edward Malet at once
saw the danger. On May 14, he telegraphed to

Lord Granville : "Knowing the feeling here (*i.e.* at Cairo) I fear that if the Sultan's implied co-operation is not secured and made known, and if he does not give his countenance at the beginning to the action of the Powers, there is a risk that the Chamber and the army may again coalesce and offer resistance, which would otherwise, I think, be impossible." The Khedive was no less anxious to obtain the moral support of the Sultan. On May 20, he asked Sir Edward Malet "to beg the English Government to induce the Porte to send him a telegram approving of his entering into negotiations with us for the restoration of his authority, and the maintenance of the *status quo*. He wished for it as a lever to act on the deputies, and dissipate the idea, which was then taking root with them and the military, that the Sultan opposed the action of the Powers." A frank explanation of the intentions of the Powers might perhaps, even at this late hour, have ensured the cordial co-operation of the Sultan. As it was, he was irritated by the action taken by the British and French Governments, more especially by the despatch of an Anglo-French squadron to Alexandria. The Turkish Ambassadors at Paris and London were instructed to protest. The despatch of the squadron also gave offence to the other Powers, who thought that they should have been previously consulted on the subject, and, therefore, declined to join in the Anglo-French recommendation to the Sultan that he should abstain from all interference in Egypt.

The dislike of the French Government to Turkish intervention was, however, such as to render it impossible to obtain the full advantage which might otherwise possibly have been derived from the co-operation of the Sultan. On May 19, M. de Freycinet told Lord Lyons that "there were very

strong objections to speaking openly at that moment
either at Constantinople or elsewhere of the agreement to call in Turkish troops, in case military intervention in Egypt should be unavoidable." On
May 22, therefore, Lord Granville telegraphed to
Sir Edward Malet : "The French Government are
nervous lest the conditional consent they have
given to Turkish intervention may be publicly
announced at Cairo or Constantinople, and produce
an explosion of public feeling at Paris." Under
these circumstances, all that could be done was to
send a somewhat vague explanatory telegram to
the British and French representatives at Berlin,
Rome, St. Petersburg, Vienna, and Constantinople.
"It was never proposed," Lord Granville said, "to
land troops or to resort to a military occupation of
the country. Her Majesty's Government intend,
when once calm has been restored, and the future
secured, to leave Egypt to herself, and to recall
their squadron. If, contrary to their expectations,
a pacific solution cannot be obtained, they will
concert with the Powers and with Turkey on the
measures, which shall have appeared to them and
to the French Government to be the best." At
the same time (May 23), Lord Dufferin told the
Minister for Foreign Affairs at Constantinople that
if "instead of helping to terminate the crisis in the
desired manner, the Porte complicates the situation
by falsifying facts and running counter to our
advice, we shall double the number of our ships
at Alexandria, and their stay will be indefinitely
prolonged." Lord Dufferin "had already hinted
to Said Pasha confidentially that if the Ottoman
Government acted in a loyal and reasonable
manner, the first-fruits of their moderation might be
the countermanding of the additional ships of war
which were under orders to join the squadron."

In the meanwhile (May 19), the British and

French Consuls-General had been instructed "to advise the Khedive to take advantage of a favourable moment, such, for instance, as the arrival of the fleets, to dismiss the present Ministry and to form a new Cabinet under Chérif Pasha, or any other person inspiring the same confidence." Sir Edward Malet replied (May 20) that he and M. Sienkiewicz had considered these instructions. "Until the supremacy of the military party is broken," he added, "the Khedive is powerless to form a new Ministry. No one will accept the task until this is effected." He, therefore, proposed to enter into negotiations with Arábi and his three principal coadjutors with a view to inducing them to leave the country. Sultan Pasha, the President of the Chamber of Deputies, consented to act as intermediary. He questioned the Consuls-General as to "whether there was any infringement of the Porte's sovereign rights in the action of England and France." Sir Edward Malet replied that "the intention of the two Governments was to respect those rights and in no way to infringe them." The negotiation failed. Arábi positively refused "either to retire from his position or from the country." An Egyptian Colonel said, in the presence of a member of the French Consular service, that "the officers would hew Arábi in pieces if he deserted them." A Cabinet Council was held at which it was decided that the Government should reply "to any official demands made upon them that they did not admit the right of the English and French Governments to interfere, and that they recognised no ultimate authority but that of the Sultan." At the same time, the President of the Chamber informed the French Consul-General that "he could no longer rely upon the deputies, on account of the feeling against the intervention of the two Powers which was gaining ground." It was, in

fact, clear that the fears which Sir Edward Malet
had expressed on May 14 had been realised.   The
reluctance of the French Government to appeal to
the authority of the Sultan had cast suspicion on
the intentions of the Western Powers, and had
again united the civil and military elements of the
Egyptian movement.   More than this, the jealousy
shown by the French of Turkish intervention had
resulted in strengthening the unnatural alliance
between Arábi and the Sultan.   Essad Effendi, a
confidential agent of the Sultan, arrived at Cairo.
It was certain that the defiant attitude adopted by
the Egyptian Ministers was in a great measure due
to the messages brought by this individual from
Constantinople.

Meanwhile, in anticipation of the failure of the
negotiations with Arábi, Sir Edward Malet and
M. Sienkiewicz had, on May 21, suggested to their
respective Governments that they should be
authorised to make an official demand that Arábi
and his principal coadjutors should leave the
country.   When, however, they saw the decided
attitude taken up by the leaders of the military
party, they hesitated to adopt so strong a measure
on their own authority.   On May 23, Sir Edward
Malet telegraphed to Lord Granville in the
following terms: "M. Sienkiewicz and I hesitate
to make an official demand to the Ministers, which
we know beforehand will be met with refusal, until
we are in a position to declare what would be the
consequences of such a refusal, and I accordingly
venture to beg Your Lordship to favour me with
further instructions.   The present situation has
been brought about by the Ministers and the
people persisting in a belief that the two Powers
will not despatch troops, and that the opposition of
France renders a Turkish intervention impossible.
In the meanwhile, military preparations are being

carried on, and a fanatical feeling against foreigners is sedulously fostered.   I am still of opinion that if the Sultan declares himself at once, and if it be known that troops are ready to be despatched, we may succeed without the necessity for landing them." On receipt of this message, Lord Granville telegraphed (May 24) to Lord Lyons in the following terms : " Tell M. de Freycinet that the news from Cairo is disquieting.   Time is all important. Propose to him that the two Governments should telegraph a Circular to the Powers, requesting them to join in asking the Sultan to have troops ready to send to Egypt under strict conditions."

No immediate answer was sent to Sir Edward Malet's telegram, but the two Governments authorised their Consuls-General to take whatever steps they considered possible to ensure the departure from Egypt of Arábi and his principal partisans, and the nomination of Chérif Pasha to be President of the Council.

When this telegram reached Cairo, a document was being circulated amongst the officers and soldiers of the army in which it was stated that the British and French Governments insisted on the following points : All the Ministers were to be exiled ; all the officers on the Army List were to leave Egypt ; the entire army was to be disbanded ; Egypt was to be occupied by foreign troops ; the Chamber was to be dissolved.   " The French representative and I," Sir Edward Malet telegraphed on May 25, " persuaded that the situation would become still further complicated, and even dangerous to the lives of foreigners, if these conditions were believed to be true ones, determined upon the official step from which we had hitherto shrunk."   They handed an official Note to the President of the Council, in which the following demands were set forth :—

" 1. The temporary retirement from Egypt of Arábi Pasha, with the maintenance of his rank and pay. 2. The retirement into the interior of Egypt of Ali Pasha Fehmi and Abdul-Al Pasha, who will also retain their rank and pay. 3. The resignation of the present Ministry."

The Note added that "the intervention of the two Powers, being divested of all character of vengeance and reprisal, they will use their good offices to obtain from the Khedive a general amnesty, and will watch over its strict observance."

In consequence of the delivery of this Note, the Ministers resigned on May 26. At the same time, they addressed a letter to the Khedive stating that as His Highness had accepted the conditions proposed by the two Powers, he had acquiesced in foreign intervention in contradiction to the terms of the Firmans. The Khedive replied that he accepted the resignation of the Ministry because it was the will of the nation, and that, as regards the rest, it was a matter between him and the Sultan, whose rights he would always respect.

For a moment, there appeared some hope that the crisis was over. Sir Edward Malet reported (May 27) that the Ministers "perceived that, were they to reject the conditions which the Khedive had accepted, they would be in overt, instead of covert rebellion, a position from which they shrank. The retirement of the Ministry was, therefore, due to the decisive and firm attitude assumed by His Highness." The French Government were elated. They now answered the proposal made by Lord Granville on May 24, to the effect that the Powers should be addressed with a view to Turkish troops being held in readiness to proceed to Egypt. M. Tissot, the French representative in London, wrote to Lord Granville in the following terms: "M. de Freycinet telegraphs to me that the Council of

Ministers, to whom he has submitted your proposal, have been unanimous in thinking that nothing in the present situation of affairs would justify an appeal to Turkish troops. A Note was delivered by our Consuls-General on the 25th instant; the Ministry has just tendered its resignation, the elements of resistance are manifestly in process of disorganisation; there is, therefore, every motive for awaiting the course of events. It appears impossible to M. de Freycinet that you should not be struck with the justice of these considerations, and that, taking into account the recent events which have taken place at Cairo, you should not, yourself, my dear Lord, recognise the uselessness of the step which you at first proposed to him."

This elation was short-lived. On May 27, Sir Edward Malet telegraphed that Chérif Pasha had been asked to form a Ministry, but had refused to do so, "on the ground that no Government was possible so long as the military chiefs remained in the country." The Khedive, Sir Edward Malet added, "will now endeavour to form another Ministry, although he has faint hope of being able to get an efficient one, if he can form one at all." Sir Edward Malet urged that the Sultan should be called upon to exercise his authority, and especially that he should despatch an officer to Egypt with as little delay as possible. The Khedive also thought that "a Turkish Commissioner could make himself heard and restore tranquillity." Toulba Pasha, one of Arábi's principal associates, had an interview with the Khedive, at which "he stated that the army absolutely rejected the Joint Note and awaited the decision of the Porte, which was the only authority they recognised." There was, in fact, little doubt that the Ministers were acting in collusion with the Porte.

On May 28, the Grand Vizier telegraphed to

the Khedive stating that a Turkish Commissioner would be sent if an official request to that effect were made. The Khedive asked the British and French Consuls-General what he was to do. His position was, indeed, one of the utmost difficulty. The officers of the regiments and of the Police force stationed at Alexandria had telegraphed to him on the previous day (May 27) that "they would not accept the resignation of Arábi Pasha, and that they allowed twelve hours to His Highness to consider, after which delay they would no longer be responsible for public tranquillity." Moreover, Sultan Pasha and other deputies told the Khedive in the presence of the British and French Consuls-General, that "unless he agreed to reinstate Arábi as Minister of War, his life was not safe." Nevertheless, Sir Edward Malet reported, "His Highness refused." As regards the request for a Turkish Commissioner, Sir Edward Malet telegraphed: "I stated that, if His Highness's life were in danger, I could not give any advice against the step he proposed, if it appeared to be the only chance of safety. M. Sienkiewicz limited himself to saying 'that he would request instructions from the French Government,' and we left without giving any further answer, although the Khedive urged the necessity of immediately making some reply to the Grand Vizier." Well might Sir Edward Malet say: "The position of the Khedive is a most painful one. Threatened with death, prevented by us from going to Alexandria while there was yet time,[1] and not allowed to appeal to the only quarter from which effectual assistance can come, he must feel bitterly the apparent result at present of following our

[1] The Khedive had, a short while previously, wished to go to Alexandria, but he was urged by the British and French Governments to remain at Cairo.

advice and relying upon our support." The
necessity for action was, indeed, so apparent that
Lord Granville, without waiting to consult the
French Government, telegraphed both to Lord
Dufferin at Constantinople and to the Ambassadors
at the other courts of Europe that "Her Majesty's
Government considered it most desirable that no
time should be lost by the Sultan, who should send
an order to support the Khedive, to reject the
accusation of the fallen Ministry with regard to
His Highness, and to order the three military
chiefs, and perhaps also the ex-President of the
Council, to come and explain their conduct at
Constantinople." M. de Freycinet, when he was
informed of what had been done, sent similar
instructions to the French representatives abroad,
but he evidently did so with reluctance.

In the meanwhile, Cairo and Egypt generally
remained in the hands of the military party. On
May 29, Admiral Sir Beauchamp Seymour (afterwards Lord Alcester), who commanded the British
fleet, which had by this time arrived at Alexandria, telegraphed: "Alexandria is apparently controlled this morning by the military party." It
was clear that, in the absence of any effective help
from without, the Khedive would be obliged to
yield to the wishes of the mutinous army. On
May 28, Sir Edward Malet telegraphed to Lord
Granville in the following terms: "This afternoon,
the Chiefs of religion, including the Patriarch, and
the Chief Rabbi, all the deputies, Ulema and others,
waited on the Khedive, and asked him to reinstate
Arábi as Minister of War. He refused; but they
besought him, saying that, though he might be
ready to sacrifice his own life, he ought not to
sacrifice theirs, and that Arábi had threatened them
all with death if they did not obtain his consent.
The Colonel of the Khedive's Guard stated that

the guard of the Palace had been doubled, that
orders had been given to them to prevent his
leaving the Palace for his usual drive, and to fire
if he attempted to force his way. Under these
circumstances, the Khedive yielded, not to save
himself, but to preserve the town from bloodshed."
At the same time, the Khedive made a formal
demand to the Sultan that a Commissioner should
be sent to Egypt.

The situation at the end of May was, therefore,
as follows : An attempt had been made to free the
Khedive from the dictatorship of the military party.
In spite of the support accorded by the British and
French Governments, the attempt had completely
failed. Arábi and his associates had again
triumphed. British diplomacy, although somewhat
more free in action than previous to the accession
to power of M. de Freycinet, was still hampered
by its association with France. No frank appeal
could be made to the Sultan that he should exercise
his authority, although both Lord Granville and Sir
Edward Malet saw that in such an appeal lay the
only chance of avoiding military intervention of
some sort. M. de Freycinet was almost as much
opposed as his predecessor to Turkish intervention.
The result of all this vacillation was that the policy
of England and France was suspected on all sides,
— by the Sultan, who was greatly irritated ; by the
other Powers ; and by the Egyptians. The Khedive,
in the meanwhile, had so far found that Anglo-
French support was a weak reed on which to lean
in time of necessity.

The end, however, was not far off. It was
daily becoming more clear that Arábi could be
suppressed by nothing but force. If no one else
would use the requisite force, the task would
necessarily devolve on England.

APPENDIX

Note on the relations between Mr. Gladstone and Mr. Wilfrid Blunt.

THE overestimate of Mr. Wilfrid Blunt's influence was in no small degree due to the fact that he was known to be in communication with Mr. Gladstone. As Mr. Blunt in his *Secret History* has narrated at length his dealings with Mr. Gladstone, who, he says (p. 369), was, in his opinion, "capable of any treachery and any crime," I think that, in justice to the memory of that distinguished statesman, I should furnish whatever evidence is in my possession as to the manner in which he regarded the question of his relations with Mr. Blunt. At a later period of Egyptian history (October 23, 1883), Lord Granville wrote to me privately, forwarding a letter addressed by Mr. Blunt to Sir Edward Hamilton, Mr. Gladstone's Private Secretary, with the following remarks:

Gladstone sent me this letter, condemning Blunt, but suggesting that I might send it on to you.

I declined, and expressed a hope that Hamilton would not answer him at all; that there was no knowing what use he might make of the fact of his being in correspondence with any one in Downing Street.

But as Gladstone returns to the charge, I forward it to you privately.

He writes:

"There are certain parts of Blunt's letter which, indifferently as I think of him, I certainly should have wished Baring to see. My rule has always been to look in the declarations of even the extremest opponents for anything which either may have some small percentage of truth in it, or ought not to be let pass without contradiction (private in this case) I know not how it is that he writes to Hamilton, but you see it is personal and *tutoyant*, not official."

Gladstone's principle is plausible, but I fancy it often gets him into unnecessary difficulties.

You have seen Blunt, and heard all he had to say.

I replied on November 5, in the following terms:

I would just as soon that Mr. Blunt was not in correspondence with any one connected with the Government; if it were known, it might be misinterpreted.

The principle of not neglecting criticisms which come from an opponent is a very sound one, and I always endeavour to follow it.   But, in this case, we may have the advantage of knowing what Blunt has to say without corresponding with him. He will not hide his light under a bushel.   You may feel sure that before long it will burn brightly in the pages of some magazine.

I also, for Mr. Gladstone's information, replied at some length to Mr. Blunt's criticisms, but neither his letter, nor my reply, are of sufficient importance or interest to warrant their reproduction.

CHAPTER XVI

THE BOMBARDMENT OF ALEXANDRIA

MAY–JULY 1882

State of the country—Vacillation of the Porte—A Conference proposed—Dervish Pasha and Essad Effendi sent to Egypt—The Alexandria massacres—Failure of Dervish Pasha's Mission—Panic in Egypt—The Conference meets—The Ragheb Ministry—The British Admiral demands that the construction of batteries at Alexandria shall cease—The French decline to co-operate—The bombardment of Alexandria—The town abandoned and burnt.

ARÁBI's reinstatement was "looked upon by the natives as a sign that the Christians were going to be expelled from Egypt, that they were to recover the land bought by Europeans or mortgaged to them, and that the National Debt would be cancelled." Great numbers of Christians left the interior. The British residents at Alexandria called upon their Government to provide means for the protection of their lives. "Every day's delay," Sir Charles Cookson telegraphed on May 30, "increases the dangerous temper of the soldiery, and their growing defiance of discipline." The officers of the army were "obtaining by threats signatures to a petition praying for the deposition of the Khedive." The President of the Chamber requested the deputies to go to their homes "in order to save them from being compelled to sign the petition." Official business, except at the Ministry of War, was at a standstill. The whole country was in a state of panic. Sir Edward Malet warned the

British Government (May 31) that "a collision might at any moment occur between the Moslems and the Christians."

It was abundantly clear by this time that the question of protecting European financial interests in Egypt had fallen completely into the background. It was also clear that the national movement was entirely under the control of the military party. Foreign intervention of some sort had become necessary.

For years past, the Ottoman Government had been longing to regain their hold over Egypt. The chanceries of Europe were filled with notes and protests embodying the querulous complaints made by the Porte against the intervention of the European Powers in Egyptian affairs, and against the insufficient recognition accorded to the sovereign rights of the Sultan. The Turkish opportunity had at last come. The force of circumstances had fought in favour of Turkish pretensions. The Khedive and the two Western Powers had endeavoured to settle the affairs of Egypt independently of the Sultan. They had signally failed in the attempt. All the Powers of Europe, with the exception of France, were in favour of employing the authority of the Sultan as the executive arm by which order should be restored in Egypt. Even French opposition was much modified. The *République Française*, indeed, which was inspired by M. Gambetta, strongly opposed any idea of Turkish intervention. "Il faut maintenir," it said on May 31, "l'indépendance de l'Égypte, en interdire l'approche aux Commissaires aussi bien qu'aux troupes du Sultan." But M. Gambetta was no longer in office. "Je ne m'expliquerai point à la tribune," M. de Freycinet said in the French Chamber on June 1, "sur les divers moyens auxquels on pourrait être conduit, mais il y a un moyen que j'exclus;

ce moyen c'est une intervention militaire Française en Égypte." This declaration, which produced an explosion of indignation from M. Gambetta, was almost tantamount to publicly admitting the possibility of Turkish intervention.

It is one of the peculiarities of the vacillating and tortuous policy invariably pursued by the Porte that Turkish statesmen are rarely able to seize the favourable moment for action in support of their most cherished views. The Khedive had asked for the despatch of a Turkish Commissioner to Egypt. The British and French Governments viewed the proposal more or less favourably. It might reasonably have been supposed that the Sultan would seize with avidity the opportunity for asserting his sovereign rights which was thus afforded him. He did nothing of the kind. He was inclined to show his resentment at the way in which he had been enjoined not to intervene at the commencement of the Egyptian troubles, by refusing to act at the instance of England and France when they were favourably disposed towards his intervention. A suggestion was ostentatiously promulgated that the withdrawal of the allied fleet from Alexandria must be a preliminary condition to the despatch of a Turkish Commissioner. The Sultan had yet to learn that his assistance, though desirable, was not indispensable.

In the meanwhile, M. de Freycinet, under the pressure of circumstances, had in some degree overcome his objections to international action. On May 30, he telegraphed to M. Tissot that " there could no longer be any reasonable hope of a pacific solution through the moral influence of the French and English squadrons, and the good offices of the two agents at Cairo." He therefore proposed to Lord Granville that a Conference should be summoned. Lord Granville at once intimated his

concurrence in this proposal, which was well received
by the other Powers.   Prince Bismarck thought
the idea of a Conference "a very good expedient
for covering the change of policy on the part of
the French Government in regard to the admissi-
bility of Turkish intervention."   The Sultan was
pressed to join the Conference.   "I expressed my
hope," Lord Granville wrote on June 2, "that
Musurus Pasha would represent to his Government
the expediency of acting in cordial co-operation
with England.   I remarked that if the Sultan were
to make difficulties and raise obstacles, it would be
difficult to find arguments to meet the pressure
that would be put upon us to take immediate and
independent action in consideration of the pressing
nature of the circumstances and engagements under
which we lay."

The idea of assembling a Conference was distasteful to the Sultan, and the proposal was sufficient
to overcome his hesitation about the despatch
of a Turkish Commissioner to Egypt.   Dervish
Pasha left Constantinople for Alexandria on June 4.
The Porte "confidently hoped that the mission of
Dervish Pasha would suffice to restore the normal
situation in Egypt to the general satisfaction,"
and Musurus Pasha was instructed to express to
Lord Granville a hope that the project of the Conference would be abandoned.   He was told in reply
that if it were found that there were good hopes
of a settlement being speedily attained by the un-
assisted efforts of Dervish Pasha, there would be
no objection to the Conference adjourning for a
short time in order that the result of his mission
might be watched.

Any beneficial results, which might possibly
have accrued from the despatch of the Turkish
mission to Egypt, were frustrated by the conditions
under which it was sent.   It would have been

contrary to the traditions and to the existing practice of Turkish diplomacy to have selected one capable Commissioner, in whom confidence might be reposed, and to have traced clear and straightforward instructions for his guidance. Whilst Dervish Pasha was to act on lines friendly to the Khedive and hostile to Arábi, his colleague, Essad Effendi, was to be guided by diametrically opposite principles. He was to hold out the hand of fellowship to the mutineers. Moreover, in order to guard against the possibility of common action on the part of the two Commissioners, each of them was to communicate independently with the Sultan. The end to be obtained by each of the Commissioners was, indeed, identical, though the method of attaining it was more explicitly set forth in Dervish Pasha's instructions than in those of Essad Effendi. The latter was merely told that the principal object he should bear in mind was to " faire échouer les entreprises et intrigues pernicieuses des étrangers." Dervish Pasha, on the other hand, was told that " in order to create a rivalry amongst the Consuls, he was to attach himself to the Consuls of Germany, Austria, and Italy, by pretending to invite them to decisive deliberations, and to promise to take their advice."

Save in respect to this point of principle, the instructions given to each of the two Commissioners differed widely.[1] Dervish Pasha was ordered, if necessary, to arrest Arábi and his principal followers and to send them to Constantinople, to abolish the Chamber of Notables, to curtail the powers of the Khedive, to extend those of the Sultan, and, lastly, to call for troops if necessary.

[1] The instructions to each Commissioner were, of course, secret. But there can be no doubt of the accuracy of the facts here stated in connection with them. See also the testimony of Mr. Wilfrid Blunt, who was probably well-informed on the point under discussion.—*Secret History*, etc., p. 305.

Essad Effendi, on the other hand, was instructed
to thank the "Notables et hommes de marque de
l'Égypte pour le dévouement dont ils ont fait
preuve," and to assure every one that the Sultan
had no intention of curtailing the powers granted
to the Khedive by the Firmans.   "Quant à l'envoi
d'une force armée," it was added, "ce n'est qu'une
invention pernicieuse et malveillante."   It was, in
fact, certain that the Sultan was reluctant to bring
his troops into collision with the population of
Egypt.   He preferred to pose as their defender
against European aggression.   Under these circumstances, it is not surprising that the bewildered
Essad Effendi should, shortly after his arrival at
Cairo, have reported that the policy of Dervish
Pasha was in entire contradiction to the instructions he had himself received.   He asked, but
asked in vain, for some clear indication of what he
was to do.

Dervish Pasha, however, lost no time in acting
on his instructions.   He resolved to assert his
authority.   On June 10, he received a deputation
from the Ulema of Cairo.   "One of them," Sir
Edward Malet reported, " well known as a follower
of Arábi, proceeded to deliver a speech, extolling
the course pursued by the army in having preserved the country from falling into the hands of
infidels.   Upon this, the Commissioner rose from
his seat, and, in forcible language, reminded those
present that he had come to issue orders and not
to listen to preaching.   The offending Alim was
thereupon seized and forced to retire by an
attendant of colossal stature who appears always
at hand."

It was, to say the least, a curious coincidence
that at the moment when it appeared possible
that the rulership of Egypt would slip from the
hands of the military clique, which then exercised

supreme power, an incident should have occurred which showed that without the aid of Arábi and his colleagues public tranquillity could not be preserved. For some while past, the population of Alexandria had shown unusual signs of effervescence. Europeans had been hustled and spat upon in the streets. A Sheikh had been crying aloud in the public thoroughfares, "O Moslems, come and help me to kill the Christians!" On June 9, a Greek was warned by an Egyptian to "take care, as the Arabs were going to kill the Christians either that day or the day following." On the 10th, some low-class Moslems went about the streets calling out that "the last day for the Christians was drawing nigh."[1] On June 11, the storm burst. It is needless to give the details of the riot which took place on that day. It will be sufficient to say that disturbances broke out simultaneously in three places. Some fifty Europeans were slaughtered in cold blood under circumstances of the utmost brutality. Many others, amongst whom was Sir Charles Cookson, the British Consul, were severely wounded and narrowly escaped with their lives. "Whenever a European appeared in sight, the mob cried out 'O Moslems! Kill him! Kill the Christian!'"

Both the Khedive and Arábi have at times been accused of having instigated the Alexandria massacres.[2] So calm and impartial an observer

---

[1] Royle's *Egyptian Campaigns of 1882 to 1885*, vol. i. p. 88.

[2] Mr. Wilfrid Blunt (*Secret History*, pp. 497-534) gives at great length the evidence on which he relies to incriminate the Khedive. After a careful examination of all the facts, I have come to the conclusion that this evidence is altogether valueless. It is unnecessary that I should give my reasons at length.

Lord Randolph Churchill made himself the principal mouthpiece in Parliament of the charges against the Khedive. Papers on the subject were laid before P.rliament (see *Egypt*, No. 4, 1884). They were forwarded to Sir Edward Malet on August 6, 1883, by Lord Granville with the following remarks: "A full examination of the papers and arguments adduced by Lord Randolph Churchill leads to the conclusion

as Sir Edward Malet, however, held that both
accusations were devoid of foundation, and that
the massacres were the natural outcome of the
political effervescence of the time.   There can
be little doubt that this view of the question is
correct.   A considerable moral responsibility, however, rested on Arábi and his colleagues for the
blood which was shed.   For a long time past, they
had done their best to arouse the race hatred and
fanaticism of the cowardly mob at Alexandria.[1]
The natural result ensued.

The effect of the riot was instantaneous.   Sir
Edward Malet reported to Lord Granville, on
June 13, that Dervish Pasha's mission had altogether failed in its object.   The Sultan's Commissioner was obliged to bow to the authority of
Arábi.   He informed the representatives of the
Powers that "under the urgent circumstances of
the case, he would assume joint responsibility with
Arábi Pasha for the execution of the orders of the
Khedive."   Dervish Pasha distributed decorations
alike to the Arábists and to the Khedivial party,
but his influence was gone.   None of the officers
of the army went to see him.   It was only by "a
remnant of politeness" that Arábi answered the
letters which Dervish Pasha addressed to him.

It was about this moment that the Sultan
informed Lord Dufferin that "Arábi Pasha had
made a complete submission, and that the *status
quo* was about to be established."   Musurus Pasha
also told Lord Granville that the Sultan had
conferred on Arábi the Grand Cordon of the

that no *prima facie* evidence (either legal or moral) exists in support of
the charges which have been preferred against His Highness Tewfik
Pasha."

As regards Arábi, Sir Charles Wilson, who watched his trial,
expressed the opinion that "there was no evidence to connect Arábi
with the massacre at Alexandria on June 11."

[1] Abundant evidence in support of this statement was adduced at
Arábi's trial.

Medjidieh, and that Arábi "had expressed his gratitude and had reiterated his assurances of fidelity and devotion to the Sultan." His Majesty thought that there was "no longer occasion for anxiety." The alarm which had prevailed had been due to insubordination on the part of the military, but these acts of submission and the restoration of tranquillity "removed all difficulties and rendered any measures of rigour useless." The extent of Arábi's submission may be gathered from the fact that, on July 5, Arábi "intimated to Dervish Pasha that he had better quit Egypt," and that when, on July 8, he was summoned, through Essad Effendi, to proceed to Constantinople "he refused to comply with the invitation of His Majesty." Then, at last, Lord Dufferin extorted from the unwilling Minister for Foreign Affairs at the Porte the admission that "Arábi had taken the bit in his teeth and that it was evident something must be done."

Manifestly something had to be done, for the whole framework of society in Egypt was on the point of collapsing. By June 17, 14,000 Christians had left the country, and some 6000 more were anxiously awaiting the arrival of ships to take them away. On June 26, ten Greeks and three Jews were murdered by a fanatical mob at Benha. Arábi, following perhaps unconsciously the example of the French Jacobins, proposed to the Council that the property of all Egyptians leaving the country should be confiscated.[1] On June 29, Mr. Cartwright, Sir Edward Malet's *locum tenens*,[2]

---

[1] It is possible that Arábi designedly copied the proceedings of the Jacobins. I have been informed on good authority that at this period he devoted a good deal of attention to the literature of the French Revolution.

[2] Ill-health obliged Sir Edward Malet to leave Egypt at this time. He subsequently came to the conclusion that the sudden illness by which he was prostrated was the result of a plot to poison him.—See his letter in the *Times* of October 12, 1907.

reported to Lord Granville : " The exodus of Europeans and the preparations for flight continue with vigour. . . . It is impossible to conceive the collapse and ruin which have so suddenly overtaken the country. . . . The natives, even the religious Sheikhs, are now raising their voices against the military party, and a large number of respectable Arabs are leaving the country. The departure of Turkish families is taking large proportions."

The effect of the massacre at Alexandria was to quicken the slow pace of European diplomacy. M. de Freycinet thought it "more than ever imperative that the Conference should be constituted without the least delay." On June 13, the British and French Governments instructed their representatives at the various courts of Europe to propose that "the Sultan, as Sovereign, shall, in case of necessity, be jointly invited by the Powers united in Conference to be prepared to lend to the Khedive a sufficient force to enable His Highness to maintain his authority ; the Sultan to be requested to give a positive assurance that these troops should only be used for the maintenance of the *status quo*, and that there should be no interference with the liberties of Egypt secured by the previous Firmans of the Sultan, or with existing European agreements ; the troops not to remain in Egypt for a longer period than a month, except at the request of the Khedive, and with the consent of the Great Powers, or of the Western Powers as representing Europe ; the reasonable expenses of the expedition to be borne by the Egyptian Government." This was quickly followed by a proposal that the Conference should meet immediately " with or without Turkey." The Sultan declined to join the Conference. He thought it unnecessary, as "Dervish Pasha was succeeding in his efforts to fulfil his mission in

Egypt." The result was that, after some diplomatic skirmishing, the Conference met at Constantinople on June 23 without the Porte being represented.

It is unnecessary to dwell at length on the tedious proceedings of the Conference. It was clear, as Lord Salisbury said in the House of Lords on July 24, that the "European concert was rather a phantasm." On the one side, was the British Government, represented at the Conference by one of the most able diplomatists of the day. Lord Granville and Lord Dufferin thoroughly understood what they wanted. They wished for order to be maintained in Egypt, and they were alive to the fact that, without the employment of material force, order could not be maintained. European public opinion had been irritated by the "tortuous and occult devices" of the Sultan. If the Sultan refused to send troops, it would be necessary to "resort to an armed, occupation of Egypt other than through the instrumentality of Turkey." On the other side, were the various Powers of Europe, watchful of their own interests, but unwilling to incur any responsibility. On June 30, Lord Dufferin reported that so far the Conference had "done absolutely nothing," and that, unless something could speedily be settled, "the prolongation of its existence would seem useless." By July 2, the Conference had only got so far as to consider "the object to be attained by the armed Turkish intervention in Egypt," and the united Ambassadors had come to the sage but somewhat impotent conclusion that, if the Porte refused an invitation to send troops, "the Conference reserved the right to express an opinion as to what should be done at the opportune moment."

In the meanwhile, the bewildered ruler, whose battalions it was proposed to use in order to keep the peace, held aloof from the Council Chamber,

being at times willing and at times unwilling to
act. He wished to know what Lord Granville
meant when he referred to "the safe improvement of the internal administration of Egypt."
He was anxious to have some explanations on this
point, for his suspicions had been excited by the
fact that the Conference had been invited to consider how "the prudent development of Egyptian
institutions" might best be effected. "What,"
Lord Dufferin reported, "has excited His Majesty's
mistrust, is evidently the allusion to Parliamentary
Government, which he imagines to be shadowed
forth in the word 'institutions.'"

Eventually, on July 6, the Conference got so
far as to invite the Sultan to send troops under
certain conditions, which were specified in general
terms, and which, in the event of the invitation
being accepted, were to be embodied in a subsequent agreement between the six Powers and
Turkey.

Whilst these discussions were taking place,
matters had been going from bad to worse in
Egypt. On June 26, Mr. Cartwright wrote:
"The exclusive influence of Arábi Pasha is best
shown by the unbroken ascendancy, the intolerable
pretensions, and the threatening attitude of the
army." A mock inquiry was instituted into the
massacres of June 11, but the English member of
the Commission soon withdrew from the proceedings, and the Minister of War told the Khedive's
private secretary that "he would not allow any
Arab to be executed, unless for every Arab, a
European was hung." No one dared to give evidence which might be distasteful to the military
party.

The Austrian and German representatives in
Egypt urged the formation of a Ministry approved
by the military party. Prince Bismarck thought

that Arábi had become a power "avec lequel il fallait compter."

The German and Austrian proposals were not viewed with disfavour in Paris. M. de Freycinet spoke about "the possibility of patching up the Egyptian question by making terms with Arábi," but was at once met with the decisive statement that, in the opinion of the British Government, no

satisfactory or durable arrangement was possible, without the overthrow of Arábi Pasha and the military party in Egypt."

Under the pressure exerted by the Austrian and German Consuls-General, the Khedive, on June 17, nominated Ragheb Pasha, an effete old man, to be President of the Council, with Arábi as his Minister of War. The result was what might have been expected. On June 28, Mr. Cartwright reported to Lord Granville : " Ragheb Pasha meets with great difficulties in his endeavour to control the military element in his Ministry. I hear that His Excellency is greatly disheartened at his want of success, and finds the officers too much occupied with warlike designs and preparations to pay any serious attention to reassuring measures, or to the need of serious steps with a view to the establishment of order and a more normal state of affairs."

For some while past, both British public opinion and the British Government had shown a disposition to break through the diplomatic cobwebs which were hindering all effective action and allowing Arábi to defy Europe. The opportunity for doing so now presented itself. So early as June 3, the Admiralty was informed that batteries were being raised at Alexandria with the intention of using them against the British fleet. The Sultan gave orders that the construction of these batteries should cease, and for the time being his order was obeyed. A month later, the works were recommenced. The garrison of Alexandria was reinforced. Arábi urged upon his colleagues the desirability of a *levée en masse.* On July 5, Mr. Cartwright reported : "At a Council of Ministers held yesterday, Arábi Pasha made a very violent speech against the Sultan. He has, moreover, ordered the officers of the Egyptian army to discontinue all communication with Dervish Pasha, who is to be told that his mission in Egypt is terminated." On July 3, Lord Alcester was instructed to prevent the continuance of work on the fortifications. If not immediately discontinued, he was to " destroy the earthworks and silence the batteries if they opened fire." The French Government were informed of the issue of these instructions and invited to co-operate. The other Powers of Europe were also informed. On July 5, M. de Freycinet told Lord Lyons that "the French Government could not instruct Admiral Conrad to associate himself with the English Admiral in stopping by force the erection of batteries or the placing of guns at Alexandria. The French Government considered that this would be an act of offensive hostility against Egypt, in which they could not take part without violating the constitution, which prohibits their making war without the consent of the Chamber." On July 6, M. de Freycinet, in answer to a question addressed to him by M. Lockroy in the Chamber of Deputies, "repeated emphatically the assurance that the arms of France would not be used without the express consent of the Chamber." On July 6, Lord Alcester sent a note to the commandant of the garrison demanding that the work of fortification and the erection of earthworks should be discontinued. He was informed in reply that no guns had recently been added to the forts, or military preparations made. The truth of this statement was confirmed by Dervish Pasha. On the 9th, however, work on the fortifications recommenced. Guns were mounted on Fort Silsileh. At daybreak on July 10, Lord Alcester gave notice to the Consuls resident at Alexandria that he would "commence action twenty-four hours after, unless the forts on the isthmus and those commanding the entrance to the harbour were surrendered." The different Cabinets of Europe were informed of this step.

The views of the Austrian Government on a matter of this sort are of special importance, on account of the interest possessed by Austria in any step which menaces the integrity of the Ottoman Empire. When Sir Henry Elliot, the British Ambassador at Vienna, informed Count Kalnoky of the measures about to be taken by the British Admiral, "His Excellency replied without hesitation that he thought Her Majesty's Government perfectly right in the step that was being taken, and nothing could be more complete and cordial than the manner in which he declared the action to be perfectly legitimate, as it was impossible for us to permit the threatening preparations to be carried on without interference."

The bewilderment of the Sultan was at this moment extreme. Baron de Ring, who had been formerly French Consul-General in Egypt and whose Arábist sympathies were well known, was at Constantinople, and had given the Sultan to understand that France would be glad to see some compromise effected with Arábi's party. Under these circumstances, the Sultan was inclined to join the Conference. Indeed, on July 10, he informed the German Chargé d'Affaires at Constantinople that "a Turkish Commissioner would join the Conference the next day but one." It was, however,

clear that the work of restoring order in Egypt
was about to be taken out of the hands of
the Conference. When, on July 10, the Sultan
was informed of the intended bombardment of
Alexandria, he told Lord Dufferin that he "would
send a categorical answer to his communication by
five o'clock to-morrow (July 11)." In the meanwhile, he asked that the bombardment should be
delayed, and he appointed a new Prime Minister,
who at once called on Lord Dufferin and said
that "to-morrow (the 12th) he would be able to
propose a satisfactory solution of the Egyptian
question." Lord Dufferin forwarded the Sultan's
request to London and to Alexandria, but he "held
out no hope that the line of action determined
upon would be modified." He also pointed out
"the folly, when such great interests were at stake,
of postponing diplomatic action till it became
materially impossible to interfere with the course
of events."

The Sultan was, as usual, too late. The
patience both of the British Government and of
the British public was exhausted. For the last
year and a half, every one had been agreed that
something should be done, but no one could agree
as to what should be done. At last, something
effectual was done. "At 7 A.M., on the 11th," Lord
Alcester stated in his report on the bombardment,
"I signalled from the *Invincible* to the *Alexandra*
to fire a shell into the recently armed earthworks
termed the Hospital Battery, and followed this by
a general signal to the fleet 'Attack the enemy's
batteries,' when immediate action ensued between
all the ships in the positions assigned to them, and
the whole of the forts commanding the entrance to
the harbour of Alexandria." By 5.30 P.M., the
batteries were silenced. On the afternoon of the
following day, the Egyptian garrison retreated,

having first set fire to the town, which was pillaged by the mob. Several Europeans were murdered. On the evening of the 13th, 150 marines, with a Gatling gun, were landed from the fleet, but re-embarked after remaining on shore for about half an hour. On the morning of the 14th, a further force was landed. In the course of the next day or two, reinforcements having arrived, effective possession was taken of the town and something like order restored. On July 18, Europeans and Egyptians began to return to Alexandria.

It has been frequently stated by critics hostile to England that Alexandria was set on fire by the shells from the British fleet. For this statement there is not a shadow of foundation.[1] There is no

[1] Mr. Wilfrid Blunt's testimony on Egyptian affairs generally is of very little value, but it may perhaps be quoted on this special point His first impressions are recorded in the following words (*Secret History, etc.*, p 372): "July 14th. Went to see Gregory. He is frightened at Alexandria's being burnt, and will have it that Arábi did not order it. I say he ordered it, and was right to do so. This is the policy of the Russians at Moscow, and squares with all I know of their intentions." Somewhat later, Mr. Blunt wrote (pp. 390-91): "With regard to the burning of Alexandria, I have never been able to make up my mind exactly what part, if any, the Egyptian army took in it. Arábi has always persistently denied having ordered it, and an act of such great energy stands so completely at variance with the rest of his all-too supine conduct of the war that I think it may be fairly dismissed as improbable. . . . Ninet, who was present at the whole affair, attributes the conflagration primarily to Seymour's shells, and this is probably a correct account. . . . I do not consider the question of any great importance as affecting the moral aspect of the case, it being clearly a military measure. . . . Historically, however, it is of importance, and I therefore say that on a balance of evidence I am of opinion that the retreating army had its share in it, not in consequence of any order, but as an act of disorder."

Mr. Broadley, who defended Arábi at his trial, evidently had strong suspicions that the burning of Alexandria was his handiwork On November 27, 1882, he wrote to Mr. Blunt: "*Nothing* presents difficulties but the burning of Alexandria As regards this, I believe the proof will fail as to Arábi's orders, but many ugly facts remain, viz : (1) No efforts to stop conflagration and loot. (2) Continued intimacy with Suliman Sami *afterwards.* (3) No punishment of offenders. (4) Large purchases of petroleum. (5) Systematic manner of incendiarism by soldiers. This is *the rub* Could Arábi have not stopped the whole thing? Besides, some of his speeches have a very burning appearance "—*Secret History, etc.*, p. 468.

doubt that the conflagration was the deliberate work of incendiaries.

At the time, the British Government were severely blamed for not taking prompt measures immediately after the bombardment to stop the conflagration and to restore order in the town. So early as July 7, the Khedive pointed out that the bombardment should be immediately followed by the landing of a military force. The War Office and the Admiralty were desirous to land troops, but their advice was overruled by the Cabinet on political grounds. Mr. Gladstone stated in the House of Commons that the landing of a force was objectionable, because it would have involved "the assumption of authority upon the Egyptian question," and would have been " grossly disloyal in the face of Europe and the Conference." It is difficult to conceive the frame of mind of any one who considers that firing several thousand shot and shell into Egyptian forts did not involve an "assumption of authority," whereas landing some men to prevent a populous city from being burnt to the ground did involve such an assumption. These technicalities, which are only worthy of a special pleader, were the bane of the British Government in dealing with the Egyptian question during Mr. Gladstone's Ministry. No foreign Power would have had any reasonable ground for complaint if, immediately after the bombardment, a force sufficient to preserve order had been landed at Alexandria.

The question remains whether, apart from the details in the execution, the bombardment was justifiable. There can be no doubt that it was perfectly justifiable, not merely on the narrow ground taken up by the British Ministry, namely, that it was necessary as a means of self-defence, but because it was clear that, in the absence of effectual Turkish or international action, the duty of crushing Arábi devolved on England.[1]

---

[1] The bombardment of Alexandria led to the retirement from Mr. Gladstone's Cabinet of Mr. Bright, "the colleague who in fundamentals stood closest to him of them all" (Morley's *Life of Gladstone*, iii. p. 83). The arguments by which Mr. Gladstone defended the action taken at Alexandria are given in a letter addressed at the time to Mr. Bright (p. 84). Save to those who hold that, under no circumstances is the use of force justifiable, they would appear to be conclusive.

CHAPTER XVII

TEL-EL-KEBIR

JULY–SEPTEMBER 1882

State of the country—British policy—Vote of credit—Negotiations with France—Fall of the Freycinet Ministry—France declines to co-operate—Negotiations with Italy—Italy declines to co-operate—Negotiations with Turkey—Tel-el-Kebir—General remarks.

AFTER the bombardment of the forts, Arábi retired to Kafr-Dawar, a few miles distant from Alexandria, whence he issued a Proclamation stating that "irreconcilable war existed between the Egyptians and the English, and all those who proved traitors to their country would not only be subjected to the severest punishment in accordance with martial law, but would be for ever accursed in the future world." On July 22, the Khedive formally dismissed Arábi from the post of Minister of War, but it was not till August 27, that a new Ministry under the presidency of Chérif Pasha, with Riaz Pasha as Minister of the Interior, was formed at Alexandria. In the meanwhile, the condition of the provinces was one of complete anarchy. The towns of Tanta, Damanhour, and Mehalla were plundered, and the European inhabitants massacred.

The history of the next two months may be summarised in a single sentence. England stepped in, and with one rapid and well-delivered blow crushed the rebellion. But it will be interesting to the student of diplomatic history to know in somewhat greater detail how it was that the British Government were left to act alone in the matter.

After the bombardment of Alexandria, British public opinion was thoroughly roused. On July 22, Mr. Gladstone stated the policy of the British Government in the House of Commons. "We feel," he said, "that we should not fully discharge our duty if we did not endeavour to convert the present interior state of Egypt from anarchy and conflict to peace and order. We shall look during the time that remains to us to the co-operation of the Powers of civilised Europe, if it be in any case open to us." But, Mr. Gladstone added, amidst the cheers of the House, "if every chance of obtaining co-operation is exhausted, the work will be undertaken by the single power of England." Parliament granted, by a majority of 275 to 19, the money (£2,800,000) for which the Government asked. 15,000 men were ordered to Malta and Cyprus. A force of 5000 men was ordered to be sent to Egypt from India. Sir Garnet (afterwards Lord) Wolseley was placed in chief command. He was to go to Egypt " in support of the authority of His Highness the Khedive, as established by the Firmans of the Sultan and existing international engagements, to suppress a military revolt in that country."

Simultaneously with the military preparations, diplomatic negotiations were actively carried on. The French Government were "firmly resolved to separate the question of protecting the Suez Canal from that of intervention properly so - called." They would "abstain from any operation in the interior of Egypt except for the purpose of re-pelling direct acts of aggression. If, therefore, the English troops thought fit to undertake such operations, they must not count on French co-operation." Amongst other reasons for adopting this course, it was stated that the Ministers of War and Marine considered that the season was most unfavourable, and that at least half the troops would perish from sickness, if operations were undertaken before November. At the same time, the French Chargé d'Affaires in London told Lord Granville "that it was certain that M. de Freycinet wished it to be understood that the French Government had no objection to our (*i.e.* the British) advance if we decided to make it." M. de Freycinet, however, was not unwilling to take action in common with England for the defence of the Canal. On July 19, the French Chamber granted to the Government, by a majority of 421 to 61, the navy credits for which they asked, amounting to about £313,000. In the course of the debates on this vote, it became clear that much difference of opinion existed in the Chamber. M. Gambetta denounced in the strongest terms the despatch of Turkish troops to Egypt, and spoke eloquently in support of the Anglo-French alliance. "Au prix des plus grands sacrifices," he said, "ne rompez jamais l'alliance Anglaise. Et précisément — je livre toute ma pensée, car je n'ai rien à cacher—précisément ce qui me sollicite à l'alliance Anglaise, à la co-opération Anglaise, dans le bassin de la Méditerranée, et en Égypte, et ce que je redoute le plus, entendez-le bien, outre cette rupture néfaste, c'est que vous ne livriez à l'Angleterre et pour toujours, des territoires, des fleuves, et des passages où votre droit de vivre et de trafiquer est égal au sien."[1]

---

[1] To a limited extent, M. Gambetta was a true prophet, although time alone can show how far he was right in using the words *pour toujours*. In the meanwhile, it may be remarked that the "right to live and to trade" in Egypt has been as fully, indeed, perhaps somewhat more fully assured to the French since the British occupation than was the case before the occurrence of that event. According to a

M. Clémenceau, on the other hand, was animated with a very different spirit. He congratulated the Government on not having taken part in the bombardment of the forts at Alexandria, he approved of the Conference, and he deprecated any active French interference in Egypt. Speaking with a manifest suspicion of the policy and intentions of Germany, he said that it appeared to him that endeavours were being made to get the French forces scattered over Africa, and that, as Austria had been pushed into Bosnia and Herzegovina, so France had been pushed into Tunis, and was now being pushed into Egypt.

Active preparations were now made in the French dockyards. The French Admiral at Port Said was instructed to concert measures with Rear-Admiral Hoskins for the protection of the Suez Canal. But both the French Government and the French Chamber were haunted by the idea that France would be isolated in Europe. M. de Freycinet wished to have a distinct mandate from the Conference deputing England and France to watch over the Canal. The British and French Ambassadors at Constantinople were, therefore, instructed to propose to their colleagues that the Conference should designate the Powers who, failing any effective action on the part of Turkey, should be charged in case of need to take whatever measures were necessary for the protection of the Canal. It soon became apparent that it would be impossible to obtain a mandate from the Powers. Prince Bismarck "was afraid of giving the question greater proportions by such a step, and of converting it into a war between the Christian Powers of Europe and the Mohammedan countries." Count

statement published in the *Journal Officiel* in 1903, French capital to the extent of over 57 millions sterling was at that time invested in Egypt. I do not doubt that this amount has now been exceeded.

Münster, however, assured Lord Granville that, in the event of the British Government taking action on their own initiative, they would receive the moral support of Germany, although Prince Bismarck was not prepared to go to the length of a formal mandate. The Austrian Government shared the views set forth by Germany.

In the meanwhile, the feeling in France against any intervention in Egypt grew apace. The partisans of non-intervention and those of intervention united against the Suez Canal Credit Bill. The opposition was increased by a communication made by the German Ambassador in Paris to M. de Freycinet, which favoured Turkish intervention as the best means for safeguarding the Canal. This communication was regarded as one of many steps said to have been recently taken by Prince Bismarck with a view to keeping M. de Freycinet in office. Resentment at the interference in their internal affairs implied, as the French conceived, in the undisguised support Prince Bismarck was supposed to give to M. de Freycinet, had been rankling for some while in French minds. The suspicions entertained of Germany found expression in a report made by the Committee of the Chamber. Some members of the Committee thought "que l'intérêt de la France était de ne pas intervenir en Égypte et de ne point immobiliser dans une expédition lointaine une partie de nos forces militaires. Sans méconnaître que la politique de non-intervention avait ses périls, ils ont exposé que la politique d'intervention leur paraissait plus dangereuse encore dans la situation actuelle de l'Europe." M. Clémenceau, in the final debate on the Bill, expressed himself as follows: "Messieurs, la conclusion de ce qui se passe en ce moment est celle-ci: L'Europe est couverte de soldats, tout le monde attend, toutes les Puissances se réservent leur liberté pour l'avenir ; réservez la liberté d'action de la France." A division took place on July 29, with the result that the Government were defeated by a large majority, the numbers being 416 to 75. This vote brought about the fall of the Freycinet Ministry, and finally settled the question of French intervention in Egypt. A new Government was formed under the presidency of M. Duclerc, who, on August 8, informed the Chamber that "le Gouvernement s'inspirera de la pensée qui est dictée par ce vote et y conformera sa politique."

For the time being, the attitude of the French Government and people was dignified and friendly to England. There was, indeed, no reason for the display of any unfriendly feeling. Whether it was or was not wise that France should intervene actively in the affairs of Egypt, might be an open question. But one point was clear. The British Government had done all in their power to ensure French co-operation; their want of success in obtaining it was due to the action of the French Government and of the French people, speaking through their constitutional representatives. When, a little later, British military preparations were in a more advanced stage, M. Grévy, the President of the French Republic, told the British Chargé d'Affaires at Paris "that it was not only out of goodwill to England that he hoped for the prompt success of our arms, it was also in the interest of France. Pan-Islamism was a factor of great weight in the future ; and he considered it of the highest importance that there should be no doubt, even for a moment, that Musulman or Arab troops could not resist Europeans in the field. The action of the Chamber had prevented the French Government from giving practical proof of their desire for our success, but he could assure me (in spite of what some few might say to the contrary) that France wished well to England in this matter, and would sincerely rejoice at the success of her arms." The *Temps*, which was supposed to be the organ of the French Government, pointed out that, even if England established herself in Egypt, as France had done in Tunis, "la France y gagnerait autant qu'elle." The main point was to keep out the Turk. "Nous avons," the same newspaper said, "des intérêts de diverses sortes en Égypte : la liberté du Canal, le paiement de nos créanciers, la sécurité de ceux de nos nationaux qui habitent le pays—autant d'intérêts que ne menace aucunement l'Angleterre, mais nous avons, sur le Nil, un intérêt infiniment supérieur à ceux-là ; c'est que le Turc ne change pas sa domination nominale contre un pouvoir réel, c'est que la puissance Ottomane, au lieu d'y remporter un avantage, y reçoive un échec."

Immediately after the battle of Tel-el-Kebir, the French Minister for Foreign Affairs congratulated the British Government on the victory, and "expressed his sincere hope for the prompt and complete success of the British forces in Egypt." "There was," M. Duclerc said a day or two later (September 15), "no doubt in France a certain general spirit of Chauvinism (which personally he did not share) which must have an outburst when fighting is going on anywhere without France being in it, and which was inclined to flare up at any moment. He trusted, however, that Her Majesty's Government knew the right value to attach to the outpourings of some portion of the Paris press. The sober good sense of France felt that the success of England against Arábi was also a solid gain to the rulers of Algeria."

In spite, however, of all this apparent cordiality, it was evident that there were rocks ahead. The force of circumstances had unfortunately severed the *entente cordiale* between England and France. Internal dissension and mistrust of Germany had paralysed French action at a critical moment. But, whatever may have been the causes, the fact that the French had lost their former footing of equality in Egypt was not calculated to make them easier to deal with when the final arrangements to be adopted in the valley of the Nile came to be discussed. Signs of the coming estrangement were, indeed, already visible to observers behind the scenes.

Foiled in their endeavours to obtain the co-operation of the French, the British Government turned to Italy. Italian jealousy had been set ablaze at the prospect of British, and still more of Anglo-French, intervention in Egypt. The policy of England was attacked with virulence by the Italian press. The Anglo-French Control had, it was said, brought about the ruin of Egypt. A sedative was evidently required. On July 24, Sir Augustus Paget, the British Ambassador at Rome, was authorised "to join with his French colleague in the application to be made to the Italian Government to co-operate with England and France in the steps to be taken for the protection of the Suez Canal; and he was at the same time to express the great satisfaction of Her Majesty's Government should Italy agree to be associated with England in this important work." This was immediately (July 25) followed by a further instruction to Sir Augustus Paget to invite the co-operation of Italy without waiting for action on the part of the French Ambassador. On July 26, the British Government went still farther. They no longer limited their invitation to co-operation in order to secure the safety of the Canal. Lord Granville informed the Italian Ambassador in London that "Her Majesty's Government would also welcome the co-operation of Italy in a movement in the interior, which they were of opinion could no longer be delayed, and for which they were making active preparations." Lord Dufferin was also instructed to state to the Conference that "while reserving to themselves the liberty of action which the pressure of events might render expedient and necessary, Her Majesty's Government would be glad to receive the co-operation of any Powers who were ready to afford it."

At this moment, the Sultan, after much vacillation, had signified his readiness to send Turkish troops to Egypt. On July 29, General Menabrea informed Lord Granville that " under these circumstances, the Italian Government would be open to a charge of contradiction if they were to negotiate with a view to the intervention of any other Power, and that it only remained for them, therefore, to express their thanks to the British Cabinet for having entertained the idea that the friendship of Italy for England might take the form of an active co-operation." Although, therefore, these negotiations produced no practical result, they had the effect of calming Italian irritation. Henceforward, Italian policy in Egypt was conducted on lines which were consistently friendly to England.

In view of the restless ambition displayed at times by the Italian Government and their desire, which has frequently been manifested, to extend their influence in the Mediterranean, the refusal of Italy to co-operate with the British Government in Egypt appears at first sight strange. It is not probable that M. Mancini, who was then in power, could have attached much importance to Turkish promises, or that he could have believed to any great extent in the efficacy of Turkish assistance.

The real reasons for Italian inaction must be sought elsewhere than in a desire to spare the susceptibilities of the Porte. Something may, without doubt, be attributed to a reluctance on the part of Italy to separate herself from the European concert. Something was also due to the fact that, from a naval and military point of view, the Italian Government was not ready to take prompt action. But the main reason was to be sought in the mistrust of France, which then existed in Italy, and in fear of ultimate collision with the French, which engendered a reluctance to co-operate with them. Whatever may have been the reasons, the decision of the Italian Government was unquestionably a wise one. It relieved Italy from a heavy responsibility. It removed the risk of complications whether with France or England. It left the care of Italian interests in Egypt in the hands of a Power traditionally and necessarily friendly to Italy, and it enabled the Italian Government to devote themselves to the study of internal questions.

Turning from Paris and Rome to Constantinople, it will not be wholly unprofitable to trace in some detail the tortuous windings of Turkish diplomacy.

Immediately after the bombardment of Alexandria, the Sultan again brought forward his favourite solution of the Egyptian question. Tewfik Pasha should be deposed, and Halim Pasha should be installed in his place. The latter would be "an excellent ruler." His nomination would "prevent the effusion of blood and satisfy everybody." This proposal was summarily rejected by the British Government, and the Sultan was told that "he was only wasting time by putting forward such suggestions."

Pressure was brought to bear on the Porte to

join the Conference, with the result that on July
20, Said Pasha and Assim Pasha were named to
be the Turkish representatives.

After much hesitation, the Sultan consented to
send troops to Egypt under conditions which were
generally of a nature to keep Turkish intervention
under the control of the Powers of Europe. On
July 26, Said Pasha informed the Conference that
troops were on the point of starting. At the
same time, he "expressed a hope that the military
intervention of the foreign Powers in Egypt would
no longer be necessary." In reply, Lord Granville
stated that "Her Majesty's Government would
accept the arrival and co-operation of Turkish
forces in Egypt, provided the character in which
they came was satisfactorily defined and cleared
from all ambiguity by previous declarations of
the Sultan."

It was evident that the conditions under which
Turkish co-operation was promised were far from
being free from ambiguity. Moreover, the Sultan
would not issue any Proclamation against Arábi.
The Grand Vizier told Lord Dufferin that he
"did not think it would be advisable to issue a
Proclamation until after the troops were landed."
Lord Dufferin replied that "if the Sultan desired
to co-operate with Her Majesty's Government it
was necessary he should first clearly define the
attitude he intended to assume towards Arábi and
the rebellious faction."

Whilst the Sultan, acting apparently under the
erroneous impression that his assistance was indispensable, was thus endeavouring to intervene
without the restraints imposed upon him by the
Powers, the reluctance to call in Turkish aid in
any shape was increasing, notably in Egypt. On
July 31, the Khedive told Sir Auckland Colvin
that he "was very apprehensive of Turkish

intrigue, and trusted that the Turks would be closely controlled."

Preparations were now made for the despatch of 5000 Turkish troops to Egypt, and on August 2, Said Pasha undertook to submit to the Conference a draft Proclamation, denouncing Arábi as a rebel. Besides the Proclamation, which was necessary as a guarantee of the Sultan's intentions, it was essential that, before Turkish troops landed in Egypt, a Military Convention should be framed indicating the manner in which they were to be employed. On August 5, therefore, Lord Dufferin informed Said and Assim Pashas, "that unless the Sultan would issue a Proclamation of a satisfactory character, and unless the Turkish Government would consent to enter into a Military Convention with Her Majesty's Government, the Ottoman troops would not be allowed to land." At the same time, the British Admiral was instructed, in the event of any vessel with Turkish troops appearing at an Egyptian port, to inform the officer in command, "with the utmost courtesy, that the despatch of Turkish troops must be premature and due to some misunderstanding, and that his orders were to request the officer commanding to proceed to Crete or elsewhere, and to apply to the Turkish Government for further instructions, as he was precluded from inviting them to land in Egypt." The Admiral was, at the same time, instructed "to prevent their landing if they declined to comply with his advice." The result of adopting this firm attitude was that, at a meeting of the Conference held on August 7, the Ottoman Delegates made the following declaration: "The Sublime Porte accepts the invitation for military intervention in Egypt made to it by the Identic Note of July 15, as well as the clauses and conditions contained therein." At the same time,

a promise was made to Lord Dufferin that a
Proclamation declaring Arábi to be a rebel should
be at once drawn up and communicated to
him. On August 9, the Proclamation was sent
to Lord Dufferin. On the 10th, the text of
the Proclamation was accepted by the British
Government with some slight modifications.

In the never-ceasing jar of Palace intrigue, which
always goes on at Constantinople, the party which
was in favour of an understanding with England
appeared for the moment to have got the upper
hand. The question of the Proclamation having
been apparently settled, negotiations were set on
foot with a view to the arrangement of a Military
Convention between England and Turkey. A
draft Convention was communicated by Musurus
Pasha to Lord Granville on August 10. It provided that the British troops should not pass
beyond the zone which they then occupied in
Alexandria and its neighbourhood, that they should
not remain more than three months, that all
persons arrested should be handed over to the
Khedive's authorities, and that all further details
should be settled between the Ottoman Commissioners and the British Commander-in-Chief on
the spot. It was obvious that these terms were
unacceptable. The Sultan now made an effort to
get the Military Convention before the Conference,
instead of treating separately with the British
Government. This attempt, however, failed. It
had, indeed, now become clear to everybody,
except the Sultan, that it was useless to prolong
the sittings of the Conference. At a meeting
held on August 14 "the Representatives of the
Powers unanimously expressed their opinion that
the moment had come to suspend the labours of
the Conference." The Sultan, however, who but
a short time previously had resisted the meeting of

the Conference, and who had only been persuaded with difficulty to allow an Ottoman representative to attend its meetings, now gave a further instance of the perversity which appears always to attend Turkish diplomacy. He was anxious that the Conference should continue to sit, thinking, without doubt, that there would be a greater chance of dissension amongst the Powers if the Conference were sitting, than would be the case if it suspended its labours. The Ottoman delegates were, therefore, instructed to say that "they did not share the opinions of the Representatives of the Powers." They reserved the right of fixing a date for the next meeting of the Conference. The date was, however, not fixed. The Conference was never formally closed. It died a natural death.

Foiled in his attempt to bring the Military Convention before the Conference, the Sultan fell back on negotiations with the British Government. On August 18, Lord Dufferin spent five hours in discussing the matter with Said and Assim Pashas, with the result that the Turkish delegates agreed to a Convention subject to the approval of the Sultan. On the following day, the Sultan rejected the draft Convention, and made counter proposals which Lord Dufferin declined to discuss. At the same time, the Ottoman Government refused permission for the embarkation at Smyrna of some mules purchased for the use of the British troops in Egypt. The action was characterised by Lord Granville as "most unfriendly." In view of all these circumstances, Lord Dufferin wrote to Said Pasha and begged him "to consider as void and *non avenues* whatever friendly assurances and expressions of confidence in relation to the Egyptian question he might have addressed to him outside the Conference."

After the lapse of a few days, the negotiations

were renewed. Munir Bey, an officer of the Sultan's household, was sent to Lord Dufferin to assure him "that it was from no unfriendly feeling towards England that the prohibition against the export of mules had been insisted upon, and that, in order to show his friendly feelings, His Majesty had ordered it to be removed." Lord Dufferin "took the opportunity of again repeating to Munir Bey some very earnest words of warning as to the gravity of the situation."

On the same day (August 23), Lord Dufferin, at the request of Said Pasha, paid him a visit and discussed the question of the Convention again with him and Assim Pasha. The result of this discussion was that the Turkish delegates agreed to all the clauses of the Military Convention proposed by the British Government, except that the latter wished the Turkish troops to disembark at Aboukir, Rosetta, and Damietta, whilst the Sultan attached great importance to the disembarkation taking place at Alexandria. Lord Dufferin then alluded to the Proclamation against Arábi, which, although the text had been arranged between the two Governments, had not yet been issued. What followed had best be related in Lord Dufferin's words. "Said Pasha," Lord Dufferin telegraphed, "then began with much hesitation, and evidently against his will, to suggest to me, in a roundabout manner, that the Proclamation agreed upon should not be issued at all in the first instance, but that another Proclamation of a different character, containing a final appeal to Arábi's sense of loyalty, should precede it. This impudent repudiation of his former engagements made me so angry that I got up and left the room, simply saying that it was impossible to negotiate either a Convention or anything else under such circumstances. On this, the two Pashas followed me downstairs and into the street, accompanied by their secretaries and dependants, calling to me that they withdrew every word of what they had said, that I must consider it altogether as *non avenu*, and that they would never again allude to the proposal. On concluding our interview in a more amicable mood, I told them that I could not sign any Convention until the Proclamation had been officially communicated to me in French and Arabic, and that not a single Turkish soldier would be allowed to land until it had been proclaimed in Egypt. The two Pashas seemed heartily ashamed of themselves, and admitted that they had been compelled to make the proposal very much against their will." On this interview being reported to London, Lord Granville telegraphed to Lord Dufferin that "Her Majesty's Government were unable to make any further changes in the provisions of the proposed Military Convention." Lord Dufferin was, at the same time, instructed to intimate to the Porte that, "under the present pressure of circumstances, it would not be well for the dignity of either England or Turkey that the negotiations should be indefinitely prolonged."

On August 24, Said and Assim Pashas paid a further visit to Lord Dufferin, and endeavoured to obtain some modifications in the draft Convention. On the 25th, an incident occurred which showed how little in earnest the Sultan was in the friendly assurances given to the British Government. Lord Dufferin telegraphed to Lord Granville: "I regret to have to inform your Lordship that although the Prime Minister and the Foreign Minister had actually written a letter ordering the release of the shepherds and muleteers engaged by the contractors to proceed to Egypt in charge of the live stock which had been shipped at Odessa and Smyrna for the use of our army, a subsequent order from the Palace annulled their decision.   A further order from the Palace has threatened with imprisonment the artificers who have undertaken to supply the contractors with the six hundred pack-saddles we require."

The time during which Turkish co-operation would have been useful, was now rapidly passing away.   On August 25, Sir Edward Malet telegraphed to Lord Granville: "The action of the Sultan has been such as to prevent the possibility of the rebels believing that the Sultan is really anxious to assist us ; and thus the moral support, which an alliance with Turkey might have given us, cannot any longer be attained.   Both Chérif Pasha and Riaz Pasha have expressed confidentially their extreme anxiety to obviate the difficulties which the arrival of Turkish troops would entail, and they are especially apprehensive of the complications which may ensue hereafter from their presence in the country."

On August 27, the Turkish delegates again waited on Lord Dufferin and informed him that they would unconditionally accept the Convention in the terms to which the British Government had agreed.   Directly the Convention was signed, the Proclamation denouncing Arábi as a rebel would be published in Egypt and communicated officially to the British Ambassador.   It was known that the Austrian Government was anxious that England and Turkey should come to terms. It was more in deference to the views of that Government than for any other reason, that, on August 28, Lord Granville telegraphed to Lord Dufferin authorising him to agree to the Convention on the following conditions: That the animals, supplies, and persons for the British

expedition should be immediately released, and
that a promise should be given by the Porte to
assist in forwarding the same to Egypt; that an
assurance should be given that no further impedi-
ments would be offered hereafter; that the
Proclamation declaring Arábi a rebel should be
issued immediately; and that British officers, who
should be sent either to Crete (where the Turkish
force was then collected) or to Constantinople,
as the Porte might prefer, should concert with
Turkish officers as to the military operations to
be undertaken. The matter appeared now at last
to be settled. On August 31, Lord Granville
telegraphed to this effect to Sir Edward Malet.

On the same day, Said Pasha made an earnest
appeal to Lord Dufferin that the British Government should "allow the disembarkation of Turkish
troops to take place at Alexandria, on condition
that the troops should merely file through the
town, and march at once to Aboukir." The
Sultan, Lord Dufferin said, was "on his knees."
"I would venture," Lord Dufferin added, "most
earnestly to urge Her Majesty's Government to
acquiesce in His Majesty's prayers." In spite of
the little faith Lord Dufferin had in Turkish
sincerity, he thought that a real chance of
establishing good relations with the Porte had
now presented itself. "The Sultan promised to
do everything Her Majesty's Government desired
in regard to the Proclamation, and to ensure an
altered tone in the press." On September 1, Lord
Granville telegraphed to Lord Dufferin that his
recent message "altered the situation," but that
the British Government could not agree to disembarkation at Alexandria. They "would prefer
that the landing should take place in the Suez
Canal." On September 2, Lord Dufferin was
able to telegraph the final text of the Convention

to Lord Granville, and to state that it was ready
for signature. On September 3, Lord Dufferin
saw the Sultan. "His Majesty confirmed, in
a perfectly explicit manner, all the propositions
made by Said Pasha." The Proclamation, the
Sultan said, was being translated into Arabic
and would be communicated to Lord Dufferin
immediately. On September 4, Lord Dufferin
was authorised to sign the Military Convention
as soon as the Proclamation against Arábi was
published.

Strong representations were again made by the
Khedive and Chérif Pasha against the landing of
Turkish troops in Egypt. Nevertheless, Lord
Granville decided to adhere to his arrangement
with the Sultan. This was all the more loyal on
the part of the British Government, inasmuch as
evidence was forthcoming to show that even at
this late hour the Sultan contemplated treating
with Arábi behind the backs both of the British
Government and the Khedive.

By September 6, the Proclamation was ready
and was published in the newspapers before being
communicated to Lord Dufferin. It was found
that the text did not tally with the draft to
which the British Government had agreed. Lord
Dufferin thereupon telegraphed to Lord Granville :
"I at once stated to the Minister of Foreign
Affairs that, in presence of such an inconceivable
act of bad faith as the publication without warning
of a different document from that which had been
formally agreed upon between the two Governments, I must decline signing the Convention ;
that I should report what had happened to my
Government ; and that I should not be surprised
if it declined to continue negotiations. Said
Pasha fully admitted that he had been guilty of
an act of what he called 'heedlessness,' but he

said that the fault had been committed through an excess of zeal, as the denunciation of Arábi in the new Proclamation was still stronger than in the old. He undertook . . . that an official correction of what had been published in the *Vakit* should be inserted in that paper. He begged me to do my best to mitigate the indignation, which I led him to understand this intolerable mode of procedure would arouse in the mind of the British Government." On September 10, Lord Granville telegraphed to Lord Dufferin accepting some of the changes made in the Proclamation, but objecting to others. Sir Edward Malet was, at the same time, informed that, in consequence of the difficulties which had been raised about the Proclamation, the signature of the Military Convention had been deferred. On the same day (September 10), the Turkish Plenipotentiaries met Lord Dufferin, bringing with them copies of a draft Convention and of a new Proclamation. Even at this late hour, however, further difficulties were raised. Said Pasha explained to Lord Dufferin "with much earnestness" that it was most desirable that the words "se rendront à Port Said," which had been struck out of the Convention, should be maintained. After much discussion, it was settled that the words should only be interpreted in the following sense, viz. that the Turkish ships should "direct their course to Port Said, in order to enter the Canal." Lord Granville was asked by telegraph to agree to this modification.

At the moment when the Porte was pressing for the signature of the Convention, another act was committed which showed how little confidence could be placed in the assurances of the Sultan. A number of porters, who had been engaged at Lord Wolseley's request for service with the army in Egypt, were imprisoned by order of the Porte. They were only released after Lord Dufferin had made a strong representation on the subject. Indeed, Lord Dufferin was at one time authorised to break off all diplomatic relations with the Porte.

On the afternoon of September 13, Lord Granville telegraphed to Lord Dufferin that he might sign the proposed Military Convention. On the morning of the same day, however, the battle of Tel-el-Kebir was fought. The French Government, who had always looked upon the presence of the Turks in Egypt with great disfavour, were the first to suggest that a Military Convention with the Porte was now no longer necessary. The Khedive also told Sir Edward Malet that "if anything could enhance the value of the victory, it was that it removed all pretext for the signature of a Convention with Turkey. He said that he looked back with dismay at the danger which Egypt would have incurred, if the Sultan, through the presence of his troops, had obtained a footing in the country." Under these circumstances, Lord Granville telegraphed to Lord Dufferin that he "presumed that the emergency having passed, His Majesty the Sultan would not now consider it necessary to send troops to Egypt."

Before this message could arrive, the Sultan sent for Lord Dufferin and kept him eleven hours at the Palace discussing a variety of further changes, which he wished to have made both in the Convention and the Proclamation. Finally, matters were brought to a close on September 18 by the despatch of the following telegram from Lord Granville to Lord Dufferin: "Her Majesty's Government greatly appreciate the fact that a substantial accord exists between the Government of the Sultan and that of Her Majesty on the Egyptian Question, and especially as to the rebellion of Arábi Pasha and the position of His Highness the Khedive. The occasion of the proposed Military Convention between this country and Turkey having now passed away, Her Majesty's Government rejoice that it is no longer necessary to discuss the difficulties which have been raised by His Majesty. Your Excellency is, therefore, authorised to convey to the Sultan, in the most courteous terms, the permission given you to drop the negotiations on this question."

In summing up the history of these events, Lord Dufferin said: "I can only reiterate that, from first to last, I have used every means at my disposal to induce the Turkish Government to move quickly, and to settle the matter out of hand. . . . Their conduct was so obviously contrary to their interests, that Europe had begun to misjudge the situation. While ruining my reputation as an honest man, they were enhancing it as a diplomatist, for it had begun to be believed that the delay in signing the Convention could not possibly result from their own incomprehensible shortsightedness, but must have been artificially created by the Machiavellian astuteness of the English Ambassador."

Lord Granville also summed up the Egyptian negotiations in a despatch to Lord Dufferin, dated October 5, 1882, which concluded with the following words: "This summary of events will show that the isolated action which has been forced upon Her Majesty's Government was not of their seeking. From the first moment when it became apparent that order could not be re-established in Egypt without the exercise of external force, they maintained that that force should be supplied by the Sultan as Sovereign of Egypt. They proposed this solution to the Conference, and Your Excellency lost no opportunity of urging it upon His Majesty and his advisers. Our efforts to induce them to intervene in Egypt, under conditions which would satisfy Europe, proved unavailing, and when it became necessary to make immediate provision for the safety of the Suez Canal, we prepared to undertake this duty jointly with France, with the co-operation of any other Powers who might be prepared to join us. We addressed a special invitation to Italy to take part in the arrangements. The progress of the rebellion having destroyed the authority of the Khedive, and reduced Egypt to a state of anarchy, we invited France and Italy to act with us in suppressing it; and when those Powers declined to do so, we still urged the Porte to send troops, insisting only on such conditions as were indispensable to secure unity of action. But, before the Turkish Government carried out its agreement to sign the Military Convention, the success of our arms had put an end to the insurrection."

The details of these negotiations have been stated at some length because they afford an admirable instance of the diplomatic procedure ordinarily adopted by the Ottoman Government. The Turks, as a nation, possess many fine, though perhaps somewhat barbaric qualities. But a species of paralysis appears to affect most Turks in high positions. The duplicity and shortsightedness of the Ottoman Government come out strongly in every incident of these negotiations.

It is unnecessary to give a detailed account of the military operations by which the insurrection in Egypt was crushed. They have been described in a book published by the British War Office, and in other works. It will be sufficient to say that Lord Wolseley arrived at Alexandria on

August 13. Previous to this, some desultory operations had taken place in the neighbourhood of Alexandria. Lord Wolseley decided to move on Cairo by way of Ismailia.[1] The Canal was seized in spite of the querulous cries of M. de Lesseps. On September 13, the Egyptian army was totally routed at Tel-el-Kebir.[2] A small force of cavalry was at once pushed on to Cairo, which was captured without a blow being struck. Kinglake's prophecy had been fulfilled. "The Englishman"—in the person of Major Watson, R.E., with two squadrons of the 4th Dragoon Guards and a detachment of Mounted Infantry, who occupied the Citadel on the evening of September 14—"planted a firm foot on the banks of the Nile, and sat in the seats of the faithful." Arábi and his associates, who throughout the whole affair do not appear to have displayed a single quality worthy of respect or admiration, surrendered.[3]

It is always a somewhat unprofitable proceeding to speculate on what might have been in politics, but I cannot close this portion of the narrative without hazarding a conjecture as to whether any foreign occupation of Egypt could have been avoided. Mistakes were, without doubt, committed. The true nature of the Arábi revolt was

---

[1] Arábi was warned by Mr. Wilfrid Blunt that he would probably be attacked from the side of Ismailia. "I believe," Mr. Blunt writes (*Secret History*, p. 228), "that it was in consequence of this hint that the lines of Tel-el-Kebir were begun to be traced by Arábi."

[2] At this time, I was in India. On August 22, Lord Wolseley wrote to me from Ismailia: "I hope to hit Arábi very hard about the 10th or 12th of September at latest." Lord Wolseley was only twenty-four hours out in his prediction.

[3] Mr. Wilfrid Blunt, in spite of his sympathy with Arábi, says, in speaking of the fact that he did not attempt to handle the Egyptian troops in the field: "His abstention on this head has been attributed by his detractors to physical cowardice, and it is difficult to avoid the conclusion that there was some truth in this."—*Secret History, etc.*, p. 385.

misunderstood.[1] It was more than a mere military mutiny. It partook in some degree of the nature of a *bona fide* national movement. It was not solely, or, indeed, mainly directed against Europeans and European interference in Egyptian affairs, although anti-European prejudice exercised a considerable influence on the minds of the leaders of the movement. It was, in a great degree, a movement of the Egyptians against Turkish rule. Although previous to the issue of the Joint Note some hope might have been entertained of guiding the movement, and although I am distinctly of opinion that an effort to guide it should have been made, it must be admitted that the chances of failure predominated over those of success. Leaving out of account questions of detail, and speaking with some knowledge of the various classes of Egyptian society, I ask myself, where were the elements for the formation of any stable government to have been found when, in pursuance of the policy of "Egypt for the Egyptians," there had been eliminated, as would probably have been the case, first, the Europeans, with all their intelligence, wealth, and governing power; secondly, the Khedive in whose place some illiterate Egyptian, of the type of Arábi or Mahmoud Sami, would have been appointed; thirdly, the Syrians and Armenians, with all their industry and capacity for sedentary employment; fourthly, the native aristocracy, largely composed of Turks, who were at that time the principal large landowners in the country, and amongst whom, in spite of many defects, the habits and traditions of a governing class still

---

[1] Sir Donald Mackenzie Wallace, who accompanied Lord Dufferin to Egypt and who had exceptionally good opportunities for forming an opinion on this subject, says: "There can be no longer any reasonable doubt that the English Government totally misconceived the real nature of the Egyptian revolutionary movement."—*Egypt and the Egyptian Question*, p. 365.

lingered; when, in fact, the nationalists and mutineers had got rid of all the classes, who then
governed, and who for several centuries had governed
the country? The residue would have consisted,
first, of the mass of the fellaheen population, who
were sunk in the deepest ignorance, who cared little
by whom they were governed provided they were
not overtaxed, and whose main idea throughout the
Arábi movement was to tear up the bonds of the
Greek or Syrian usurer; secondly, of a certain
number of small proprietors, village Sheikhs,
Omdehs, etc., who constituted the squirearchy of
the country, and who, in point of knowledge and
governing capacity, were but little removed from
the fellaheen; thirdly, of the Copts, whose religion
would certainly, sooner or later, have prevented
them from acting in complete harmony with the
Arábists, and who, even if tolerated by the
Mohammedan population, could neither have obtained any influence over the Mohammedans, nor,
even if that influence had been obtained, could
have used it to the general advantage of the
country; fourthly, of the hierarchy, consisting principally of the Ulema of the El-Azhar Mosque.
The latter, though numerically the smallest, was by
far the most important and influential of the four
classes to which allusion is made above. The spirit
which animated them would, in the first instance
at all events, have been infused into the masses
below. They would have been the Jacobins of the
movement, which, whether nationalist or military,
would certainly have been reactionary in so far
as it would have tended to destroy whatever germs
of civilisation had been implanted into Egypt.
Like their prototypes in France, they would, had
no strong hand intervened, have maintained their
supremacy until, possibly after an acute and disastrous period of transition, their incapacity for

government had been clearly demonstrated. The corruption, misgovernment, and oppression, which would have prevailed, if the influence of this class had become predominant, would probably have been greater than any to which Egypt had been exposed at previous periods. An attempt would have been made to regulate, not only the government, but also the social life of the country upon those principles of the Mohammedan faith which are most antiquated, obsolete, and opposed to the commonplace ideas of modern civilisation.

Egypt may now almost be said to form part of Europe. It is on the high road to the far East. It can never cease to be an object of interest to all the Powers of Europe, and especially to England. A numerous and intelligent body of Europeans and of non-Egyptian Orientals have made Egypt their home. European capital to a large extent has been sunk in the country. The rights and privileges of Europeans are jealously guarded, and, moreover, give rise to complicated questions, which it requires no small amount of ingenuity and technical knowledge to solve. Exotic institutions have sprung up and have taken root in the country. The Capitulations impair those rights of internal sovereignty which are enjoyed by the rulers or legislatures of most States. The population is heterogeneous and cosmopolitan to a degree almost unknown elsewhere. Although the prevailing faith is that of Islam, in no country in the world is a greater variety of religious creeds to be found amongst important sections of the community.

In addition to these peculiarities, which are of a normal character, it has to be borne in mind that in 1882 the army was in a state of mutiny; the Treasury was bankrupt; every branch of the administration had been dislocated; the ancient and arbitrary method, under which the country

had for centuries been governed, had received a
severe blow, whilst, at the same time, no more
orderly and law-abiding form of government had
been inaugurated to take its place.

Is it probable that a Government composed of
the rude elements described above, and led by
men of such poor ability as Arábi and his coadjutors, would have been able to control a complicated machine of this nature? Were the
Sheikhs of the El-Azhar Mosque likely to
succeed where Tewfik Pasha and his Ministers,
who were men of comparative education and
enlightenment, acting under the guidance and
inspiration of a first-class European Power, only
met with a modified success after years of patient
labour? There can be but one answer to these
questions. Sentimental politicians may consider
that the quasi-national character of Arábi's movement gives it a claim to their sympathies, but
others who are not carried away by sentiment
may reasonably maintain that the fact of its having
been a quasi-national movement was one of the
reasons which foredoomed it to failure; for, in
order to justify its national character, it had to
run counter, not only to the European, but also
to the foreign Eastern elements of Egyptian government and society. Neither is it in the nature of
things that any similar movement should, under
the present conditions of Egyptian society, meet
with any better success. The full and immediate
execution of a policy of "Egypt for the Egyptians,"
as it was conceived by the Arábists in 1882, was,
and still is impossible.

History, indeed, records some very radical
changes in the forms of government to which a
State has been subjected without its interests being
absolutely and permanently shipwrecked. But it
may be doubted whether any instance can be

quoted of a sudden transfer of power in any civilised or semi-civilised community to a class so ignorant as the pure Egyptians, such as they were in the year 1882. These latter have, for centuries past, been a subject race. Persians, Greeks, Romans, Arabs from Arabia and Baghdad, Circassians, and finally, Ottoman Turks, have successively ruled over Egypt, but we have to go back to the doubtful and obscure precedents of Pharaonic times to find an epoch when, possibly, Egypt was ruled by Egyptians. Neither, for the present, do they appear to possess the qualities which would render it desirable, either in their own interests, or in those of the civilised world in general, to raise them at a bound to the category of autonomous rulers with full rights of internal sovereignty.

If, however, a foreign occupation was inevitable, or nearly inevitable, it remains to be considered whether a British occupation was preferable to any other. From the purely Egyptian point of view, the answer to this question cannot be doubtful. The intervention of any European Power was preferable to that of Turkey. The intervention of one European Power was preferable to international intervention. The special aptitude shown by Englishmen in the government of Oriental races pointed to England as the most effective and beneficent instrument for the gradual introduction of European civilisation into Egypt. An Anglo-French or an Anglo-Italian occupation, from both of which we narrowly and also accidentally escaped, would have been detrimental to Egyptian interests and would ultimately have caused friction, if not serious dissension, between England on the one side and France or Italy on the other.

The only thing to be said in favour of Turkish

intervention is that it would have relieved England from the responsibility of intervening. It has been shown in the course of this narrative that, in the early stages of the proceedings, the policy of the two Western Powers, which was guided by the anti-Turkish sentiments prevalent in France, was not of a nature to invite or encourage Turkish co-operation. At a later period, the shortsightedness of the Sultan was such as to cause the Porte to commit political suicide in so far as decisive Turkish action was concerned. Perhaps it was well that it did so, for it is highly probable that armed Turkish intervention in Egypt, accompanied, as it might well have been, by misgovernment, paltry intrigue, corruption, and administrative and financial confusion, would only have been the prelude to further, and possibly more serious international complications.

By a process of exhausting all other expedients, we arrive at the conclusion that armed British intervention was, under the special circumstances of the case, the only possible solution of the difficulties which existed in 1882. Probably also it was the best solution. The arguments against British intervention, indeed, were sufficiently obvious. It was easy to foresee that, with a British garrison in Egypt, it would be difficult that the relations of England either with France or Turkey should be cordial. With France especially, there would be a danger that our relations might become seriously strained. Moreover, we lost the advantages of our insular position. The occupation of Egypt necessarily dragged England to a certain extent within the arena of Continental politics. In the event of war, the presence of a British garrison in Egypt would possibly be a source of weakness rather than of strength. Our position in Egypt placed us in a disadvantageous diplomatic position, for any Power, with whom we had a difference of opinion about some non-Egyptian question, was at one time able to retaliate by opposing our Egyptian policy. The complicated rights and privileges possessed by the various Powers of Europe in Egypt facilitated action of this nature.

There can be no doubt of the force of these arguments. The answer to them is that it was impossible for Great Britain to allow the troops of any other European Power to occupy Egypt. When it became apparent that some foreign occupation was necessary, that the Sultan would not act save under conditions which were impossible of acceptance, and that neither French nor Italian co-operation could be secured, the British Government acted with promptitude and vigour. A great nation cannot throw off the responsibilities which its past history and its position in the world have imposed upon it. English history affords other examples of the Government and people of England drifting by accident into doing what was not only right but was also most in accordance with British interests. Δεῖ δὲ σκοπεῖν μὲν καὶ πράττειν ἀεὶ τὰ δίκαια, συμπαρατηρεῖν δ' ὅπως ἅμα καὶ συμφέροντα ἔσται ταῦτα.[1] Such was the advice Demosthenes gave to his fellow-countrymen. In spite of some mistakes of detail, it was on this sound principle that, broadly speaking, the British Government acted in dealing with Egyptian affairs in 1882.

---

[1] Oration *For the Megalopolitans.*

CHAPTER XVIII

THE DUFFERIN MISSION

SEPTEMBER 1882–AUGUST 1883

British policy—Trial of Arábi—Resignation of Riaz Pasha—Exile of political prisoners—Courts-martial—The Alexandria Indemnities —The abolition of the Dual Control—Rupture of the Anglo-French understanding—Lord Dufferin's Report—My arrival in Egypt.

KINGLAKE'S prophecy was that the Englishman would plant his foot firmly in the valley of the Nile. It had so far been fulfilled that the Englishman had planted his foot, but he had not planted it firmly. Hardly, indeed, had his foot been planted when, fearful of what he had done, he struggled to withdraw it. A few hours after the battle of Tel-el-Kebir had been fought, Sir Edward Malet was instructed to send to London "as soon as possible, suggestions as to army, finance, and administration for the future." Lord Dufferin was, at the same time, informed that "Her Majesty's Government contemplated shortly commencing the withdrawal of the British troops from Egypt."

The British Government were, at a subsequent period, blamed for not having at once proclaimed a Protectorate. A petition signed by 2600 Europeans residing at Alexandria was presented to Lord Dufferin in favour of a permanent British occupation of Egypt. The Egyptians generally also viewed British intervention with unmixed satisfaction.

It cannot be doubted that if the position of the British Government had been more strongly asserted directly after the occupation, many of the obstacles which have stood in the path of the reformer would have been swept away. On the other hand, the adoption of a policy of this sort would have constituted a breach of faith with Europe. It is extremely doubtful whether it would have met with adequate support in England. It may be said, therefore, that the execution of this policy was, for all practical purposes, both undesirable and impossible.

Moreover, it is to be observed that the mere proclamation of a Protectorate would not in any degree have impaired the rights and privileges of Europeans resident in Egypt,[1] and it was these which so much hampered the progress of reform in the early days of the occupation. In order to ensure this result, annexation, either permanent or temporary, would have been necessary.

At the same time, it must be admitted that the situation in Egypt was misunderstood both by the British Government and by British public opinion of

[1] The French Government established a Protectorate over Tunis in 1884, but subsequent negotiations with the Powers were necessary before the régime of the Capitulations could be modified. The difficulties which the existence of the Capitulations threw in the way of the French administration of Tunis have been described by a very competent authority, who wrote under the pseudonym of P.H.X., in the following terms :—" Les difficultés que devait faire cesser l'organisation de la réforme financière et de notre contrôle sont relativement peu de chose auprès des complications inextricables et des abus que la multiplicité comme la toute-puissance des juridictions Européennes en Tunisie avaient fait naître. Sous prétexte de protéger les Européens contre l'arbitraire et le désordre du Gouvernement Beylical, les Capitulations leur assuraient des privilèges qui s'étaient étendus démesurément à mesure que l'autorité locale s'affaiblissait ; ce qui n'était à l'origine qu'une exception était devenue plus fort que la règle, en sorte que l'administration indigène, eût-elle été animée des meilleures intentions du monde, s'était trouvée peu à peu complètement paralysée" (La Politique Française en Tunisie, p. 360).

the time. Moreover, party politics cast their baneful spell over the English proceedings, and obscured the real issues at stake. Two alternative policies were open to the British Government. These were, first, the policy of speedy evacuation; and, secondly, the policy of reform. It was not sufficiently understood that the adoption of one of these policies was wholly destructive of the other. The withdrawal of the British troops connoted severity in the treatment of the rebels, the establishment of some rough prætorian guard composed of foreigners, who would have quelled all disturbance with a high hand, the re-establishment of an arbitrary rule, and the abandonment of all attempts to introduce the various reforms which follow in the train of European civilisation. On the other hand, the adoption of a policy of reform connoted an indefinite prolongation of the British occupation, and an increase of European interference, without which no progress was possible.

It was natural and praiseworthy that public opinion in England should have been opposed to handing the Egyptians over to the uncontrolled rule of the Turkish Pashas, but it was characteristic of the want of consistency, which so often distinguishes English politics, that the same people who cried out most loudly for control over the Pashas, were also those who most strenuously opposed the adoption of the only method by which Pashas could be effectively controlled. They wished to withdraw the British troops, and, at the same time, to secure all those advantages which could only be obtained by their continued presence in the country. Party politicians had not failed to dwell constantly and in condemnatory terms on the number of Europeans employed in Egypt. It was a good *ad captandum* cry, for at the time the British public did not appreciate the extent to which European agency was necessary if a policy of reform was to be adopted. The attempt to attain two objects, which were irreconcilable one with the other, naturally rendered the policy of the British Government vacillating and uncertain.

This vacillation showed itself immediately after the occupation in the treatment accorded to Arábi and the other leaders of the rebellion. There could be no doubt that, as a subject of the Khedive, Arábi had been guilty of treason and rebellion, and that, as an officer of the army, he had been guilty of mutiny. Had he been tried by Court-martial and shot directly after he was taken prisoner, no injustice would have been done. On the other hand, he was regarded by some few Englishmen as a hero, and, from a purely political point of view, it was more than questionable whether it was wise to elevate him to the rank of a martyr. Moreover, it is not easy, as a matter of public morality, to state precisely at what point the sacred right of revolution begins or ends, or to say at what stage a disturber of the peace passes from a common rioter, who is an enemy to society, to the rank of a leader in a political movement set on foot for the attainment of ends which command at least a certain degree of sympathy. The commonplace standard of success is not a bad test by which to decide this question. It is difficult to justify unsuccessful rebellion, or to maintain that those who have been instrumental in bringing it about should not suffer the extreme consequences of their own conduct. Even from this point of view, however, it was not easy to decide on Arábi's fate. Had he been left alone, there cannot be a doubt that he would have been successful. His want of success was due to British interference. The British Government had, therefore, a perfect right to decide on his fate. Their decision could not be doubtful. British public opinion condemned the execution of prisoners for political offences, and the British Government would naturally follow public opinion on a point of this sort. "Her Majesty's Government," Lord Granville wrote, "were disposed to recommend to the Khedive to adopt the more humane practice of modern times, and to exercise his prerogative of mercy," if it were found that Arábi could not be charged with any other crimes than those of treason and rebellion.[1] It was, from the first, doubtful whether any "crime which, according to the practice of civilised nations, called for the extreme penalty of the law" could be brought home to Arábi, and it was certainly not worth while to prolong the proceedings, and thus keep the country in a ferment, whilst a lengthy inquiry into this point was going on. The best plan would have been for the British Government to have decided at once that Arábi and his principal associates should be exiled.

Unfortunately, this was not done. The fiction was maintained that the fate of the prisoners depended, not on the strong Government which had suppressed the revolt, but on the weak Government which had proved itself powerless to suppress it. Arábi and his fellow-prisoners were made over to the Khedive. There might have been some slight justification for the adoption of this course if the cession had been real, and if, in view of the early withdrawal of the British troops which was then contemplated, the British

---

[1] The following statement, for which, of course, there is not the smallest foundation, is one amongst very numerous illustrations which might be given of the little value to be attached to Mr. Wilfrid Blunt's testimony on Egyptian affairs. He writes (*Secret History*, p. 443) that "Gladstone had made up his mind that Arábi should be executed no less than had the Foreign Office."

Government had stood aside whilst, under the
protection of British bayonets, the Turkish party
wreaked its vengeance on the Arábists, and struck
terror into the hearts of future revolutionists.
But this was obviously both undesirable and impossible. The cession was, therefore, made unreal.
The Khedive was to have the appearance of
dealing with Arábi, but he was not to move a
step without the consent of the British Government. More than this, when the Egyptian
Government established a court to try Arábi,
it was thought, and, without doubt, rightly
thought, that the trial would be a mockery.
Hence arose an unseemly wrangle, in which the
Egyptian Government endeavoured to create a
condition of things which would increase the
chances of Arábi being condemned to death,
whilst the British Government insisted on a fair
trial conducted in public, and with European
counsel to defend the prisoners. The Egyptian
Government were, of course, obliged to yield.
After long discussions, the conditions under which
the trial was to be conducted were settled. On
November 7, Lord Dufferin, who had been deputed
on a special mission to Egypt, arrived in Cairo.
He saw at a glance that it was essential to bring
the Arábi proceedings to a close. A preliminary
inquiry had rendered it clear that no charge,
except that of rebellion, could be established
against Arábi. Lord Dufferin, therefore, arranged
that Arábi should plead guilty to the charge of
rebellion, that he should be sentenced to death,
and that, immediately after the sentence was
pronounced, it should be commuted into perpetual
exile. This arrangement was carried out. Several
places were suggested to which Arábi might be
sent. It was finally settled that he should go to
Ceylon. A special ship was chartered, and he

and his six principal associates left Suez on December 26.[1]

In the meanwhile, Riaz Pasha resigned his position in the Ministry, ostensibly on the ground of ill-health. It was, however, well known that the real reason for his resignation was that he could not reconcile himself to the idea of Arábi having escaped capital punishment. Neither would it be fair to ascribe this attitude to vindictive feelings. Without doubt, Riaz Pasha thought that the execution of Arábi was not merely an act of justice but a State necessity.

In a report addressed to Lord Granville on December 12, Lord Dufferin described the effect produced in Egypt by the commutation of the capital sentence on Arábi and his principal followers. The Europeans and the Pashas condemned the leniency with which they had been treated. On the other hand, the mass of the people approved of the commutation of the sentences.

In addition to the leaders of the rebellion, about 150 persons were condemned, some to exile from Egypt, and some to residence in the provinces under police supervision for various terms. On January 1, 1883, a Decree was issued granting an amnesty to all other prisoners charged with political offences.

"The *débris* of the late rebellion having thus been cleared away," Lord Dufferin expressed a hope that "the stage was cleared for reconstruction." Unfortunately, however, some months were yet to elapse before the whole of these *débris* were fully cleared away. The prisons were crowded with persons who were charged with murder, pillage, and arson. At Tanta, from seventy to eighty Christians, mostly Greeks and Syrians, had been massacred, on July 13, by a mob of Moslem

[1] In 1901, Arábi was allowed to return to Egypt.

fanatics under circumstances of great brutality. On the same day, eight Italians had been killed at Mehallet-Kebir, and, on July 14, fourteen Christians and one Jew had been killed at Damanhour and its neighbourhood. In all these places, the houses and shops of the Christians had been pillaged. It was impossible to allow crimes of this nature to remain unpunished. Commissions were, therefore, appointed to make preliminary inquiries and to send accused persons, against whom a *prima facie* case had been established, for trial before a Court-martial. There was little risk of injustice being committed. " The persons dealt with by the Commissioners," Lord Dufferin pertinently remarked, "and by the Court-martial were Musulman Egyptians accused of murdering and pillaging Christians, principally European Christians. My experience of the East has long since convinced me that an Oriental court of justice may be safely trusted not to strain either law or evidence when the cause lies between a Musulman culprit and his Christian victim. During all the time I was in Egypt, Major MacDonald [1] was principally preoccupied in noting the tendency of the Court to unduly favour the prisoners ; and Your Lordship may rest assured that whatever miscarriages of justice may have occurred have been occasioned by the escape of the guilty, and not by the condemnation of any innocent persons." These were wise words, but the advice of the impartial and experienced diplomatist was unheeded by party politicians in England, who saw in the Egyptian trials an opportunity for attacking the Government of the day. The fate of Suleiman Sami, a miscreant who was largely responsible for the burning of Alexandria and who was deservedly

---

[1] Major (subsequently Sir Claude) MacDonald was Lord Dufferin's Military Attaché. He was charged with the duty of watching the proceedings of the Court-martial.

hanged, attracted a special degree of fictitious sympathy, and was characterised by Lord Randolph Churchill in the House of Commons as "the grossest and vilest judicial murder that has ever stained the annals of Oriental justice." Both the British Government and the authorities in Egypt, however, stood firm in the face of these attacks. In a few cases, capital punishment was inflicted. Others were condemned to various terms of penal servitude and imprisonment. A large number of accused persons were released after a preliminary inquiry. Eventually, on October 9, 1883, a Decree was issued abolishing the Special Commissions and the Court-martial.

The punishment of the principal offenders was not the only burning question which the rebellion left in its wake. A large amount of valuable property had been destroyed at Alexandria. After some lengthy negotiations, a Decree appointing an International Commission to assess the claims was issued on January 13, 1883. The delay in the settlement of this question caused great irritation and discontent.

The final rupture of the Anglo-French *entente,* which followed immediately after the occupation, increased the difficulties of the situation. On September 20, M. Duclerc told the British Chargé d'Affaires in Paris, "that he thought it would be in the interest of England to give at an early date some notion of what her future intentions were with regard to Egypt." It was impossible at that moment to state, save in the most general terms, what were the intentions of England as regards Egypt, and it soon became apparent that the only point to which for the moment the French Government attached any real importance, was the continuance of the Anglo-French Control, as it existed previous to the occupation. The Egyptian Government, on the other hand, wished the institution to be abolished on the ground that its dual nature and semi-political character had caused great inconvenience. Public opinion in England pronounced strongly in favour of its abolition. In spite of considerable pressure exerted by France, the British Government wisely stood firm and declined to accede to the French wishes on this point. The presidency of the Commission of the Debt was offered to France, but was declined on the ground that it was not "consistent with the dignity of France to accept as an equivalent for the abolition of the Control, a position which was simply that of cashier." Eventually, after some sharp diplomatic skirmishing, the negotiations were dropped, and the French Government "resumed its liberty of action in Egypt." From that moment, until the signature of the Anglo-French Agreement in 1904, French action in Egypt was more or less persistently hostile to England.

On January 3, 1883, Lord Granville addressed a circular to the Powers in which he expressed himself in the following terms: "Although for the present a British force remains in Egypt for the preservation of public tranquillity, Her Majesty's Government are desirous of withdrawing it as soon as the state of the country and the organisation of proper means for the maintenance of the Khedive's authority will admit of it. In the meanwhile, the position in which Her Majesty's Government are placed towards His Highness imposes upon them the duty of giving advice with the object of securing that the order of things to be established shall be of a satisfactory character, and possess the elements of stability and progress." Lord Dufferin was sent to Egypt to report upon the measures which were necessary in order that "the administration of affairs should be reconstructed on a basis which would afford satisfactory guarantees for the maintenance of peace, order, and prosperity in Egypt, for the stability of the Khedive's authority, for the judicious development of self-government, and for the fulfilment of obligations towards the Powers."

It is unnecessary to dwell on Lord Dufferin's detailed proposals. A few remarks on the main framework of his plan will suffice.

It was not the first time that an endeavour had been made on the banks of the Nile to make bricks without straw. The task, which Lord Dufferin was called upon to perform, was, in fact, impossible of execution. He was asked to devise a plan for the complete rehabilitation of the country, and, at the same time, one which would not be inconsistent with the policy of speedily withdrawing the British garrison. It can be no matter for surprise that, in spite of the qualities of statesmanship, political foresight, and literary skill, all of which Lord Dufferin possessed in an eminent degree, he should have failed to accomplish the impossible. It is, moreover, difficult to read Lord Dufferin's report without entertaining a suspicion that he was aware that the policy of the British Government was incapable of execution. There was only one practicable method by which the Egyptian administration could be reformed. That was to place the government more or less under British guidance. Lord Dufferin's statesmanlike eye saw this clearly enough. His remarks on this point form, indeed, the most valuable portion of his report. "I cannot," he said, "conceive anything which would be more fatal to the prosperity and good administration of the country than the hasty and inconsiderate extrusion of any large proportion of the Europeans in the service of the

Government, in deference to the somewhat unreasonable clamour which has been raised against
them. For some time to come, European assistance in the various Departments of Egyptian
administration will be absolutely necessary. . . .
It is frightful to contemplate the misery and
misfortune which would be entailed on the population, were the Financial, the Public Works, and
analogous Departments to be left unorganised
by a few high-minded European officials. The
Egyptian Government would quickly become a
prey to dishonest speculators, ruinous contracts,
and delusive engineering operations, from which
they are now protected by the intelligent and
capable men who are at hand to advise them in
reference to these subjects. This is especially
true in regard to financial matters. The maintenance of Egypt's financial equilibrium is the
guarantee of her independence."

Without doubt, Lord Dufferin was right. But
in what manner was the ascendency of European
influence to be secured ? It could only be secured
by the prolongation of the British occupation.
Lord Dufferin's instructions, however, forbade him
to state in clear and positive terms the inevitable
inference to be drawn from his own proposals.

In the meanwhile, in deference, to a great
extent, to British public opinion, a certain development of free institutions was proposed. But
Lord Dufferin appears to have had little confidence that he would succeed in "creating a
vitalised and self-existent organism, instinct with
evolutionary force." "A paper constitution," he
said, "is proverbially an unsatisfactory device.
Few institutions have succeeded that have not
been the outcome of slow growth, and gradual
development; but in the East, even the germs of
constitutional freedom are non-existent. Despotism

not only destroys the seeds of liberty, but renders the soil, on which it has trampled, incapable of growing the plant. A long-enslaved nation instinctively craves for the strong hand of a master, rather than for a lax constitutional régime. A mild ruler is more likely to provoke contempt and insubordination than to inspire gratitude."

It was, without doubt, desirable to make some beginning in the way of founding liberal institutions, but no one with any knowledge of the East could for one moment suppose that the Legislative Council and Assembly, founded under Lord Dufferin's auspices, could at once become either important factors in the government of the country, or efficient instruments to help in administrative and fiscal reform.

> Where Order deigns to come,
> Her sister, Liberty, cannot be far.[1]

What Egypt most of all required was order and good government. Perhaps, *longo intervallo*, liberty would follow afterwards. No one but a dreamy theorist could imagine that the natural order of things could be reversed, and that liberty could first be accorded to the poor ignorant representatives of the Egyptian people, and that the latter would then be able to evolve order out of chaos. In the early days of the struggles which eventually led to Italian unity, Manzoni said that "his country must be morally healed before she could be politically regenerated."[2] The remark applied in a far greater degree to Egypt in 1882 than it did to Italy in 1827. Lord Dufferin was certainly under no delusion as to the realities of the situation. In the concluding portion of his report, he said that one of the main points to

---

[1] Akenside, *Pleasures of the Imagination*.
[2] Bolton King, *History of Italian Unity*, vol. i. p. 112.

consider was "how far we can depend upon the continued, steady, and frictionless operation of the machinery we shall have set up. A great part of what we are about to inaugurate will be of necessity tentative and experimental. . . . Before a guarantee of Egypt's independence can be said to exist, the administrative system of which it is the leading characteristic must have time to consolidate, in order to resist disintegrating influences from within and without, and to acquire the use and knowledge of its own capacities. . . . With such an accumulation of difficulties, native statesmanship, even though supplemented by the new-born institutions, will hardly be able to cope, unless assisted for a time by our sympathy and guidance. Under these circumstances, I would venture to submit that we can hardly consider the work of reorganisation complete, or the responsibilities imposed upon us by circumstances adequately discharged, until we have seen Egypt shake herself free from the initial embarrassments which I have enumerated above." In other words, Lord Dufferin, without absolutely stating that the British occupation must be indefinitely prolonged, clearly indicated the maintenance of the paramount influence of the British Government for an indefinite period as an essential condition to the execution of the policy of reform.

Lord Dufferin threw out another important hint. "If," he said, "I had been commissioned to place affairs in Egypt on the footing of an Indian subject State, the outlook would have been different. The masterful hand of a Resident would have quickly bent everything to his will." After detailing the advantages to be derived from this system of government, Lord Dufferin added: "The Egyptians would have justly considered these advantages as dearly purchased at the expense of their domestic independence. Moreover, Her Majesty's Government and the public opinion of England have pronounced against any such alternative." Public opinion in England, however, had not pronounced strongly against this alternative. On the contrary, many people were of opinion that the course indicated by Lord Dufferin was the best to adopt. It is, moreover, possible, in spite of the forced condemnation which he pronounced, that Lord Dufferin was of a somewhat similar opinion. It was, indeed, clear that for some long while to come, the representative of the British Government in Egypt would of necessity be more than an ordinary diplomatic agent. "The title-deeds of all political authority," it has been truly said, "are elastic."[1] Their elasticity was about to be put to the test in Egypt.

The question of who should be the man then arose. I was at that time in India. Sir Edward Malet was promoted to be Minister at Brussels. The British Government did me the honour of inviting me to become his successor. I accepted the invitation and arrived in Cairo on September 11, 1883.

[1] Oliver's *Alexander Hamilton*, p. 169.

PART III

THE SOUDAN

1882–1907

The difficulties of the case have passed entirely beyond the limits of such political and military difficulties as I have known in the course of an experience of half a century.

Mr. GLADSTONE, *Speech in the House of Commons on Soudan affairs, February 23, 1885.*

CHAPTER XIX

THE HICKS EXPEDITION

January–November 1883

Extent of Egyptian territory—Misgovernment in the Soudan—Slave-hunting—Said Pasha's views—Colonel Stewart's Report—The Mahdi—Military and financial situation—Interference from Cairo—Attitude of the British Government—Destruction of General Hicks's army.

THE affairs of the Soudan exercised a very important influence on the course of events in Egypt, more especially during the years which immediately followed the British occupation of the country. They will, therefore, be treated separately.

At the time when this narrative commences, the nominal authority of the Khedive extended over an area stretching from Wadi Halfa on the north to the Equator on the south, a distance of about 1300 miles, and from Massowah on the east to the western limit of the Darfour province on the west, a distance of about 1300 miles—that is to say, he ruled, or attempted to rule, over a territory twice as big as France and Germany together.

The worst forms of misgovernment existed over this vast tract of country. Sir Samuel Baker, on the occasion of his second visit to the Soudan in 1870, wrote: "I observed with dismay a frightful change in the features of the country between Berber and the capital since my former visit. The rich soil on the banks of the river, which had a few years since been highly cultivated, was abandoned.

. . . There was not a dog to howl for a lost master.
Industry had vanished; oppression had driven the
inhabitants from the soil."[1]   The taxes, which
were excessive in amount, were collected by Bashi-
Bozouks.   These agents were described by Colonel
Stewart, who was sent to the Soudan in the winter
of 1882-83 to report on the state of the country, as
" swaggering bullies, robbing, plundering, and ill-
treating the people with impunity."   In addition,
moreover, to the evils attendant on a thoroughly
bad and oppressive system of government, the
Soudan suffered from a scourge peculiar to itself.
It was the happy hunting-ground of the Arab
slave-dealer.   "The entire country," Sir Samuel
Baker wrote, "was leased out to piratical slave-
hunters, under the name of traders, by the
Khartoum Government."

Even assuming that Ismail Pasha was sincere
in his desire to suppress slavery and to govern
the Soudan well, nothing is more certain than
that he was powerless to do so.   *Qui trop
embrasse, mal étreint.*   In extending his dominions
to the centre of Africa, the Khedive had undertaken a task which was far beyond the military
and financial resources, as well as the administrative capacity of the Egyptian Government.
His predecessor, Said Pasha, saw this, although
during his time the area, over which the Khedive
of Egypt was supposed to exercise authority,
was far smaller than in 1883.   In 1856, Said
Pasha visited Khartoum.   "After due consideration he had almost decided to abandon the country,
and was only restrained from doing so by the
Sheikhs and Notables pointing out the inevitable
anarchy that would result from such a measure."
Twenty-seven years later, Colonel Stewart saw
that the only hope of improvement lay in abandon-

[1] *Ismailia*, p. 11.

ing some of the outlying provinces of the Soudan, and thus bringing the ambitious task, which the Egyptian Government had set itself to perform, within comparatively manageable limits. "It is generally acknowledged," he wrote, "that the Soudan is, and has for many years been, a source of loss to the Egyptian Government. . . . Putting, however, the financial view of the question aside, I am firmly convinced that the Egyptians are quite unfit in every way to undertake such a trust as the government of so vast a country with a view to its welfare, and that both for their own sake and that of the people they try to rule, it would be advisable to abandon large portions of it. The fact of their incompetence to rule is so generally acknowledged that it is unnecessary to discuss the question."

There is a tradition in the Mohammedan world that, at some future time, a Mahdi[1] will appear on earth, upon whose coming the world will be converted to the Mohammedan religion. A variety of unauthorised rumours are current amongst the lower orders of Mohammedans as to the appearance and qualities of the true Mahdi, such as, for instance, that he will have very long hands; but these are discarded by the more learned classes. A work written at Mecca in 1883 by a Sherif of that place, and entitled *The Conquests of Islam*, contains what may be considered as an authorised version of the conditions which the true Mahdi must fulfil. "The greatest of the signs," it is said, "shall be that he shall be of the line of Fatma (*i.e.* a Sherif, or descendant of the Prophet); that he shall be proclaimed Mahdi against his will, not seeking such proclamation for himself, and not causing strife amongst the Faithful to obtain it, nor even yielding to it till threatened with death by them.

[1] The literal meaning of the word "Mahdi" is one who is "conducted in the right path."

He shall be proclaimed in the Mosque of Mecca,
not elsewhere; he shall not appear save when there
is strife after the death of a Khalifa; he shall
neither come nor be proclaimed until such time as
there is no Khalifa over the Moslems.   His advent
shall coincide with that of Anti-Christ, after whom
Jesus will descend and join himself to the Mahdi.
These are the great signs of his coming.   The
others are imaginary or disputed, and whosoever
shall, of his own will, declare himself to be Mahdi
and try to assert himself by force, is a pretender,
such as have already appeared many times."

In August 1881, a man named Mohammed
Ahmed proclaimed himself to be the Mahdi in
the Soudan.[1]   He was born in 1843 in the
province of Dongola.   As a young man he was
apprenticed to his uncle, a boatbuilder in Sennar,
but the tendency which, from his earliest child-
hood, he had shown towards religious studies, led
him to abandon trade, and to enter a religious
school at Khartoum.   His mission, as explained
in his various Proclamations, was to gain over
the Soudan to his cause, then to march on Egypt,
overthrow the heretical Turks, and convert the
whole world.   All who opposed his mission were to
be destroyed, whether Christians, Mohammedans,
or Pagans.

Mohammed Ahmed was at once branded by

---

[1] Many persons had appeared in Egypt prior to 1881 claiming to be
the Mahdi. See, for instance, Colonel Burgoyne's *History, etc., 1798 to
1801*, p. 13. In Ismail Pasha's time, a Mahdi appeared in Upper Egypt.
He and his followers were put to death (see Lady Duff Gordon's
Letters from Egypt, p. 342). In the Koran, no allusion is made to the
coming of the Mahdi. The belief in a future Mahdi is based on a
Hadith, that is to say, one of the traditionary sayings of the Prophet,
which were recorded by Abu Bekr and others. It is confined to the
Sunnis. According to the Shiahs, the Mahdi has already appeared
in the person of Mohammed Abu el Kasim, the twelfth Imam, who is
believed to be concealed in some secret place until the day of his
manifestation before the end of the world.—Hughes's *Dictionary of
Islam*, p. 305.

orthodox Mohammedans in Egypt and elsewhere as a False Mahdi (Mutemahdi). Neither, in spite of the credulity and ignorance of the population of the Soudan, is it probable that he would have met with any success even in that province, had not the prevailing discontent predisposed the inhabitants against the Egyptian Government. It was, however, Colonel Stewart wrote, "a melancholy fact that the Government was almost universally hated and abhorred." The people, therefore, flocked to the standard of the Mahdi, whose prestige was increased by some successes gained over the Egyptian troops in the early days of the insurrectionary movement. It soon became apparent that the Egyptian Government had to deal, not with any petty disturbance which must sooner or later succumb to superior force, but with a formidable rebellion, the suppression of which would tax to the utmost their military and financial resources. What, therefore, was the nature of those resources?

The army was in a deplorable condition. "The troops in garrison here (at Khartoum)," Colonel Stewart wrote on January 5, 1883, "are working at elementary drill and tactics, and are making some progress. It is, however, very uphill work; the officers are so ignorant and so incapable of grasping the meaning of the simplest movement. Quite one-third of the troops are also ignorant of the use of the rifle, and they would be more formidable as adversaries were they simply armed with sticks. Many have also superstitious ideas of the power of the Mahdi." A little later (February 27), Colonel Stewart wrote: "It is impossible for me to criticise too severely the conduct of the Egyptian troops, both officers and men, towards the natives. Their general conduct and overbearing manner is almost sufficient to cause a rebellion. When to this conduct cowardice is added, it is impossible for me to avoid expressing my contempt and disgust." Moreover, the soldiers were imbued with Arábist sympathies; their loyalty to the Khedive was doubtful. "The question," Colonel Stewart wrote on February 16, "is whether they will remain faithful, or whether their cowardice may not induce them to desert, knowing, as they will, that the Mahdi will not harm them. . . . At one or two of the late skirmishes, they were heard exclaiming, 'Oh, Effendina Arábi! If you only knew the position Tewfik has placed us in!'"

The financial position was as bad as the military. The Soudan revenue for 1882 was estimated at £E.507,000, and the expenditure at £E.610,000, thus leaving a deficit of £E.103,000. There is little use in endeavouring to ascertain what the real revenue of the Soudan was at this time. No trustworthy accounts were kept. It is certain, however, that it had for years been the practice to overestimate the revenue, and it was obvious in the then condition of affairs that little or no revenue of any kind was to be expected. " There can be no doubt," Colonel Stewart wrote, " that the deficits of many provinces are very far in excess of those stated. Probably, no revenue whatever has been collected in the province of Kordofan. Much the same can also be said of Dara and Fashoda. Sennar, with perhaps Darfour, must also be in pretty much the same plight."

Several British officers, chief amongst whom was General Hicks, were appointed to the staff of the Soudan army in the spring of 1883. Shortly after his arrival at Khartoum in March 1883, General Hicks made an appeal to Cairo for help.

Those who have followed the account which

has already been given of the financial situation in
Egypt at that time, will be able to judge of the
degree of pecuniary assistance which it was possible
for the exhausted Treasury at Cairo to afford to
General Hicks.   Nevertheless, an effort was made
to provide funds for the Soudan.   General Hicks
was told that up to the end of the year 1883 the
Egyptian Government would provide him with
£E.147,000.   The pecuniary aid thus afforded,
though sufficient to cause embarrassment to the
Egyptian Treasury, was wholly inadequate to
meet General Hicks's wants.   It only amounted
to enough to provide for the pay of the men to
the end of the current year.   "The native Bashi-
Bozouks," General Hicks pointed out, "are still
months in arrears of pay.   The men on the Blue
Nile are in some cases two years in arrear."

The position, therefore, in the spring of 1883
was as follows:—The Treasury was exhausted;
the army was unpaid, undisciplined, untrained,
partially disloyal, and, therefore, worthless as a
fighting machine.

Under such conditions, the Egyptian Government had to face a formidable rebellion, which
drew its strength from two potent forces, namely:
first, the religious fervour of a credulous, fanatical,
but courageous population; secondly, the well-
merited hatred engendered by a long course of
misgovernment.   The difficulty of the task was
enhanced by the fact that the scene of the rebellion
was remote from the headquarters of the Government, and that the physical difficulties of communication with the base of operations were very great.
It was a task which would have taxed the resources
of a civilised Government whose affairs were conducted by men of the utmost energy and intelligence.   It was altogether beyond the strength of
the inexperienced Cairene administrators, who had

themselves only just emerged from an internal revolution which, but for foreign aid, would have been successful.

The Horatian maxim *Versate diu, quid ferre recusent, quid valeant humeri,* holds good of politics as well as of poetry. The first thing which the Egyptian Government ought to have done was to have considered whether their strength was proportionate to the task which they had undertaken. The main question to be decided was whether the Egyptian Government should, for the time being at all events, abandon the more remote parts of the Soudan and stand on the defensive at Khartoum, or whether an expedition should be sent into Kordofan, which had become the chief centre of rebellion, in the hope of dealing a crushing blow to the rising power of the Mahdi. The importance of the decision in this matter was realised by the British authorities on the spot, more especially by Colonel Stewart, who could speak with high authority on Soudan affairs. On December 27, 1882, that is to say, whilst El Obeid, the capital of the Kordofan province, was still besieged and Abdul-Kader Pasha, who was Governor-General of the Soudan, was preparing an expedition for its relief, Colonel Stewart wrote : "I would beg to point out how very important it is that the present expedition should prove a success. A failure would probably entail the total loss, if not of the Soudan, of at any rate many provinces. This truth can hardly be brought home with too much force to the Egyptian Government." At that time, Colonel Stewart thought that "Abdul-Kader had every right to expect a success." A little later (January 9), when Colonel Stewart had seen more of the Egyptian troops and had become strongly convinced of their inefficiency, he spoke less hopefully. Alluding to various small engagements in which the Egyptian troops had behaved badly, he wrote : "It is very evident that the matter will become exceedingly serious should the troops continue to exhibit such pusillanimity.   It will be quite hopeless to expect to cope successfully with the rebellion, and it will only remain with the Egyptian Government to make the best terms they can with the Mahdi." On January 16, he recurred to the same subject. "This move of Abdul-Kader," he wrote to Sir Edward Malet, "is a critical one, for, should he meet with any reverse, it will probably be a decisive one, as far as Egyptian authority in this country is concerned."

On February 16, when the fall of El Obeid was imminent, Colonel Stewart wrote : "The question now arises, 'What should be done in this crisis?' I think the first thing the Government will have to decide on will be whether the Kordofan expedition should leave or not.   My own opinion, from what I am told and know of the Egyptian soldiers, is that to send it would be to run a very great risk, and if the expedition were defeated, the probability is that the Soudan would be lost.   Should it be decided to give up the expedition, I would then suggest that orders should be at once sent to Slatin Bey, the Governor of Darfour, to destroy all his stores and retreat as best he can on the Bahr-el-Ghazal Province.   There is, of course, a chance that Khartoum may be beleaguered, but I can hardly fancy that even 10,000 Egyptian soldiers, if they remain faithful, and are commanded by some energetic officers, will allow themselves to be shut up."   Two days later (February 18), the news of the fall of El Obeid reached Khartoum.   On February 20, Colonel Stewart wrote : "I am strongly of opinion that to advance now on Kordofan would be exceedingly injudicious, and that the alternative policy of remaining on the defensive,

vigorously putting down any attempted rising on
this bank of the Nile, and waiting to see what
will happen, is the true one. To advance now with
our miserable troops against an enemy flushed with
recent success, well supplied with arms, and worked
up to a pitch of fanaticism, would be but to risk a
disaster with no corresponding advantage now that
Obeid has fallen. A serious disaster or, indeed, a
check, would also very probably involve the loss of
the whole of the Soudan." Speaking of the "utter
worthlessness of the Egyptian infantry," Colonel
Stewart added: "It is almost impossible for me
to convey an idea of the contempt with which all
classes of people here regard them. The negro
troops will not associate with them, nor will,
curiously enough, the Egyptian officers in command of those troops."[1]

It was unfortunate that Colonel Stewart's advice
was not followed. Both Lord Dufferin and Sir
Edward Malet shared his views. On April 2,
1883, Lord Dufferin had an interview with Ibrahim
Bey, the head of the Soudan Department at Cairo,
in which he said that "if the Egyptian Government
were wise, it would confine its present efforts to
the re-establishment of its authority in Sennar, and
would not seek to extend its dominion beyond that
province and the bordering river banks." In his
general report on Egypt, Lord Dufferin, whilst
deprecating the abandonment of the whole of the
Soudan, no necessity having as yet arisen for so
heroic a remedy, added: "I apprehend, however,

---

[1] In a letter dated September 1, 1883, Mr. Power, the British Consular Agent at Khartoum, wrote: "In three days, we march on a
campaign that even the most sanguine look forward to with the greatest
gloom. We have here 9000 infantry that fifty good men would rout
in ten minutes, and 1000 cavalry (Bashi-Bozouks) that have never learnt
even to ride, and these, with a few Nordenfelt guns, are to beat the
69,000 men whom the Mahdi has got together. . . . That Egyptian
officers and men are not worth the ammunition they throw away, is
well known."—Power's *Letters from Khartoum*, p. 20.

that it would be wise on the part of Egypt to abandon Darfour and perhaps part of Kordofan, and to be content with maintaining her jurisdiction in the provinces of Khartoum and Sennar." On June 5, when General Hicks was urging the Egyptian Government, through Sir Edward Malet, to give him more men and more money, the latter telegraphed to Lord Granville : "Your Lordship is aware that it is already impossible for the Egyptian Government to supply the funds demanded for the Soudan, and the proposed operations will run a considerable risk of failure unless they are conducted on a large scale, and unless the army is well supplied in every respect. Under these circumstances, a question arises as to whether General Hicks should be instructed to confine himself to maintaining the present supremacy of the Khedive in the region between the Blue and White Niles." Sir Edward Malet added that he "had furnished Chérif Pasha with a copy of General Hicks's telegram, as requested, but without comment or expression of opinion upon its contents."

What, however, was the opinion of General Hicks, the officer who was to command the expedition about to be sent against the Mahdi ? General Hicks's position was one of great difficulty. The Government at Cairo had not learnt the elementary lesson that, in dealing with a state of affairs such as that which then existed in the Soudan, the first essential and preliminary condition to success was to entrust the supreme command to one individual and to support him cordially. Ala-el-Din Pasha was sent to Khartoum to supersede Abdul-Kader Pasha, of whom Colonel Stewart thought highly ; but when he arrived (February 1883) he did not, in the first instance, declare his mission. "Although," Colonel Stewart wrote, "nominally

he has no official position, his presence is sufficient
to neutralise the influence of Abdul-Kader, with
the result that practically no one is in command."
It is easy to believe that the position of the
Governor-General at Khartoum was thus rendered
extremely difficult. Suleiman Pasha Niazi, who is
described by Colonel Stewart as "a miserable-look-
ing old man of seventy-four or seventy-five," was
sent up in nominal command of the troops, with
the understanding "that he was to defer in all
things to his subordinate (General Hicks), who was
held responsible for the direction of all preparations and operations." In addition to the confusion
caused by these arrangements, much harm resulted
from the inveterate habit, which was at that time
common to many high Egyptian authorities, of
giving orders direct to subordinate officials over
the heads of their superiors. After mentioning
a flagrant instance of this sort, Colonel Stewart
added (January 26): "I need hardly point out
how deplorable is this independent action of the
Khedive's. Should it continue, we shall not alone
have all the authorities here quarrelling with each
other, but it will be also quite impossible to carry
out any concerted plan. The Khedive must entrust
some one here with supreme authority (Dictator)
and then leave him alone. To telegraph what he
should do or not do, or to correspond with his
subordinates over his head, is only to make his
position quite untenable, and to insure a disastrous
termination to the campaign." Colonel Stewart's
letters written at this time, are full of complaints
of the "backstairs influence" exerted at Cairo, and
of the "unbusinesslike interference of the Cairo
Government in Soudan affairs." "Until matters,"
he wrote on February 27, "are conducted in a
businesslike, straightforward, and honest way, it is
hopeless to expect any amelioration in the Soudan."

The difficulties of a British officer suddenly thrust into the middle of these paltry intrigues can easily be imagined. General Hicks soon found his position intolerable. Suleiman Pasha in no way considered his own office as a sinecure. On the contrary, he paid no attention to the opinions expressed by General Hicks. At last, after making a series of complaints to which little attention was paid, General Hicks telegraphed, on July 16, to Sir Edward Malet: "My orders and arrangements here are quite disregarded ; promises are made that they shall be carried out, but nothing whatever is done. Suleiman Pasha disregards them altogether. It is useless to keep me here under these conditions, and it is a position which I cannot hold. I beg you will have me recalled." This telegram brought matters to a crisis. General Hicks was appointed Commander-in-Chief in the Soudan with the rank of General of Division. Suleiman Pasha was recalled from Khartoum, but any good effect, which might otherwise have been produced by this measure, was marred owing to his being at once named Governor of the Eastern Soudan. His new appointment, General Hicks telegraphed, was "looked upon as promotion."

In view of the intrigues which surrounded General Hicks, of the wretched material of which his army was composed, and of the fact that the Egyptian Government could not comply with his requests for men and money, it is scarcely conceivable that he should have been confident of success. But he seems to have underrated the difficulties of the task which lay before him. He was perhaps unduly elated at some trifling successes gained during the early stages of the rebellion over the forces of the Mahdi. He thought (June 23) that as he advanced, the tribes, though "afraid of commencing hostilities against the Mahdi,

would join him as camp-followers." It does
not appear that at any time General Hicks
was definitely asked by the Egyptian Government to state his views as to the wisdom of
undertaking the expedition, though it might have
been supposed that ordinary prudence would have
dictated the necessity of obtaining, in official form,
a very distinct expression of his opinion on this
momentous question. But on June 18, that is to
say about three months before he started into
the Kordofan desert, he telegraphed to General
Valentine Baker, who was at the time at the head
of the Egyptian Police: "In my telegram of the
3rd of June to Malet, I pointed out what I thought
was necessary to ensure success in Kordofan and
guard against all possible eventualities.[1] At the
same time I am prepared to undertake the campaign
with the force available; the risks are, as I have
said, in case of a mishap, but I think this is not
at all probable. Khartoum ought to be safe from
outside under any circumstances."

Looking to the terms of this telegram, it is
not difficult to judge of General Hicks's frame of
mind. In view of the fact that the expeditionary
force, as it eventually started, was below the
strength which he recommended, and that the
material of which the army was composed was of
the worst possible description, it can scarcely be
conceived that he felt sanguine of success. It

---

[1] The telegram to which allusion is here made runs as follows:
"The force we have is not nearly sufficient to undertake the Kordofan
campaign. . . . It should be 10,000 men. What number of men will
it be possible for the Government to send me in augmentation? When
we consider that a defeat might mean not only the loss of Darfour and
Kordofan, but also of Sennai, and possibly Khartoum, I think no risk
should be run." It was this telegram which elicited the opinion
expressed by Sir Edward Malet (vide ante, p. 359) that General Hicks
should confine his operations to the country lying between the Blue
and White Niles. But the telegram was sent on to Chérif Pasha "without comment or expression of opinion." The natural result ensued.
General Hicks's weighty opinions were never properly considered.

may be surmised that his qualified expression of willingness to undertake the campaign was inspired, not so much by any heartfelt confidence of success based on a full consideration of the whole of the facts, as by the reluctance naturally felt by a gallant soldier to appear to shrink from a dangerous undertaking.

The truth is that the decision in this matter should not have been left to General Hicks. It was from no fault of their own that the Government which then existed at Cairo were powerless to provide the resources, whether in men or money, which were necessary in order to suppress the rebellion. The helplessness of the Khedive's Government was the result of the misgovernment of the Khedive's predecessor. But it behoved the Egyptian Ministers to look the facts with which they had to deal fairly in the face, and to bring the objects, which they sought to attain, into harmony with the means which they possessed for attaining them. They did nothing of the sort. They drifted on, until at last they brought on their heads a catastrophe, which involved the collapse of Egyptian authority over the whole of the Soudan.

There was only one method by which the realities of the situation might have been brought home to the minds of the Khedive and his Ministers. The British Government should have insisted on the adoption of a rational and practicable policy. Unfortunately, they abstained from all interference. They appear, indeed, to have seen that the wisest plan for the Egyptian Government would have been to stand on the defensive at Khartoum. But they did nothing to enforce this view.

The British Government had, in fact, been led much against their will into the occupation of Egypt. They were now fearful that they might unconsciously drift into military intervention in the Soudan. Lord Granville was determined to guard against this danger. He refused to have anything to say to Soudan matters. The fact that General Hicks's telegrams were sent to the various Egyptian authorities through Sir Edward Malet roused him to a sense of danger. He thought that the British representative, by allowing himself to become the medium of communication between Cairo and Khartoum, might involve his Government in some degree of responsibility. On May 7, Lord Granville, therefore, telegraphed to Mr. Cartwright, who temporarily occupied Sir Edward Malet's place: "Her Majesty's Government are in no way responsible for the operations in the Soudan, which have been undertaken under the authority of the Egyptian Government, or for the appointment or actions of General Hicks." This disclaimer of responsibility was repeated in a letter addressed by Sir Edward Malet to Chérif Pasha on May 22, when forwarding another telegram addressed by General Hicks to Lord Dufferin. "In this particular instance," Sir Edward said, "I desire to guard against any supposition on the part of Your Excellency that my sending a copy of the telegram to Your Excellency indicates any expression of opinion with regard to the recommendations contained in it."

A little later, Lord Granville was again alarmed at the continuance of communication between Sir Edward Malet and General Hicks. On August 8, he wrote to Sir Edward Malet: "It appears that General Hicks continues to communicate with you respecting the financial difficulties which he meets with in the Soudan, under the impression that you will exert your influence with the Egyptian Government to induce them to give favourable consideration to his wishes. I need not remind you that Her Majesty's Government assume no responsibility whatever in regard to the conduct of affairs in the Soudan, and it is desirable that General Hicks should understand that, although they are glad to receive information as to the progress of the campaign, it is their policy to abstain as much as possible from interference with the action of the Egyptian Government in that quarter." Sir Edward Malet informed Lord Granville that his action had been in strict conformity with the instructions he had received on this subject. He took steps, also, to render the position clear to General Hicks. On August 18, he telegraphed to General Hicks: "I congratulate you on your appointment as Commander-in-Chief and General of Division. The act is spontaneous on the part of the Egyptian Government, for although I am ready to transmit to them telegrams that come from you, I am debarred by my instructions from giving advice with regard to action on them, the policy of Her Majesty's Government being to abstain as much as possible from interference with the action of the Egyptian Government in the Soudan."

The objections to British military intervention were obvious, neither was the danger against which Lord Granville sought to guard imaginary. It might well have happened that, almost before the Government were aware of it, they might have found themselves in a situation which would have obliged them to assert their authority by force of arms in the Soudan. The history of the rise of British power in the East served as a warning that one forward step in the direction of territorial extension often leads to another, until at last a goal is reached far more distant than any which was originally contemplated. Moreover, when once a question, such as the state of the Soudan,

becomes a matter for public discussion in England,
there are not wanting many who, partly from the
love of adventure natural to most Englishmen,
partly from a keen sense of the benefits which
would be conferred locally by British interference,
and partly from a great, perhaps an exaggerated
idea of England's mission as a civilising agent in
the world, are prone to push on the Government
to action without sufficient consideration of the
ultimate consequences of their proposals. Under
these circumstances, it behoved a wise statesman to
move cautiously. Nevertheless, looking back over
the course of events as we now know them, it
must be admitted that the line of action which Lord
Granville adopted was very unfortunate. It is to
be regretted that he did not by timely interference
save the Egyptian Government from the consequences of their own want of foresight. Had he,
acting on the views expressed by the various
British authorities in Egypt, stepped in and for-
bidden the despatch of the Hicks expedition to
Kordofan, not only would thousands of lives and
the large sums of money, which were subsequently
squandered, have been saved, but he would have
deserved the gratitude of the Egyptian people, and
would have saved his own country from that interference which he so much dreaded, and which was
eventually precipitated by the negative policy
adopted in the early stage of the proceedings.
Lord Granville appears to have thought that he
effectually threw off all responsibility by declaring
that he was not responsible. There could not have
been a greater error. The responsibility of the
British Government for the general conduct of
affairs in Egypt did not depend on a few phrases
thrown into a despatch and subsequently published
in a parliamentary paper. It was based on the
facts that the British Government were in military

occupation of the country, that the weakness and inefficiency of the native rulers were notorious, and that the civilised world fixed on England a responsibility which it was impossible to shake off so long as the occupation lasted. "Those," Lord Salisbury said in the House of Lords (February 12, 1884), "who have the absolute power of preventing lamentable events, and knowing what is taking place, refuse to exercise that power, are responsible for what happens." Lord Granville failed to see this. Instead of recognising the facts of the situation, he took shelter behind an illusory abnegation of responsibility, which was a mere phantasm of the diplomatic and parliamentary mind. The result was that the facts asserted themselves in defiance of diplomacy and parliamentary convenience.

It may, however, be urged in defence of the policy adopted by Lord Granville that he does not appear to have received sufficient warning of the possible, and, indeed, probable consequences of inaction. What was most of all required was that an alarm-bell should be rung to rouse the British Government from its lethargy, and show that the consequences of inaction might be more serious than those of action.[1] But no sufficient warning appears to have been given. The result was that the Egyptian Government blundered on headlong to their own destruction, and that the British Government, like the frail beauty of Byron's poem, whilst vowing that they would ne'er consent to a policy of intervention in the Soudan, consented but a short time afterwards to a degree

---

[1] "I am not of the opinion of those gentlemen who are against disturbing the public repose; I like a clamour when there is an abuse. The fire-bell at midnight disturbs your sleep, but it keeps you from being burned in your bed. The hue-and-cry alarms the country, but it preserves all the property of the province."—Burke's *Speech on the Prosecution for Libels.*

of intervention far greater than would have been necessary had the true facts of the situation been in the first instance recognised.

On September 8, 1883, that is to say, three days before my arrival in Egypt, General Hicks started on the expedition, which was to terminate in so disastrous a manner. At Cairo, news from the Soudan was anxiously awaited, but no one contemplated the possibility of the disaster which shortly ensued. I remember speaking to Chérif Pasha as to the desirability of giving up the outlying provinces of the Soudan. He was not disinclined to give up Darfour; on the other hand, he held strongly to Kordofan. But, he added, with the light-heartedness characteristic of a Gallicised Egyptian, "Nous en causerons plus tard; d'abord nous allons donner une bonne raclée à ce monsieur" (*i.e.* the Mahdi).[1]

Chérif Pasha was soon undeceived. On November 22, news reached Cairo that on the 5th General Hicks's army had been totally destroyed. "Hardly anything was known of the country into which the army was venturing, beyond the fact that it was the driest in the Soudan." The last communication received from General Hicks spoke of the want of water and of the intense heat. The final catastrophe is described by Colonel Colville in the following words: "On advancing to Kasghil, the army was led astray by the guides, who were Mahdi's men, and who, when they were sure that it was thoroughly lost in the bush, deserted it. After wandering three days and

---

[1] On January 4, 1884, Sir Charles W. Wilson wrote: "When Hicks Pasha left Cairo, it was not intended that he should do more than clear Sennar of rebel bands, a work he accomplished with ease, and protect Khartoum. It is useless to inquire what madness made the Egyptian Government order Hicks Pasha to attempt the reconquest of Kordofan; it was a hazardous operation, and with the troops employed, of whom Colonel Stewart has given a faithful picture, disaster was an almost foregone conclusion."

nights without water, they came upon a force of the enemy near Kasghil. But many hundreds had already died from thirst, and the remainder were too feeble to offer any determined resistance, and were soon despatched by the enemy. A brilliant charge was made by Hicks Pasha and his staff, who all died fighting like men." [1]

It was not until twenty-two years later that the site of the Hicks disaster was visited by any European. Sir Reginald Wingate went over the ground in the course of a tour through Kordofan during the winter of 1905-6. He recorded his impressions in the following words :—

I visited the battlefield where the late General Hicks Pasha and his force were almost entirely annihilated by the Dervish hordes in 1883, despite the fact that within a mile of the spot where the thirst-stricken troops were overwhelmed was a large pool of water, of which they were apparently in complete ignorance. The locality is in the depths of a huge forest some thirty miles south of El Obeid, and I have no hesitation in hazarding the opinion that, had the efforts to relieve El Obeid been conducted by a far more numerous and efficient force, the result would have been the same. It is abundantly evident that the Government of that period neither realised the situation nor appreciated the enormous difficulties attendant on the movement of a large force through such country; the dispatch of the expedition, under the circumstances, can only be characterised as an act of extreme folly.

Thus, the whole edifice of territorial aggrandisement in Africa, which Ismail Pasha and his predecessors, in an evil moment for their country, had planned, toppled to the ground. It was built on no sure foundation. The power gained by semi-civilised skill over the wild tribes of the Soudan had been grossly misused. Slave-hunting Pashas, and corrupt and extortionate tax-collectors, had

[1] *History of the Soudan Campaign*, p. 16.

rendered the name of Egypt hateful to the people. A despotism, which is neither strong nor beneficent, must perforce fall directly it is exposed to serious attack. The bubble Government established by Ismail Pasha and his predecessors in the Soudan collapsed directly it was pricked by the religious impostor who was now to rule the country, neither amongst the population whose fate was at stake in the combat was a voice raised or a sword drawn to avert its downfall.

CHAPTER XX

THE ABANDONMENT OF THE SOUDAN

NOVEMBER 1883–JANUARY 1884

My position—I press the British Government to depart from a passive attitude — Lord Granville's reply — The Egyptian Government decide to hold Khartoum — Colonel Coetlogon recommends a retreat on Berber—Opinions of the military authorities at Cairo —The Egyptian Government wish to invoke the aid of the Sultan—The British Government recommend withdrawal from the Soudan—The Egyptian Ministers resign—Nubar Pasha takes office—Observations on the policy of withdrawal from the Soudan.

I HAVE so far been dealing with a period of Egyptian history during which I either played a subordinate part, or was in no way connected with Egypt. I have occasionally criticised the acts of those who were responsible for the conduct of Egyptian affairs at this time. I now reach another period. It would be false modesty not to recognise that from this time forward I was myself one of the principal actors on the Egyptian stage, not, of course, to the extent of being responsible for the general policy of the British Government, but rather to the extent of being mainly responsible for the management of local affairs in Egypt. This latter responsibility I accept, only begging that it should be borne in mind that my action had of necessity to conform itself to the lines of general policy adopted in London.

During the period when I represented the

British Government in Egypt, Egyptian affairs frequently formed the subject of public discussion. My own conduct was at times sharply criticised. Any one engaged in English public life must expect at times to receive some hard knocks. I believe I know, perhaps better than any one else, the mistakes which I committed, and I shall use my best endeavours to deal with them at least as unsparingly as I have dealt with what appear to me to be the mistakes of others. *Se judice, nemo nocens absolvitur.*

The first step of any importance taken in connection with Soudan affairs after my arrival in Egypt was on November 19, 1883, on which day I sent the following telegram to Lord Granville: "The position of affairs in the Soudan is becoming very serious. . . . Nothing definite has been heard of Hicks since September 27. He only had provisions for two months. The Egyptian Government are very anxious, and evidently anticipate bad news. Giegler Pasha, who was with Gordon in the Soudan, and whom I saw to-day, says that if Hicks is beaten, Khartoum will probably fall. In fact, the Egyptian Government have no money, and excepting Wood's and Baker's forces,[1] they have sent almost their last available man to the Soudan. If Hicks's army is destroyed, I have little doubt that, unless they get assistance from outside, they will lose the whole of the Soudan. Neither, if once they begin to fall back, is it easy to say where along the valley of the Nile they could arrest the rebel movement. From some observations which Chérif Pasha let drop to me this morning, I think it not at all improbable that before long he will ask for the assistance of English or Indian troops. He said

---

[1] Sir Evelyn Wood commanded the Egyptian army then in course of formation. General Valentine Baker commanded the Gendarmerie.

to me, 'I suppose Her Majesty's Government would not like to see Turks intervene in the Soudan?' Shall I be right in telling him, if the occasion arises, that under no circumstances must he look for the assistance of British or Indian troops in the Soudan? As regards Turkish assistance, I should be glad to receive instructions as to the attitude I am to adopt. It is a question which course the Egyptian Government would dislike most—to call in the Turks, or to abandon the Soudan. My own opinion is that, if Hicks be beaten, the wisest course for the Egyptian Government to adopt is to accept defeat and fall back on whatever point on the Nile they can hold with confidence, although the adoption of this course would certainly give a great impulse to the Slave Trade. But it will not be easy to persuade them of this. Turkish intervention would, I think, be most undesirable. . . . I may now, at any moment, be forced to discuss these Soudan affairs with Chérif Pasha, and it is, therefore, desirable that I should receive some indications of Your Lordship's views. It will be very difficult, under the circumstances, to maintain a purely passive attitude, and to give no advice whatsoever."

To this telegram Lord Granville replied, on November 20, in the following words: "We cannot lend English or Indian troops. . . . It would not be for the advantage of Egypt to invite Turkish troops into the Soudan. If consulted, recommend the abandonment of the Soudan within certain limits."

The principal object which I had in view in sending my telegram of November 19 was to draw the British Government out of the passive attitude which they had hitherto adopted. A short residence in the country had been sufficient to convince me that it was neither possible nor

desirable to leave the Egyptian Government to
manage Soudan affairs without any advice or
assistance.[1]   My object had been attained.   It
is true that I was instructed only to give
advice "if consulted," but as I was sure to be
consulted, the reserve placed on my action did
not practically hamper me.   I had obtained a
definite expression of opinion as to the Soudan
policy which commended itself to the British
Government in the event of a disaster happening
to General Hicks's army.   They would not afford
military aid to reconquer the Soudan; they were
also averse to the employment of Turkish troops.
Under these circumstances, the only possible
course to pursue would be to abandon the Soudan
within certain limits.   This is the policy which,
as has been already mentioned, commended itself
to Lord Dufferin, Sir Edward Malet, and Colonel
Stewart; but the telegram which I sent on
November 19, was, so far as I am aware, the first
occasion upon which the British Government were
strongly pressed to express a decided opinion on the
subject.   I consider myself, therefore, largely responsible for initiating the policy of withdrawal from
the Soudan.   On Mr. Gladstone's Government rests
the responsibility of approving that policy.

So early as November 18, a report reached
Cairo that General Hicks's army was surrounded
and in want of provisions.   But it was not till

---

[1] On November 22, I wrote privately to Lord Granville : "I fully
understand the policy of the Government, which is not to be drawn
into affairs in the Soudan.   I see no reason why this policy should not
be carried out.   On the other hand, it is quite impossible to separate
the Egyptian question from the Soudan question altogether."   In
another letter, dated December 23, I said: "The separation of the
Soudan question from the question of Egypt proper was always well-
nigh impossible on financial grounds.   Now, it has become quite
impossible.   I think the policy of complete abandonment is, on the
whole, the best of which the circumstances admit ; but I am not sure if
the extreme difficulty of carrying it out, or the consequences to which
it must almost inevitably lead, are fully appreciated at home."

the 22nd that intelligence was received of the destruction of the army.

I did not at once press any advice on the Egyptian Government. In the first place, contradictory reports continued to be received regarding the fate of General Hicks's army, and, indeed, some weeks elapsed before all doubts as to the occurrence of the disaster were removed. In the second place, it was necessary to consult the military authorities, who naturally required time to study the facts of the case before expressing any opinion as to the course to be adopted. In the third place, I wished to give the Egyptian Government time in order to see whether they would be able to devise any practicable policy of their own.

The first decision at which the Egyptian Government arrived was "to try and hold Khartoum, and to reopen the route between Suakin and Berber." In reporting this decision to Lord Granville, on November 23, I said that "according to several telegrams received from Khartoum, there appeared to be a general opinion on the spot that it would be impossible to hold the town, and that it would be necessary to fall back on Berber."

On November 26, Colonel Coetlogon, an officer of General Hicks's army who had remained at Khartoum, telegraphed to Sir Evelyn Wood in the following terms: "I think it right to let you know the situation. Khartoum and Sennar cannot be held. In two months' time, there will be no food. All supplies are cut off. To save what remains of the army in the Soudan, a retreat on Berber should be made at once, and, by a combined movement from Berber and Suakin, that route should be opened. Reinforcements arriving could not reach Khartoum except by land, and for that a very large force is necessary. . . . The troops that are left are the refuse of the army, mostly old and blind. Again I say, the only way of saving what remains is to attempt a general retreat on Berber. This is the real state of affairs here, and I beg of you to impress it on His Highness the Khedive."

By December 3, I had obtained the views of the principal British military authorities in Cairo, and I was able to report to Lord Granville on the situation. "The most important question for the moment," I said, "is to know whether the Egyptian Government will be able to maintain themselves at Khartoum. I have had the advantage of fully discussing this question with General Stephenson, Sir Evelyn Wood, and General Baker.[1] All these high military authorities are of one opinion. They consider that, if the Mahdi advances, it will be impossible for the Egyptian Government to hold Khartoum, I mean, of course, with any forces of which they now dispose, or are likely to dispose. I leave out of account the contingency of despatching forces to Khartoum belonging either to Her Majesty the Queen or His Imperial Majesty the Sultan. Your Lordship has informed me that Her Majesty's Government are not prepared to send English or Indian troops to the Soudan. I will not now attempt to discuss

---

[1] Sir Frederick Stephenson then commanded the British army of occupation. General Baker left for Suakin during the course of these discussions. He did not see my despatch before he left Cairo. I, therefore, wrote to him with a view to ascertaining whether I had rightly interpreted the opinions which he had expressed to me verbally. He replied on January 7, 1884, in the following terms: "1. I did not believe that, without the aid of exterior power, Egypt could reconquer or hold the Soudan. 2. I believed that the loss of the Soudan would be a disastrous blow to Egypt, and that the expenditure necessary for the defence of Egypt proper would be ruinous to her financially in the future, and far in excess of the sum which the Soudan had cost in the past. 3. I thought it necessary that both England and Egypt should immediately adopt a definite policy, and that the latter should prepare to withdraw from the Soudan, unless England could afford such aid as would enable her to recover it and hold it." This, of course, really meant that General Baker wished the British Government to undertake the reconquest of the Soudan.

the possible contingency of troops belonging to His Imperial Majesty the Sultan being sent to the Soudan. The adoption of this last-named measure involves serious political considerations, which I must leave to the appreciation of Her Majesty's Government.

"The reasons which have led General Stephenson, Sir Evelyn Wood, and General Baker to the conclusions that, if the Mahdi advances, it will be impossible for the Egyptian Government to hold Khartoum are that the garrison is demoralised, that they have little or no confidence in the fighting qualities of the soldiers, that the Egyptian Government have no adequate reinforcements to send, and that the difficulty of provisioning the place, whether from the north or the south, is very great, as are also the difficulties of maintaining a line of communications. It is also very doubtful whether General Baker will be able by force to open up the Suakin-Berber route.[1] . . . General Stephenson and Sir Evelyn Wood are of opinion that if the Egyptian Government be left to rely exclusively on their own resources, and the Mahdi advances, Khartoum must fall. They think that an endeavour should be made to open out the Berber-Suakin route, not because the mere establishment of communication between those two points will enable the Egyptian Government, with the forces at their disposal, to hold Khartoum, but because the success of General Baker's undertaking will afford the best hope of retreat to the garrisons of Khartoum and the immediate neighbourhood.

"If Khartoum is abandoned, they think that the whole valley of the Nile down to Wadi Halfa or thereabouts will probably be lost to the Egyptian Government.

[1] General Baker's expedition to Suakin will be described in a subsequent chapter.

"I have dwelt especially on the opinions of General Stephenson and Sir Evelyn Wood, because, as they have seen this despatch, I am confident that I am rightly interpreting their views. I may, however, add that I have gathered, in communication with Baker Pasha, that his views on the military situation do not differ materially from those of General Stephenson and Sir Evelyn Wood.

"My own views on the points which I have so far discussed are, relatively speaking, of little value. But I should wish to say that, in view of the facts with which we have to deal, it appears to me scarcely possible to arrive at any other conclusions than those of General Stephenson and Sir Evelyn Wood. Their views are also shared by Mr. Clifford Lloyd,[1] who has been present at many of our discussions.

"I need hardly say that these views are, not unnaturally, very unpalatable to the Egyptian Government. I hardly think that Chérif Pasha believes that he will be able to hold Khartoum if the Mahdi advances, but neither he nor his colleagues can make up their minds to abandoning it."

Whilst this despatch was on its way to London, daily discussions took place in Cairo about the policy which was to be pursued. It became clearer every day that, if the Egyptian Government were left to themselves, they would never decide upon any definite and practicable policy. On December 10, I sent the following private telegram to Lord Granville: "I have not telegraphed for fresh instructions as I thought it useless to do so until events had developed somewhat, and I had something definite to recommend. But it is quite clear to me that more

---

[1] Mr. Clifford Lloyd had been sent to Egypt to reorganise the Department of the Interior.

definite instructions must shortly be sent as to the
attitude of Her Majesty's Government and as to
the advice to be given to the Egyptian Government. At present, they are drifting on without
any very definite or practical plan of action, and
will continue to do so unless they are told what
course to pursue." This was followed, on
December 12, by an official telegram in which I
informed Lord Granville that Chérif Pasha had
called upon me and informed me that "the Khedive
had held a Council of Ministers and that they had
resolved to place themselves absolutely in the hands
of Her Majesty's Government." The Egyptian
Government thought that the best solution of the
question was to invite the aid of the Sultan. They
wished the British Government to arrange the conditions under which Turkish aid would be afforded,
the principal of these conditions being that the
Sultan's troops should leave the country when
their presence was no longer required. Chérif
Pasha pointed out that as the rebellion in the
Soudan was a religious movement, it would probably gather strength if British or Indian troops
were employed.

On December 13, Lord Granville replied in the
following terms: "Her Majesty's Government
have no intention of employing British or Indian
troops in the Soudan. Her Majesty's Government
have no objection to offer to the employment of
Turkish troops, provided they are paid by the
Turkish Government, and that such employment
be restricted exclusively to the Soudan, with their
base at Suakin. Excepting for securing the safe
retreat of the garrisons still holding positions in
the Soudan, Her Majesty's Government cannot
agree to increasing the burden on the Egyptian
revenues by expenditure for operations which, even
if successful, and this is not probable, would be

of doubtful advantage to Egypt. Her Majesty's Government recommend the Ministers of the Khedive to come to an early decision to abandon all territory south of Assouan, or, at least, of Wadi Halfa. They will be prepared to assist in maintaining order in Egypt proper, and in defending it, as well as the ports of the Red Sea."

On December 16, I informed Lord Granville that I had communicated to Chérif Pasha the leading features of the policy of the British Government in respect to Soudan affairs. Chérif Pasha told me that he saw considerable objections to the abandonment of the territory south of Wadi Halfa. He promised that he would communicate to me a written Memorandum on the subject. On December 22, Chérif Pasha gave me this Memorandum. The Egyptian Government, it was said, "cannot agree to the abandonment of territories which they consider absolutely necessary for the security, and even for the existence, of Egypt itself." Chérif Pasha reiterated his proposal that Turkish troops should be sent under conditions to be negotiated in concert with the British Government.

The impression left on my mind during the course of these discussions was that the Egyptian Government were only half in earnest in their desire to invoke Turkish aid. My belief at the time was that they wished to use the suggestion about the employment of Turkish troops as an instrument by which to force the hand of the British Government, and oblige the latter to employ British troops. Moreover, the condition laid down by the British Government to the effect that the Ottoman Treasury should bear the cost of the expedition, was practically prohibitive. In telegraphing the substance of Chérif Pasha's note to Lord Granville, I, therefore, added the following remarks : "If negotiations are commenced with the Porte on the basis of the latter paying, they are, I conceive, almost certain to fail. I believe that the policy recommended by Her Majesty's Government is, on the whole, the best of which the very difficult circumstances admit. . . . No amount of argument or persuasion will make the present Ministry adopt the policy of abandonment. The only way in which it can be carried out is for me to inform the Khedive that Her Majesty's Government insist on its adoption, and that if the present Ministers will not carry it out, he must name others who will do so. Further, I am not sure that any Egyptian Ministers can be found who will be willing to carry out the policy, and capable of doing so. If, therefore, it is forced on the Egyptian Government, Her Majesty's Government must be prepared to face the possible contingency of appointing English Ministers temporarily."

Some delay ensued before any answer was sent to this telegram. In the interval, Chérif Pasha presented me, on January 2, 1884, with a further Note. In this Note, it was stated that the Egyptian Government proposed to apply to the Porte for 10,000 men. In the event of their request being refused, they wished to restore the Eastern Soudan and the ports of the Red Sea to the Sultan, and to endeavour with their own resources to hold the valley of the Nile up to Khartoum. In forwarding this proposal to Lord Granville, I said: "I can only say that I entirely disbelieve that any Egyptian force, which can be got together, will be capable of defending the whole length of the valley of the Nile from Khartoum downwards."

On January 4, I received Lord Granville's reply. It was to the effect that the British Government had no objection to the Sultan being asked to send troops to Suakin provided that there was no increase of Egyptian expenditure, and provided also that the decision to be taken by the Egyptian Government as regards its own movements was not retarded. Her Majesty's Government concurred in the proposal that, in the event of the Sultan declining to send troops, the administration of the shores of the Red Sea and of the Eastern Soudan should be given back to the Porte. As regards the suggestion that, with the frontiers thus reduced, the Egyptian Government should endeavour to hold the Nile up to Khartoum, Her Majesty's Government, it was said, "do not believe it to be possible for Egypt to defend Khartoum, and whilst recommending the concentration of the Egyptian troops, they desire that those forces should be withdrawn from Khartoum itself, as well as from the interior of the Soudan, and you will so inform Chérif Pasha."

Simultaneously with this telegram, a further confidential message was sent to me for use should occasion require. It was to the following effect: "It is essential that in important questions affecting the administration and safety of Egypt, the advice of Her Majesty's Government should be followed, as long as the provisional occupation continues. Ministers and Governors must carry out this advice or forfeit their offices. The appointment of English Ministers would be most objectionable, but it will no doubt be possible to find Egyptians who will execute the Khedive's orders under English advice. The Cabinet will give you full support."

On communicating the views of the British Government to Chérif Pasha, I found, as I had anticipated, a strong determination to reject the policy of withdrawal from Khartoum. I was, therefore, obliged to make use of the instructions contained in Lord Granville's confidential telegram.[1] The result was that, on January 7, Chérif Pasha tendered his resignation to the Khedive.

My position at this moment was one of considerable difficulty. The policy of withdrawal from the Soudan was very unpopular in Egypt. Riaz Pasha was asked to form a Ministry, but declined to accept the task. A rumour reached me that I should be told that no Ministry could be formed to carry out the policy of withdrawal from the Soudan; thus, it was hoped, the hand of the British Government would be forced, and Chérif Pasha would of necessity have returned to office to carry out his own policy. I had warned the British Government that they might have to face the possibility of nominating English Ministers. This, however, they were unwilling to do. My instructions were to get an Egyptian Ministry appointed. If, however, no Egyptian Ministry could be formed to carry out the policy recommended by the British Government, I intended to take the government temporarily into my own hands, and then telegraph to London for instructions. The Egyptians had, I know, some inkling of what was likely to happen, as, without making any official or private communication to the Ministers, I purposely allowed my intention to be known. The Khedive became alarmed at the prospect of my programme being carried into execution. He, therefore, decided to yield. On the night of January 7, he sent for me and informed me that he had accepted the resignation of his Ministers, and had sent for Nubar Pasha. He added that he "accepted cordially the policy of abandoning the whole of the Soudan, which, on mature reflection, he believed to be the best in the interests of the

---

[1] Although I was unable to agree with Chérif Pasha about Soudan affairs, my personal relations with him during all this period were excellent. On the day following his resignation, he dined at my house, to the great astonishment of all the gossips of Cairo.

country." On January 8, I was able to telegraph
to Lord Granville that Nubar Pasha had consented
to form a Ministry, and that "he entirely concurred in the wisdom of abandoning the Soudan,
retaining possession of Suakin."

Thus the general policy, which was to be
pursued, was definitely settled. It was, indeed,
high time to come to some decision. Mr. Power
telegraphed from Khartoum on December 30:
"The state of affairs here is very desperate." On
January 7, Colonel Coetlogon telegraphed to the
Khedive: "I would strongly urge on Your Highness the great necessity for an immediate order for
retreat being given. Were we twice as strong as
we are, we could not hold Khartoum against the
whole country, which, without a doubt, are one
and all against us."

Few measures have formed the subject of more
severe criticism than the policy adopted by Mr.
Gladstone's Government in 1883-84 in connection
with the Soudan. On February 12, 1884, a vote
of censure on the Government was moved by
Lord Salisbury in the House of Lords and by Sir
Stafford Northcote in the House of Commons.
It was couched in the following terms: "That
this House . . . is of opinion that the recent
lamentable events in the Soudan are due in a great
measure to the vacillating and inconsistent policy
pursued by Her Majesty's Government." Care
was evidently taken not to base the attack on the
Government upon any specific objections to the
policy of withdrawal from the Soudan. Lord
Salisbury, indeed, said: "We may think it was a
right policy to maintain the Soudan, or we may
think it was a right policy to abandon it; but we
must, whatever opinion we hold, condemn the
policy of the Government." Looking back on

what occurred, and making allowance for the fact
that the necessities of party warfare often involve
an expression of condemnation or of approval in
somewhat exaggerated terms, it must be admitted
that the censure, which the leading Conservative
statesmen wished to pass on the Government,
though severe, was not altogether undeserved.
Unquestionably, the state of affairs, which then
existed in the Soudan, was in some measure due
to the policy of the British Government. But if
we inquire in what measure it was due to that
policy, the answer is clear. The British Government could have used their paramount influence in
Egypt to stop the departure of General Hicks's
expedition, and they did not do so. Had they done
so, it is not only possible but also probable that the
advance of the Mahdi would have been arrested at
Khartoum. Putting aside points of detail, that is
the sum total of the charge which can be brought
against Mr. Gladstone's Government. I do not
know of any answer to this charge save that which is
contained in the commonplace, but extremely true
remark that it is easy to be wise after the event.[1]

Turning to the criticisms made, not so much by
responsible party leaders as by the general public,
it is to be observed that the view which was at the
time freely expressed, and which has to some extent
floated down the tide of history, was that the British
Government were responsible for the relapse of the
Soudan into barbarism, and that not only might
that country have been preserved to Egypt, but that
it would have been so preserved had the Egyptian
Government been allowed to follow their own devices. General Gordon did a good deal to propagate

---

[1] Mr. Morley (*Life of Gladstone*, vol. iii. p. 72) very appropriately
prefaces his chapter on Egypt by the following characteristic remark
made by the Duke of Wellington: "I find many very ready to say
what I ought to have done when a battle is over; but I wish some of
these persons would come and tell me what to do before the battle."

this idea. His Journal abounds with statements
fixing the responsibility for the abandonment of the
Soudan on the British Government. I maintain
that this view is entirely erroneous. Save in respect
to one sin of omission, that is to say, that no veto
was imposed on the Hicks expedition, the British
Government were in no way responsible for the loss
of the Soudan. They were responsible for obliging
the Egyptian Government to look the facts fairly in
the face. Now the main fact was this,—that after
the defeat of General Hicks's army, the Soudan
was lost to Egypt beyond any hope of recovery,
unless some external aid could be obtained to effect
its reconquest. That external aid could only come
from two countries, England or Turkey. The
British Government decided that the troops of
Great Britain should not be used to reconquer
the Soudan. This decision was ratified by British
public opinion, neither am I aware that any one,
who could speak with real authority on the subject,
was at the time found to challenge its wisdom. It
must be borne in mind that, if British troops had
been sent to the Soudan in 1883, they would have
been obliged to stay there in considerable numbers.
The Egyptian Government could not, with their
own resources, have held the country even after
the forces of the Mahdi had been defeated. The
conditions of the problem which awaited solution
were, therefore, essentially different from those
which obtained some thirteen years later when
the reconquest of the Soudan was taken in hand.
Turning to the other alternative, it may be said
that, although the proposal to utilise the Sultan's
services gave occasion to some diplomatic trifling,
no one seriously wished Turkish troops to be
employed. Every one felt that the remedy would
be worse than the disease. The Egyptian Government, as in the days of Arábi, were afraid that if

Turkish troops once came into the country, they would not leave it again.   The British Government gave a half-hearted assent to the employment of a Turkish force, but coupled their assent with conditions which were impossible of execution.   Even supposing that the Sultan would have been able to reconquer the country, which is a bold assumption, it was notorious that the misgovernment of Turkish Pashas had caused the rebellion, and it might be safely predicted that, whatever temporary success might be gained, no permanent settlement could be hoped for if Turkish authority were re-established. It must also be remembered that to take so important a step as that of immediately sending troops to the Soudan would have been quite inconsistent with the character of the Sultan.   It is highly improbable that he would have consented to render any prompt and effective assistance.   For all these reasons, it cannot be doubted that the decision not to call in Turkish aid was wise.[1]

[1] About four years later, the question of handing over Suakin to the Turks was again raised.   I did not like the proposal, but the difficulties of the whole Egyptian situation were at that time so great, that I was rather disposed to support it, as a choice of evils.   Lord Salisbury, however—very wisely, I think—rejected the idea, and, as subsequent events proved, it was fortunate that he did so.   His opinion was conveyed to me in the following very characteristic letter, dated December 22, 1888 : "At first, your proposal to hand over Suakin to the Turk seemed to me very alluring.   It would be such a blessing to be rid of it, both for Egypt and for us; and in the light of that hope, the conditions which it would be necessary to obtain from the Turks did not seem insuperable obstacles, but only difficulties to be overcome.   But as time went on—and especially after we had been able to watch the impression caused by Grenfell's easy success—we felt the task was not so easy.   It is as material that we should look at the matter from an English, as that you should look at it from an Egyptian point of view.   Unluckily, the English point of view is not only in practice the most important, but it is also the most difficult to understand.   The misfortune—the root-difficulty—we have in dealing with questions like those which beset Egypt is that public opinion in its largest sense takes no note of them.   Unless some startling question appealing to their humanity arises, the constituencies are quite indifferent   The result is that the Members of the House of Commons are each like a ship without an anchor.   They drift as any chance current may drive them.   Yet the combined resultant of

If, therefore, neither British nor Turkish troops were to be employed, withdrawal from the Soudan was imposed on the Egyptian Government as an unavoidable although unpleasant necessity. This, in fact, was the conclusion to which all the responsible authorities on the spot arrived at different stages of the proceedings. I have already given the opinions expressed by Lord Dufferin,

their many drifting wills is omnipotent and without appeal. If they vote wrong on an Irish question, a hint from their electoral supporters will bring them right. If they vote wrong on an Egyptian question, there is no such appeal. The result is that we are at the mercy of any fortuitous concurrence of fanaticisms or fads that chance may direct against us. This preamble is necessary to enable you to understand the importance I attach to the next remark: if we withdrew our own and the Egyptian troops from Suakin in favour of Turkey, we should be assailed by three separate feelings—the Turcophobists, still very strong ; the military or jingo feeling, which simply desires to annex, and objects to evacuating in all cases ; and the curious collection of fanatics who believe that by some magic wave of the diplomatic wand the Soudan can be turned into a second India. The superficial philanthropy of the day runs in this channel, and by its side, as is often the case, a current of decided roguery There are promoters, and financiers, and contractors of various kinds, who know perfectly well that there is as much chance of colonising the Sahara as the Soudan, but who see a prospect of sweeping a shoal of guileless shareholders into their net, and are longing to take advantage of the prevailing delusion. All these people would grumble fiercely if we gave Suakin to the Turks ; but if we could have done with it, the riddance would be well worth a few grumbles. But the Turks would commit every possible blunder. They would oppress the Arabs, destroy all possibility of any trade, except the Slave Trade, to which they would give every facility ; and, having caused the hostility of the natives to the utmost by taxation and misgovernment, would allow the garrison of Suakin to fall into so weak a state in regard to command, numbers, and equipment, that some fine day a lieutenant of the Khalifa would rush the fortresses. If such a thing happened, the combined forces to which I have referred would have their opportunity. They would dominate the House of Commons The political air would be rent with tales of the inefficiency and the brutality of the Turks, and with praises of the virtues of the Soudanese, only requiring Home Rule under the ægis of Great Britain to develop them into an equatorial Arcadia. The whole evil would be attributed to the evacuation, which must be immediately reversed. I need not go any farther. There would be endless complications with foreign Powers, and a great deal of waste of blood and money with no result It might go much farther still, for there is a good deal of loose powder about on the shores of the Red Sea. On these grounds alone, we have come to the conclusion that a Turkish occupation presents more dangers than advantages."

Sir Edward Malet, and Colonel Stewart prior to the occurrence of the Hicks disaster, and those of Sir Frederick Stephenson, Sir Evelyn Wood, General Baker, and myself expressed subsequent to that event. Sir Auckland Colvin, who knew Egypt well, wrote to me from India, in December 1883, advocating the policy of abandoning the Soudan. Mr. Power, also, put the matter in homely and forcible language. Writing to his mother on February 9, 1884, he said : "Holding Khartoum is bosh. . . . This is, indeed, a 'land of desolation,' as Baker called it. We must give it up." I would now speak of the opinions of General Gordon. Colonel Stewart was, I think, a better authority on Soudan affairs, as they then existed, than General Gordon ; but the public attached great weight to General Gordon's opinions. What, therefore, were those opinions ?

General Gordon so frequently expressed at short intervals opinions which were opposed to each other, that it is not easy to answer this question with confidence. In a pamphlet issued by the *Pall Mall Gazette* in 1885 and entitled *Too Late*, it was stated that General Gordon's "personal views as to the impolicy of abandoning Khartoum were notorious" ; and in the *Pall Mall Gazette* of January 11, 1884, an account is given of an interview between General Gordon and a representative of that newspaper. General Gordon is alleged to have condemned the policy of evacuation. "You must either," he said, "surrender absolutely to the Mahdi or defend Khartoum at all hazards." I do not call in question the fact that General Gordon used language of this sort, but it was certainly opposed both to what he wrote about the same time officially, and to what he said when he was on the point of starting for Khartoum.

On January 22, 1884, whilst on his way to Egypt,

General Gordon wrote a Memorandum which he sent to Lord Granville, and in which the following passage occurs: "The Soudan is a useless possession, ever was so, and ever will be so. . . . I think Her Majesty's Government are fully justified in recommending the evacuation, inasmuch as the sacrifices necessary towards securing a good government would be far too onerous to admit of such an attempt being made." Colonel Stewart, after reading General Gordon's Memorandum, wrote as follows: "I have carefully read over General Gordon's observations and cordially agree with what he states. . . . I quite agree with General Gordon that the Soudan is an expensive and useless possession. No one who has visited it can escape the reflection: 'What a useless possession and what a huge encumbrance on Egypt.'"

Further evidence can be produced, which is even more conclusive as regards General Gordon's views. When he arrived in Cairo in January 1884, I had to prepare certain instructions for him. One passage of those instructions ran as follows: "You will bear in mind that the main end to be pursued is the evacuation of the Soudan. This policy was adopted after very full discussion by the Egyptian Government on the advice of Her Majesty's Government. I understand, also, that you entirely concur in the desirability of adopting this policy." When I went through the draft instructions with General Gordon, I well remember stopping at this passage and asking him whether I was right in saying that he agreed in the policy adopted by the Egyptian Government on the advice of the British Government. Without the smallest hesitation, General Gordon expressed in the strongest terms his entire concurrence in that policy. Indeed, he insisted that a phrase should be added stating that in his opinion the policy, which had

been adopted, "should on no account be changed."
This was accordingly done.

It seems to me that this evidence is conclusive.
I think that I have every right to assume that
when General Gordon, at a momentous period of
his life, gave his opinion deliberately in official
form, and with a due sense of the responsibility
he was taking, what he then said must be regarded
as his true opinion, and that it cannot be gainsaid
by any *obiter dicta* let fall in conversation at other
times.

Mere appeal to authority is, however, a weak
argument. Reason, it has been truly said, and
not authority, should determine the judgment. I
maintain that, judged by the standard of reason,
the arguments in favour of the policy adopted at
the time are irrefragable. I am, of course, merely
speaking of the general policy, not of the details
of its execution, in respect to which, as I shall
subsequently show, many errors were committed.
The only practical question was, not whether it
was or was not desirable to hold Khartoum, but
whether it was possible to hold Khartoum. To
this question there could only be one answer.
The Egyptian Government, with the resources of
which they disposed, were unable to hold Khartoum. No one, therefore, has a right to criticise
the policy which was actually adopted, unless he is
prepared to advocate that the reconquest of the
Soudan should have been effected by British,
British-Indian, or Turkish troops. For my own
part, I may say that, although during the period
I represented the British Government in Egypt
I may have made many mistakes, there is one
episode to which I look back without the least
sense of personal regret. Time and reflection
have only served to convince me more strongly
than ever that I acted rightly in advocating

withdrawal from the Soudan in 1883-84. It was the adoption of that policy which allowed the Egyptian and British Governments, after a painful period of transition, to devote themselves to the work of reorganisation and reform in Egypt proper, a work which could not have been undertaken at that time with any prospect of success so long as the Soudan hung like a dead-weight round the necks of Egyptian reformers. Whatever else may be said against the Egyptian policy of Mr. Gladstone's Government, my conviction is that they deserve the eternal gratitude of the Egyptian people for coming down with a heavy hand on all the vacillations of the Cairene administrators, and obliging the Egyptian Government to look the facts of the case fairly in the face.[1]

There is, however, another criticism which was directed against the conduct of the British Government at this time and to which some allusion should be made. It was stated that, even suppos-

---

[1] In a private letter to me, dated December 28, 1883, Lord Granville stated the case in characteristic language. "It takes away," he said, "somewhat of the position of a man to sell his racers and hunters, but if he cannot afford to keep them, the sooner they go to Tattersall's the better." I have a large number of private letters from Lord Granville. Some of them are very interesting. His light touches on serious questions were inimitable, and his good humour and kindness of heart come out in every line he wrote. It was possible to disagree with him, but it was impossible to be angry with him. It was also impossible to get him to give a definite answer to a difficult question when he wished not to commit himself. His power of eluding the main point at issue was quite extraordinary. Often did I think that he was on the horns of a dilemma, and that he was in a position from which no escape was possible without the expression of a definite opinion. I was generally mistaken. With a smile and a quick little epigrammatic phrase, Lord Granville would elude one's grasp and be off without giving any opinion at all. I remember on one occasion pressing him to say what he wished me to do about one of the numerous offshoots of the general tangle, which formed the Egyptian Question. The matter was one of considerable importance. All I could extract from him was the Delphic saying that my "presence in London would be a good excuse for a dawdle."

I remember once comparing notes with Lord Goschen on this subject. He told me that on one occasion, when he was at Constantinople, after many unsuccessful endeavours to obtain definite

ing that withdrawal from the Soudan was necessary, the policy of the Government should not have been publicly announced. This view was advocated by Lord Salisbury. Speaking in the House of Lords on February 27, 1885, he said : "As soon as they (the British Government) made up their minds that the Soudan was to be evacuated, their first course was to retire the garrisons as rapidly as they could, and when this was done they might announce their policy as loudly as they please. But it was an unfortunate announcement when the men were in deadly danger, — a policy of crass folly, which almost amounts to a crime." This criticism, though strongly expressed, sounds reasonable in substance ; and, in fact, if the policy advocated by Lord Salisbury had been possible, it would unquestionably have been the best to pursue. Can any one, however, suppose that, when the British press and the British Parliament were actively engaged in discussing Egyptian

answers to certain important questions which he had addressed to Lord Granville, he wrote a very lengthy and very strong private letter, intimating that unless clear answers were sent, he would resign. The only reply he received from Lord Granville was as follows: "My dear Goschen—Thank you a thousand times for expressing your views so frankly to your old colleagues." The dawdling policy, or, to put the case in another way, the policy of not having a policy at all, is often very good diplomacy, particularly when it is carried out by a man of Lord Granville's singular tact, quickness, and diplomatic experience. This line of action, which involves delaying any important decision until the last moment and not looking far ahead, is rather in conformity with English customs and habits of thought It was generally practised by many of the English statesmen and diplomatists of Lord Granville's generation. Unfortunately, Lord Granville, during the latter portion of his career, fell on times when, under the auspices of Prince Bismarck, a directness, I might almost say a brutality, had been introduced into European diplomacy, which did not exist before. Lord Granville always seemed to me to make the mistake of confounding the cases in which the dawdling *laissez-faire* policy was wise, with those in which it was necessary to take time by the forelock and have a clearly defined policy at an early date. This, in a Foreign Minister, is a great fault. He becomes to too great a degree the sport of circumstances, and inspires foreign Governments with a belief that the policy of his country is vacillating and uncertain.

affairs, when keen party opponents were constantly
pressing the Government for a declaration of their
intentions, when Cairo was full of newspaper
correspondents, when the policy of withdrawal
could only be enforced by the heroic remedy
of a change of Ministry in Egypt, when it is
remembered that such a thing as official secrecy
is almost unknown in Egypt, and when it is
further remembered that numerous agents, some
of whom, especially General Gordon himself,[1] were
not remarkable for reticence of speech, necessarily
had to be taken into the confidence of the Government,—can any one suppose for one moment that,
under all these circumstances, the adoption of a
policy of withdrawal could have been kept secret?
Secrecy was, in fact, impossible, and it mattered
little whether any public announcement was or
was not made, at all events in Europe or in Egypt
proper.

This, therefore, is all I have to say about the
policy of withdrawal from the Soudan. In spite
of the vehemence with which every one connected
with the adoption of this policy was at one time
assailed, I believe it to have been the only wise policy
possible under the circumstances. Further, in spite
of some obvious drawbacks, and of many mistakes
in the execution, I believe the adoption of this
policy to have been beneficial to Egypt itself and
to the accomplishment of the general aims of England in that country. If I am asked whether the
policy of withdrawal from the Soudan was desirable or the reverse, and, if undesirable, why it was
adopted, I have no hesitation in answering these
questions. As a mere academic question, I think
that the policy of withdrawing from Khartoum was

---

[1] It will presently be explained (pp. 467-471) that General Gordon
was himself responsible for spreading in the Soudan the news that the
Egyptian Government intended to withdraw from the country.

undesirable, but I decline to consider that, in view of the circumstances which then existed, the question of the desirability or undesirability of withdrawal was at the time one of any practical importance. A long course of misgovernment had culminated in a rebellion in the Soudan, which the Egyptian Government were powerless to repress. They, therefore, had to submit to the time-honoured law expressed in the words *Vae victis.* The abandonment of the Soudan, however undesirable, was imposed upon the Egyptian Government as an unpleasant but imperious necessity for the simple reason that, after the destruction of General Hicks's army, they were unable to keep it. This, as it appears to me, is the residuum of truth which may be extracted from all the very lengthy and somewhat stormy discussions which have taken place on this subject.

CHAPTER XXI

THE REBELLION IN THE EASTERN SOUDAN

AUGUST 1883–MARCH 1884

Prevailing discontent—Annihilation of a force sent to Sinkat—And of one sent to Tokar—Defeat of the Egyptians at Tamanieb—It is decided to send the Gendarmerie and some black troops under Zobeir Pasha to Suakin — Instructions to General Baker — He arrives at Suakin—His instructions are modified—Zobeir Pasha retained at Cairo—General Baker advances to Tokar—His defeat—Fall of Sinkat—It is decided to send a British force to Tokar—Fall of Tokar—General Graham advances—Action at El Teb—The British troops return to Suakin—Battle of Tamai—Results of the operations.

THE events already narrated could not fail to have a great effect in the Eastern Soudan. There also a long course of misgovernment had produced its natural result. The people were ripe for rebellion against the Egyptian Government. When, therefore, towards the middle of 1883, the Mahdi issued a Proclamation to the inhabitants of the Eastern Soudan, inviting them "to advance against the Turks and drive them out of the country," they were well disposed to respond to his appeal. A former slave-dealer at Suakin, named Osman Digna, was appointed to be the Mahdi's Emir. He was a man of considerable ability, and was destined in the near future to play a leading part in the affairs of the Eastern Soudan.

At this time, an Egyptian garrison was posted at Sinkat, a spot situated about fifty miles from

Suakin. The road from Suakin to Sinkat passes through some rocky defiles, which present great facilities for defence against any force advancing from the coast. The geographical position of Sinkat renders it devoid of military importance. A wise foresight would have dictated its abandonment and the retreat of the garrison to Suakin at an early stage of the rebellion. Unfortunately, this was not done ; the result was disastrous. The garrison of Sinkat was commanded by Tewfik Bey, an officer of courage and ability, who is described by Mrs. Sartorius as "the one grand and noble man who stands forth so prominently amongst the horde of Egyptian officials."[1]

The first overt act of rebellion took place on August 5. On that day, Osman Digna appeared with 1500 men before Sinkat and demanded, in the name of the Mahdi, that both Sinkat and Suakin should be delivered up to him. These demands being refused, Osman Digna attacked the outskirts of Sinkat. He was repulsed with considerable loss. Two of his nephews were killed, and he was himself wounded.

On September 9, Tewfik Bey again defeated the rebels at Handoub, a spot on the road leading from Suakin to Berber.

These successes were, however, but the prelude to a series of disasters which were about to befall the Egyptian arms. Towards the middle of October, a force of about 160 men sent by Suleiman Pasha, the Governor of Suakin, to the relief of Sinkat, was attacked and totally defeated by the Dervishes. The women and children, who accompanied the soldiers, alone escaped to become the slaves of their captors.

---

[1] *The Soudan*, p. 81. Mrs. Sartorius was the wife of Colonel Sartorius, who was General Baker's principal staff officer. She accompanied her husband to Suakin.

The result of this engagement was to increase the prestige of the Mahdi and of Osman Digna, and to encourage amongst their followers the belief that they were fighting in a cause which would render them invincible. Another event soon followed tending in the same direction.

On November 3, an Egyptian force of about 550 men was despatched from Suakin to Trinkitat, a seaport lying about forty-five miles to the south. The object of this expedition was to relieve Tokar, situated some twenty miles from the coast, which place was at that time invested by the Mahdist forces. Captain Moncrieff, R. N., the British Consul at Jeddah, accompanied the expedition. The force left Trinkitat on the morning of November 4. After marching for about an hour and a half, they were attacked by the Dervishes. "The Egyptian troops formed square, the front and right of the square commenced firing, but by some means the left of the square was broken into by eight or ten Arabs, which immediately created a panic amongst the troops and caused a general stampede." In this action, Captain Moncrieff and 160 Egyptian officers and men were killed. The attacking force only amounted to about 200 men.

A worse disaster was to follow. Suleiman Pasha and Mahmoud Tahir Pasha, who commanded the troops at Suakin, were fearful of the effect which would be produced at Cairo when the news arrived of the recent defeat near Tokar. They were aware that an expedition was to be sent from Cairo to Suakin under the command of General Baker. They determined, therefore, "to try another throw of the dice with a fine regiment of 600 Soudanese, under Major Kassim, that had been hurriedly sent from Massowah." This regiment was attacked and cut to pieces. Of the whole force, only 2 officers and 33 men returned to Suakin.

These successive victories established the power of Osman Digna in the Eastern Soudan. On November 19, 1883, I telegraphed to Lord Granville: "It is clear that Egyptian authority in the Eastern Soudan does not extend beyond the coast, and is even threatened there."

After the defeat of General Hicks's army, the military authorities at Cairo were of opinion that an endeavour should be made to open out the Berber-Suakin route with a view to facilitating the retreat of the garrison of Khartoum. The question then arose as to what troops should be employed to attain this object.

The British Government objected to the employment of the Egyptian army, then being organised by Sir Evelyn Wood. There were valid grounds for their objection. The army was intended for service in Egypt proper. Its organisation was at that time defective. None of the men had served for more than one year. Sir Evelyn Wood and the officers serving under him had not as yet had time to fashion into shape the raw material at their disposal. The employment of the Egyptian army might not improbably have led to a further disaster. The British War Office authorities felt this so strongly that, at a subsequent period when British troops were employed, they declined to allow any portion of the Egyptian army to take part in the expedition.

Under these circumstances, the only force available was the Egyptian Gendarmerie commanded by General Baker. A few British officers were attached to this force, but with, I think, one exception (Colonel Sartorius), they were not on the active list of the British army, and it was held, perhaps somewhat illogically, that the Egyptian Government possessed a greater degree of liberty of action in respect to the employment of this force than was the case in respect to the army. The Gendarmerie were fairly well equipped, but, with the exception of some 200 Turks, who were good soldiers, the force was composed of bad fighting material.

It was with the utmost hesitation that I consented to the despatch of General Baker's force to Suakin. I was under no delusion as to the quality of the troops which he would command. Moreover, I feared that Baker Pasha would be led into the committal of some rash act. He was a gallant officer, and it was certain that his military instincts would revolt at inaction, more especially when Sinkat and Tokar were being beleaguered in the immediate vicinity of Suakin. There were also special reasons which made me doubtful as to the wisdom of sending General Baker. He had been obliged to leave the British army under circumstances on which it is unnecessary to dwell. He was ardently attached to his profession, and it was well known that the main object of his life was to regain his position in the British army, which he hoped to do by distinguished service in the field. Before he left Cairo, I impressed upon him strongly that the necessity of avoiding any disaster must come before all other considerations, and that if he did not feel sufficient confidence in his troops to advance, he must remain and defend Suakin, however painful the consequences might be as regards the garrisons of Sinkat and Tokar. General Baker expressed to me his entire concurrence in these views, and promised that he would act up to them. I was not, however, content with mere verbal instructions. On the advice of Sir Evelyn Wood and myself, a letter, which contained the following passage, was written to General Baker by the Khedive on December 17: " The mission entrusted to you, having as its object the pacification of the regions designated in my above-mentioned order, and the maintenance, as far as possible, of communication between Berber and Suakin, I wish you to act with the greatest prudence on account of the insufficiency of the forces placed under your command.

"I think it would be hazardous to commence any military operations before receiving the reinforcements which shall be sent to you with Zobeir Pasha. . . . If, in the event of the situation improving, you should consider an action necessary, I rely on your prudence and ability not to engage the enemy except under the most favourable conditions. . . . My confidence in your prudence enables me to count upon your conforming to these instructions."

On December 27, General Baker arrived at Suakin. Almost simultaneously with his arrival, the change of Ministry narrated in the last chapter took place at Cairo. The result of this change was the issue, on January 11, 1884, of the following further instructions to General Baker by Sir Evelyn Wood, acting on behalf of the Khedive :—

1. All that portion of your instructions which gives you discretion to open the Suakin-Berber route westward of Sinkat by force, if necessary, is cancelled.

2. If it is absolutely necessary to use force in order to extricate the garrisons of Sinkat and Tokar you can do so, provided you consider your forces sufficient and you may reasonably count on success.

The enforced submission of the men who have been holding out at these two places would be very painful to His Highness the Khedive; but even such a sacrifice is better, in his opinion, than that you and your troops should attempt a task which you cannot fairly reckon to be within your power.

3. You are directed to continue to use every effort possible to open the route up to Berber by diplomatic means.

About this time, another change of importance was made. On December 9, I wrote to Lord Granville : "The Egyptian Government propose to send Zobeir Pasha to Suakin. Your Lordship, without doubt, is aware of Zobeir Pasha's antecedents. He has been intimately connected with the Slave Trade. Under ordinary circumstances, his employment by the Egyptian Government would have been open to considerable objection, and I should have thought it my duty to remonstrate against it. Under present circumstances, however, I have not thought it either necessary or desirable to interfere with the discretion of the Egyptian Government in this matter. Whatever may be Zobeir Pasha's faults, he is said to be a man of great energy and resolution. The Egyptian Government consider that his services may be very useful in commanding the friendly Bedouins who are to be sent to Suakin, and in conducting negotiations with the tribes on the Berber-Suakin route and elsewhere. I may mention that Baker Pasha is anxious to avail himself of Zobeir Pasha's services. Your Lordship will, without doubt, bear in mind that, up to the present time, the whole responsibility for the conduct of affairs in the Soudan has been left to the Egyptian Government. It appears to me that, under present circumstances, it would not have been just, while leaving all the responsibility to the Egyptian Government, to have objected to that Government using their own discretion on such a point as the employment of Zobeir Pasha. I make these remarks as the employment of Zobeir Pasha may not improbably attract attention in England."

Every Englishman is justly proud of the part which his country has borne in the suppression of Slavery and the Slave Trade ; few will be disposed to challenge the distinguished part played by the

Anti-Slavery Society in this humane work. The Society, however, is not without its defects. Concentration of thought and action on one subject, together with a certain want of imagination which occasionally characterises the conduct of Englishmen in dealing with foreign affairs and which is perhaps in some degree due to their insular habits of thought, produce their natural effect. The members of the Anti-Slavery Society appear sometimes to be unable to look at any question save from a purely anti-slavery point of view, and, even from that point of view, they are often liable to error through failure to judge accurately of the relative importance of events. It is certain that the action of the Society in connection with Soudan affairs in 1883-84, though well intentioned, was mischievous. The main question, whether from the general or the anti-slavery point of view, was how to quiet the Soudan. The establishment of the Mahdi's domination in that country could not fail to give an impulse to the Slave Trade. Every measure which tended to counteract the Mahdi's authority should, therefore, have been welcomed by the Anti-Slavery Society, even although it might have been open to some objections in detail. The Society failed to see this. They were so taken up with the objections to the detail, that they forgot the main principle. In deference to the opinions which the Society was known to entertain, it was decided not to send Zobeir Pasha to Suakin. The consequences of this decision are thus described by Mrs. Sartorius: "As a matter of fact Zobeir never came down. . . . This was another grand blunder that rendered the Suakin expedition almost hopeless from the first. The black troops required to be led in their own fashion ; they had no idea of drill or discipline. There was no time to lick them into shape. With Zobeir Pasha at their head, they would have been formidable antagonists to the Soudanese, and have fought in precisely the same fashion. Without him, they were wasted."

On January 31, telegraphic communication with Suakin was established. General Baker reported that he was at Trinkitat, and hoped to move on the following day to Tokar. Some little delay, however, occurred. On February 2, General Baker telegraphed that he would advance on the morning of the 3rd with 3200 men. "There is," he added, "every chance of success." I awaited the result with anxiety. On the 6th, General Baker telegraphed: "I marched yesterday morning with 3500 men towards Tokar; we met the enemy, after two miles' march, in small numbers, and drove them back about two miles nearer the wells of Teb. On the square being only threatened by a small force of the enemy, certainly less than 1000 strong, the Egyptian troops threw down their arms and ran, carrying away the black troops with them, and allowing themselves to be killed without the slightest resistance. More than 2000 were killed. They fled to Trinkitat. Unfortunately, the Europeans who stood suffered terribly. . . . The troops are utterly untrustworthy except for the defence of earthworks."

I remember the bitter disappointment with which I received this telegram. My worst fears had been realised. General Baker had evidently been led into undertaking a task which was beyond the powers of the inefficient force at his disposal. I remember also that my first impression was that, after the strong manner in which I had spoken to him and after the assurances he had given to me at Cairo, General Baker would reproach himself for having advanced on Tokar. It was with this feeling uppermost in my mind that I at once telegraphed to the Consul at Suakin : "Tell General Baker that I feel sure that he did all that could be done, that he has my entire confidence, and that I shall continue to do all I can to help and support him."

When this matter was subsequently (February 12) discussed in England, Lord Derby, speaking on behalf of the British Government, said : "We may have known—we did know—that the composition of General Baker's force was not very good, but I venture to affirm that nobody supposed that a body of men calling itself a regular army would run away, almost without a shot fired, from half its own number, or less than half, of savages under no discipline whatever. It is a thing, I should imagine, new in war. It is a misfortune, but it is a misfortune for which we, sitting in London, can hardly hold ourselves responsible."

I agree in this view. I do not think that the British Ministers were responsible for the despatch of General Baker's force to Suakin except in so far that, by not offering any other form of assistance, they practically obliged the Egyptian Government either to utilise the Gendarmerie or to remain altogether inactive. Manifestly, they could form no independent opinion of the military value of General Baker's force. The main responsibility, therefore, rests on the authorities at Cairo, and notably on myself.

Mr. Gladstone stated in the House of Commons : "Baker Pasha was under no military necessity to undertake this expedition. He was not enlisted for that purpose, and was under no honourable or military obligation to undertake it unless he thought it hopeful. . . . I say he went with a belief that the means at his command were adequate means for the purpose which he had in view. . . . Baker Pasha stated that he was very confident that the means at his disposal, though not sufficient to relieve all the garrisons, were sufficient for Tokar, which would have been most important. On the 2nd of February, three days before the calamity which overtook him, Baker Pasha telegraphs that he will advance to the relief of Tokar to-morrow with every chance of success." All this is perfectly true. I have heard it stated that General Baker was induced to advance by one of his staff officers against his own judgment. How far this statement is correct, I cannot say. There can, however, be no doubt that he made an error in advancing. He saw the hopelessness of endeavouring to relieve Sinkat,[1] but he was too confident of success in the direction of Tokar.

Whilst, however, the accuracy of Mr. Gladstone's statement may be admitted, he did not, as it appears to me, state the whole case ; neither, indeed, was he in possession of sufficient information to have enabled him to do so. Mrs. Sartorius had the best possible opportunities of learning the opinions current amongst the officers at Suakin. This is what she says: "I still say that the military and other authorities at Cairo should not have allowed General Baker to advance ; they ought not to have left it to him, for they could not but know that he had no choice." Regarded by the light of subsequent events, there is much force in this criticism. Either General Baker should not have been sent to Suakin, or, if sent, he should have received no discretionary power to advance ; in fact, it would have been better that he should have received positive orders not to advance. I was principally responsible for this mistake, that is

---

[1] "A most painful decision has lately been arrived at, namely, that we ourselves cannot relieve Sinkat, for it would be madness to trust our troops in a broken and mountainous country like that through which the Sinkat road runs. We intend to do what we can in the Tokar direction."—*The Soudan*, p. 210.

to say, I could have prevented General Baker from
going to Suakin, and, although I knew the risk I
was running and although I thought seriously of
imposing a veto on the expedition, I eventually
decided not to do so.   I remember the nature of
the arguments which led me to take this decision.
I was not influenced by the consideration that
General Baker's force would be able to open up
the Berber-Suakin route.   I never believed that
he would be able to do so, and, as has been
already stated, this portion of his instructions
underwent considerable modifications immediately
after the change of Ministry took place in Cairo.
The way I reasoned the matter was this: here are two
garrisons, one at Sinkat and one at Tokar, shut up
within a short distance of the coast ; moreover, the
administration at Suakin is so bad, and the troops
there are so demoralised, that the Egyptian
position at Suakin itself may at any moment be
endangered ; the British Government will not
afford any military aid, neither will they allow the
Egyptian Government to use their own army ; I
daresay they are right in these decisions, but the
position thus created for the Egyptian Government and its British advisers is, to say the least, a
painful one ; are we not only to refuse assistance,
but are we also to impose a veto on the Egyptian
Government employing the only remaining force at
their disposal, with the certainty that in doing so
Suakin itself will be endangered and that any hope
of relieving the beleaguered garrisons of Sinkat and
Tokar will have to be abandoned ?   I answered
this question at the time in the negative.   Subsequent events showed that I should have answered
it in the affirmative.   I should have stated the
case to the British Government, and have informed
them that the Egyptian Government had no
trustworthy force at their disposal with which to

act, and that they must decide whether or not to defend Suakin, and to send a British force to relieve the two garrisons. It was, however, difficult at the time to take up this line. I felt sure that the British Government would do nothing to help the beleaguered garrisons, although they would have afforded naval protection to Suakin. Indeed, so early as November 23, Admiral Hewett was ordered to maintain Egyptian authority at the Red Sea ports. Moreover, however acute the pressure and however painful the consequences of inaction might be, I sympathised with the reluctance of the British Government to be drawn into military operations in the Soudan. Once begun, it was difficult to say where they would end.

Then, again, in view of the instructions, written and verbal, which General Baker had received before leaving Cairo, and in view of the whole tenor of his conversation, I believed that I might rely on him not to advance unless success was well-nigh absolutely certain, and, indeed, I thought it probable that, when he arrived at Suakin and had studied the situation, he would tell me that the risk of advancing either to Sinkat or Tokar with the troops under his command was too great to be undertaken. In reasoning thus, I was mistaken. General Baker's military instincts, the natural reluctance of a gallant officer to leave the beleaguered garrisons to their fate without making an effort to help them, the pressure which was probably brought to bear on him by the younger and less responsible British officers at Suakin to advance, and the special personal inducement which existed in his case to distinguish himself by heading a daring and successful military exploit, all acted in a sense contrary to the conclusions formed when discussing the matter calmly in my room at Cairo.

For these reasons, I think I was wrong in allowing General Baker's expedition to go to Suakin.

Sinkat had for long been in great straits. With the defeat of General Baker's force, the last hope of relief disappeared. On February 12, news reached Suakin that Tewfik Bey, despairing of all succour and finding his provisions exhausted, had made the desperate resolution to evacuate Sinkat and fight his way to Suakin. He made a brave fight for life and killed large numbers of the enemy, but eventually his whole force, with the exception of about thirty women and six men, was annihilated. Thus, another was added to the list of disasters in the Soudan.

The defeat of General Baker's force caused a panic at Suakin. Manifestly, the first thing to do was to provide for the safety of the town. Admiral Hewett landed a small force. He was placed in civil and military command. I was, at the same time, authorised to inform the Egyptian Government that "in the event of an attack on Suakin on the part of the rebels, the town would be defended by a British force."

In the meanwhile, British public opinion was greatly excited about Soudan affairs. Party politicians were sure not to allow so good an opportunity for attacking the Government to escape. Chauvinists and humanitarians alike swelled the ranks of the opposition. A meeting was called at the Mansion House to condemn the policy of the Government. No inconsiderable section of British public opinion was disposed to push the Government on to a policy of reconquering the Soudan without much regard either to the difficulties of the task, or to the ulterior consequences which would have ensued had such a course been adopted. Mr. Forster, who was a leading member of the Anti-Slavery Society and the chief of the party of bellicose philanthropy, attacked the Government. When, eventually, it was decided to send an expedition to Suakin, Mr. Forster said (February 14): "I rejoice that the Government have taken their present policy. By that, they are more likely to strike a blow against slavery than anything we have yet done." There was no mistaking this language. The Government were invited to undertake a military campaign against slavery.

Thus, there was a risk that the Government, which had been too fearful of assuming responsibility during the early stages of the Soudan troubles, would now, under the pressure of excited and ill-informed public opinion in England, be forced into the assumption of more serious responsibilities than they were aware of, or than it was desirable that they should assume. On February 12, I repeated to Lord Granville the following telegram which I had received from General Gordon, who was then on his way to Khartoum: "I sincerely hope that you will be reassured as to the situation, in spite of all that has happened." I added, "I entirely agree on all points with General Gordon, and trust that, in spite of the panic which appears to prevail in London, Her Majesty's Government will not change any of the main points of their policy." I followed this up by a further telegram on the same day in which I said: "I am altogether opposed to sending troops to Suakin except to hold the town." I held this opinion because I did not believe that British troops would arrive in time to save Tokar.

The pressure on the Government was, however, too strong to be resisted. It was decided to send a force to the relief of Tokar.

By February 28, about 4000 British soldiers, under the command of Major-General Sir Gerald

Graham, were collected at Trinkitat. A week before that date, however, a report arrived to the effect that the garrison of Tokar was about to capitulate.

The British Government were singularly unfortunate. From this time forth, the stock argument of their opponents was that their action was invariably "too late." This was the title given to a pamphlet published a year later on the Gordon mission; amongst party politicians, Lord Randolph Churchill, more especially, used his remarkable oratorical powers to place before the public the aspect of Soudan affairs represented by these words. The facts of the case had, however, to be faced. It was clear that the expedition would not be able to accomplish the only object with which it had been sent. What, therefore, was to be done? On February 24, Sir W. Hewett telegraphed to the Admiralty that the news of the fall of Tokar had been confirmed; but, he added, with all the conviction and impetuosity of a fighting sailor who was longing for action, "we must move on there with our men. Rebels are sure to stand; they are in considerable numbers mustering. Our forces landed. Decisive victory will re-establish order amongst the tribes round here." I remember Sir Frederick Stephenson, coming into my room on the morning of February 23 and saying to me, "Well! Tokar has fallen, but of course we must go on." He subsequently telegraphed to Lord Hartington, who was at that time Secretary of State for War: "News just received that rebels are in force on Baker Pasha's late battlefield, eager to fight and confident of victory. I strongly recommend that Graham should be ordered to advance towards Tokar, should this prove true."

It was clear that the soldiers and sailors were

like greyhounds straining at the leash. They were almost within sight of their enemy, and at the last moment it appeared that they might not be allowed to attack. They were naturally disappointed, and I trust that the same spirit will always animate the British army and navy. My view, however, at the time was that the soldiers and sailors should not be allowed to decide the question. As Tokar had already fallen, I could not see what was the object of expending a number of valuable lives under the pretence of relieving the garrison. I, therefore, telegraphed to Lord Granville on the evening of February 23 in the following terms, "If the troops are not to advance on Tokar, the War Office should send out orders without a moment's delay. The soldiers are, of course, longing for a fight, and will advance if there is the smallest excuse for doing so. I can scarcely entertain a doubt that Tokar has fallen. In that case, I think a useless effusion of blood should be stopped; that enough troops should be left to garrison Suakin; and that the remainder should come back here. I would on no account send a British force to Kassala." At the same time, I repeated to Lord Granville a telegram which I had received from General Gordon, in answer to a message despatched by me telling him of the report that Tokar had fallen. "I think," he said, "if Tokar has fallen, Her Majesty's Government had better be quiet, as I see no advantage to be now gained by any action on their part. Let events work themselves out. The fall of Tokar will not affect in the least the state of affairs here (*i.e.* at Khartoum)."

It was, without doubt, difficult for the Government to act on the advice of General Gordon and myself. To have landed a force at Trinkitat, and then to have brought it away without achieving anything whatever, would have rendered the Government ridiculous, and would have exposed them to further attacks in Parliament. The lives of the officers and men who subsequently fell at the battle of El Teb, were, in reality, sacrificed to public clamour and the necessities of the Parliamentary situation. On February 15, Lord Granville wrote privately to me telling me that the papers on the subject were about to be presented to Parliament. "I have," he said, "cut out your opinion unfavourable to the expedition. You might as well try to stop a mule with a snaffle bridle as check the feeling here on the subject. Our great object must now be to get them (*i.e.* the troops) back as soon as possible." When, eventually, the Soudanese were beaten, the Government, which had been violently attacked from one quarter for inaction, were attacked from another quarter for their activity. On March 14, Lord Granville wrote to me: "We are very nearly stalemated in the Soudan by the bloody victories."

Sir Gerald Graham was consulted. On February 24, the following telegram was sent to him from the War Office: "Assuming Tokar to have fallen, what course would you recommend, remembering that no distant expedition will be sanctioned? Could the force march to Teb, protect fugitives, bury the English dead, and return by land to Suakin? If a movement on Suakin is threatened, you may take the offensive from Trinkitat or Suakin, as you think best. Report fully on the position." There could be no mistaking the spirit of this message. It meant that the Government wanted Sir Gerald Graham to suggest action of some sort, so that the policy of sending the expedition to Suakin might in some degree be justified. This, of course, tallied with the views of the soldiers. After receiving Sir Gerald

Graham's report, Lord Hartington sent him the following instructions : "You should, if practicable, before attacking, summon the chiefs to disband their forces and attend Gordon at Khartoum for the settlement of the Soudan. Say that we are not at war with the Arabs, but must disperse force threatening Suakin." This telegram was first communicated to me by Sir Frederick Stephenson. I felt convinced that the proposed summons to the tribal leaders to go to Khartoum would not be productive of any result. I, therefore, telegraphed privately to Lord Granville (February 27) : "Stephenson has shown me the War Secretary's telegram to Graham. I do not think that you can stop Graham advancing now. It is too late."

On the morning of February 29, Sir Gerald Graham advanced with his entire available force. He found the Dervishes entrenched at El Teb; they were attacked and driven from their position with heavy loss. The British loss amounted to 189 of all ranks, killed and wounded.

On March 3, Sir Gerald Graham advanced to Tokar, which was reached without any further fighting. On the 4th, the whole force returned to Trinkitat, and on the 5th embarked for Suakin. Admiral Hewett telegraphed to the Admiralty : "Tokar expedition most successful." The success or failure of the expedition must be a matter of opinion. Its original object was to relieve the garrison of Tokar. This object had not been accomplished. It had been shown, not for the first time in history, that a small body of well-disciplined British troops could defeat a horde of courageous savages. But no other important object had been attained. Osman Digna had received a severe blow, but his power in the Soudan was by no means broken. Osman Digna's own view on the subject may be gathered from a letter written by him at the time and found some years afterwards at Tokar. "The English," he said, "did not stay long. God struck fear into their hearts, and they went back the next morning, staying only one night at the Mamurieh, and then they started back in their steamers."

The question now arose of whether any further operations should be undertaken by Sir Gerald Graham's force. On March 2, Admiral Hewett telegraphed to the Admiralty recommending that the troops should be assembled at Suakin, and that Osman Digna, who was still in the neighbourhood, should be attacked. "That," he said, "will quiet the whole of this country." On March 7, Lord Granville telegraphed to me: "Her Majesty's Government have approved the recommendation of Admiral Hewett and General Graham to land a force at Suakin to give effect to their Proclamation calling upon the rebel chiefs to come in and denouncing Osman Digna as an impostor. They will march on Osman's camp to disperse force if the Proclamation is ineffectual."

The Proclamation produced no effect, and, on March 13, General Graham's force advanced on Tamai, a few miles from Suakin, which was occupied by a Mahdist force estimated at 12,000 men. On the following morning, an engagement ensued. After an obstinate fight, 2000 Dervishes were killed; the remainder fled to the hills. In this action, the British loss was 18 officers and 208 men, killed and wounded.

On the following day (March 15), Osman Digna's camp was burned, and the British force returned to Suakin. On the 17th, Sir Gerald Graham telegraphed to the War Office: "The present position of affairs is that two heavy blows have been dealt at the rebels and followers of the Mahdi, who are profoundly discouraged. They say, however, that the English troops can do no more, and must re-embark and leave the country to them."

It will be as well to break off the narrative of events in the Eastern Soudan at this point. The subsequent operations depended upon the course of events in the valley of the Nile, to which it is now time to revert. It will be sufficient for the present to say that the whole of the episode narrated in this chapter is not one to which any Englishman can look back with either pride or pleasure. Many valuable lives were lost. A great slaughter of fanatical savages took place. But no political or military result was obtained at all commensurate with the amount of life and treasure which was expended.

CHAPTER XXII

THE GORDON MISSION

DECEMBER 1883–JANUARY 1884

The situation in Egypt—Sir Frederick Stephenson—General Earle—
Sir Edgar Vincent—Sir Evelyn Wood—Foreign Office support—
First and second proposals to send General Gordon—They are
rejected—Third proposal to send General Gordon—It is accepted
—No British officer should have been sent to Khartoum—General
Gordon should not in any case have been chosen—The responsi-
bility of the British press—And of the British Government—
General Gordon's optimism—My regret at having assented to the
Gordon Mission.

DURING the course of an official career which
extended over a period of nearly fifty years, I at
times had some hard work. But I never had such
hard work, neither was I ever in a position of such
difficulty, or in one involving such a continuous
strain on the mind, the nerves, and, I may add, the
temper, as during the first three months of the year
1884. I was rarely able to leave my house. I
had a very small staff to help me. I was generally
hard at work from daybreak till late at night.
Without doubt, mistakes were made during this
period, but looking back to the difficulties of the
situation and remembering the confusion which
then reigned in Egyptian affairs, I cannot help
reflecting that it was quite as much by luck as by
good management that the mistakes were not more
numerous and more serious. I had, fortunately,
one qualification for dealing with the situation, and

that was a strong constitution. Without that, I should certainly have broken down altogether.

Without entering into any detail, I will describe the broad features of the Egyptian situation, as it then existed.

The Egyptian question alone, by which I mean the work of reorganisation in Egypt proper, presented difficulties of no common order. On to this was now grafted the Soudan question, which by itself was one of the utmost importance, and which for the time being exercised a paramount, though indirect influence on the solution of all other Egyptian questions. The Government Treasury was well-nigh bankrupt. It seemed at the time as though a whole or partial repudiation of the Egyptian debt was imminent, and, if this had happened, very troublesome international complications would have ensued. The Europeans were discontented because trade was depressed, and because the indemnities due to them for their losses during and after the Alexandria bombardment had not yet been paid. The Pashas were in a morose and sullen condition because their privileges were threatened. The people were discontented because they had not as yet reaped the benefits which they had expected from the British occupation. The old arbitrary system of government by the courbash had been abolished, but nothing had as yet been instituted to take its place. The Arábist rebellion had profoundly shaken the authority of the ruling classes. The reorganisation of the army and of the police had only just been commenced. A large force of Gendarmerie had been withdrawn for service at Suakin, whence such of them as did not leave their bones to whiten on the sands of Trinkitat were to return discomfited and demoralised. The Anglo-Egyptian officials were for the most part new to their work. With some rare exceptions, the Egyptian officials were not only useless but often obstructive. A severe epidemic of cholera had but recently swept over the country, leaving behind it a variety of troublesome quarantine questions, the settlement of which involved considerable diplomatic difficulties. Every man's hand was against the British Government. French hostility was never more active. The other Powers of Europe, with the exception of Italy, were animated with no very friendly sentiments towards England. Prince Bismarck disliked the Liberal Government in England; moreover, he was at this time making an effort, which ended in failure, to conciliate France, a policy which naturally led Germany to adopt a hostile attitude towards England in Egypt. The Sultan again came forward with his favourite idea of deposing Tewfik Pasha and substituting Halim in his place, an idea which was, as on former occasions, at once nipped in the bud by the British Government. Nubar Pasha was unpopular in the country. The attitude which he assumed on matters connected with internal reform, increased the difficulties of the situation. His main object at this time was to get rid of Mr. Clifford Lloyd, who was endeavouring to reorganise the Department of the Interior. An international question of considerable importance had also to be dealt with during this period. The powers of the Mixed Courts had expired, and the conditions under which they were to be renewed had to be discussed. This subject afforded a wide field for petty international intrigue. In England, the Government were exposed to constant attacks from party politicians. The incidents of this party warfare necessitated frequent reference to Cairo for information, the collection of which often caused great trouble and waste of valuable time,[1] which I grudged all the more because I was aware that, when the information had been collected, it would be of little real utility and that, in fact, it was only demanded with a view to affording a handle to Parliamentary attack or defence. The Government themselves did not know their own mind. Every British official in Egypt turned to me for advice and guidance about the affairs of his Department, and in each Department numerous troublesome questions of detail were constantly cropping up for settlement. I was myself new to the work and had not had sufficient time to take stock of the situation, which was greatly changed since I left the country in 1880, or to fully understand the characters of the principal people with whom I had to deal. Looking at the situation as a whole, it seemed as if Isaiah's prophecy had been fulfilled. "The Lord hath mingled a perverse spirit in the midst thereof, and they have caused Egypt to err in every work thereof, as a drunken man staggereth in his vomit." There were, however, some redeeming features in the situation.

In the first place, the presence of a British army in the country afforded a solid guarantee that, in spite of administrative disorder and foreign intrigue, nothing could occur of a nature calculated to endanger seriously the stability of the Khedive's rule. The behaviour and discipline of the British troops were alike excellent. Moreover, they were commanded by an officer (Sir Frederick Stephenson) who combined in a high degree all the qualities necessary to fill with advantage to his country a post of such exceptional difficulty as the command

[1] On this subject, and, indeed, on all others, I received the utmost personal consideration from Lord Granville. On February 8, 1884, he wrote to me: "I keep over the references to you as much as possible, and I hope you fully understand that questions do not mean complaints."

of an army of occupation in a foreign country. The French residents in Egypt resented the presence of a British army in their midst. They were in a state of nervous irritability, which rendered them prompt to take offence at the smallest real or imaginary provocation. At any moment, some paltry squabble might have occurred between the officers and soldiers of the army of occupation on the one hand, and the population on the other hand, which, if any Frenchman had been concerned, might have caused much trouble. The General Officer in command of the troops was thus called upon to exercise great tact, firmness, patience and judgment. These qualities Sir Frederick Stephenson possessed in a high degree; it was largely due to him that such difficulties as arose never assumed proportions which it was beyond the resources of local diplomacy to settle satisfactorily. Sir Frederick Stephenson won for himself the admiration even of those who were most hostile to the British occupation.

General Earle occupied at Alexandria much the same position as that held by Sir Frederick Stephenson at Cairo. A first-rate soldier, a clearheaded and vigorous man of business, endowed with exceptional tact, good manners, and judgment, he was respected and liked by the whole population of Alexandria. A statue, now standing in the principal square of the town, was erected by public subscription to his memory, and bears witness to the honour in which he was universally held. The Dervish bullet, which subsequently cut short this promising career, deprived the Queen and the country of a servant of the highest merit.

Another bright spot on the otherwise dark horizon was that, in spite of occasional jars, reliance could always be placed on the loyalty and devotion of the British officials in the service of the Egyptian Government. Of the services of those officials, I shall have to speak more fully at a later period. For the present, I need only allude to the work performed by Sir Edgar Vincent and by Sir Evelyn Wood. The former was using all the resources of a mind endowed with singular fertility of resource to struggle with a financial situation which appeared well-nigh desperate. Sir Evelyn Wood was reconstructing the Egyptian army out of materials which appeared at the time to be very unpromising. Moreover, his advice on the military aspects of the Soudan question, on which the policy of the Government mainly depended, was of great value. He loyally supported me in enforcing a course of action, which, although obviously dictated by reason, was at the time extremely unpopular with almost all classes whether in England or in Egypt.

There was yet a third consideration from which I derived a certain amount of consolation during this stormy and difficult period. It has often been my fate to disagree with the Government which I was serving, but I have seen something of the relations between foreign Governments and their representatives abroad. So far as is possible for any one who has never sat in the House of Commons, I think I can appreciate the difficulties of Parliamentary life,—difficulties which, owing to a variety of circumstances, have increased in magnitude during the last few years. Looking to the whole of the facts, my experience leads me to the conclusion that British Ministers, whether Liberal or Conservative, are good masters to serve.

Of course, the exigencies of Parliamentary warfare are sometimes too much even for the most loyal of Ministers. They are occasionally obliged to trim their sails to a Parliamentary breeze; during the Soudan discussions, indeed, the breeze rose almost to the force of a hurricane; and, when this happens, the character and reputation of their representative abroad may suffer. But even then, it will probably only suffer for a time if he has a fairly good case to show. Not only British Ministers, but British public opinion are fair and just in the long run, although both the fairness and the justice are at times obscured in the midst of a sharp party conflict. I often disagreed with Lord Granville during his tenure of office; but I always felt that, if I got into any real difficulty, he would support me to the best of his ability.

On December 1, 1883, I received the following telegram from Lord Granville: "If General Charles Gordon were willing to go to Egypt, could he be of any use to you or to the Egyptian Government, and, if so, in what capacity?"[1] I did not at that time know General Gordon well, but I had seen a little of him, and I had, of course, heard much of him. My first impression was decidedly adverse to his employment in the Soudan. Moreover, when I spoke to Chérif Pasha on the subject, I found that he entertained strong objections to the proposal. I was unwilling to put forward my own objections, which were in some degree based on General Gordon's personal unfitness to undertake the work in hand. In replying to Lord Granville, therefore, I only dwelt on the objections entertained by the Egyptian Government, which were reasonable, and, I thought, calculated to produce an impression in London, without bringing in the awkward question of personal fitness. It was with these feelings uppermost in my mind that, on December 2, I telegraphed to

---

[1] Sir Henry Gordon (*Events, etc.*, p. 322) says that if General Gordon had gone to Khartoum six weeks earlier the result of his mission "would most likely have been a complete success." This conclusion is, of course, a mere conjecture and is incapable of proof. I see no reason to believe that the despatch of General Gordon to Khartoum early in December would have materially altered the course of events.

Lord Granville: "The Egyptian Government are very much averse to employing General Gordon, mainly on the ground that, the movement in the Soudan being religious, the appointment of a Christian in high command would probably alienate the tribes who remain faithful. I think it wise not to press them on the subject."[1]

The idea of sending General Gordon to the Soudan was then allowed to drop for a while, but his employment continued to be warmly advocated by the press in England, more especially by the *Pall Mall Gazette*, a newspaper which took a leading part in the discussion of Egyptian affairs at that time.

On December 22, I sent to Lord Granville a telegram advising that the British Government should insist on the withdrawal of the Egyptian troops from the Soudan.[2] I indicated that Chérif Pasha would probably resign, and I added : "Also, it will be necessary to send an officer of high authority to Khartoum with full powers to withdraw the garrisons and to make the best arrangements he can for the future of the country."

On January 7, the Ministry of Chérif Pasha resigned, and a new Ministry was formed under the presidency of Nubar Pasha. On January 10, Lord Granville telegraphed to me : "Could General Charles Gordon or Sir Charles Wilson be of assistance under altered circumstances in Egypt ?" I had had further time to think over this proposal since sending my telegram of December 22. The more I thought of it, the less was I inclined to send General Gordon, or, indeed, any Englishman to Khartoum. I discussed the matter with Nubar

---

[1] There was reason in the objection taken by the Egyptian Government. On March 4, 1884, General Gordon telegraphed from Khartoum : "My weakness is that of being foreign and Christian, and peaceful."

[2] *Vide ante*, p. 381.

Pasha, and we both came to the conclusion that the best plan would be to send Abdul-Kader Pasha. He had been a former Governor-General of the Soudan. He had been highly spoken of by Colonel Stewart. He had the reputation of being a courageous and capable soldier. It was under these circumstances that, on January 11, I telegraphed to Lord Granville: "I have consulted with Nubar Pasha, and I do not think that the services of General Gordon or Sir Charles Wilson can be utilised at present." I had thus twice rejected the proposal to send General Gordon to Khartoum. Would that I had done so a third time!

On January 14, Lord Granville telegraphed to me: "Can you give further information as to prospects of retreat for army and residents at Khartoum, and measures taken?" On the following day (January 15), Lord Granville telegraphed to me privately: "I hear indirectly that Gordon is ready to go straight to Suakin without passing through Cairo on the following rather vague terms. His mission to be to report to Her Majesty's Government on the military situation of the Soudan, and to return without any further engagement towards him. He would be under you for instructions and will send letters through you under flying seal. You and Nubar Pasha to give him all assistance and facilities as to telegraphing, etc. Egyptian Government to send Ibrahim Bey Fauzi to meet him at Suez, with a writer to attend on him. He might be of use in informing you and us of the situation. It would be popular at home, but there may be countervailing objections. Tell me your real opinion with or without Nubar Pasha."[1]

[1] Mr. Morley (*Life of Gladstone*, vol. iii. p. 149) says that, on January 14, Lord Granville wrote to Mr. Gladstone as follows: "If Gordon says he believes he could, by his personal influence, excite the tribes to

On January 16, I sent two telegrams to Lord Granville, one official, and the other private. The official telegram was as follows : " I hope soon to be able to telegraph fully, as the subject of the withdrawal from Khartoum is now being discussed. There can be no doubt, however, that very great difficulties will be encountered. It was intended to despatch Abdul-Kader, the new Minister of War, to Khartoum ; he at first accepted, but now declines to go. The Egyptian Government would feel greatly obliged if Her Majesty's Government would select a well-qualified British officer to go to Khartoum instead of the War Minister. He would be given full powers, both civil and military, to conduct the retreat." At the same time, I sent the following private telegram : " My official telegram of to-day, and your private telegram of yesterday. Gordon would be the best man if he will pledge himself to carry out the policy of withdrawing from the Soudan as quickly as is possible consistently with saving life. He must also fully understand that he must take his instructions from the British representative in Egypt and report to him.[1] He was at Brussels early this month and is now believed to be in England. If so, please see him. I would rather have him than any one else, provided there is a perfectly clear understanding with him as to what his position is to be and what line of policy he is to carry out. Otherwise, not. Failing him, consider Stewart. Whoever goes

escort the Khartoum garrison and inhabitants to Suakin, a little pressure on Baring might be advisable." Mr. Gladstone replied by telegraph that he agreed. Hence, the telegram from Lord Granville to me given above.

I have been told on good authority that Mr. Gladstone was, in the first instance, much opposed to the despatch of General Gordon to Khartoum, and that he only yielded with great reluctance to the pressure which was brought to bear on him by some of his colleagues.

[1] The reason why I said this was that I knew something of General Gordon's erratic character, and I thought that the only chance of keeping him to his task was to appeal to his sense of discipline.

should be distinctly warned that he will undertake
a service of great difficulty and danger."

On January 18, Lord Granville informed me
by telegraph that General Gordon and Colonel
Stewart would leave London that evening for
Egypt. On the same day, Lord Granville wrote
privately to me : " I was glad to get your approval
of Gordon. He may possibly be of great use, and
the appointment will be popular with many classes
in this country. He praises you very highly and
expressed a wish to be placed entirely under you."

General Gordon's own account of how he came
to go to the Soudan is as follows: " At noon he,
Wolseley, came to me and took me to the Ministers.
He went in and talked to the Ministers, and came
back and said : ' Her Majesty's Government want
you to undertake this. Government are determined to evacuate the Soudan, for they will not
guarantee future government. Will you go and
do it ? ' I said : 'Yes.' He said : 'Go in.' I went
in and saw them. They said : 'Did Wolseley tell
you your orders ? ' I said : ' Yes.' I said : ' You
will not guarantee future government of the
Soudan, and you wish me to go up and evacuate
now.' They said : ' Yes,' and it was over, and I
left at 8 P.M. for Calais."[1]

General Gordon's appointment, the *Pall Mall
Gazette* said, with perfect truth, "was applauded
enthusiastically by the press all over the country
without distinction of party." I was reproached
for having too "tardily discovered that Gordon was
the best man," and the Government were sharply
criticised for not having utilised his services at an
earlier date.

Mr. Gladstone's Government made two great
mistakes in dealing with Soudan affairs in their

[1] *Letters to the Rev. J. Barnes, 1885.*

early stages.   Of these one was a sin of omission,
and the other a sin of commission.   The sin of
omission was that the Government did nothing to
stop the departure of the Hicks expedition.   The
sin of commission was the despatch of General
Gordon to Khartoum.   Looking back at what
occurred after a space of many years, two points are
to my mind clear.   The first is that no Englishman
should have been sent to Khartoum.   The second
is that, if any one had to be sent, General Gordon
was not the right man to send.

The reasons why no Englishman should have
been sent are now sufficiently obvious.   If he were
beleaguered at Khartoum, which was possible and
even probable, the British Government might be
obliged to send an expedition to relieve him.   The
main object of British policy was to avoid being
drawn into military operations in the Soudan.
The employment of a British official at Khartoum
involved a serious risk that it would be no longer
possible to adhere to this policy, and the risk was
materially increased when the individual chosen to
go to the Soudan was one who had attracted to
himself a greater degree of popular sympathy than
almost any Englishman of modern times.   General
Gordon, Lord Cairns said (February 14) amidst
the cheers of the House of Lords, "is one of our
national treasures," and, although possibly party
politicians used the popular sympathy with General
Gordon as a card in the political game, Lord Cairns's
expression faithfully represented the general tone of
British public opinion at that time.

The Government scarcely realised the gravity
of the decision at which they had arrived.   I
believe I am correct in stating that the question
was not discussed at a Cabinet Council.   Some
years afterwards, Sir Charles Dilke, who was then
a member of the Government, gave me the follow-

ing extract from his Journal: "January 18, 1884.
—Meeting at War Office. Ld. G., Hartington,
Northbrook, and self. Decided to send Colonel
Gordon to Suakin to report on the Soudan."[1]

I think I may say that I saw the danger more
clearly than the Ministers in England, and it was
on that account that I wished to send an Egyptian
official to Khartoum, but I did not realise it so
fully as I should have done.

If, however, it was a mistake to send any
Englishman to Khartoum, it was a still greater
mistake to choose General Gordon as the man to
send.

It happens to most men engaged in public life
that their conduct gives rise to some differences of
opinion. General Gordon's actions were rarely
subjected to this healthy form of criticism. A
wave of Gordon *cultus* passed over England in
1884. His personal character, which was in many
respects noble, the circumstances connected with
his mission to the Soudan, the perilous position
in which he was placed at Khartoum, his heroic
defence of the town, and his tragic death, all
appealed powerfully to the imagination of a people,
who are often supposed to be pre-eminently cold

---

[1] On January 18, Lord Northbrook wrote privately to me as follows:
"I got a summons to-day to the W. O. to meet Chinese Gordon with
Granville, Hartington, and Dilke. The upshot of the meeting was that
he leaves by to-night's mail for Suakin to report on the best way of
withdrawing the garrisons, settling the country, and to perform such
other duties as may be entrusted to him by the Khedive's Government
through you. He will be under you, and wishes it. He has no doubt
of being able to get on with you He was very hopeful as to the state
of affairs, does not believe in the great powers of the Mahdi, does not
think the tribes will go much beyond their own confines, and does not
see why the garrisons should not get off. He did not seem at all
anxious to retain the Soudan, and agreed heartily to accept the policy
of withdrawal."
    The following entry occurs in Sir Mountstuart Grant Duff's *Notes
from a Diary 1896-1901*, vol. ii. p. 75 : "Northbrook said that, if he
had previously read Gordon's book, nothing would have induced him
to consent to his going anywhere. It was the book of a madman!"

and practical, but who in reality are perhaps more led by their emotions than any other nation in Europe.[1]   During this stage of national excitement, any one who had attempted to judge General Gordon's conduct by the canons of criticism which are ordinarily applied to human action, would have failed to obtain a hearing.   His melancholy death also silenced the voice of criticism.   Five years after its occurrence, a critic, who was disposed to be hostile to General Gordon (Colonel Chaillé Long), wrote to Mr. Gladstone, with a view to eliciting an expression of his opinion on General Gordon's conduct.   Mr. Gladstone, with the magnanimity of a true statesman and the delicate feelings of a gentleman, declined to enter into any discussion on the subject.[2]

The public enthusiasm which General Gordon's name evoked led to some disastrous consequences, yet I cannot bring myself to condemn it.   It was, in fact, eminently creditable to the British public. There was nothing mean or self-seeking about it. It was a genuine and generous tribute to moral worth, and it showed that, even in this material age, moral worth has a hold on the public opinion of at least one great civilised country.   It may be that the Gordon of real life did not always act quite up to the standard of the idealised hero who was present to the public mind, but, after all, this is merely to say that he was human and fallible. More than this, whatever may have been General Gordon's defects, the main lines of his character were really worthy of admiration.   I do not speak so much of his high courage and fertility in mili-

---

[1] It was, I think, Lord Beaconsfield who said that the English were the most emotional people in Europe, and Lord Beaconsfield was a keen observer of human nature.   Lord Salisbury once wrote to me: "It is easier to combat with the rinderpest or the cholera than with a popular sentiment."

[2] *Belford's Magazine*, September 1890, p. 549.

tary resource, though in these respects he was remarkable, but of his moral qualities. His religious convictions, though eccentric, were sincere. No one could doubt the remarkable purity of his private life, or his lofty disinterestedness as regards objects, such as money and rank, which usually excite the ambition of mankind. His aims in life were unquestionably high and noble.

Besides his moral qualities, there was another point in General Gordon's character, which was eminently calculated to attract the sympathy of the British public. He was thoroughly unconventional. He chafed under discipline, and was never tired of pouring forth the vials of his wrath on the official classes.[1] Mistrust of Government officials is engrained in the English character, and I may add that I hope the dislike of being over-governed will ever continue to exist in England.

It is dangerous when either an individual or a nation allow their imagination to predominate over their reason, and this is what the British nation did under the spell of General Gordon's name. But it is perhaps better that the national imagination should even run riot at times in a good cause rather than that a dull level of practical utility should invariably be maintained, and that the imaginative qualities should be discarded altogether. Enthusiasts are troublesome to politicians and diplomatists, but the world would be dull without them. The enthusiastic and emotional classes found, or thought they had found their

---

[1] General Gordon, who had a keen sense of humour, was fully aware of his own unfitness for official employment. "I own," he wrote in his Journal (p. 59), "to having been very insubordinate to Her Majesty's Government and its officials, but it is my nature, and I cannot help it. I fear I have not even tried to play battledore and shuttlecock with them. I know if *I* was chief I would never employ *myself*, for I am incorrigible. To men like Dilke, who weigh every word, I must be perfect poison."

ideal type in General Gordon, and accordingly
they bestowed on him extreme, sometimes extravagant eulogy.[1]

General Gordon was no friend to the particular
official class to which I belonged. "I must say,"
he wrote, "I hate our diplomatists. I think, with
few exceptions, they are arrant humbugs; and I
expect they know it." Acting on this general
principle, General Gordon in his Journal which,
when it was first published, was probably read
by almost every educated man in England, held
up Mr. (subsequently, Sir Edwin) Egerton,[2] myself,
and others to odium and ridicule. To all this,
acting on Mr. Gladstone's principle, I shall not
attempt to reply, more especially as I feel sure
that, had he lived, no one would have regretted
what he wrote more than General Gordon himself.
But I must, for the elucidation of this narrative,

---

[1] Unquestionably, officialism and enthusiasm—notably undisciplined
enthusiasm—*ne se marient pas*, as the French would say. At the same
time, strange as it may appear to some sections of the public, it is
quite possible to have a genuine sympathy for suffering humanity
without constantly mouthing the catchpenny phrases which form to
so large an extent the stock-in-trade of the professional "friends of
humanity." These latter are usually not over-charitable to those who
cannot accept, and at once carry into execution, the whole of their
idealist programmes. There appears to be much truth in Mr. John
Morley's remark (*Robespierre*, p. 59), that "the most ostentatious faith
in humanity in general seems always to beget the sharpest mistrust of
all human beings in particular." I should term most of the leading
British officials in Egypt humanitarians under any reasonable interpretation of that term, but the responsible nature of their position
naturally obliges them to look at the questions with which they
have to deal from many, and not merely from one point of view.

[2] Mr. Egerton acted as my *locum tenens* when I was temporarily
absent from Cairo in 1884.
I saw General Gordon's Journal in manuscript before it was printed.
I know that I am correct in saying that the Government would have preferred that the Journal should have been published without any omissions.
At the instance, however, of General Gordon's friends and family, a
good deal of violent and very foolish abuse of Lord Granville—and, if I
remember rightly, of others—was omitted. It is, in my opinion, to be
regretted that this was done. The publication of the Journal, as it was
originally written, would have enabled the public to judge more accurately of the value of General Gordon's criticisms, than was possible
when only an expurgated edition was issued.

state why I think it was a mistake to send General Gordon to Khartoum.

"It is impossible," I wrote privately to Lord Granville on January 28, 1884, "not to be charmed by the simplicity and honesty of Gordon's character." "My only fear," I added, "is that he is terribly flighty and changes his opinions very rapidly. I am glad that Stewart, who impressed me favourably, is going with him, but I do not think Gordon much likes it himself. He said to me: 'They sent him (Stewart) with me to be my wet-nurse.'"[1] Impulsive flightiness was, in fact, the main defect of General Gordon's character, and it was one which, in my opinion, rendered him unfit to carry out a work which pre-eminently required a cool and steady head. I used to receive some twenty or thirty telegrams from General Gordon in the course of the day when he was at Khartoum, those in the evening often giving opinions which it was impossible to reconcile with others despatched the same morning. Scarcely, indeed, had General Gordon started on his mission, when Lord Granville, who does not appear at first to have understood General Gordon's character, began to be alarmed at his impulsiveness. On February 8, Lord Granville wrote to me: "I own your letters about Gordon rather alarm. His changes about Zobeir are difficult to understand.[2] Northbrook consoles me by saying that he says all the foolish things that pass through his head, but that his judgment is excellent." I am not prepared to go

---

[1] Whilst on his way to Khartoum, Colonel Stewart wrote me a letter, from which it was clear that, at one time, the relations between him and General Gordon were much strained. He asked me to tear it up directly I had read it, without showing it to any one. This I accordingly did. Subsequently, they appear to have been fully reconciled, but it was only natural that there should have been occasional jars between two men of such very different characters and habits of thought.

[2] This is an allusion to circumstances which took place at Cairo, and which will be presently narrated.

so far as to say that General Gordon's judgment was excellent. Nevertheless, there was some truth in Lord Northbrook's remark. I often found that, amidst a mass of irrelevant verbiage and amidst many contradictory opinions, a vein of sound common sense and political instinct ran through General Gordon's proposals. So much was I impressed with this, and so fearful was I that the sound portions of his proposals would be rejected in London on account of the eccentric language in which they were often couched, that, on February 12, I telegraphed to Lord Granville: " In considering Gordon's suggestions, please remember that his general views are excellent, but that undue importance must not be attached to his words. We must look to the spirit rather than the letter of what he says."

In spite of General Gordon's high qualities, however, I do not think that a man of his peculiar character was a proper person to send on such an extremely difficult mission as that of arranging for the evacuation of the Soudan. The task was, indeed, so difficult that it is probable that no one could have carried it out successfully, but I believe that a better chance of success would have presented itself if Colonel Stewart had been sent without General Gordon. It is singular how entirely General Gordon's reputation has overshadowed that of Colonel Stewart. I have rarely come across anybody who impressed me more favourably than this cool, sagacious, and courageous soldier. His premature death was a great loss both to England and to Egypt.

One further point remains to be considered. Who was responsible for sending General Gordon ?

In a sense, the main responsibility rests with the press of England, and, notably, with the *Pall Mall Gazette*. The people of England, as represented by the press, insisted on sending General Gordon to the Soudan, and accordingly to the Soudan he was sent. "Anonymous authorship," one of the wisest political thinkers of modern times has stated, "places the public under the direction of guides who have no sense of personal responsibility."[1] The arguments in favour of newspaper influence are too commonplace to require mention. But newspaper government has certain disadvantages, and these disadvantages were never more clearly shown than in the incident now under discussion.

The attitude of the British press, however, though it may be pleaded in palliation of the mistake which was made, does not, of course, exonerate the Government from responsibility. The truth is, that Mr. Gladstone's Government did not fully realise the importance of the step they were taking. Whilst entirely agreeing in the policy of evacuating the Soudan, I had pressed upon the Government the extreme difficulty of carrying the policy into execution. I had told Lord Granville that any one who went to the Soudan would "undertake a service of great difficulty and danger." But these warnings fell unheeded, neither can it be any matter for surprise that they should have done so, for the one person who the Government were told on all sides was the highest authority on Soudan affairs, namely, General Gordon himself, did not share my apprehensions in any degree; neither was any danger-signal hoisted by Colonel Stewart. There can be no doubt that when General Gordon was in London, his views were far too optimistic. He did not rightly appreciate either the state of affairs which then existed in the Soudan, or the difficulties of the task which he had undertaken. Being deceived himself, it was natural that he should,

---

[1] Sir G. Cornewall Lewis, *On the Influence of Authority in Matters of Opinion*, p. 355.

quite unintentionally, have deceived the Government, and should have encouraged them in the optimism to which all Governments are somewhat prone.[1] On January 28, after having seen General Gordon, I wrote to Lord Granville : "Gordon speaks very hopefully of being able to do the whole thing in three or four months." So late as February 20, that is to say, two days after his arrival at Khartoum, General Gordon wrote to Colonel Coetlogon : "I have proposed to you to go back to Cairo because, in my belief, there is not the least chance of any danger being now incurred in Khartoum, which I consider as safe as Cairo. . . . You may rest assured that you leave a place which is as safe as Kensington Park."

To sum up,—the main defence of the Government, for what it is worth, is contained in the saying of the French revolutionary leader when he was reproached for obeying the dictates of the Jacobin mob : "Je suis leur chef; il faut que je les suive." The Government did not attempt to guide public opinion. They followed it. Nevertheless, the opinions which General Gordon entertained, may be pleaded as some justification for the line of policy adopted by the Government. If the British Ministers erred on the side of optimism, it is certain that their optimistic views were shared by General Gordon, and, indeed, were largely based on what he said both before leaving London and whilst on his way to Khartoum.

So far as my personal responsibility is concerned, I can plead no such justification, or, at all events, I can only plead it to a less degree. I was never

---

[1] On September 28, 1884, General Gordon wrote in his Journal (p. 110): "The Government may say that they had reasonable hopes that I would succeed ; I will neither say I gave them such assurance or that I did not give it. I think I was neutral in giving or in not giving such an assurance." When General Gordon wrote this, he must have forgotten many of his previous utterances.

under any delusion as to the difficulties of the task which General Gordon had undertaken, or as to the personal danger which he and Colonel Stewart would run. More than this, I mistrusted General Gordon's judgment, and I was in reality adverse to his employment. I am not now making use of *ex post facto* arguments. I have such a vivid recollection of my own frame of mind at that time, that I can state very positively why it was that, after having twice refused to utilise General Gordon's services, I yielded on being pressed a third time by Lord Granville. I believed that at that time I stood alone in hesitating to employ General Gordon. Public opinion in England was calling loudly for his employment. Lord Granville's telegrams, though couched in language from which it might be inferred that the Government would defer to my opinion, showed, nevertheless, clearly enough a strong wish on the part of the Government that General Gordon should be employed. Nubar Pasha concurred in this view. I did not, however, attach much importance to his opinion on the special point at issue. Sir Evelyn Wood's opinion carried more weight with me. He was favourable to the employment of General Gordon. So also was Colonel Watson, who was at that time on the staff of the Egyptian army, and who spoke with the authority of one who knew General Gordon well, having served under him in the Soudan.

With this array of opinion against me, I mistrusted my own judgment. I did not yield because I hesitated to stand up against the storm of public opinion. I gave a reluctant assent, in reality against my own judgment and inclination, because I thought that, as everybody differed from me, I must be wrong. I also thought that I might be unconsciously prejudiced against General Gordon from the fact that his habits of thought and modes of action in dealing with public affairs differed widely from mine.

In yielding, I made a mistake which I shall never cease to regret. It may well be that, had I not yielded, the result would have been the same. The public feeling in favour of sending General Gordon was so strong as to be almost irresistible. But this consideration does not constitute any consolation to me. By yielding, I rendered myself in some degree responsible for all the valuable lives which were lost, and the treasure which was subsequently expended in the Soudan.

The whole incident left a strong impression on my mind. Unquestionably, much harm has been done at times by Governments failing to yield, or yielding too late, to a clear and unmistakable expression of public opinion. Nothing, in fact, can be more foolish or hurtful than that officials should unreasonably oppose a stiff barrier of bureaucratic obstruction to the views of the outside public. If they do so, they are liable to be swept away. But occasions do occur, which in these democratic days are becoming more rather than less frequent, when the best service a Government official can render to his country is to place himself in opposition to the public view. Indeed, if he feels certain that he is right, it is his bounden duty to do so, especially in respect to questions as to which public opinion in England is ill-informed. Such an occasion presented itself when there was a question of sending General Gordon to the Soudan. It was worth while to incur a good deal of unpopularity and misrepresentation in order to save the Government and the nation from making so great a mistake. " A man," it has been truly said, " who never disagrees with his countrymen, and who shrinks from unpopularity as the worst of all evils, can never have a share in moulding the traditions of a virile race, though for a time he may make its fashions."[1]   I repeat, therefore, that I shall never cease to regret that I did not stand to my guns and maintain, to the best of my ability, my original objections to the Gordon mission.   Had I known General Gordon better, I should certainly never have agreed to his employment.

[1] Oliver's *Alexander Hamilton*, p. 436.

CHAPTER XXIII

GORDON AT CAIRO

JANUARY 24-26, 1884

General Gordon wishes to go to Suakin—He goes to Cairo—Consequences which resulted from the change of route—General Gordon's views as to the Soudan—His London instructions—Instructions issued at Cairo—General Gordon appointed Governor-General of the Soudan—And furnished with certain Proclamations—Reasons why General Gordon's instructions were changed—The Darfour Sultan—General Gordon proposes that Zobeir Pasha should accompany him—Interview between General Gordon and Zobeir Pasha—It is decided not to employ Zobeir Pasha—General Gordon leaves Cairo.

WHEN, on January 18, Lord Granville informed me that General Gordon and Colonel Stewart were about to proceed to Egypt, he added that General Gordon was anxious not to go to Cairo, and that he would go through the Suez Canal straight to Suakin. I was requested to meet him at Ismailia. The reason why General Gordon did not wish to visit Cairo was obvious. He had publicly criticised the conduct of the Khedive in no measured terms, and did not wish to meet him.

The road from Suakin to Berber was at this time blocked. The tribes were in a state of open rebellion, and had gained a series of successes over the Egyptian troops. It was certain that General Gordon would never be able to reach Khartoum by the Suakin route. I, therefore, telegraphed to Lord Granville, on January 19, urging the desirability of General Gordon's coming to Cairo. Lord Granville supported my view. The result was that General Gordon came to Cairo. He arrived on the evening of January 24.

If I had not interfered as regards General Gordon's route, a point which seemed at the time to be one of detail, the course of history in the Soudan would have been changed and many valuable lives, including probably that of General Gordon himself, would have been saved. General Gordon would possibly never have got to Khartoum, and it would not, therefore, have been necessary to send any British expedition to the Soudan. It is probable, indeed almost certain, that in a few weeks he would have returned to England without having effected anything of importance towards the accomplishment of his mission. I remember that it crossed my mind that I had better not interfere, but leave General Gordon to work out his plans in his own way. It was, however, clear that, in going to Suakin, General Gordon would foredoom his mission to failure, and that he would never have made any such proposal had he been well acquainted with the state of affairs then existing in the Eastern Soudan. I had, therefore, excellent reasons for interfering, but, looking back upon events as they subsequently occurred, I regret that I did so.

On the morning of January 25, General Gordon accompanied me to the Ismailia Palace to see the Khedive. Colonel Stewart wrote in his journal: "Gordon apologised to Tewfik for his former brusque behaviour, and the interview went off very well."

The question of General Gordon's instructions then had to be discussed. I shall have to deal with this matter at some length, as it has formed the subject of much misapprehension.[1]

---

[1] For instance, Sir William Butler (*Charles George Gordon*, p. 200) says : "Few persons are aware that the English Government knew

On January 23, whilst on his way to Egypt, General Gordon wrote a Memorandum setting forth the line of policy which he proposed to pursue in the Soudan. It contained the following passage:

"My idea is that the restoration of the country should be made to the different petty Sultans, who existed at the time of Mehemet Ali's conquests, and whose families still exist; that the Mahdi should be left altogether out of the calculations as regards the handing over of the country, and that it should be optional with the Sultans to accept his supremacy or not. As these Sultans would probably not be likely to gain by accepting the Mahdi as their sovereign, it is probable that they will hold to their independent positions. . . . The most difficult question is how, and to whom, to hand over the arsenals of Khartoum, Dongola, and Kassala, which towns have, so to say, no old-standing families, Khartoum and Kassala having sprung up since Mehemet Ali's conquest. Probably it would be advisable to postpone any decision as to these towns till such time as the inhabitants have made known their opinion."

Colonel Stewart in recording his "cordial agreement" with General Gordon's views, added: "Handing back the territories to the families of the dispossessed Sultans is an act of justice both towards them and their people. The latter, at any rate, will no longer be at the mercy of foreign mercenaries, and if they are tyrannised over, it will be more or less their own fault. Handing back the districts to the old families is also a politic act, as raising up a rival power to that of the Mahdi. As it is impossible for Her Majesty's Government to

nothing of the appointment of their officer as Governor-General of the Soudan, or of the change of his destination from Suakin to the Nile route, until some days after both had been effected by our Minister in Cairo." Both of these statement are devoid of foundation.

foresee all the eventualities that may arise during the evacuation, it seems to me as the more judicious course to rely on the discretion of General Gordon and his knowledge of the country."

The policy of setting up the local Sultans to govern the country appeared at the time wise and politic; but, looking at events with an after-knowledge of what subsequently happened, it is evident that General Gordon both underrated the power of the Mahdi, and overrated the influence of the local Sultans. The most powerful and warlike tribes in the Soudan were partisans of the Mahdi. The families of the local Sultans, who had governed the Soudan in former times, had lost all hold on the public opinion of the country.

Moreover, General Gordon himself indicated one great difficulty in the way of giving effect to this policy. It was that, in respect to Khartoum, Dongola, and Kassala, there were "no old-standing families." Now, whoever holds Khartoum, dominates a large part of the Soudan; unless, therefore, the policy in question could be carried into execution as regards Khartoum, it was almost sure to fall to the ground altogether.

When General Gordon arrived in Egypt, I received a copy of the instructions, dated January 18, which were given to him in London by Lord Granville. The principal portion of these instructions was as follows :—

"Her Majesty's Government are desirous that you should proceed at once to Egypt to report to them on the military situation in the Soudan, and on the measures which it may be advisable to take for the security of the Egyptian garrisons still holding positions in that country, and for the safety of the European population in Khartoum.

"You are also desired to consider and report, upon the best mode of effecting the evacuation of

the interior of the Soudan, and upon the manner
in which the safety and the good administration
by the Egyptian Government of the parts on the
sea-coast can best be secured. . . .

"You will consider yourself authorised and
instructed to perform such other duties as the
Egyptian Government may desire to intrust to
you and as may be communicated to you by Sir
E. Baring."

On the morning of January 25, a meeting took
place to consider whether, acting on the authority
I had received from Lord Granville, I should issue
further instructions to General Gordon. At this
meeting were present Nubar Pasha, General Gordon,
Colonel Stewart, Sir Evelyn Wood, and myself.
After a long discussion, the meeting was adjourned
till the following afternoon. It was arranged
that, in the interval, I was to embody in a letter
addressed to General Gordon the conclusions at
which we had arrived.

On the occasion of the second meeting, I went
through the draft instructions which I had prepared, and discussed them with General Gordon
and the others who were present. A few
changes were made. The following extracts will
be sufficient to show the leading features of these
instructions :—

"It is believed that the number of the Europeans at Khartoum is very small, but it has been
estimated by the local authorities that some
10,000 to 15,000 people will wish to move northwards from Khartoum only when the Egyptian
garrison is withdrawn. These people are native
Christians, Egyptian employés, their wives and
children, etc. The Government of His Highness
the Khedive are earnestly solicitous that no effort
should be spared to ensure the retreat both of these
people and of the Egyptian garrison without loss

of life. As regards the most opportune time and
the best method for effecting the retreat, whether
of the garrisons or of the civil populations, it is
neither necessary nor desirable that you should
receive detailed instructions. . . .

"You will bear in mind that the main end to be
pursued is the evacuation of the Soudan. This
policy was adopted, after very full discussion, by
the Egyptian Government, on the advice of Her
Majesty's Government. It meets with the full
approval of His Highness the Khedive, and of the
present Egyptian Ministry. I understand, also,
that you entirely concur in the desirability of
adopting this policy, and that you think it should
on no account be changed.[1] You consider that it
may take a few months to carry it out with safety.
You are further of opinion that 'the restoration of
the country should be made to the different petty
Sultans who existed at the time of Mehemet Ali's
conquest, and whose families still exist; and that
an endeavour should be made to form a confedera-
tion of those Sultans.' In this view, the Egyptian
Government entirely concur. It will, of course, be
fully understood that the Egyptian troops are not
to be kept in the Soudan merely with a view to
consolidating the power of the new rulers of the
country. But the Egyptian Government have the
fullest confidence in your judgment, your knowledge of the country, and your comprehension of
the general line of policy to be pursued. You are,
therefore, given full discretionary power to retain
the troops for such reasonable period as you may
think necessary, in order that the abandonment
of the country may be accomplished with the least
possible risk to life and property.

"A credit of £100,000 has been opened for you

---

[1] The last part of this sentence was added at Gordon's own request
(*vide ante*, p. 390).

at the Finance Department, and further funds will
be supplied to you on your requisition when this
sum is exhausted."

Simultaneously with the issue of these instructions, a letter was addressed by the Khedive to
General Gordon appointing him Governor-General
of the Soudan. General Gordon was, at the same
time, furnished with two Proclamations from the
Khedive addressed to the inhabitants of the Soudan.
In one of these, the appointment of General Gordon
to be Governor-General was notified, and the people
were invited to obey his orders. In the other
Proclamation, more distinct allusion was made to
the intention of the Government to evacuate the
Soudan. "We have decided," it was said, "to
restore to the families of the kings of the Soudan
their former independence."

"General Gordon," I wrote to Lord Granville
on February 1, "has authority and discretion to
issue one or other of these Proclamations whenever
he may think it desirable to do so. He fully
understands that he is going to Khartoum for the
purpose of carrying out the policy of evacuation,
and has expressed to me his fullest concurrence in
the wisdom of this policy. Your Lordship will
have seen, by my instructions to him, that no
doubt is left on this point, and these instructions
were drafted at the request and with the entire
approval of General Gordon himself. It was,
however, thought desirable, after full discussion
here, that the widest discretionary powers should
be given to General Gordon as regards the manner
of carrying out the policy, and as to the best time
and mode of announcing it at Khartoum."

It has been frequently stated, first, that the
instructions which General Gordon received at Cairo
differed so widely from those which were given
to him in London as to alter entirely the character

of his mission; and, secondly, that the change in
his instructions was effected by myself without
any reference to London. These statements were
freely made by the press. They were echoed by
Mr. Egmont Hake, Sir William Butler, and others
who have written on the Gordon Mission. The
British Government, also, wrote to me a despatch
in which, though they approved of the instructions given to General Gordon, they confirmed the
erroneous popular impression that the London
instructions had been materially altered by me,
acting on my own authority, without reference to
the Foreign Office. "Her Majesty's Government,"
it was said, "bearing in mind the exigencies of the
occasion, concurred in these instructions, which
virtually altered General Gordon's mission from
one of advice to that of executing, or at least
directing, the evacuation not only of Khartoum,
but of the whole Soudan, and they were willing that General Gordon should receive the very
extended powers conferred upon him by the
Khedive to enable him to effect this very difficult
task."

The statement that the instructions, which
General Gordon received in Cairo, altered the
character of his mission is substantially correct.
The statement that I altered General Gordon's
instructions without authority from the British
Government is wholly devoid of foundation.

I never cared to go into this subject at the
time, because my hands were full of other work,
and, moreover, by the time the discussions to
which I allude took place, the question merely had
an historic interest. But I may now state what
occurred.

In the first place, I have to observe that the
importance of this question has been exaggerated.
In reality, it mattered little what instructions

General Gordon received, because he was not the
sort of man to be bound by any instructions.[1]

In the second place, the instructions, which
General Gordon received in London, were manifestly
written without a due appreciation of the necessities of the situation. The Egyptian Government
had asked for "a well-qualified British officer to
go to Khartoum with full powers, both civil and
military, to conduct the retreat." It would have
been a mere mockery if, instead of an executive
officer, they had been given some one whose sole
duty it would have been to write a report. There
had already been a sufficient number of reports
about the Soudan. The moment had arrived
when it was necessary to cease writing and to
act. It would have been particularly ridiculous
to send General Gordon, of all men in the world,
as a "mere reporter upon a difficult situation."[2]
General Gordon was essentially a man of action.
No one, who knew anything of his character,
could have supposed for one moment that he
would confine himself to mere reporting.

The idea, however, appears to have originated
with General Gordon himself. On January 15,
Lord Granville telegraphed to me that General
Gordon was prepared to go to the Soudan on certain
"rather vague terms," the principal of which was that
he was to "report to Her Majesty's Government on
the military situation of the Soudan." Moreover,
on February 14, Sir Charles Dilke stated in the
House of Commons: "General Gordon drafted
his own instructions. . . . Believing him to be
the highest authority, that he knew more of the
conditions, and that he was better able to form a

---

[1] On January 21, 1884, I wrote to Lord Granville: "It is as well
that Gordon should be under my orders, but a man who habitually
consults the Prophet Isaiah when he is in a difficulty is not apt to
obey the orders of any one."

[2] *Too Late*, p. 4.

judgment on the subject than anybody else, we
asked him to draft his own instructions." In spite
of this fact, however, nothing can be more certain
than that General Gordon never considered his
mission to be that of a simple reporter. Indeed,
on the day (January 18) on which General Gordon
received his London instructions, Lord Granville
telegraphed to me: "Gordon suggests that it may
be announced in Egypt that he is on his way to
Khartoum to arrange for the future settlement of
the Soudan for the best advantage of the people."
Nothing was said of reporting. If General Gordon
was to arrange for "the future settlement of the
Soudan," I fail to see how he could do so without
exercising some executive authority.

In the third place, it is to be observed that
the proposal that General Gordon should be made
Governor-General of the Soudan did not emanate
from any one in Cairo. It was made by General
Gordon himself, whilst he was on the journey from
London to Egypt, and was communicated to me by
Lord Granville who, on January 22, telegraphed to
me certain "suggestions made by Gordon as to the
steps which should be taken with regard to the
present state of affairs in the Soudan."[1] The first
of these suggestions was that the Khedive should
issue a Proclamation to the people of the Soudan,
in the following terms: "To the people of the
Soudan! The immense distances which have
separated me from you have given rise to disorders
which have resulted in revolt against my authority.
This revolt has cost much blood and treasure, far
beyond any adequate compensation, and has thrown

---

[1] See *Egypt*, No. 2 of 1884, p. 4 A short despatch from Lord
Granville to me is published in this Parliamentary paper. From this
despatch it appears that certain suggestions of General Gordon's
were telegraphed to me, and that I was authorised to carry them out.
But the suggestions themselves were not published. If they had been
published, no misapprehension on the point now under discussion would
have been possible.

burdens on Lower Egypt which are intolerable. I have, therefore, determined to restore to the various Sultans of the Soudan their independence, and for this purpose I have commissioned General Gordon, late Governor-General of the Soudan, to proceed there as my representative, and to arrange with you for the evacuation of the country and the withdrawal of my troops. Her Majesty's Government, being most desirous of your welfare, have also appointed General Gordon as their Commissioner for the same purpose. *General Gordon is hereby appointed Governor-General for the time necessary to accomplish the evacuation.*"[1]

The second suggestion was that a Proclamation should be issued in General Gordon's name, announcing that he had "*accepted the post of Governor-General of the Soudan.*"[1] "I recommend," General Gordon said in his telegram to Lord Granville, which was repeated to me, "that these Decrees and Proclamations should be published as soon as possible in the Soudan." In forwarding General Gordon's recommendations to me, Lord Granville added : "Her Majesty's Government have not sufficient local knowledge to enable them to form an opinion as to the practicability of these suggestions, and I therefore authorise you, as time is valuable, either immediately to make the arrangements suggested, or to await General Gordon's arrival, and consult with him as to the action to be taken." As, when I received this telegram, General Gordon had already left Brindisi, I did not think it desirable to act upon the authority given to me to cause these Proclamations to be issued at once. I decided to await General Gordon's arrival. When he arrived, I moved the Khedive to name him Governor-General of the Soudan. This was in accordance with General

---

[1] The italics are not in the original.

Gordon's own suggestion, upon which I had been authorised by Lord Granville to act. Further, as I have already mentioned,[1] certain Proclamations were prepared and given to General Gordon with discretionary power to use them should he think fit to do so. These Proclamations did not differ materially from those which had been communicated to me in Lord Granville's telegram of January 22.

Under these circumstances, it was with some surprise that, on February 4, I received a telegram from Lord Granville asking me whether "General Gordon had accepted any appointment from the Khedive." And it was with still greater surprise that I found myself accused, not only by the public, but also to a certain extent by the Government, of having altered the character of General Gordon's mission without any authority to do so. The documents quoted above are sufficient to show that this accusation was altogether groundless. Indeed, so little importance did I attach to the changes in the instructions, which had been made at Cairo, that on January 28, I wrote privately to Lord Granville: "You will see that I gave Gordon, at his own request, additional instructions, of which I hope you will approve. They really amount to nothing more than what he had already received, but they give him a little latitude as to the time at which the troops shall be withdrawn." Looking to the fact that, on the face of the thing, it was absurd to send General Gordon as a mere reporter, to the further fact that General Gordon, who had just arrived from London, never said one word to me to induce the belief that such was the intention of the Government, and also to the fact that Lord Granville had himself authorised me to secure General Gordon's

[1] *Vide ante*, p. 446.

nomination as Governor-General of the Soudan, it never occurred to me that I was departing from the wishes and instructions of the British Government by one hair's-breadth. The explanation of all this confusion is, however, very simple. I believe that the original intention of the British Government was that General Gordon should limit himself to reporting, and that Lord Granville did not see that, in authorising General Gordon to accept the appointment of Governor-General of the Soudan, he changed the spirit of the instructions which he had issued on January 18. He was, therefore, surprised to find out what he had done.

Leaving aside, however, the personal and, therefore, unimportant question of who is responsible for naming General Gordon Governor-General of the Soudan, I wish to say that, in my opinion, the decision was a wise one. General Gordon was about to depart on a very difficult and dangerous mission. He had resided for some while in the Soudan, and was supposed to be well acquainted with the affairs of that country. The only chance of success lay in following his advice, and adopting such measures as he thought most likely to conduce to the accomplishment of his task. He wished to be named Governor-General, and he was obviously right. Otherwise, he would have exercised no authority.

To resume the narrative. It has been already mentioned that one of the main difficulties, which stood in the way of re-establishing the rule of the local Sultans in the Soudan, was that in some of the most important portions of the country there were no old-standing families. This difficulty did not, however, exist in respect to Darfour. Only ten years had elapsed since that province had been annexed by Egypt. Before that period, the country had been governed by a line of Sultans which had existed for more than four hundred years. When the annexation took place, the surviving members of the reigning family were deported to Cairo. The Egyptian Government doled out allowances to them. In respect to Darfour, therefore, there seemed to be some prospect of carrying into execution the policy advocated by General Gordon.

There were several members of the Darfour family at Cairo. It was no easy matter to decide which to choose. The position of a *Roi en exil* is not under any circumstances calculated to ennoble the character. When the ex-monarch happens to be an ignorant barbarian leading a slothful life in a semi-civilised Oriental capital, such as Cairo, and dependent on the charity of the Government for his subsistence, no element is wanting to hasten the process of moral decadence. The uses of adversity had not been turned to account by the Darfour family. The materials from which a choice had to be made were, therefore, unpromising. However, a choice was made. The individual chosen was Emir Abdul-Shakour, son of the late Sultan Abdul-Rahman. He is described in Colonel Stewart's Journal as a " common-looking, unintelligent, and badly-dressed native." He was given " £E.2000, a well-embroidered coat, and the biggest decoration that could be found." He at first wished to remain in Cairo for several days in order to make preparations for his departure, but General Gordon was in a hurry to be off, and the Darfour Sultan was with some difficulty induced to start with him. Colonel Stewart, speaking of General Gordon's departure from Cairo on the night of January 26, wrote in his Journal : " Some delay was caused at starting by the numerous retinue of the Darfour Sultan. Extra carriages had to be put on for the accommodation of his twenty-three wives and a quantity of baggage. At the last moment, his gala uniform was almost forgotten, and there was some commotion until it was found."

Altogether, it did not look much as if an " unintelligent native " with twenty-three wives and a quantity of baggage, who was, as it subsequently appeared, inordinately proud of his decoration and of his "gala uniform," would be very helpful in inaugurating the new policy.

One further incident of importance occurred whilst General Gordon was in Cairo.

In the course of this narrative allusion has already been made to Zobeir Pasha.[1] It is needless to dwell at length on the history of his previous relations with General Gordon. It will be sufficient to say that Zobeir Pasha's social position,[2] the wealth which he had amassed in slave-hunting, his courage, ability, and force of character, had at one time won for him a position of commanding influence in the Soudan. In June 1878, Zobeir Pasha's son, Suleiman, raised a revolt in the Bahr-el-Ghazal province, and killed 200 of the Egyptian regular troops. General Gordon's lieutenant, Gessi, was sent against him, and, in the beginning of 1879, the rebellion was crushed. Suleiman was taken prisoner and shot. A letter from Zobeir Pasha was found in Suleiman's possession, in which the father incited the son to revolt. Zobeir Pasha's property was confiscated. In 1884, he was residing at Cairo. He was detained there, but was allowed his personal liberty and received an allowance from the Egyptian Government. Under these circumstances, it was natural that there should be enmity between General Gordon and Zobeir Pasha.

On January 22, whilst General Gordon was on his way to Egypt, I received the following telegram

---

[1] *Vide ante*, pp. 402-404.
[2] Zobeir Pasha is a descendant of the Abbaside dynasty of Khalifa.

from Lord Granville: "Gordon considers it most
important that Zobeir should be well watched by a
European to prevent his sending emissaries or letters
to the Soudan.   He has suggested that Zobeir
should be sent to Cyprus, but there is no legal
power to detain him if sent."   On receiving this
telegram, I took steps to have Zobeir Pasha watched.

On January 25, whilst paying a visit to Chérif
Pasha, General Gordon accidentally met Zobeir
Pasha.   A short conversation ensued between the
two, with the result that General Gordon expressed a wish that he and Zobeir Pasha should
meet in my presence with a view to the latter
stating his complaints.

On the morning of the 26th, I received a written
Memorandum from General Gordon, in which,
after sketching the history of the events which led
to Zobeir Pasha's expulsion from the Soudan, he
went on to express himself as follows:—

"Zobeir, without doubt, was the greatest slave-
hunter who ever existed.   Zobeir is the most able
man in the Soudan, he is a capital general, and has
been wounded several times.   Zobeir has a capacity
of government far beyond any other man in the
Soudan.   All the followers of the Mahdi would, I
believe, leave the Mahdi on Zobeir's approach, for
the Mahdi's chiefs are ex-chiefs of Zobeir.   Personally, I have a great admiration for Zobeir, for he
is a man, and is infinitely superior to those poor
fellows who have been Governors of the Soudan.
But I question in my mind, 'Will Zobeir ever
forgive me the death of his son?' and that question
has regulated my action respecting him, for I have
been told he bears me the greatest malice, and one
cannot wonder at it, if one is a father.   I would
even now risk taking Zobeir, and would willingly
bear the responsibility of doing so, convinced as I
am that Zobeir's approach ends the Mahdi, which

is a question which has its pulse in Syria, the Hedjaz, and Palestine.

"It cannot be the wish of Her Majesty's Government, or of the Egyptian Government, to have an intestine war in the Soudan on its evacuation, yet such is sure to ensue, and the only way which would prevent it is the restoration of Zobeir, who would be accepted on all sides, and who would end the Mahdi in a couple of months. My duty is to obey the orders of Her Majesty's Government, *i.e.* to evacuate the Soudan as soon as possible *vis-à-vis* the safety of the Egyptian employés. To do this, I want no Zobeir. But if the addenda is made that I leave a satisfactory settlement of affairs, then Zobeir becomes a *sine qua non.* Therefore, the question resolves itself into this, does Her Majesty's Government, or Egyptian Government, desire a settled state of affairs in the Soudan after the evacuation? Do those Governments want to be free of this troublesome fanatic? If they do, then Zobeir should be sent; if the two Governments are indifferent, then do not send him, and I have confidence we will get out the Egyptian employés in three or four months, and will leave a cockpit behind us. It is not my duty to dictate what should be done. I will only say—

"1. I was justified in my action against Zobeir.

"2. That if Zobeir bears no malice personally against me, I would take him at once, as a humanly certain settler of the Mahdi and of those in revolt.

"I have written this Memorandum, and Zobeir's story may be heard. I only ask that after he has been interrogated, I may be questioned on such subjects as his statements are at variance with mine. I would wish the inquiry to be official, and in such a way that whatever may be the decision come to, it may be come to in my absence.

"With respect to the Slave Trade,[1] I think nothing of it, for there will be Slave Trade always as long as Turkey and Egypt buy the slaves, and it may be Zobeir will or might see his interests to stop it in some manner.

"I will, therefore, sum up my opinion, viz. that I would willingly take the responsibility of taking Zobeir up with me, if after an interview with Sir E. Baring and Nubar Pasha, they felt the mystic feeling I could trust him, and which mystic feeling I felt I had for him to-night when I met him at Chérif Pasha's house. Zobeir could have nothing to gain in hurting me, and I would have no idea of fear. In this affair my desire, I own, would be to take Zobeir. I cannot exactly say why I feel towards him thus, and I feel sure that his going would settle the Soudan affair to the benefit of Her Majesty's and Egyptian Governments, and I would bear the responsibility of recommending it."

The interview between General Gordon and Zobeir Pasha took place on the afternoon of January 26 in the presence of Nubar Pasha, Sir Evelyn Wood, Colonel Stewart, Colonel Watson, Giegler Pasha, and myself.[2] A shorthand writer and an interpreter were present. The scene was dramatic and interesting. Both General Gordon and Zobeir Pasha were labouring under great excitement and spoke with vehemence. Zobeir Pasha did not deny that his son had rebelled against the Egyptian Government, but he denied his own complicity in the rebellion. General Gordon's case rested mainly upon the letter addressed by Zobeir

[1] General Gordon's instructions given to him in London, contained the following passage: "You should pay especial consideration to the question of the steps that may usefully be taken to counteract the stimulus which it is feared may possibly be given to the Slave Trade by the present insurrectionary movement, and by the withdrawal of the Egyptian authority from the Interior."

[2] A full account of this interview is given in *Egypt*, No. 12 of 1884, pp. 38-41.

Pasha to his son, which was found by Gessi. This letter could not be produced at the time, but I saw a copy of it subsequently. If genuine, it afforded sufficient proof of Zobeir Pasha's complicity in his son's rebellion.

After this interview was over and Zobeir Pasha had retired, General Gordon's Memorandum, in which he had proposed that Zobeir Pasha should accompany him to Khartoum, was discussed. All present, more especially Colonel Stewart, were opposed to sending him. I had always been rather in favour of employing Zobeir Pasha in the Soudan. Moreover, I saw that the main difficulty in the way of carrying out General Gordon's policy was the absence of any strong local men to whom to entrust the future government of the Soudan, and especially of Khartoum. I believed that, by giving Zobeir Pasha money and an influential position, it might be possible to secure his friendship towards General Gordon; and there could be no doubt that, if this friendship could be secured, he would prove a valuable instrument in the execution of General Gordon's policy. The arguments on the other side were, however, strong.

In the first place, the employment of Zobeir Pasha would be sure to raise an outcry in England. I should not have minded this, if I could have felt certain that his employment was desirable. But was it desirable? I was not at that moment prepared to take the responsibility of answering this question in the affirmative. The weight of authoritative opinion was decidedly against sending him to the Soudan. My wish was to follow General Gordon's lead, but he himself hesitated as to what course to pursue. It was impossible to say how far this impulsive man was animated, not so much by a consideration of the political necessities of the case, as by a chivalrous feeling that possibly

in former times he might have done some injustice
to Zobeir Pasha, and that he wished to atone for
such injustice by giving his old adversary an opportunity of retrieving his position. The argument,
however, which convinced me that, for the time
being at all events, it was undesirable to employ
Zobeir Pasha, was that forty-eight hours before I
received General Gordon's Memorandum proposing
that Zobeir Pasha should accompany him to the
Soudan, I had received, through Lord Granville, a
proposal, also emanating from General Gordon, that
Zobeir Pasha should be deported to Cyprus.[1]   A
few minutes' conversation with Zobeir Pasha, and
a "mystic feeling" which that conversation had
engendered, had led General Gordon to jump from
one extreme to the other.   Instead of being considered as an enemy, Zobeir Pasha was to be treated
as a trusted ally, on whose conduct the success of
the mission was to depend.   I have no confidence
in opinions based on mystic feelings.   Colonel
Stewart subsequently (March 11) wrote to me from
Khartoum: "I never saw or met any one whose
mind and imagination are so constantly active as
Gordon's.   For him to grasp an idea is to act on it
at once."   Short as my personal acquaintance had
been with General Gordon, it was clear to me that
his various *obiter dicta* were not to be regarded
as expressions of his matured opinions.   It might
eventually be desirable to employ Zobeir Pasha,
but it was necessary to give General Gordon more
time to think over the matter before taking action.

Under these circumstances, I had no hesitation
in deciding against the immediate employment of
Zobeir Pasha.   "At General Gordon's suggestion,"
I wrote to Lord Granville, "I informed Zobeir Pasha
that he would be allowed to remain in Cairo, and
that the future treatment he would receive at the

[1] *Vide ante*, p. 455.

hands of the Egyptian Government depended in a great measure upon whether General Gordon returned alive and well from the Soudan, and upon whether, whilst residing at Cairo, Zobeir Pasha used his influence to facilitate the execution of the policy upon which the Government had determined." Thus the matter was settled for the moment.

On the night of January 26, General Gordon and Colonel Stewart left Cairo on the ill-fated expedition from which they were destined never to return. General Gordon was in excellent spirits and hopeful of success. My own heart was heavy within me. I knew the difficulties of the task which had to be accomplished. I had seen General Gordon. Nothing could have been more friendly than his behaviour. The main lines of his policy appeared wise and practical. Nevertheless, I was not relieved of the doubts which I originally entertained as to the wisdom of employing him. Manifestly, in spite of many fine and attractive qualities, he was even more eccentric than I had originally supposed. However, the die was cast. A comet of no common magnitude had been launched on the political firmament of the Soudan. It was difficult to predict its course. It now only remained for me to do my best to help General Gordon, and to trust to the shrewd common sense of his companion, Colonel Stewart, to act in some degree as a corrective to the impulsiveness of his wayward chief.[1]

---

[1] I may mention that during the short period whilst General Gordon and Colonel Stewart were at Cairo I was most unfortunately afflicted with a severe sore throat, which well-nigh deprived me of any powers of speech. The health of individuals in responsible positions, more especially at critical moments, has a more serious bearing on public affairs than is often supposed. During the Egyptian Conference, which sat in London in the summer of 1885, the course of events was, I am inclined to think, a good deal influenced by the fact that Lord Granville had a rather unusually severe attack of gout. Further, I may mention that whilst the question of Zobeir Pasha's despatch to the Soudan was under discussion, Mr. Gladstone was ill in bed. (See further remarks on this subject, p. 531.)

CHAPTER XXIV

Contradictory nature of General Gordon's proposals—The Darfour Sultan—General Gordon proposes to visit the Mahdi—Or to retire to the Equator—He issues a Proclamation announcing the independence of the Soudan — The Slavery Proclamation — General Gordon arrives at Khartoum—He is sanguine of success—Colonel Stewart's warning.

ON February 1, Colonel Stewart wrote to me from Korosko : "I shall be very glad when we are actually at Khartoum and face to face with the situation. Gordon is so full of energy and action that he cannot get along without doing something, and at present he revenges himself for his enforced inactivity by writing letters, despatches, etc., and sending telegrams."

Now, in fact, began a period during which I received a large number of very bewildering and contradictory messages from General Gordon. They began immediately after he left Cairo. Sir Henry Gordon subsequently wrote : "It was no part of General Gordon's character to form a definite opinion from imperfectly known facts, and to adhere obstinately to that opinion, notwithstanding the evidence of altered circumstances and new elements." Much may be forgiven to fraternal affection. The truth, however, is that General Gordon's main defect was that he was constantly forming strong opinions on imperfectly known facts. Extreme consistency in political matters is certainly not a cardinal virtue. It has, indeed, been characterised by Emerson as "the hobgoblin of little minds." But the peculiarity of General Gordon was that, in great things as in small, his revulsions of opinion were so rapid and so complete that it was almost impossible to follow him. On March 11, Colonel Stewart wrote to me from Khartoum: "I most sincerely congratulate you on the interruption in the telegraphic communication.[1] The shower of telegrams which we have been sending you of late must have acted somewhat like a cold *douche*. Yesterday, I told Gordon that his numerous communications might tend to confuse you, but he replied that he was merely giving you different aspects of the same question." General Gordon's communications did, indeed, tend to confuse me. In addition to the other difficulties of the situation, this further difficulty was now superadded, that I had, if I may be allowed to coin such an expression, to learn Gordonese. I had to distinguish between such proposals of General Gordon as represented his matured opinions, and others which were mere bubbles thrown up by his imaginative brain, probably forgotten as soon as made, and, therefore, unworthy of serious attention. I do not say that I always succeeded in eliminating the dross in order to arrive at the valuable residuum. I can only say that the task was one of great difficulty, and that I did my best to accomplish it.

---

[1] Before telegraphic communication between Khartoum and Cairo was permanently interrupted, several temporary breaks took place owing to the line being in a very bad condition. Lord Granville expressed much the same idea as Colonel Stewart. On March 21, he wrote to me: "I am not sure that the stoppage of communication with Gordon for a time is the greatest of misfortunes either for himself or us."

The policy of setting up the local Sultans did not begin well. The Darfour Prince, who accompanied General Gordon, was a wretched creature. On January 29, General Gordon telegraphed to me: "The Emir Abdul-Shakour has taken to drinking." On the 30th, Colonel Stewart wrote in his diary: "The Darfour Sultan decided to get out here (Assouan) and not to come with us any farther." Two days previously (28th), Gordon wrote to me: " Please listen to no telegrams from the Sultan of Darfour's family. I have explained to him that, having placed him at Dongola, whence clear roads exist to Darfour, we wash our hands of him, for it is his work to raise the tribes in his favour. We have nought to do with him and will not support him, for we cannot do so." The Darfour Prince was manifestly deficient in the qualities necessary to carry out a policy such as that projected by General Gordon. He got as far as Dongola, where he remained for some months, and then returned to Cairo.

Whilst General Gordon was on his way from Brindisi to Port Said, he gave the following message for Mr. Clifford Lloyd to an English officer, who was a fellow-passenger on the same ship: "Tell Lloyd, no panics. It is possible that I may go to the Mahdi and not be heard of for two months, for he might keep me as a hostage for Zobeir. You can tell Lloyd this when you get to Cairo, so that he can publish it at the right time, if necessary." Owing to Mr. Clifford Lloyd being confined to his house through illness, I did not hear of this message until General Gordon was half-way to Khartoum. Looking to General Gordon's very singular character, I thought it not impossible that he would carry out the idea of going to the Mahdi. Had he done so, he would certainly have been detained a prisoner for life, unless a

British force had been sent to release him. I, therefore, telegraphed to him : "I hope you will give me a positive assurance that you will on no account put yourself voluntarily in the power of the Mahdi. The question is not a personal one. There would, in my opinion, be the strongest political objections to your risking a visit to the Mahdi." In reply, General Gordon telegraphed to me that he had no intention of visiting the Mahdi. I do not believe that he ever seriously contemplated this step. It was merely an idea which flashed through his brain for a moment. But, had he gone, the consequences both to himself and, possibly, to his country, would have been so serious that it was as well to obtain from him an assurance that he would not give effect to this hare-brained project.

I turn to another incident which occurred about this time. On February 1, General Gordon wrote to me from Korosko enclosing a letter for the King of the Belgians. In this letter, he spoke of going up the White Nile, taking possession of the Bahr-el-Ghazal and Equatorial Provinces, and then handing them over to the King of the Belgians. I received this letter on February 9. This project did not appear to me to be feasible. Moreover, I was always afraid of General Gordon acting on the impulse of the moment without sufficient reflection. I, therefore, telegraphed to Lord Granville : "I do not think that General Gordon should be allowed, at all events for the present, to go anywhere south of Khartoum." At the same time, I sent the following private telegram to Lord Granville : "Do I understand rightly that I have full powers to give Gordon positive orders not to proceed beyond a certain point, if I think it necessary to do so ? I believe he would obey orders, but I doubt his caring much about suggestions. If he comes to any harm, it will be the worst thing that has happened yet. I am more anxious lest his total disregard for his own safety should lead to further serious difficulties than almost anything else." On February 10, Lord Granville, in reply to my inquiry, sent me the following private telegram: "You have full powers. Instruct Gordon not to proceed at present south of Khartoum." This was followed, on February 11, by an official telegram, which was to the following effect: "Her Majesty's Government are of opinion that General Gordon should not, at present, go beyond Khartoum." I communicated the views of the British Government on this point to General Gordon on February 12, and in reply received a telegram, stating that he would not go south of Khartoum without my permission.

It may be as well, for the sake of clearness, that I should anticipate this narrative so far as to state, in the present place, what subsequently occurred in connection with this particular point. On March 9, General Gordon sent me several telegrams. In one of them he proposed to resign his commission in the British army, to "take all steamers and stores up to the Equatorial and Bahr-el-Ghazal provinces, and consider those provinces as under the King of the Belgians." Later on, I shall have to deal with the reply which Lord Granville gave to the various proposals then under discussion. I need here only state that, in communicating to General Gordon the views of the British Government, I instructed him to hold on at Khartoum until I could communicate with Her Majesty's Government, and I told him that he should on no account proceed to the Bahr-el-Ghazal and Equatorial provinces. In his Journal, General Gordon complained bitterly of not having been allowed to proceed up the White Nile. Writing on October 5,

1884, he said: "Her Majesty's Government ought to have taken the bold step of speaking out and saying, *SHIFT FOR YOURSELF in March*,[1] when I could have done so, and not now when I am in honour bound to the people after six months' bothering warfare. Not only did Baring not say 'Shift for yourself,' but he put a veto upon my going to the Equator, *vide* his telegrams in Stewart's Journal."

As regards General Gordon's complaint on this subject, I have the following observations to make.

In the first place, I doubt whether General Gordon would in any case have attempted to go up the White Nile. If he had done so, he would have been obliged to abandon the garrisons of Khartoum and other places, and this, as Colonel Stewart wrote to me so early as March 4, he was "the last man in the world to do."

In the second place, if General Gordon had made the attempt, I believe he would have failed. Both he and his followers would almost certainly have been taken prisoners by the Mahdi.

In the third place, in spite of the entry in General Gordon's Journal, to which I have alluded above, it is clear that, as a matter of fact, the instructions received from me on this particular point did not hamper his action. I received an undated telegram from him, on April 16, 1884, which was to the following effect: "I consider myself free to act according to circumstances. I shall hold on here as long as I can, and if I can suppress the rebellion, I shall do so. If I cannot, I shall retire to the Equator." Colonel Stewart, at the same time, telegraphed that he did not think it would be possible to get to Berber. "I am inclined," he

---

[1] In this and other quotations from General Gordon's Journal, the capitals and italics, have in a few cases to which attention is specially drawn, are in the original.

added, "to think my retreat will perhaps be safer
by the Equator. I shall, therefore, follow the
fortunes of General Gordon." Mr. Power, the
British Consular Agent at Khartoum, telegraphed
to the same effect. These messages constitute a
sufficient proof that, in spite of my telegram of
February 12, General Gordon did not think himself
precluded from retiring up the White Nile, should
he have thought fit to do so.

It will be borne in mind that General Gordon
took with him two Proclamations, one of which
stated that the Egyptian Government had decided
to withdraw their troops from the Soudan, whilst
in the other it was stated that General Gordon
was appointed Governor-General of the Soudan.[1]

On February 1, Colonel Stewart wrote to me
from Korosko: "It seems to me that at present
the most suitable plan is not to publish abroad
throughout the Soudan that we mean to leave.
Before doing so, we ought at any rate to place
the kinglets in their several districts. Whether
it will be possible to induce Gordon to remain
silent in the matter is, however, more than
doubtful."

On February 11, General Gordon and Colonel
Stewart arrived at Berber. The following entry
occurs in Colonel Stewart's Journal, dated February
12: "I was called up at 5 A.M. by General Gordon,
who, having pondered deeply all night, had come to
the decision of opening the Pandora box, and openly
proclaiming the divorce of the Soudan from Egypt,
and the forming of local militias, and the appointment of Soudan officials in every important post.
At 8 A.M., Hussein Pasha Khalifa, and Mohammed
Tahir, the judge of the civil court, a man we
have every reason to believe is a bosom-friend of
the Mahdi, made their appearance. With their

[1] *Vide ante,* p. 446.

assistance, and after showing them the secret
Firmans, which the General thought necessary
to show them to allay their alarm at the over-
turning of the Khedive's authority, a Proclamation
was drawn up. This Proclamation appointed a
Committee, or provisional Government consisting
of six of the most influential Notables of the
Mudirieh, and proclaimed that the Mudirieh was
from henceforth independent of Cairo, but subject
to General Gordon as Governor-General and
Commissioner of the British Government. The
Proclamation was affixed to the gate, and caused
a good deal of excitement; so far as I am able
to judge, the people appeared to approve of it."

On February 13, the following further entry
occurs in Colonel Stewart's Journal: "At 2 P.M.,
Hussein Pasha Khalifa and the leading men of the
province assembled in secret conclave, and General
Gordon, after a speech, showed them the secret
Firman. This document caused the most profound
astonishment, but in so far as one could judge from
what they said, nothing could exceed their delight.
We have tried to fathom what those present really
thought, and we are told that it was a mistake
to have shown it. We are told that the probable
effect will be to lead those who read the Firman to
conclude that all the concessions made by General
Gordon, viz.:—half-tax (*sic*), were made merely
with a view to getting the troops out of the
country without danger, and to leave the people
to stew in their own juice. On consideration, it
may perhaps have been a mistake to show this
Firman, but General Gordon says that, as the
object of his mission is to get out of the country
and to leave them independent, that he could not
have put a sharper spur into them to organise
their government than by this action. It is
certain that they fondly believe that by some

means or other they would be rid of the Cairo Government, and remain independent under General Gordon, who would give them greater local liberties and not interfere with their darling slave-trade. As regards my own opinion on the matter, I fully admit that the question of showing or not showing the Firman is a difficult one to answer. Perhaps I should have preferred following Nubar Pasha's advice and delaying any action in the matter till a later period, when I could have better judged what would have been the result, or at any rate, till the political situation had become clearer."

In a letter to me of the same date, February 13, Colonel Stewart wrote: "You will see by my Journal that Gordon has taken his leap in the dark and shown his secret Firman. How it will act, and what will be the result, goodness only knows. At any rate, the deed is done and we must now abide by the result and hope for the best."

General Gordon says in his Journal (p. 285) that the Khedive's Firman — by which he meant the Proclamation which was given to him in Cairo—was not "promulgated" in the Soudan, and the same statement is repeated by the editor of the Journal (Mr. Egmont Hake) in a note on p. 309. It is clear, however, from the facts narrated above, that, after the events which took place at Berber, the existence of the Firman must have been known throughout the Soudan.

There can be little doubt that General Gordon committed an error of judgment in showing the Firman at Berber. News of the intended abandonment of the Soudan had, indeed, reached Khartoum prior to that date. But it was only half believed. It was not till after the events which took place at Berber on February 12 and 13, that the intentions of the Egyptian Government became widely

known.	Sir Reginald Wingate[1] alludes to the
"fatal Proclamation which gave the Soudan
away," and he has informed me verbally that his
researches have led him to the conclusion that
General Gordon's difficulties were greatly increased
by the action taken at Berber.

If General Gordon had not stated the fact himself,
and if we did not know something of his peculiar
character, it would be almost incredible that he
should have shown such an important document
as the Khedive's Firman to the Sheikhs at Berber
without having fully mastered its contents.	Such,
however, is the case.	He appears subsequently to
have seen that he made a mistake in showing the
Firman, for, on November 9, 1884, the following
entry occurs in his Journal (p. 309) : " If the
Mahdi got this (*i.e.* the Firman), he would have
crowed, though he may know of it,[2] for I showed

[1] *Mahdiism, etc.*, p. 121.	Father Ohrwalder also says : "Gordon
himself committed a mistake by which he gave a death-blow to himself
and his mission.	On his way to Khartoum, he stopped at Berber and
interviewed the Mudir Hussein Pasha Khalifa ; he imprudently told
him that he had come up to remove the Egyptian garrisons, as Egypt
had abandoned the Soudan.	At Metemmeh also . . . he committed a
similar imprudence, by giving the same information to Haj Ali Wad
Saad, the Emir of Metemmeh."—*Ten Years' Captivity in the Mahdi's
Camp*, p. 123.

[2] On October 22, *i.e.* eighteen days before General Gordon made this
entry in his Journal, he had received a letter from the Mahdi (Appendix
to *Journal*, p. 522), in which the latter gave a list of the documents which
had fallen into his possession at the time of Colonel Stewart's death.
Inter alia, the Mahdi wrote : "Also we have seen your telegram dated
August 28, 1884, stating that, as for the Firman emanating from the
Khedive to all the Nobles and Notables and people of the Soudan,
announcing the withdrawal of the troops of the Government from it,
and their evacuation of the country, and leaving it to the Soudanese to
appoint rulers of the country from among the natives,—you had not been
able to communicate it, or to show it to any one on account of what
had taken place."	The receipt of this letter is recorded in General
Gordon's Journal (p. 220) in the following characteristic words written
on October 22, 1884 : "The Mahdi's letter is to relate how he captured
the post, etc., *Abbas* (the steamer in which Stewart went down the
Nile), etc.	My answer was that I did not care who had surrendered
and who had been captured.	As for these letters, I cannot make head
or tail of them, so I leave them to the Arabic scholars of the Univer-
sities."	General Gordon knew very little Arabic, neither does he appear

it, *not knowing well its contents*,[1] to Hussein Pasha
Khalifa (*vide* Stewart's Journal, which went down
and in which I criticised my having done so)."

I now turn to another episode. In 1877, a
Convention was signed between the British and
Egyptian Governments having for its object the
abolition of slavery and of the Slave Trade in Egypt.
The Convention was not to come into operation
in the Soudan till the year 1888. It would, under
any circumstances, have been very difficult to apply
the Convention to the Soudan. General Gordon
knew this. So early as October 11, 1883, Lord
Granville wrote privately to me : " About slavery,
I was very keen at first, and the first cold water
I got was, of all people in the world, from Colonel
Gordon, who seemed to me sensible on the matter."
In other words, in spite of his anti-slavery sympathies, and although he had himself been a witness
of the horrors of the Slave Trade, General Gordon
recognised the facts of the situation more fully than
his friends, who, in so far as the incident about to
be narrated is concerned, became his critics.

On February 12, Colonel Stewart, who was
then at Berber, made the following entry in his
Journal : " A deputation of the Notables came to
inquire whether the Treaty, which had been printed
and published by General Gordon, in November
1877, by which all slaves would be freed in 1889,
was in his present programme. General Gordon,
knowing the utter futility of saying ' Yes,' replied
' No,' and published a Proclamation to this effect.
It is probable that this Proclamation interested and
pleased the people more than anything else."

A few days later, the Proclamation was published

to have taken pains to get Arabic documents properly translated to him.
This, added to his habitual carelessness in the transaction of business,
led him into the committal of many mistakes which might have been
avoided.

[1] The italics are not in the original.

in Khartoum. It was to the following effect: "My sincerest desire is to adopt a course of action which shall lead to public tranquillity, and knowing your regret at the severe measures taken by the Government for the suppression of the slave traffic, and the seizure and punishment of all concerned, according to the Convention and Decrees, I confer upon you these rights, that henceforth none shall interfere with your property; whoever has slaves, shall have full right to their services and full control over them. This Proclamation is a proof of my clemency towards you."

This Proclamation naturally caused some excitement in England. That a man who had heretofore been considered a champion of the anti-slavery cause, should, immediately on his arrival at Khartoum, sanction slavery and thus run counter to the traditions of his previous career, seemed, indeed, astonishing. The special supporters of the anti-slavery movement were up in arms. Party managers, moreover, were not likely to let slip such a good opportunity for attacking the Government. On February 18, Sir Stafford Northcote, speaking in the House of Commons, asked, amidst the "loud cheers" of his supporters, whether "General Gordon's powers extended to the issue of such a Proclamation?"

The Government were, in fact, in an embarrassing position. It was obvious from the first that, if the Soudan were abandoned, a stimulus would be given to slavery and the Slave Trade. Nothing General Gordon could have said or done could have acted as an antidote. He rightly judged that he had to look to the main object of his mission, which was to evacuate the Soudan. He sought, therefore, to make some capital out of permitting the continuance of an abuse which he was powerless to arrest. Without doubt, under ordinary circumstances, it would have been better, if he could not remedy the evil, at all events not to have given the sanction of his name to its continuance. But the circumstances in which General Gordon was placed were far from being ordinary. The difficulties of carrying out his task were such that he could not afford to miss a point in the game. He was free from the peculiar feature which, according to many foreign critics, is such a prominent defect in the English character, and which, if it be not cant, is nearly allied to cant. I mean that particular phase of thought which, although it cannot deny that certain unpleasant facts exist, hesitates to draw the logical conclusion from their existence, and hesitates still more to make any open acknowledgment of their existence. General Gordon probably reasoned thus: "As I cannot stop slavery, there can be no harm in my saying so, and in acting accordingly." A section of British public opinion, on the other hand, reasoned somewhat as follows: "We know that you cannot stop slavery, but you had better hide the unpleasant fact from the eyes of the world."

General Gordon's action in this matter appeared to me to be justifiable. I, therefore, determined to support him to the best of my ability. On February 21, General Gordon telegraphed to me as follows: "Several telegrams have been sent from the press asking about what I said respecting slaves. The question asked me was this: Did I insist on the liberation of slaves in 1889, as per Treaty of 1877? I answered that the Treaty would not be enforced in 1889 by me, which, considering the determination of Her Majesty's Government respecting the Soudan, was a self-evident fact. The question is one of slave-holding, not of slave-hunting, and, in my opinion, that Treaty of 1877 will never be carried out in Cairo as to slave-holding."

I sent the following reply: "About your Slavery Proclamation, I am sure I quite understand your reasons. I have telegraphed home to say that I think you are quite right. You are doing admirably, and may rely on my full support in everything."

At the same time (February 21), I sent the following telegram to Lord Granville: "It is only natural that the Proclamation issued by General Gordon at Khartoum should have caused a good deal of surprise in England. But in reality his declaration with regard to the buying and selling of slaves is of very little practical importance, and it is easy enough to understand his reasons for making it.

"It was obvious from the first that a revival of slavery in the Soudan would result from the policy of abandonment. Nothing that General Gordon can do at Khartoum will prevent this revival; knowing that he is powerless to stop slavery in the future, General Gordon evidently intends using it as a concession to the people which will strengthen his position in other matters. I consider that he has succeeded admirably so far, and I sincerely trust that he will be allowed full liberty of action to complete the execution of his general plans. I have informed him that my personal opinion is entirely in his favour, and that I will give him all the support in my power.

"As to the best means of preventing slavery, the subject will have to be considered carefully and discussed afresh, in view of the altered circumstances of the situation."

After this, the subject was allowed to drop. The *Pall Mall Gazette* wrote: "The Government stood by their agent with commendable courage, and, as is usual when responsible authorities well-informed as to facts resist the clamour of ill-informed public opinion, the cry promptly subsided."

On February 18, General Gordon reached Khartoum. His arrival was announced to me by Mr. Power, in the following telegram: "Gordon arrived here this morning, and met with a wonderful demonstration of welcome on the part of the population. The state of affairs here, since it was heard that Gordon was coming, gives every promise of the speedy pacification of this portion of the Soudan. His speech to the people was received with the greatest enthusiasm."

On the following day (February 19) Mr. Power sent me another telegram. "Gordon," he said, "met with a great reception yesterday. Has ordered all white troops to leave for Cairo. Soudani soldiers kept in Khartoum. Has formed Council of twelve Notables, Arabs, to sit with him. Burned all old records of debts against people, and instruments of torture in Government House. Colonel Stewart at prison striking irons off all prisoners of war, debtors, and men who have long ago served their sentences. Gordon sends Ibrahim Pasha down with detachment of white troops. Everything is now safe here for troops and Europeans. He is giving the people more than they expected from the Mahdi."

General Gordon was at this time hopeful as regards the future. Without doubt, he was over-sanguine, but at the time a reasonable prospect seemed to exist that he would be able to carry out his mission successfully. He had begun well. On February 12, he telegraphed to me: "Do not fear for the Khartoum garrison. It can come by Berber, if necessary, but neither the men who attacked Baker, nor those who attacked Hicks, will ever leave tribal limits. What had to be feared was the rising of other peoples, which I trust I have prevented by liberal concessions." Again, on February 14, he telegraphed to me : "I believe you need not give yourself any further anxiety about this part of the Soudan. The people, great and small, are heartily glad to be free of a union which only caused them sorrow."

To a certain extent, General Gordon was right in his view of the situation. The tribes round Khartoum were wavering. If they openly joined the Mahdi, the difficulties of the situation would be greatly increased. The only chance of ensuring their friendship was by making liberal concessions. General Gordon had made such concessions. He had issued a Proclamation sanctioning slavery, which, although it caused consternation in London, was hailed with delight at Khartoum. He had remitted taxes. He had destroyed the bonds of the usurers—always a most popular proceeding in an Oriental country. He had released prisoners who were unjustly confined. His mere presence at Khartoum was interpreted as a guarantee that the future government of the Soudan would be less oppressive than that of the past. Lord Granville's buoyant spirits at once rose. On February 15, he wrote privately to me : "It was an anxious moment while Gordon was in the desert. When he gets at the head of 6000 men, it becomes more of a normal situation. It looks as if he would succeed."[1]

---

[1] On another occasion (December 28, 1883), speaking of Egyptian affairs generally, Lord Granville wrote to me : "I was delighted to see that you do not feel the alarm, which is felt here, and apparently in Egypt. I am perpetually reproaching myself with being too optimistic. The difficulties are great, especially the enormous one of finance, but they ought not to be insurmountable." I do not think that I was ever very optimistic about Egyptian affairs. Indeed, as regards finance, I at one time erred somewhat on the side of undue pessimism. What I felt during this period was that, amidst all the excitement that then prevailed, and which resulted in some very wild and ill-considered suggestions being occasionally made, it was necessary for me to keep my head, to ascertain so far as was

The shrewd Scotchman, who accompanied General Gordon, was not, however, carried away by the jubilation of the moment. On February 17, Colonel Stewart wrote to me: "The problem of evacuating the Soudan is continually in our minds. I must confess the more one looks at it, the more difficult it becomes. However, perhaps, when actually tackled, it will resolve itself somehow or other."

I have already stated that it was, in my opinion, a mistake ever to have sent General Gordon to the Soudan. Once sent, however, the best chance of success lay in adopting the course advocated by the *Pall Mall Gazette.* General Gordon should have had "*carte blanche* to do the best that could be done," so long as he conformed to the broad lines of the policy which he was sent to carry out. I saw this from the first, and regulated my conduct accordingly. My difficulty lay in discovering, amidst the numerous contradictory opinions that emanated from General Gordon, what it was he really wished should be done. Unfortunately, a section of the British public did not realise sufficiently the importance of giving General Gordon a free hand. In spite of his popularity, directly he made proposals which ran counter to the current of preconceived public opinion, a chorus of disapprobation was raised, in which some of General Gordon's warmest friends and supporters joined.

---

possible the real facts of the case, to consider carefully the merits of any proposal before acting upon it, and especially to avoid the use of sensational or exaggerated language. On April 13, 1884, General Gordon sent me a telegram which I did not receive till six years later (March 26, 1890), and in which he exhorted me to depart "from that delicious diplomatic calm which is Paradise." He frequently used language of a somewhat similar description in his Journal. The "diplomatic calm" existed in a somewhat less degree than General Gordon supposed. Its appearance was mainly due to the fact that, in my opinion, the greater the difficulties, the more does it behove any one in a responsible position to maintain a clear judgment, and not be carried away by sentiment or rash advice.

The Government accepted the principle that they must follow General Gordon's advice. Mr. Gladstone, speaking in the House of Commons, on February 12, said that it was the duty of the Government "to beware of interfering with General Gordon's plans generally." They adhered to this principle, at all events in respect to the Slavery Proclamation, with the result that the agitation against it speedily died a natural death.

The Soudan question was, indeed, as Colonel Stewart said, to be solved "somehow or other," but its solution was to bring to the British Government the political discredit which always attaches itself to failure. It was to cause a great waste of public treasure and to involve the sacrifice of many valuable lives, including those of the two brave men on whose actions the attention, not only of England and Egypt, but it may also be said of all Europe was then fixed.

CHAPTER XXV

ZOBEIR PASHA

FEBRUARY 18–MARCH 16, 1884

The turning-point of General Gordon's Mission—General Gordon's
Memorandum of February 8—Change in General Gordon's views
—He asks for Zobeir Pasha—I advise that Zobeir Pasha should be
General Gordon's successor—The Government reject this proposal
—General Gordon proposes to "smash up" the Mahdi—Conflicting
policies advocated by General Gordon—His Proclamation stating
that British troops were coming to Khartoum—General Gordon's
neglect of his instructions—I again urge the employment of Zobeir
Pasha—Difficulty of understanding General Gordon's telegrams—
Colonel Stewart recommends that Zobeir Pasha should be sent—I
support this view—General Gordon recommends that the Berber-
Suakin route should be opened—The Government object to the
employment of Zobeir Pasha—I again urge the employment of
Zobeir Pasha—General Gordon's communications to the *Times'*
correspondent—The tribes round Khartoum waver—The Government reject the Zobeir proposal—I instruct General Gordon
to hold on to Khartoum—I again urge on the Government the
necessity of employing Zobeir Pasha—The proposal is rejected—
I remonstrate—Final rejection of the Zobeir proposal—Were the
Government right in their decision?

EVERYTHING of political importance connected
with General Gordon's Mission took place within a
few weeks of his arrival at Khartoum. The essential
facts connected with the history of those eventful
weeks can be summed up in a few words. General
Gordon proposed that Zobeir Pasha should govern
the Soudan as a feudatory of the Egyptian Government. Colonel Stewart and myself at first hesitated
as to the desirability of sending Zobeir Pasha to
the Soudan, but after a brief interval we came

round to General Gordon's opinion. The British Government would not agree to the employment of Zobeir Pasha. Subsequently, the tribes round Khartoum rose. General Gordon and Colonel Stewart were besieged. It was clear that General Gordon's political mission had failed, and from that moment there only remained an important military question to decide, viz., whether a British military force should or should not be sent to the relief of Khartoum.

The broad facts of the case are already well known. They were set forth in the Parliamentary papers, which were published at the time. I am not, however, aware that any attempt has as yet been made to give so clear a *précis* of the whole of the correspondence as to enable a thorough appreciation to be formed of the parts played respectively by those who were the principal actors in this political drama—I might almost say political tragedy. I propose, at the risk of being tedious, to make such a *précis*.

On February 8, General Gordon, who was then at Abu Hamed, addressed to me an important Memorandum. He wrote: "In spite of all that has occurred, I feel satisfied that the prestige of the Cairo Government, except in so far as the conduct of their troops in the field is concerned, is not seriously shaken, and that the people still continue to look up to the Cairo Government as the direct representatives of the Sultan as Khalif, and would look with horror on a complete separation." He proposed that the Egyptian Government "should continue to maintain their position as a Suzerain Power, nominate the Governor-General and Moudirs"—who were to be Soudanese—"and act as a supreme Court of Appeal. Their controlling influence should, however, be a strictly moral one, and limited to giving advice." "I would, therefore," he added, "earnestly beg that evacuation, but not abandonment, be the programme to be followed, and that the Firman, with which I am provided, be changed into one recognising moral control and suzerainty."

Accompanying this Memorandum, were some remarks by Colonel Stewart upon General Gordon's proposals, to which he gave a qualified support. He said that he "did not quite agree with General Gordon that the prestige of Cairo had not been greatly diminished." General Gordon's Memorandum and Colonel Stewart's observations did not reach me till February 23.

In the meanwhile, I had received a private letter from Colonel Stewart, dated Korosko, February 1, in which the following passage occurred : "Gordon is apparently still hankering after Zobeir, says he feels a sympathy for him, etc. It is impossible to say that he may not of a sudden request him to be sent up. Should such be the case, I trust you will not let him leave Cairo unless under very cogent reasons. I am convinced his coming up would be a dangerous experiment. It is also quite possible that he may not have the influence attributed to him, now that it is said his Bazingers (slave soldiers) have ceased to exist." On the other hand, General Gordon wrote to me from Abu Hamed on February 8 : "With respect to Zobeir, he is the only man who is fit for Governor-General of the Soudan if we wish it to be quiet, and as for his touching me, he would have no object to do so. I wish you would see more of this remarkable man. . . . I wish Lady Baring would see him."

There can be no doubt that, as General Gordon approached Khartoum and as he became better informed of the situation in the Soudan, not only did the optimism of the views, which he had previously held, fade away, but also his sympathy

for the people of the country led him to forget the
main object for the accomplishment of which he
had been sent to the Soudan.   But a few months
were to elapse before the same man who had
insisted that, in his instructions, it should be
stated that the policy of evacuating the Soudan
"should on no account be changed," was to write
in his Journal : "I hate her Majesty's Government
for their leaving the Soudan after having caused
all its troubles."

The first indication I got of the rapid change
which was to take place in General Gordon's views
was contained in a letter from Colonel Stewart,
dated Berber, February 13, in which he wrote :
"Gordon is so full of sympathy for these people
that he is inclined to use every effort to mitigate
the effect of our withdrawal, but I am convinced
no effort of his will prevent the reign of anarchy.
Personally, although I regret the unavoidable, still
I am persuaded that the evacuation policy is the
right one, and that it will probably be in the end
the best for all parties."

Immediately upon his arrival at Khartoum, on
February 18, General Gordon sent me the following
telegram : "In a previous Memorandum,[1] I alluded
to the arrival of an epoch when whites, fellaheen
troops, civilian employés, women and children of
deceased soldiers—in short, the Egyptian element
in the Soudan—will be removed; when we shall
be face to face with the Soudan administration,
and when I must withdraw from the Soudan.   I
have stated that to withdraw without being able
to place a successor in my seat would be the signal
for general anarchy throughout the country, which,
though all Egyptian element was withdrawn, would
be a misfortune, and inhuman.

[1] This is the Memorandum of February 8, which did not reach me
till the 23rd.   *Vide ante*, pp. 480-481.

"Also, I have stated that, even if I placed a man in my seat unsupported by any Government, the same anarchy would ensue.

"Her Majesty's Government could, I think, without responsibility in money or men, give the commission to my successor on certain terms which I will detail hereafter. If this solution is examined, we shall find that a somewhat analogous case exists in Afghanistan, where Her Majesty's Government give moral support to the Ameer, and go even beyond that in giving the Ameer a subsidy, which would not be needed in the present case.

"I distinctly state that if Her Majesty's Government gave a Commission to my successor, I recommend neither a subsidy nor men being given. I would select and give a commission to some man, and promise him the moral support of Her Majesty's Government and nothing more.

"It may be argued that Her Majesty's Government would thus be giving nominal and moral support to a man who will rule over a Slave State, but so is Afghanistan, as also Socotra.

"This nomination of my successor must, I think, be direct from Her Majesty's Government.

"As for the man, Her Majesty's Government should select one above all others, namely, Zobeir. He alone has the ability to rule the Soudan, and would be universally accepted by the Soudan. He should be made K.C.M.G., and given presents."

After stating the terms under which Zobeir Pasha should be nominated, General Gordon continued: "Zobeir's exile at Cairo for ten years, amidst all the late events and his mixing with Europeans, must have had a great effect on his character. Zobeir's nomination, under the moral countenance of Her Majesty's Government, would bring all the merchants, European and others, back to the Soudan in a short time. I have asked Stewart to give his opinions independently of mine, in order to prevent a one-sided view. He is a first-rate man." At the same time, Colonel Stewart sent me the following telegram; "With reference to Gordon's telegram of to-day, I think that the policy he urges would greatly facilitate our retirement from the country. As to whether Zobeir Pasha is the man who should be nominated, I think we have hardly yet a sufficient knowledge of the country to be able to form an opinion. It is, however, probable that whoever is nominated will be accepted for a time."

I thought that General Gordon, when at Cairo, had made his proposal to utilise Zobeir Pasha's services without sufficient deliberation. When, however, I found that, after an interval of three weeks and after having had an opportunity of judging of the situation at Khartoum, General Gordon still thought that Zobeir Pasha's services might be utilised, it appeared to me safe to assume that he was expressing something in the nature of a matured opinion, and that he was not, as so frequently happened, dashing off an ill-considered proposal on the spur of the moment. I, therefore, resolved to support him in so far as the ultimate utilisation of Zobeir Pasha's services was concerned. On the other hand, there was manifestly a risk in allowing Zobeir Pasha and General Gordon to be at Khartoum together. Moreover, General Gordon's cautious companion, Colonel Stewart, entertained considerable doubts as to the advisability of employing Zobeir Pasha. I had great confidence in Colonel Stewart's judgment. I wished to give him the time, for which he asked, to form an opinion.

On February 19, therefore, I repeated to Lord Granville General Gordon's and Colonel Stewart's telegrams of the 18th, with the following remarks of my own :—

"As regards the choice of his (General Gordon's) successor, there is, as Colonel Stewart says in his telegram, no necessity to decide at once, but I believe Zobeir Pasha to be the only possible man. He undoubtedly possesses energy and ability, and has great local influence.

"As regards the Slave Trade, I discussed the matter with General Gordon when he was in Cairo, and he fully agreed with me in thinking that Zobeir Pasha's presence or absence would not affect the question in one way or the other. I am also convinced, from many things that have come to my notice, that General Gordon is quite right in thinking that Zobeir Pasha's residence in Egypt has considerably modified his character. He now understands what European power is, and it is much better to have to deal with a man of this sort than with a man like the Mahdi.

"I should be altogether opposed to having General Gordon and Zobeir Pasha at Khartoum together. As soon as General Gordon has arranged for the withdrawal of the garrison and the rest of the Egyptian element, he could leave Khartoum, and Zobeir Pasha might shortly afterwards start from Cairo. One of my chief reasons for allowing the interview between the two men to take place was that I wished to satisfy myself to some extent of the sentiments entertained by Zobeir Pasha towards General Gordon. I would not on any account run the risk of putting General Gordon in his power.

"If Zobeir Pasha is nominated, it will be very necessary to lay down in writing and in the plainest language what degree of support he may expect from Her Majesty's Government. I cannot recommend that he should be promised the moral support of Her Majesty's Government. In the first place, he would scarcely understand the sense of the phrase, and, moreover, I do not think he would attach much importance to any support which was not material. It is for Her Majesty's Government to judge what the effect of his appointment would be upon public opinion in England, but except for that, I can see no reason why Zobeir Pasha should not be proclaimed Ruler of the Soudan with the approbation of Her Majesty's Government. It should be distinctly explained to him in writing that he must rely solely upon his own resources to maintain his position. He might receive a moderate sum of money from the Egyptian Government to begin with. His communications with that Government might be conducted through Her Majesty's Representative in Cairo, as General Gordon suggests.

"With regard to the detailed conditions mentioned by General Gordon, I think they might form the subject of further consideration and discussion, both with General Gordon and with others in authority here. I am inclined to doubt whether such conditions would be of any use; they would probably not long be observed.

"In conclusion, I may add that I have no idea whether Zobeir Pasha would accept the position which it is proposed to offer him."

On February 22, Lord Granville replied : "Her Majesty's Government are of opinion that the gravest objections exist to the appointment by their authority of a successor to General Gordon. The necessity does not, indeed, appear to have yet arisen of going beyond the suggestions contained in General Gordon's Memorandum of the 23rd ultimo,[1] by making a special provision for the government of the country.

"In any case, the public opinion of this country would not tolerate the appointment of Zobeir Pasha."

[1] *Vide ante,* p. 442.

Simultaneously with the receipt of this telegram, I received General Gordon's Memorandum written at Abu Hamed on February 8. This Memorandum, though in some respects at variance with the proposals contained in his telegram of the 18th, enabled me more fully to understand the general line of policy which he wished to advocate. I repeated to General Gordon Lord Granville's telegram of the 22nd, and at the same time I added the following remarks of my own: "The views expressed in your telegram of the 18th do not appear to me to harmonise with those contained in your letter of the 8th instant, which I received this morning, but that is of no consequence. The real difficulty is to find a man, or several men, who will take over the government of the country to the south of Wadi Halfa, especially the government of Khartoum itself. In view of the objections entertained in England against Zobeir, can you suggest any other names?"

I resolved to postpone any further communication to Lord Granville until I had received General Gordon's reply to my question. It came on February 26, and was as follows: "Telegram of the 23rd February received respecting Zobeir. That settles question for me. I cannot suggest any other. Mahdi's agents active in all directions. No chance of Mahdi's advance personally from Obeid. You must remember that when evacuation is carried out, Mahdi will come down here, and, by agents, will not let Egypt be quiet. Of course, my duty is evacuation, and the best I can for establishing a quiet government. The first I hope to accomplish. The second is a more difficult task, and concerns Egypt more than me. If Egypt is to be quiet, Mahdi must be smashed up. Mahdi is most unpopular, and with care and time could be smashed. Remember that once Khartoum belongs to Mahdi, the task will be far more difficult; yet you will, for safety of Egypt, execute it. If you decide on smashing Mahdi, then send up another £100,000, and send up 200 Indian troops to Wadi Halfa, and send officer up to Dongola under pretence to look out quarters for troops. Leave Suakin and Massowah alone. I repeat that evacuation is possible, but you will feel effect in Egypt, and will be forced to enter into a far more serious affair in order to guard Egypt. At present, it would be comparatively easy to destroy Mahdi."

I have now arrived at the moment which was the turning-point of General Gordon's mission. It will be well to pause in order that I may give a summary of the situation as it then stood.

On February 26, the date on which I received the above telegram from General Gordon, thirty-nine days had elapsed since he had left London, thirty-one days since he had left Cairo, and eight days since he had arrived at Khartoum. During that period, leaving aside points of detail, as to which his contradictions had been numerous, General Gordon had marked out for himself no less than five different lines of policy, some of which were wholly conflicting one with another, whilst others, without being absolutely irreconcilable, differed in respect to some of their most important features.

On January 18, he started from London with instructions which had been dictated by himself. His wish then was that he should be merely sent to "report upon the best means of effecting the evacuation of the interior of the Soudan." He expressed his entire concurrence in the policy of evacuation. This was the first and original stage of General Gordon's opinions.

Before he arrived in Egypt on January 24, he had changed his views as to the nature of the

functions he should fulfil. He no longer wished
to be a mere reporter. He wished to be named
Governor-General of the Soudan with full executive powers. He supplemented his original ideas
by suggesting that the country should be handed
over to "the different petty Sultans who existed
at the time of Mehemet Ali's conquest." This was
the second stage of General Gordon's opinions.

Fifteen days later (February 8), he wrote from
Abu Hamed a Memorandum in which he advo-
cated "evacuation but not abandonment." The
Government of Egypt were "to maintain their posi-
tion as a Suzerain Power, nominate the Governor-
General and Moudirs, and act as a supreme Court
of Appeal." This was the third stage of General
Gordon's opinions.

Ten days later (February 18), General Gordon
reverted to the principles of his Memorandum of
the 8th, but with a notable difference. It was no
longer the Egyptian, but the British Government
which were to control the Soudan administration.
The British Government were also to appoint a
Governor-General who was to be furnished with
a British commission, and who was to receive a
British decoration. Zobeir Pasha was the man
whom General Gordon wished the British Government to select. This was the fourth stage of
General Gordon's opinions.

Eight days later (February 26), when General
Gordon had learnt that the British Government
were not prepared to approve of Zobeir Pasha being
sent to the Soudan, he proposed that the Mahdi
should be "smashed up," and that, to assist in this
object, 200 British Indian troops should be sent
to Wadi Halfa. This was the fifth stage of
General Gordon's opinions.

In thirty-nine days, therefore, General Gordon
had drifted by successive stages from a proposal

that he should report on the affairs of the Soudan,
to advocating the policy of "smashing up" the
Mahdi. It would, he said, be "comparatively easy
to destroy the Mahdi."

It is inconceivable that General Gordon should
have thought that the Mahdi could be destroyed
with any force which the Egyptian Government
could place at his disposal. British or British-Indian
troops would have to be employed. He must have
known this. Accordingly, three days later he took
another step in advance. He proposed (February 29)
that British-Indian troops should be used to open
up the Suakin-Berber road. This, he said, "will
cause an immediate collapse of the revolt." About
the same time (February 27), he issued a Proclamation in which he stated that he had advised the
people to desist from rebellion, but, he added,
"finding that my advice had no effect on some
people, I have been compelled to use severe
measures, so much so that British troops are now
on their way to reach Khartoum."

Mr. Egmont Hake says,[1] "the statement that
British troops were on their way to Khartoum is,
of course, inexplicable. It was probably due to
the fact that Gordon had heard that British troops
were advancing along the Suakin-Berber route."
This explanation is wholly insufficient. At this
time, telegraphic communication between Khartoum
and Cairo was open. Nothing could have been
easier than for General Gordon to have asked me
whether such rumours, supposing there to have
been any, were true, and I should, of course, at
once have replied in the negative. It is clear that
General Gordon made the statement about British
troops being on their way to Khartoum knowing it
to be unfounded. He wished to exercise a moral
effect upon the population. I will not attempt to

[1] *The Story of Chinese Gordon*, pp. 82 and 153.

discuss whether, under the circumstances in which General Gordon was placed, his statement was justifiable from a moral point of view. Many a military commander before General Gordon has found it necessary to employ ruses of various descriptions. From the point of view of expediency, it would appear that General Gordon made a mistake. It was certain that, in a short time, the people would find out that no British troops were on their way to Khartoum. Thus, General Gordon would be discredited. Indeed, when eventually Lord Wolseley's expedition advanced, the news of the approach of a British force failed to obtain credence.

It can be no matter for surprise that the British Government should have been bewildered by the rapid changes in General Gordon's opinions. And this bewilderment was mixed with some alarm, for their impulsive agent appeared to be hurrying them along a path which would almost certainly lead to British armed intervention in the Soudan. Now, the Government held that one of the main objects of their policy should be to avoid any such intervention. Mr. Gladstone, speaking in the House of Commons on February 23, 1885, said : " When General Gordon left this country and when he arrived in Egypt, he declared it to be—and I have not the smallest doubt it was—a fixed portion of his policy, that no British force should be employed in aid of his mission." This statement is unquestionably correct.

The following letter from Lord Northbrook, dated February 29, contains such a clear description of the difficulties of the moment, that I give it in full :—

What a queer fellow Gordon is and how rapidly he changes his opinions !

I. Zobeir is to be sent to Cyprus before Gordon arrives in Egypt.

II. Zobeir is to rule at Khartoum.

I. The Mahdi is a good kind man, whom Gordon is to visit quietly and settle affairs with.

II. The Mahdi is to be Emir of Kordofan.

III. The Mahdi is to be smashed up.

I. The Suakin-Berber route is to be opened up, and the Hadendowa tribe is to be set upon by the other tribes.[1]

II. Suakin is to be left alone.[2]

Why should Zobeir be trusted? His antecedents are all against it. · Why should he oppose the Mahdi? He is supposed to have had a main hand in the insurrection. Why should he protect Egypt? He knows her weakness, and is just as likely to be her worst enemy.[3] Why should he like us? Gordon and you must have very good reasons, but I hope you will let us know them. There is no disposition here to negative Zobeir, simply because his nomination would undoubtedly be extremely distasteful to every one who has paid any attention to the history of the Soudan, or cares about checking the Slave Trade. But, looked at with reference to the real interests of Egypt, the arguments and probabilities against seem to me greatly to preponderate.

The Mahdi must be "smashed up." This seems to be Gordon's view now. But he gives no reasons, and it is utterly contrary to our policy hitherto. Indeed, his telegram does not differ very much from Chérif Pasha's programme of keeping Khartoum, upon which you turned him out.

Things may be in such a condition that a change may be necessary, but I cannot say I feel that confidence in Gordon's opinions, which are often most hastily expressed and constantly changed, to induce me to think without further reasons being given, that we were all wrong in January last.

---

[1] This proposal was contained in an undated Memorandum sent to me by General Gordon which I received on February 4, 1884. See *Egypt*, No. 12 of 1884, p. 61.

[2] When General Gordon was in Cairo, he wished the whole of the garrison of Suakin to be withdrawn, except 150 men. I think that this question must have formed the subject of further discussion between General Gordon and Colonel Stewart after their arrival at Khartoum, for on March 4, Colonel Stewart wrote to me: "I trust the Government will not be so ill-advised as to send away the troops from Suakin ; it would be in every way a very bad move, and very prejudicial to us."

[3] Lord Northbrook might have quoted General Gordon's own testimony in support of this view. When, early in December 1883, I favoured the idea that Zobeir Pasha should be sent to Suakin, General Gordon wrote : "Zobeir will manage to get taken prisoner and will head the revolt."—*Events, etc.*, p. 314.

If the religious movement is really so serious that the Mahdi must be "smashed up" for the safety of Egypt, how is it to be done? For my part, I can only see one way, and that is to set Musulman against Musulman, and to try and induce the Turk to take the business up. Turk against Arab it will be, and a serious business too.

Pray do not suppose that, because we hesitate to take very grave decisions involving a considerable change of policy without time to consider and without further motives upon which to form our judgment, that we have the least want of confidence in you. As to Gordon, I have great confidence in his wisdom in action—little in his steadiness in Council.

We certainly have the most difficult job to tackle between us that any men ever had, and I am sure it requires great steadiness all round.

Before General Gordon had been long at Khartoum, his combative spirit completely got the better of him. As a soldier, he could not brook the idea of retiring before the Mahdi. Moreover, as a civilised European, he winced at the idea that a country, in which some germs of civilisation had been sown, should relapse into barbarism. On April 11, 1884, he telegraphed to me :[1] "Having visited the schools, workshops, etc., it is deplorable to think of their destruction by a feeble lot of stinking Dervishes." He wished, therefore, to "smash up" the Mahdi, and perhaps it was natural that he should have done so. But in taking up this attitude, which necessarily involved armed British interference in the country, he departed from the spirit of his instructions. He was sent to evacuate the Soudan. A subsidiary portion of his instructions—I look to the spirit of those instructions rather than to the strict letter—was that, if possible, he was to leave behind him a fairly good government, which would not constitute a standing menace to Egypt. It is difficult to understand how General Gordon could have made his proposal to wage war against

[1] I did not receive this message till March 26, 1890.

the Mahdi with British troops tally with these instructions.

It was not until February 23, when I received General Gordon's Memorandum of February 8 written at Abu Hamed, that I fully understood his telegram of the 18th from Khartoum, in which he proposed to utilise Zobeir Pasha's services. I then set myself to work to consider what it was that General Gordon really wanted. I swept aside all the minor contradictions in his proposals. I did not consider that the suggestion about "smashing up" the Mahdi was worthy of serious discussion. It was obviously impracticable without employing British troops, a policy the adoption of which the British Government would certainly have rejected. It appeared to me, however, that at the bottom of all General Gordon's contradictions there was an underlying vein of common sense. He wished, in the terms of his Memorandum of February 8, to advocate a policy of "evacuation but not abandonment." The policy of setting up the local Sultans, which he had put forward at Cairo, was manifestly impossible of execution, not because it was faulty in principle, but because there were no local Sultans to set up. He wished, therefore, to carry out the same principle, but in a manner differing from that which had been originally proposed. One man, Zobeir Pasha, was to be set up, who was to govern the most important portions of the Soudan. He was to be a feudatory of the Egyptian Government. This was a serious departure from the policy of reporting, which had been adopted in London. It was not, however, a serious departure from, but rather a modification of the policy embodied in the instructions given to General Gordon at Cairo. Some two years later, Lord Northbrook wrote to me : " My own opinion of the reason of the failure is that, instead of doing as we wished, viz., withdrawing the garrison of Khartoum, Gordon, on his arrival, hankered after the *ignis fatuus* of arranging for a settled government of a country, which could not be settled excepting by a lengthened and possibly a permanent occupation in force." It may be that this view is right. But at the time it seemed to me that it would be a wise policy to establish a "buffer state" in the Soudan, which would hold much the same relation to Egypt as Afghanistan holds to British India. The policy was, I thought, at any rate worthy of a trial, and, so far as I could judge from General Gordon's utterances, he was of opinion that the difficulties in the way of its accomplishment, though great, were not altogether insurmountable.

It was with this view uppermost in my mind that, on February 28, I repeated to Lord Granville General Gordon's telegram of the 26th[1] and added the following remarks :—

" I will now submit to your Lordship my views upon the main points at issue, after having carefully considered the different proposals made by General Gordon. There are obviously many contradictions in those proposals ; too much importance should not be attached to the details. But I venture to again recommend to the earnest attention of Her Majesty's Government the serious question of principle which General Gordon has raised.

" Two alternative courses may be adopted. One is to evacuate the Soudan entirely, and to make no attempt to establish any settled government there before leaving ; the other is to make every effort of which the present circumstances admit to set up some settled form of government to replace the former Egyptian Administration.

[1] *Vide ante*, p. 487.

"General Gordon is evidently in favour of the latter of these courses. I entirely agree with him. The attempt, it is true, may not be successful, but I am strongly of opinion that it should be made. From every point of view, whether political, military, or financial, it will be a most serious matter if complete anarchy is allowed to reign south of Wadi Halfa. And this anarchy will inevitably ensue on General Gordon's departure, unless some measures are adopted beforehand to prevent it.

"With regard to the wish of Her Majesty's Government not to go beyond General Gordon's plan, as stated in his Memorandum of the 23rd ultimo, I would remark that he appears to have intended merely to give a preliminary sketch of the general line of policy to be pursued. Moreover, in that Memorandum he makes a specific allusion to the difficulty of providing rulers for Khartoum, Dongola, and other places where there are no old families to recall to power.

"It is clear that Her Majesty's Government cannot afford moral or material support to General Gordon's successor as Ruler of the Soudan, but the question of whether or not he should be nominally appointed by the authority of Her Majesty's Government appears to me to be one of very slight practical importance.

"Whatever may be said to the contrary, Her Majesty's Government must in reality be responsible for any arrangements which are now devised for the Soudan, and I do not think it is possible to shake off that responsibility.

"If, however, Her Majesty's Government are unwilling to assume any responsibility in the matter, then I think they should give full liberty of action to General Gordon and the Khedive's Government to do what seems best to them.

"I have no doubt as to the most advisable course of action. Zobeir Pasha should be permitted to succeed General Gordon. He should receive a certain sum of money to begin with, and an annual subsidy of about £50,000 for the first five years, to depend upon his good behaviour. This amount would enable him to maintain a moderate-sized army, and the whole arrangement would be an economical one for the Egyptian Government.

"The main difficulty lies in the selection of the man. It is useless to send any one who has no local influence. There are certain obvious objections to Zobeir Pasha, but I think too great weight is attached to them, and I believe that General Gordon is quite right when he says that Zobeir Pasha is the only possible man. I can suggest none other, and Nubar Pasha is strongly in favour of him.

"It is for Her Majesty's Government to judge of the importance to be attached to public opinion in England, but I venture to think that any attempt to settle Egyptian questions by the light of English popular feeling is sure to be productive of harm, and in this, as in other cases, it would be preferable to follow the advice of the responsible authorities on the spot."

On March 1, Lord Granville replied: "I have received your telegram of the 28th ultimo, informing me of General Gordon's views with regard to the proposals which he made for placing Zobeir Pasha in power at Khartoum.

"Her Majesty's Government desire further information as to the urgency of any immediate appointment of a successor to General Gordon, who they trust will remain for some time longer at Khartoum.

"If it be found necessary to make an arrange-

ment of this subject eventually, Her Majesty's
Government will carefully weigh your opinions as
to the proper person for the post.

"They are, at the same time, of opinion that
if such an appointment is made, it might be
advantageous that it should receive the confirma-
tion of the Sultan." I repeated this telegram to
General Gordon.

Lord Granville wrote me a private letter, on
February 29, which shows the views entertained
by the Government at the time this telegram was
despatched. "Pray do not," he said, "doubt our
full confidence in you, but as circumstances
naturally sometimes oblige you to change the view
you had taken when things were in a different
state, we often desire to have your opinion before
a final decision. We had a Cabinet, and although
there would have been much reluctance if we had
been obliged to answer at once categorically about
Zobeir, yet we should, probably, have yielded to
your, Gordon's and Nubar's opinion. If you
persist in it, I am certain it will be carefully
considered. The Cabinet were startled at what
appeared to be a change of front as to withdrawal
from the Soudan. I apprehend that your answer
would be that you do not propose an Egyptian
Government administering the Soudan with
Egyptian troops scattered about the desert, that
it is only proposed that an individual should be
appointed with a large salary to govern the country
as best he could, and in a friendly manner towards
Egypt. But even this offers many considerations.
As to the person, I do not doubt that Zobeir is
the only man strong enough to cope with the
Mahdi. But can you guarantee that the official
income will be a sufficient bribe to prevent his
embarking in his former lucrative pursuits, or even
of his not going over to the Mahdi?"

It was obvious that I could give no guarantee of the sort required by Lord Granville. As has been already mentioned, the attitude of the British Government in respect to Egyptian affairs was often of an exclusively negative and hypercritical character. The objections to the adoption of any particular course were clearly seen. Those objections were allowed to prevail. But as no alternative policy was adopted, the Government became the sport of circumstances. On April 18, 1884, Lord Granville wrote to me: "The misfortune during the last two years has been that we hardly ever have had anything but bad alternatives to choose from. The objectors to whatever was decided were pretty sure to have the best of it."

In the interval between the receipt of General Gordon's telegram of February 26 [1] and that of Lord Granville's reply on March 1, [2] General Gordon sent me a large number of telegrams. It was difficult to understand from them what it was he really wanted. Moreover, the language in which they were couched led me to the conclusion that he was making a number of proposals on matters of general policy without sufficient reflection. On March 2, therefore, I telegraphed to him: "I am most anxious to help and support you in every way, but I find it very difficult to understand exactly what it is you want. I think your best plan will be to reconsider the whole question carefully, and then state to me in one telegram what it is you recommend, in order that I can, if necessary, obtain the instructions of Her Majesty's Government." I added some further observations drawing attention to the main points which required consideration.

At the same time (March 2), I sent the following telegram to Colonel Stewart: "Private. As regards my long telegram to Gordon, pray make

[1] *Vide ante,* p. 487.   [2] *Vide ante,* p. 497.

him understand that my sole object is to help him
to the best of my ability, but it adds immensely to
my difficulties to receive constant and somewhat
contradictory telegrams, apparently written on the
spur of the moment, in respect to matters of
policy.　What I should like him to do is to
consider the whole question carefully and deliberately, and then to let me know what he thinks and
what he recommends.　At present, with the best
possible intentions, I can really do little to help
him, for I cannot clearly understand what it is he
wants." [1]

Prior to the despatch of this telegram to Colonel
Stewart, I had, on February 29, sent the following
private telegram to Lord Granville: "I have
received a fresh batch of telegrams from Gordon.
His statements and proposals are hopelessly
bewildering and contradictory.　I do not mean
to say that I have lost confidence in Gordon.
Such is not the case.　But in dealing with his
proposals it is often difficult to know what he
means, and still more difficult to judge what is
really worthy of attention, and what is more or less
nonsense.　It is really of no use my forwarding all
he sends home for instructions, for the difficulty
for you will be even greater than for me.　I think,
on the whole, you had better give me full authority

---

[1] On receiving this telegram, Colonel Stewart wrote to me (March 4):
"I fully sympathise with you about the many and rather divergent
telegrams you get.　Gordon telegraphs directly an idea strikes him.
There is no use in trying to stop it.　Were I you, I should always wait
for a few days before acting unless the subject matter is so evident that
there can be no doubt about it."

Matters were so urgent that I was unable to follow Colonel Stewart's
advice to the extent of "waiting for a few days before acting."　But I
rarely acted on any telegram of General Gordon's directly I received it.
I generally found a batch of them waiting for me when I began my
work in the morning.　My practice was to put them on one side and
wait till the afternoon, by which time more had generally arrived.　I
used then to compare the different telegrams, to try to extract from
them what it was that General Gordon really wanted, and then to
decide what could be done towards carrying out his wishes.

to do the best I can. I fully understand the policy
of Her Majesty's Government, and you can rely
on my doing nothing contrary to it, but, of course,
I can only do this if I feel sure I possess the
entire confidence of Her Majesty's Government. I
should, in any case, like an answer about Zobeir as a
question of principle is involved." To this telegram
Lord Granville replied on March 2 : "I am not
surprised at your private message. We have full
confidence in you and give the full discretion you
ask. When you have time, we like to know your
reasons."

I received several telegrams from General
Gordon in reply to my message of March 2. I
need not give them in full. They were to the
effect that he maintained the policy of eventually
evacuating the Soudan, including Khartoum; that,
in consequence of the evacuation, anarchy would
ensue, about which, General Gordon said, " I
would not trouble myself"; and that the immediate withdrawal of all the Egyptian employés
was impossible. General Gordon dwelt strongly
on the necessity of sending Zobeir Pasha to
Khartoum at once. "The combination," he said,
"at Khartoum of Zobeir and myself is an absolute
necessity for success, and I beg you and Lord
Granville to believe my certain conviction that
there is not the slightest fear of our quarrelling,
for Zobeir would know that the subsidy depended
on my safety. To do any good we must be
together, and that without delay. . . . Pray
abandon fear of Zobeir's hurting me. His interests
are bound up with mine. Believe me I am right,
and do not delay. . . . Things are not serious,
although they may become so if delay occurs in
sending Zobeir. My weakness is that of being
foreign and Christian and peaceful; and it is only
by sending Zobeir that that prejudice can be

removed. I wish you would question Stewart on any subject you like without hesitation and you can learn his views distinct from mine. This would please me."

General Gordon also urged that it was necessary to open up the road from Berber to Suakin. He desired that 200 British troops should be sent to Wadi Halfa. "It is not," he said, "the number, but the prestige which I need; I am sure the revolt will collapse if I can say that I have British troops at my back."

At the same time, I received the following telegram from Colonel Stewart, dated March 4: "The principal desire of General Gordon is to have Zobeir here as soon as possible. His reasons are: Zobeir is the only man with sufficient prestige to hold the country together, at any rate for a time, after the evacuation. Being a Pasha among the Shaggieh irregulars, he will be able to get at sources of information and action now closed to us. He will be opposed to the Mahdi. I agree with Gordon. It seems evident to me that it is impossible for us to leave this country without leaving some sort of established government which will last at any rate for a time, and Zobeir is the only man who can ensure that. Also, that we must withdraw the Sennar and other besieged garrisons, and here also Zobeir can greatly assist us. The principal objections to Zobeir are his evil reputation as a slave dealer and his enmity to General Gordon. As regards the first, it will have to be defended on the plea that no other course is open except British annexation or anarchy. As regards the second, if precautionary measures are taken, such as making the subsidy payable through General Gordon, I think Zobeir will see that his interests are in working with General Gordon.

"Of the secondary measures proposed by General

Gordon to assist the evacuation, they are: When the Berber-Suakin road is clear, to send a small force of Indian or British cavalry to Berber, and to send a small force of British cavalry to Wadi Halfa. These measures, showing that we had forces at our disposal, would greatly assist negotiations with rebels, and hasten evacuation. I assure you none are more anxious to leave this country than Gordon and myself, and none more heartily approve the Government policy of evacuation. Unless, however, Zobeir is sent here, I see little probability of this policy being carried out. Every day we remain, finds us more firm in the country, and causes us to incur responsibilities towards the people, which it is impossible for us to overlook."[1]

[1] Colonel Stewart's private letters give some further indication of his views at this time. On March 1, he wrote to me: "As for the future of this country, the choice of a ruler, it would seem to me, lies between Zobeir and the Mahdi. Politically and socially, I should much prefer the former. To have a religious ruler here would be a great disadvantage to us in Egypt, not to speak of the probable consequences in other parts of the Arab world. If once we establish Zobeir here, and gave him something to start upon, we might let matters slide, and act on the Darwinian principle of the 'survival of the fittest.' . . . It seems to me that the only people here who will suffer by the withdrawal of the Government are the rich Arab merchants and the Greeks. I cannot say that I have any sympathy with either class, and I should greatly grudge that any English money should be spent in supporting them. Let them make their own terms and get out of the mess as best they can. The villagers and nomad tribes have an organisation of their own, which is independent of any Government. They will probably fight and squabble amongst themselves, but that is their affair. Of the towns, such as Khartoum, Kassala, Berber, and Dongola, they are all only collections of mud-huts, which, if burnt one day, can be rebuilt the next. Of the lot, Khartoum is the best. . . . The country is only intended by nature for nomad tribes and a few scattered Arabs along the banks of the Nile. It annoys me greatly to see the blood and treasure wasted on it. . . . As regards Zobeir, I think you have no option in the matter. Unless he is sent up, I see no means of terminating the state of affairs here. . . . There is no one here we can appoint who would stand for a day; hence, I see no option but Zobeir with a small subsidy. I think by means of the subsidy you would ensure his fidelity. Of course, there is always a certain risk in the matter, but we can only do what is best. Every possible scheme has its advantages and its disadvantages. How far Gordon and Zobeir

Up to this time, I had pressed the British Government to allow Zobeir Pasha to succeed General Gordon at Khartoum, but I had opposed the idea of sending him there immediately. My reasons for making this reserve were twofold. In the first place, I feared that Zobeir Pasha's old grudge against General Gordon would endanger the latter's life. In the second place, I entertained greater confidence in the judgment of Colonel Stewart than in that of his chief. Up to March 4, Colonel Stewart hesitated as to the desirability of employing Zobeir Pasha. The telegrams which I have given above, led me, however, to reconsider the recommendations which I had so far made. It was clear that the situation at Khartoum was becoming very critical. The tribes between Berber and Khartoum were wavering. They were being driven by the force of circumstances into the arms of the Mahdi. It was evident that, if anything was to be done in the way of establishing an anti-Mahdist Government at Khartoum, no time was to be lost. General Gordon was pressing strongly for the immediate despatch of Zobeir Pasha, and argued—as I thought with great force—that, so far as his personal safety was concerned, Zobeir Pasha's interest would be in the direction of doing him no harm. Colonel Stewart also had come round to General Gordon's opinion. He now advocated, without reserve of any kind, the immediate employment of Zobeir Pasha. Judging, not only from the contents of his telegram, but also from what I knew of the character of the man, it seemed to me certain that Colonel Stewart had not changed his opinion merely in order to be agreeable to his chief, but that the

will be able to work together, time alone can say. I apprehend, however, Zobeir, like the rest of the world, knows what is to his own advantage."

change was due to a careful consideration of the facts of the situation at Khartoum. I determined, therefore, to modify my own recommendations to the British Government, and to support the proposal that Zobeir Pasha should be sent to Khartoum at once.

On March 4, I repeated to Lord Granville General Gordon's telegrams of the 2nd and 3rd and Colonel Stewart's telegram of the 4th. I added: "The general substance of General Gordon's telegram is that he presses strongly for Zobeir Pasha to be sent to Khartoum without delay. I have carefully reconsidered the whole question, and I am still of opinion that Zobeir Pasha should be allowed to succeed General Gordon. I do not think that anything would be gained by postponing a decision on this point; on the contrary, I should say that delay would be injurious.

"As regards the question of when Zobeir should be sent—in the face of the strong opinion expressed by General Gordon, I am not inclined to maintain my objection to his going at once to Khartoum. But, before giving a final opinion on this point, I should prefer to have another interview with Zobeir himself. It would be useless for me to do this until Her Majesty's Government has decided whether, apart from the question of the time of his departure, Zobeir is to be allowed to return to the Soudan at all. I await, therefore, an answer on this latter point before taking any further action."

At the same time (March 4), I sent the following private telegram to Lord Granville: "My official telegram of to-day gives the gist of some twenty telegrams from Gordon. I feel confident that I am stating his real opinion, and not a mere passing impression. Do not commit yourself to sending Zobeir at once until I have seen the man again. What I want to know is whether your objections to sending him at all are insuperable."

When I sent these telegrams, my intention was to see Zobeir Pasha, and, after hearing his language and observing his demeanour, to form a final judgment as to whether it would be desirable to send him to Khartoum at once. I should have told him that, if the withdrawal from the Soudan was conducted successfully, and especially if General Gordon and Colonel Stewart returned safely to Cairo, he would be named Governor-General of the Soudan, and that he would receive a subsidy of £100,000 a year from the Egyptian Government, so long as his behaviour was satisfactory; on the other hand, that if any harm befell General Gordon or Colonel Stewart, and in general, if at any subsequent period he adopted a hostile attitude towards Egypt, he would incur the displeasure of both the British and Egyptian Governments, and that should he fall into the hands of either, his life would possibly be forfeited. It was, however, useless for me to enter into any negotiations of this sort until I had received from the British Government a free hand to act in the matter according to the best of my judgment.

It will be observed that both General Gordon and Colonel Stewart in their telegrams of March 3 and 4 urged the desirability of opening up the Berber-Suakin road. Colonel Stewart also suggested that a force of British or Indian cavalry should be sent from Suakin to Berber. At that time, General Graham was at Suakin, and was about to advance against Osman Digna. There was some prospect that, when the latter had been defeated, Hussein Pasha Khalifa, who was then at Berber, might be able to open up the road to Suakin without further British military assistance. Moreover, so long as any prospect existed of sending Zobeir Pasha to

Khartoum, and thus settling the Soudan question by diplomacy, I was not prepared to incur the responsibility of recommending that a British force should be despatched into the interior of the Soudan. On March 4, therefore, I telegraphed to Lord Granville : " I cannot agree with the proposal mentioned in Colonel Stewart's telegram that a force of British or Indian cavalry should be sent through from Suakin to Berber."

On March 5, Lord Granville telegraphed to me as follows : " I have received your telegram of the 4th instant on the subject of the proposal that Zobeir Pasha should succeed General Gordon at Khartoum, and I have to inform you that Her Majesty's Government see no reason at present to change their impressions about Zobeir, which were formed on various grounds, amongst others on the Memoranda, dated the 23rd January, written by General Gordon and Colonel Stewart on board the *Tanjore*.[1] Unless these impressions could be removed, Her Majesty's Government could not take upon themselves the responsibility of sending Zobeir to Khartoum.

" Her Majesty's Government would be glad to learn how you reconcile your proposal to acquiesce in such an appointment with the prevention or discouragement of slave-hunting and Slave Trade, with the policy of complete evacuation, and with the security of Egypt.

" They would also wish to be informed as to the progress which has been made in extricating the garrisons, and the length of time likely to elapse before the whole or the greater part may be withdrawn.

" As Her Majesty's Government require details as to each garrison, your report should be a full one, and may be sent by mail.

[1] *Vide ante*, p. 442.

"In your telegram now under reply, no allusion is made to the proposal that the local Chiefs should be consulted as to the future government of the country, and Her Majesty's Government desire to know whether that idea has been abandoned."

I remember the feeling akin to despair with which I received this telegram. It was clear that the Government did not realise the true nature of the situation at Khartoum. I was asked to reconcile the proposal that Zobeir Pasha should be employed, (1) with the prevention or discouragement of slave-hunting and the Slave Trade; (2) with the policy of complete evacuation; and (3) with the security of Egypt. The answers were obvious.

If the Soudan were abandoned, slave-hunting and the Slave Trade could not be prevented. This was clear from the first. The fact was an unpleasant one, but no object was to be gained by a failure to recognise its existence.

Again, it could scarcely be argued that to set up Zobeir Pasha as a subsidised and semi-independent ruler of the Soudan was inconsistent with the policy of evacuation. The policy, which both General Gordon and myself were at this moment advocating, was one of "evacuation but not abandonment,"—that is to say, not complete abandonment to anarchy.

As regards the security of Egypt, the choice lay between Zobeir Pasha and the Mahdi, and the opinion of the best-informed authorities on the spot was that the former was less dangerous than the latter.

Again, I was asked to furnish information "as to the progress which had been made in extricating the garrisons, and the length of time likely to elapse before the whole or the greater part might be withdrawn."

The Government must surely have known that no progress had been made in extricating the garrisons, and that if the remote garrisons in Sennar and the Equatorial provinces were to be withdrawn, it was impossible to state what length of time would elapse before the operation could be completed. One of the objects in recommending the employment of Zobeir Pasha was to facilitate the extrication of the garrisons by preventing the wavering tribes from joining the Mahdi.

But perhaps the most deplorable part of Lord Granville's telegram was that in which the British Government, at a time when every moment was precious, asked for a full report to be sent by mail as to the details of each garrison. These details had been already furnished to the Government three months previously in a despatch which fills five pages of a blue book.[1]

My position at this time was one of great difficulty. It was clear that the situation at Khartoum was very critical. Every telegram received from General Gordon and Colonel Stewart insisted more strongly than its precursor on the necessity of sending Zobeir Pasha at once to Khartoum. On the other hand, the British Government were evidently very averse to the employment of Zobeir Pasha. Moreover, General Gordon's frequent changes of opinion, and the number and tone of his telegrams, had not unnaturally engendered the belief that he had not sufficiently considered the nature of his proposals. In spite of the messages which had been sent to London, the Government evidently thought that General Gordon and Colonel Stewart were not in any immediate danger, and that time was available to consider leisurely the future course of action in the Soudan. After weighing the matter

---

[1] See *Egypt*, No. 1 of 1884, p. 125.

carefully, I came to the conclusion that the best
course to adopt would be to make a further endeavour in the direction of utilising Zobeir Pasha's
services. I was all the more disposed to adopt
this course because just at this moment (March 7)
I received Lord Granville's private letter of
February 29,[1] from which I gathered that the
Government were open to conviction on the Zobeir
question.

It seemed to me that the best way to induce the
Government to yield was to get General Gordon
to send a carefully reasoned reply to the objections
raised in Lord Granville's telegram of March 5.
I resolved, therefore, to repeat that telegram to
General Gordon. I added the following observations : " In view of the opinions entertained by Her
Majesty's Government, it becomes your duty and
mine to reconsider very carefully the two following
points :—

"First, is it possible to choose any other man
except Zobeir ? Secondly, if it is not possible to
do so, are the arguments in favour of Zobeir's
appointment sufficient to outweigh the obvious
disadvantages ?

" As regards the first point, would it be possible
to place Hussein Pasha Khalifa at Khartoum with
a certain portion of territory northwards, and to
divide the rest of the country amongst the heads
of tribes ? I do not recommend this course. I
merely ask for your opinion on it.

"Further, will you reconsider the question of
collecting the Chiefs at Khartoum, and coming
to an agreement with them as to the future of the
country ?

" As regards the second question, the following
points require consideration.

"First, how is the proposal to nominate and

---

[1] *Vide ante,* p. 498.

subsidise Zobeir to be reconciled with the policy of evacuation ?

"Secondly, how is it to be reconciled with the prevention or discouragement of slave-hunting or the Slave Trade ?

"Thirdly, how is it to be reconciled with the security of Egypt ? In dealing with this latter question, it is desirable to consider how far Zobeir can be trusted to remain friendly to Egypt. Might he not make common cause with the Mahdi, should he become powerful, and prove a source of danger, on his own account, rather than of assistance to Egypt ? Many people think that he has instigated the revolt of the Mahdi. Have you any reasons to believe that he has done so ?

"Having answered these questions, please reply fully to Lord Granville's question as to the prospects of extricating the garrisons, including Darfour."

My object in sending this telegram was to ask General Gordon a series of leading questions, which he might answer in a form calculated to produce an effect in London. I felt, however, that some further explanation was due to him, for he might reasonably cavil at questions being addressed to him which, so far as was possible, he had already answered several times. Simultaneously, therefore, with the despatch of my official telegram, I sent him the following private message : "Please understand, as regards my long telegram of to-day, that I could answer many of the questions myself, but I want to get your opinions and then see whether they agree with mine. You can regard the Zobeir question as still under consideration, but the Home Government does not like the proposal, and requires solid reasons to be given before they can accept it. Send me a careful and well-argued answer on the different points I raise."

On March 8, I received General Gordon's reply. It was as follows: "The sending of Zobeir means the extrication of the Cairo employés from Khartoum, and the garrisons from Sennar and Kassala. I can see no possible way to do so except through him who, being a native of the country, can rally the well-affected around him, as they know he will make his home here. I do not think that the giving a subsidy to Zobeir for some two years would be in contradiction to the policy of entire evacuation. It would be nothing more than giving him a lump sum in two instalments under the conditions I have already written. As for slave-holding, even had we held the Soudan, we could never have interfered with it. I have already said that the Treaty of 1877 was an impossible one; therefore, on that head, Zobeir's appointment would make no difference whatever. As for slave-hunting, the evacuation of the Bahr-el-Ghazal and Equatorial provinces would entirely prevent it. Should Zobeir attempt, after his two years' subsidy was paid him, to take those districts, we could put pressure on him at Suakin, which will remain in our hands. I feel sure that Zobeir will be so occupied with the Soudan proper, and with consolidating his position, that he will not have time to devote to those provinces. As for the security of Egypt, Zobeir's stay in Cairo has taught him our power, and he would never dream of doing anything against Egypt. He would rather seek its closest alliance, for he is a great trader. As to progress made in extrication of garrisons, all I have done is to send down from Khartoum all the sick men, women, and children of those killed in Kordofan. Sennar, I heard to-day, is quite safe and quiet. Kassala will hold out without difficulty after Graham's victory, but the road there is blocked, as also is the road to Sennar. It is quite impossible to get the roads open to Kassala and Sennar, or to send down the white troops, unless Zobeir comes up. He will change the whole state of affairs. As for the Equatorial and Bahr-el-Ghazal provinces, they are all right, but I cannot evacuate them till the Nile rises, in two months. Dongola and Berber are quiet; but I fear for the road between Berber and Khartoum, where the friends of the Mahdi are very active. A body of rebels on the Blue Nile are blockading a force of 1000 men, which have, however, plenty of food; till the Nile rises, I cannot relieve them. Darfour, so far as I can understand, is all right, and the restored Sultan should now be working up the tribes to acknowledge him. It is impossible to find any other man but Zobeir for governing Khartoum. No one has his power. Hussein Pasha Khalifa has only power at Dongola and Berber. If you do not send Zobeir, you have no chance of getting the garrisons away; this is a heavy argument in favour of sending him. There is no possibility of dividing the country between Zobeir and other Chiefs; none of the latter could stand for a day against the Mahdi's agents, and Hussein Pasha Khalifa would also fall. The Chiefs will not collect here, for the loyal are defending their lands against the disloyal. There is not the least chance of Zobeir making common cause with the Mahdi. Zobeir here would be far more powerful than the Mahdi, and he would make short work of the Mahdi. The Mahdi's power is that of a Pope, Zobeir's will be that of a Sultan. They could never combine. Zobeir is fifty times the Mahdi's match. He is also of good family, well known and fitted to be Sultan; the Mahdi, in all these respects, is the exact opposite, besides being a fanatic. I daresay Zobeir, who hates the tribes, did stir up the fires of revolt, in hopes that he would be sent to quell it. It is the irony of fate that he will get his wish if he is sent up."

At the same time, I received some further telegrams from General Gordon, which showed that the danger of communication between Berber and Khartoum being cut off was daily becoming more imminent, although, General Gordon added, "for Khartoum itself, there is not any fear."

On March 9, I repeated to Lord Granville General Gordon's long telegram of the 8th, adding the following remarks :—

"I think that the policy of sending Zobeir to Khartoum and giving him a subsidy is in harmony with the policy of evacuation. It is in principle the same policy as that adopted by the Government of India towards Afghanistan and the tribes on the north-west frontier. I have always contemplated making some arrangements for the future government of the Soudan, as will be seen from my despatch of December 22, 1883, in which I said that it would be 'necessary to send an English officer of high authority to Khartoum with full powers to withdraw all garrisons in the Soudan, and make the best arrangements possible for the future government of the country.'

"As regards slavery, it may certainly receive a stimulus from the abandonment of the Soudan by Egypt, but the despatch of Zobeir Pasha to Khartoum will not affect the question in one way or the other. No middle course is possible so far as the Soudan is concerned. We must either virtually annex the country, which is out of the question, or else we must accept the inevitable consequences of the policy of abandonment.

"Your Lordship will see what General Gordon says about the question of the security of Egypt. I believe that Zobeir may be made a bulwark against the approach of the Mahdi. Of course,

there is a risk that he will constitute a danger to
Egypt, but this risk is, I think, a small one, and it
is in any case preferable to incur it rather than
to face the certain disadvantages of withdrawing
without making any provision for the future
government of the country, which would thus be
sure to fall under the power of the Mahdi.

"I venture to urge upon Her Majesty's Government the necessity of settling this question without
delay.   General Gordon's telegrams have latterly
caused me some uneasiness.   He evidently thinks
that there is a considerable danger of his being
hemmed in and blockaded by the rebels at Khartoum, and he appears to contemplate the despatch
of British troops to extricate him.   Moreover, so far
as I can judge, General Gordon exercises little or
no influence outside Khartoum, and, although he
was at first hailed as a deliverer, his influence is
sure to decline as time goes on."

An incident now occurred which practically
destroyed all hopes of utilising Zobeir Pasha's
services.   Up to this moment, nothing definite
was known to the public about the proposal to
send Zobeir Pasha to Khartoum.   Mr. Power was
employed by the *Times* as its special correspondent
at Khartoum.   On March 8 or 9, Mr. Moberly
Bell, who was *Times* correspondent in Egypt, communicated to me a telegram from Mr. Power for
transmission to the *Times*, from which it appeared
that General Gordon had given to him all the
information which was contained in his telegrams
to me.   I subsequently received a letter from
Colonel Stewart, dated March 8, which informed
me of what had taken place in connection with
this subject.   "The telegram," Colonel Stewart
wrote, "shown you by Bell this morning has, no
doubt, surprised you.   Gordon also sent you a telegram giving in his resignation if his views were not

carried out. Yesterday evening, he got very irritated with me because I did not at once accede to his request to send you a telegram about Zobeir and the propriety of sending him up with a British force to Berber. I said that you had already told us the chief difficulty was not at Cairo, but at London, etc.

"I did not refuse to write the telegram, I merely asked for a little time to think. G. got very impatient and finally left the table. Seeing that he was annoyed, I got up and wrote the telegram as he desired. On returning, I found him with the *Times* correspondent. The result was the telegram you have been shown. We had a discussion on the subject, but it was of no avail. He then telegraphed his resignation to you, but this I fortunately succeeded in getting put into cipher. The affair is very annoying, but I think the Ministry at home ought to let him have his wish and give him Zobeir."

General Gordon wrote in his Journal: "Baring pitched into me for indiscretion in asking *openly* for Zobeir, which I did on *purpose,* in order to save Her Majesty's Government the odium of such a step."[1] As regards the indiscretion, there can be no doubt whatever. It was not only that the publication of General Gordon's views raised a storm of opposition in England to Zobeir Pasha's appointment, but also that the difficulties of negotiating with Zobeir Pasha were greatly increased. Instead of my being able to send for him and point out to him that he had hitherto been under a cloud, but that now he had an opportunity of retrieving his reputation, he was placed in a position in which it would have appeared possible to him to dictate his own terms.

---

[1] *Journal,* September 19, 1884, vol. i. p. 57. I remember sending a telegram urging on General Gordon the desirability of reticence in his communications to the press, but I cannot lay my hands on it.

Indeed, he received advice to act in this manner from the numerous persons in Cairo who were eager to seek any and every opportunity for showing hostility to England.

As regards the effect in England, Mr. Sturge, the Chairman of the Anti-Slavery Society, wrote, on March 18, to Lord Granville that he had been instructed by a full Committee of the Society to state that they were " unanimous in the feeling that countenance in any shape of such an individual (*i.e.* Zobeir Pasha) by the British Government would be a degradation for England and a scandal to Europe. . . . As yet, however, the Committee are unable to believe that Her Majesty's Government will thus stultify that anti-slavery policy which has so long been the high distinction of England, or that they will thus discharge a trust which they have undertaken on behalf of the British people and of Europe." The action of the Anti-Slavery Society was injudicious. It can scarcely be doubted that their opposition, together with the fact that there was every indication of the matter being taken up as a party question in England, greatly contributed to the rejection of the views put forward by General Gordon, Colonel Stewart, and myself.

Before dealing with the reply which Lord Granville sent to my telegram of March 9, I must describe the further correspondence which took place between General Gordon and myself on March 9, 10, and 11.

On the 9th, General Gordon telegraphed to me : "I shall await your decision (*i.e.* the decision about Zobeir Pasha) ; if wire is cut, I shall consider your silence is consent to my propositions, and shall hold on to Khartoum and await Zobeir and British diversion at Berber." I had still some hope of being permitted to utilise Zobeir Pasha, but, in view of the fact that telegraphic communication with Khartoum might at any moment be interrupted, I did not think it was either just or desirable to leave General Gordon under the impression that the British Government had any intention of sending an expedition to Berber, when I knew that they had no such intention. I, therefore, replied at once: "So far as I know, there is no intention on the part of the Government to send an English force to Berber."

On March 10 and 11, I received a large number of telegrams from General Gordon. I need not give them in full. They were to the general effect that the Sheikh-el-Obeid was undecided whether to join the Mahdi or not,[1] that there was considerable risk of communication between Berber and Khartoum being interrupted, but that Khartoum itself was not in any danger, and that the utility of Zobeir Pasha had been greatly diminished by the delay in settling the question of his employment, "which had forced the loyal to join the enemy." "If," General Gordon telegraphed, "you mean to make the proposed diversion to Berber (of British troops), and to accept my proposal as to Zobeir, to install him in the Soudan and evacuate, then it is worth while to hold on to Khartoum.

"If, on the other hand, you determine on neither of these steps, then I can see no use in holding on to Khartoum, for it is impossible for me to help the other garrisons, and I shall only be sacrificing the whole of the troops and employés here.

"In this latter case, your instructions to me had better be that I should evacuate Khartoum, and, with all the employés and troops, remove the seat of government to Berber. You would under-

---

[1] The Sheikh-el-Obeid occupied a position of importance, as his tribal influence extended over the population lying between Khartoum and Berber. Colonel Stewart, in a letter to me, described him as "a very holy man, but a decided trimmer."

stand that such a step would mean the sacrificing of all outlying places except Berber and Dongola.

"You must give a prompt reply to this, as even the retreat to Berber may not be in my power in a few days; and even if carried out at once, the retreat will be of extreme difficulty.

"I should have to leave large stores and nine steamers, which cannot go down. Eventually, some question would arise at Berber and Dongola, and I may utterly fail in getting the Cairo employés to Berber.

"If I attempt it, I could be responsible only for the attempt to do so."

In another telegram, General Gordon said: "If the immediate evacuation of Khartoum is determined upon, irrespective of outlying towns, I would propose to send down all the Cairo employés and white troops with Colonel Stewart to Berber, where he would await your orders. I would also ask Her Majesty's Government to accept the resignation of my commission, and I would take all steamers and stores up to the Equatorial and Bahr-el-Ghazal Provinces, and consider those provinces as under the King of the Belgians.

"You would be able to retire all Cairo employés and white troops with Stewart from Berber to Dongola, and thence to Wadi Halfa.

"If you, therefore, determine on the immediate evacuation of Khartoum, this is my idea. If you object, tell me.

"It is the only solution that I can see if the immediate evacuation of Khartoum, irrespective of the outlying towns, is determined upon." [1]

Lord Granville's reply to my telegram of March 9 was despatched to me on the 11th. It

---

[1] Some of the telegrams, which Gordon sent me at this moment, did not reach me till many days later, owing to the frequent interruptions of telegraphic communication.

was to the following effect: "Her Majesty's Government have carefully considered your telegrams of the 9th instant with regard to the future government of Khartoum and the Soudan, but they do not consider that the arguments against the employment of Zobeir Pasha have been satisfactorily answered. They are prepared to agree to any other Mohammedan assistance, as well as to the supply of any reasonable sum of money which General Gordon may consider necessary in order to carry out successfully the objects of his mission.

"Her Majesty's Government are not prepared to send troops to Berber. They understand from your telegrams that General Gordon and yourself are of opinion that the withdrawal of the garrisons will take a considerable time, and that the chief difficulty arises from the uncertainty felt by the inhabitants of the Soudan with regard to the future government of the country. While attaching great importance to an early evacuation, Her Majesty's Government have no desire to force General Gordon's hand prematurely, and they propose, therefore, to extend his appointment for any reasonable period which may be necessary to enable him to carry out the objects of the mission with which he has been intrusted. You will communicate with General Gordon in the sense of this despatch."

Immediately afterwards (March 12), I received the following telegram from Lord Granville: "Her Majesty's Government desire to learn whether General Gordon's proposal as to his eventual successor refers to the whole of the Soudan, and, if not, to what districts of it. They would also be glad to receive information as to whether his proposed jurisdiction would embrace points from which Slave Trade or slave-hunting could be carried on."

I repeated Lord Granville's telegrams to General Gordon, instructing him at the same time to hold on to Khartoum until I could communicate further with the British Government. I also told him "on no account to proceed to the Bahr-el-Ghazal and Equatorial provinces."

I do not think that General Gordon ever received this message. Nevertheless, I regret that I sent it. I have already discussed this matter partially in dealing with the question of the prohibition placed on his action in respect to retiring southwards.[1] I may now add that, in view of the danger of telegraphic communication being interrupted, it would have been better for me, instead of telling General Gordon to hold on to Khartoum, to have taken upon myself the responsibility of directing him to retire at once to Berber, if he thought fit to do so. Also, it would have been better for me to have accepted the conclusion that the British Government were determined not to employ Zobeir Pasha. If it could have been announced, before the tribes between Berber and Khartoum rose, that Zobeir Pasha was to be installed as Governor-General of the Soudan with a force of black troops at his disposal to maintain order, it is possible that the Sheikh-el-Obeid and his followers would never have joined the Mahdi. But the favourable moment for influencing them in this direction had been allowed to pass by. At the time, however, I thought from the tone of Lord Granville's telegrams of the 11th and 12th of March that the employment of Zobeir Pasha was still an open question. I, therefore, repeated to him a summary of General Gordon's most recent telegrams. I also replied at length to the questions addressed to me, and at the same time I sent to him the following private telegram: "If you eventually decide to send Zobeir, please

[1] *Vide ante,* pp. 465-467.

keep it, if possible, secret, till I have dealt with him here. I am told that he will not go unless Gordon comes away, as, if Gordon came to any harm, he thinks he would be accused of causing it. The publicity, which Gordon gave to this matter, is most unfortunate. Newspaper correspondents are interviewing Zobeir, and some people here are urging him to make his own terms, as we cannot get on without him. All this will make him difficult to deal with."

Lord Granville replied immediately (March 13):

"I have received your telegram of the 13th instant on the subject of General Gordon's suggestions with regard to the appointment of Zobeir Pasha as Governor of Khartoum and the despatch of British troops to Berber. Her Majesty's Government are unable to accept these proposals. If General Gordon is of opinion that the prospect of his early departure diminishes the chance of his accomplishing his task, and that by staying at Khartoum himself for any length of time which he may judge necessary he would be able to establish a settled government at that place, he is at liberty to remain there. In the event of his being unable to carry out this suggestion, he should evacuate Khartoum and save that garrison by conducting it himself to Berber without delay.

"Her Majesty's Government trust that General Gordon will not resign his commission. He should act according to his judgment as to the best course to pursue with regard to the steam-vessels and stores."[1]

---

[1] On March 14, Lord Granville wrote to me privately: "We have had two Cabinets (at which Gladstone was not present); there was a difference of opinion as to the abstract advantages or disadvantages of Zobeir, but the unanimous opinion of the commoners in the Cabinet was that no Liberal or Conservative Government could appoint Zobeir. And the difficulty of sending troops to Berber is very great, and may entail unlimited difficulties upon us."

On March 14, I replied to Lord Granville's telegram of the 13th : "The instructions contained in your Lordship's telegram of the 13th are likely to lead to such very serious consequences that, even if the line were not still interrupted, I should hesitate to repeat them to General Gordon until I have again asked your Lordship whether the question has been fully considered in all its bearings.   When it is said that General Gordon may stay at Khartoum for any length of time which he may judge necessary to establish a settled government, is it meant that he may stay an indefinite time, and that he will be succeeded by some other Governor - General working, as before, under orders from Cairo ? This is a possible policy, but it is, of course, a reversal of abandonment.   It must lead either to the Egyptian Government endeavouring to govern the Soudan unaided (and this they cannot do, and should not be allowed to attempt), or it will lead to the appointment of a succession of English Governors-General, and probably of other English officials. This must ultimately involve the English Government becoming virtually responsible for the government of the Soudan.   I trust Her Majesty's Government will not for a moment think of adopting such a policy. If, on the other hand, it is merely intended to prolong General Gordon's period of office for a few months, then I can assure your Lordship that delay will not facilitate his task. On the contrary, the difficulty of establishing a settled government will, I believe, increase rather than diminish with time. The alternative, which General Gordon will probably adopt, of evacuating Khartoum at once and retiring on Berber, is open to very great objections, and will be most difficult to execute. It involves the certainty of sacrificing the garrisons of Sennar,

Bahr-el-Ghazal, and Gondokoro. The garrisons of Kassala and the neighbourhood may perhaps be brought down to Massowah, but it is at present impossible to speak with certainty on this point. I do not think that the retreat could be carried out without great personal risk to Gordon and Stewart. The ultimate effect will be that Khartoum must fall to the Mahdi, whose powers will be thus immensely increased, and the policy of creating a bulwark between Egypt and the Mahdi, which I cannot but think is the only wise course to follow, will have to be finally abandoned. I would beg your Lordship not to attach undue importance to some of the minor contradictions in General Gordon's telegrams. His main contentions appear to me to be perfectly clear and reasonable. They are, first, that the two questions of withdrawing the garrisons and of arranging for the future government of the country cannot be separated. Secondly, that it is most undesirable, even if it be possible, for him to withdraw without leaving some permanent man to take his place. I regret that no one but Zobeir can be found to succeed Gordon, and although I believe the opinions held in England as to the effect of Zobeir's appointment are based on an incorrect appreciation of the facts, I am nevertheless fully aware of the great difficulties which would have to be encountered in England, if the appointment is made. But the real question is, not whether the appointment of Zobeir is objectionable, but whether any other practical and less objectionable alternative can be suggested. I can suggest none. I trust your Lordship will not think that, after the repeated telegrams I have received, I am unduly pressing for the Zobeir solution. I should not again urge it, if I could see any other less objectionable way out of the present very difficult position.

On the other hand, I should not be doing my duty if I did not lay before Her Majesty's Government the grave dangers which will result from, and the objections which may be urged against the alternative set forth in your Lordship's telegram under reply."

Simultaneously with the despatch of this telegram, news arrived from Berber which left no further doubt that the Sheikh-el-Obeid had declared in favour of the Mahdi, and that the tribes between Berber and Shendy were in revolt.

On March 16, Lord Granville telegraphed to me : " I have received your telegram of the 14th instant, in which you discuss the question of the future government of the Soudan ; and after full consideration of the weighty arguments put forward therein, Her Majesty's Government adhere to the instructions contained in my telegram of the 13th. While the objections of Her Majesty's Government to Zobeir are unaltered, the prospect of good results attending his appointment seem to be diminished. The instructions to General Gordon to remain in the Soudan only apply to the period of time which is necessary for relieving the garrisons throughout the country, and for affording a prospect of a settled government. If General Gordon agrees with you that the difficulty of establishing a settled government will increase rather than diminish with time, there can be no advantage in his remaining, and he should, as soon as is practicable, take steps for the evacuation of Khartoum in accordance with the instructions contained in my telegram of the 13th instant. On evacuating Khartoum, he should exercise his discretion as to what is to be done with the steamers and stores there."

It was evidently useless to continue the correspondence. The British Government were determined not to send Zobeir Pasha, and, moreover, now that there was no longer any doubt that the tribes between Berber and Khartoum had joined the Mahdi, the favourable moment for sending him was passed.   On March 17, therefore, I sent a long telegram to General Gordon, informing him of the result of the correspondence which had taken place between Lord Granville and myself.   I added: "I think you must now regard the idea of sending Zobeir as finally abandoned, and that you must act as well as you can up to the instructions contained in Lord Granville's telegrams."   I do not think that General Gordon ever received this telegram.

On March 17, I wrote a despatch to Lord Granville in which I stated that I did not propose to continue the correspondence about the employment of Zobeir Pasha.   I added: "I regret the decision at which Her Majesty's Government has arrived, and I look forward with considerable apprehension to the results of the policy which it has now been decided to adopt.   But your Lordship may rely on my using my best endeavours to carry out the instructions which I have received."

On March 28, Lord Granville wrote to me a despatch stating at length the reasons which had induced the Government to reject the proposal that Zobeir Pasha should be employed.   The despatch alluded to the condemnatory terms which, on various occasions, General Gordon had employed in speaking of Zobeir Pasha.   It was pointed out, with perfect accuracy, that both Colonel Stewart and myself had, in the course of the correspondence, greatly modified our original opinions.   After giving a summary of the correspondence which had taken place, Lord Granville went on to say:

"If reliance could safely have been placed upon Zobeir to serve loyally with General Gordon, to act in a friendly manner towards Egypt, and to

abstain from encouraging the Slave Trade, the
course proposed was undoubtedly the best which
could have been taken under the circumstances ;
but upon this most vital point General Gordon's
assurances failed to convince Her Majesty's Government. They felt the strongest desire to comply
with his wishes, but they were bound, at the same
time, to exercise their own deliberate judgment
upon a proposal the adoption of which might
produce such serious consequences. They could
not satisfy themselves of the probability that the
establishment of Zobeir's authority would be a
security to Egypt ; on the contrary, his antecedents, and character and disposition, led them
to the conclusion that it would probably constitute
a serious danger to Egypt. There seemed to Her
Majesty's Government to be considerable risk that
Zobeir might join with the Mahdi, or if he fought
and destroyed him, that he would then turn against
Egypt. The existence of an outbreak of Musulman fanaticism was undoubted ; but the Mahdi
had not shown any personal qualifications which
threatened to convert it into a military power and
organisation. To have let loose in the Soudan a
Musulman of undoubted ability and ambition,
possessed of great military skill, and with a
grievance against the Egyptian Government,
appeared to Her Majesty's Government to be
so perilous a course that they were unable to
accept the responsibility of adopting it. They
were unable to share General Gordon's confidence
that Zobeir's blood feud with him involved no
serious danger, and they felt that the opinion
originally expressed by General Gordon, by the
Council at Cairo, and by yourself, was more likely
to be correct than the subsequent one. The
chivalrous character of General Gordon appeared
to be likely to lead him into the generous error

of trusting too much to the loyalty of a man whose interests and feelings were hostile to him.

"Besides these considerations affecting the interests of Egypt and the safety of General Gordon, Her Majesty's Government had further to consider how far it was probable that his authority might be exercised to renew the slave-hunting raids for which he was notorious. The temptation to embark in such lucrative transactions would be great to himself, and there would be the additional risk that having to rely on the support of his former friends and dependents, the slave-hunters, he would be obliged to purchase their support by connivance at their nefarious practices. Her Majesty's Government understand the reasons which compelled General Gordon to announce that the property in slaves in the Soudan would be recognised; but this is a very different thing from using the authority of Great Britain to establish a notorious slave-hunter as ruler over that country. General Gordon, indeed, proposed that the Bahr-el-Ghazal and Equatorial provinces should be excluded from Zobeir's rule, but England would have possessed no power to secure his adherence to such a stipulation.

"These were the considerations which led Her Majesty's Government to address to you the instructions of the 13th instant."

On April 14, I replied as follows to this despatch: "I trust your Lordship will permit me to say that, in my opinion, the despatch under reply contains a very fair statement of a question which I think was beset with more difficulties than any which, in the course of my experience, I have had to consider. If the arguments used in that despatch stood alone, they would, I think, be unanswerable; but the difficulty which I experienced in treating this question was to suggest some alternative which would be preferable to that which I recommended. If eventually any better solution is found, I shall be the first to admit that I was in error in proposing to send Zobeir Pasha to the Soudan."

Were the British Government right in their decision not to employ Zobeir Pasha? It is, of course, impossible to give more than a conjectural answer to this question. Reviewing the matter now, after a lapse of many years, I am still of opinion that Zobeir Pasha should have been employed.[1] I believe that if, when General Gordon sent his first telegram on the subject from Khartoum on February 18, the Government had stated that they had no insuperable objections to the employment of Zobeir Pasha, the course of events in the Soudan might possibly have been changed. When once General Gordon was supported by Colonel Stewart, I should have yielded to his pressure that Zobeir Pasha should have been despatched to Khartoum at once, to which I was at first reluctant to consent. He could have left Cairo before the end of February, or at all events very early in March. It is not improbable that the announcement of his departure would have prevented the tribes round Khartoum, who were then wavering, from joining the Mahdi. But the favourable moment was very fleeting. Regarded by the light of after events, it is evident that the discussion of this subject was prolonged for a fortnight longer than was necessary. Even if the Government had yielded when the correspondence

[1] There can be no question as to the extent of the influence which Zobeir Pasha then exercised in the Soudan, more especially over the tribes between Berber and Khartoum. When I visited the Soudan thirteen years later, I found that even the poorest classes, however ignorant of other matters, were well acquainted with Zobeir Pasha's name, and asked eagerly for news of his welfare. In the spring of 1900, he was allowed to return to the Soudan.

closed in the middle of March, no good would have
been done. The propitious moment had been
allowed to pass by.

Whilst, however, my personal opinion is that the
British Government made a mistake in not giving
General Gordon and myself a free hand in this
matter, the error was one which I do not think
that any impartial critic, even supposing he adopts
our views, will be disposed to condemn severely.
The objections which Lord Granville urged against
the employment of Zobeir Pasha were, in truth, very
forcible. Lord Northbrook, for whose calm judgment and independence of character I entertained
the highest respect, wrote to me two years later :
" I believe that to have sent Zobeir would have
been a gambler's cast, and that the probabilities
were in favour of his action against Gordon, and
of his raising a power in the Soudan, which would
have been a greater danger to Egypt than there
is now. I can say most positively that my own
conclusion, with every disposition to agree with
you, was very deliberately formed against Zobeir,
and I am still of the same opinion." Without
doubt, the risks involved in employing Zobeir Pasha
were considerable. My own opinion was, and still
is, that the advantages which might have accrued
from employing him were of a nature to counter-
balance those risks. Moreover, my main objection to the policy of the Government was that, as
so often occurred in Egyptian affairs, the British
Government confined themselves to criticism on
what was proposed without being able to suggest
any alternative and less objectionable plan. I repeat, however, that all this is conjectural. No one
can positively decide whether the British Government on the one hand, or General Gordon, Colonel
Stewart, and myself on the other hand, showed the
greater amount of foresight. All that can be said

is that disastrous circumstances ensued after the
refusal to employ Zobeir Pasha, but any one who
asserts that those circumstances were due to the
non-employment of Zobeir Pasha falls into the
post hoc ergo propter hoc fallacy.

One further point remains to be examined.
Were the British Government really averse to the
employment of Zobeir Pasha, or did they merely
act under the pressure of British public opinion?
I will endeavour to answer this question.

On March 21, that is to say, after the final
decision of the Government had been given, Lord
Granville wrote to me privately: "There was
much difference of opinion as to the abstract merits
of sending Zobeir, but there was really none as to
the vote of the House of Commons. Three of the
members of the Commons in the Cabinet who were
in favour of Zobeir,[1] were of opinion that, not only
would the House of Commons pass a censure, but
that they would do it so immediately as to stop
the possibility of his going. I should not have
minded the vote, if I had been sure the policy was
right, but I see nothing in its favour, excepting the
great authority of you, Gordon, and Nubar, and

---

[1] Mr. Morley (*Life of Gladstone*, vol. iii. p. 159) writes: "The
matter was considered at two meetings of the Cabinet, but the Prime
Minister was prevented by his physician from attending. A difference
of opinion showed itself upon the despatch of Zobeir; viewed as an
abstract question, three of the Commons members inclined to favour
it, but on the practical question, the Commons members were unanimous
that no Government from either side of the House could venture to
sanction Zobeir. Mr. Gladstone had become a strong convert to the
plan of sending Zobeir. . . . One of the Ministers went to see him in
his bed, and they conversed for two hours. The Minister, on his
return, reported with some ironic amusement that Mr. Gladstone
considered it very likely that they could not bring Parliament to
swallow Zobeir, but believed that he himself could. Whether his
confidence in this was right or wrong, he was unable to turn his
Cabinet. The Queen telegraphed her agreement with the Prime
Minister. But this made no difference. 'On Saturday 15,' Mr.
Gladstone notes, 'it seemed as if by my casting vote Zobeir was to be
sent to Gordon. But on Sunday —— and —— receded from their
ground, and I gave way.'"

two of you have supplied very strong arguments the other way."

This, without doubt, represented the real state of the case. Some members of the Government would have had the courage to face the storm of opposition if they had been convinced that it was wise to employ Zobeir Pasha. But they entertained an honest conviction that it was unwise to employ him. Others were inclined to accept the proposal of General Gordon and myself, but they would naturally hesitate to insist on the adoption of this view in a doubtful case against the adverse opinions of their colleagues. The opposition, which was certain to be encountered in Parliament and in the press, contributed to turn the scale. Whether that opposition was in reality so serious as it was represented to be is a point on which, having had no personal experience of parliamentary proceedings, I cannot express any valuable opinion. But I cannot help thinking that there is a good deal of truth in the following remarks of the *Pall Mall Gazette*: "The opposition, getting wind of Gordon's application for Zobeir, and displaying their usual anxiety to damage the Government, *coûte que coûte*, began to raise a hue and cry against Zobeir. Yet, it was pre-eminently a case in which a strong Government could and ought to have supported their agent. Public opinion, no doubt uninformed, and unaware of the arguments which were used by General Gordon and Sir Evelyn Baring, was outraged by the very suggestion of Zobeir's appointment. But, if the public had been placed in possession of the facts laid before the Government, the appointment of Zobeir would have been approved, nor would it have excited more serious opposition than the Slave-holding Proclamation."

To an outsider, indeed, the case did not seem hopeless from a parliamentary point of view. I do not say that the arguments in favour of employing Zobeir Pasha were by any means conclusive, but they were certainly strong. However high party spirit may run, there must surely always be a certain number of moderate men on both sides of the House of Commons, who would pause before, in a very serious matter of this sort with which they were imperfectly acquainted, they would deliberately reject the opinion of the best qualified authorities on the spot. From the point of view of an appeal to authority, the case was a strong one. General Gordon's name carried immense weight with the public. Both Colonel Stewart and myself were less known, and our opinions would have certainly carried far less weight with the general public than those of General Gordon. Nevertheless, we might possibly have exercised some influence over the views of those who may have felt, but were reluctant to express a certain want of confidence in General Gordon owing to the eccentricities to which allusion has been made in these pages. General Gordon's character and habits of thought differed widely from both Colonel Stewart's and mine, but, as it appears to me, the fact that these differences existed served rather to strengthen the case in so far as it depended on an appeal to authority.

Mr. Gladstone, speaking in the House of Commons on February 23, 1885, said: "It is well known, that if, when the recommendation to send Zobeir was made, we had complied with it, an address from this House to the Crown would, before forty-eight hours were over, have paralysed our action; and, although it is perfectly true that the decision arrived at was the judgment of the Cabinet, it was also no less the judgment of Parliament and of the people." Without doubt, there is much truth in this argument. But there was this notable difference between the Government on the one side, and Parliament and the people on the other side. The former were well informed of the facts and arguments; the latter were, in a great degree, ignorant of them. I believe that the final catastrophe at Khartoum might possibly have been averted if Zobeir Pasha had been employed. If I am right in this conjecture, the main responsibility must naturally devolve on Mr. Gladstone's Government. But it must in fairness be added that the responsibility must be shared by the British Parliament and by the people generally, notably by the Anti-Slavery Society. The Ministers who objected to the employment of Zobeir Pasha were perhaps in some degree wanting in imagination and elasticity of mind. They could not transport themselves in spirit from Westminster to Khartoum and Cairo. They do not appear to have shown the versatility necessary to deal with the rapidly shifting scenes in the drama which was being unfolded in the Soudan. The arguments which they applied against General Gordon and myself appear to me to be rather those of debaters trained in the art of dialectics than of statesmen whose reason and imagination enable them to grasp in an instant the true situation of affairs in a distant country widely differing from their own. Nevertheless, even supposing my appreciation of the facts to be correct, it must be admitted that in a matter of such difficulty an error of judgment is, to say the least, pardonable.

CHAPTER XXVI

THE PROPOSED DASH TO BERBER

MARCH 16–APRIL 21, 1884

Sir Gerald Graham proposes to move on Sinkat—Lord Granville approves—The proposed movement on Wadi Halfa—Proposal to send a British expedition to Berber—It is rejected—The order to move on Sinkat is cancelled—Remarks on this decision—Proposal to despatch a force to Wadi Halfa—General Gordon recommends the employment of a Turkish force—The Government reject the proposal—Necessity of preparing for a Relief Expedition.

THE decision not to employ Zobeir Pasha, coupled with the rising of the tribes between Khartoum and Berber, completely altered the aspect of affairs in the Soudan.

From that moment it became certain that, without external military aid, the Soudan must fall under the domination of the Mahdi. No such aid was available, yet without it any attempt to establish an anti-Mahdist Government at Khartoum was merely, to use Lord Northbrook's phrase, to follow a will-o'-the wisp.

This, however, did not constitute the only change in the situation. Communication with Khartoum was cut off. It became clear that the question of employing British troops might before long present itself for solution under different aspects from those which had heretofore existed. General Gordon and Colonel Stewart were surrounded by hostile tribes. It might become necessary to consider whether an expedition should be sent, not to re-establish order in the Soudan, or to relieve the beleaguered Egyptian garrisons, but to bring away the officers who had been sent by the British Government to Khartoum.

It was obviously desirable that the necessity for sending any expedition to Khartoum should be avoided. The best chance of avoiding it lay in opening up the road from Suakin to Berber at once, and thus facilitating General Gordon's retreat before the Mahdists could gather in force to oppose it. It was futile to rely any longer on diplomacy, on political concessions, or on individual influence to execute the aims of British policy in the Soudan. Diplomatists and politicians had had their say. Whether their efforts had been skilfully or unskilfully directed, was now immaterial. The political concessions made by General Gordon immediately after his arrival at Khartoum merely produced a temporary effect. His influence, although considerable on those with whom he was brought into personal contact, was manifestly confined to the walls of Khartoum. It had proved powerless to prevent the neighbouring tribes from throwing in their lot with the Mahdi. It was becoming daily more and more clear that it was only by the use of force that anything effective could be done to help General Gordon.

The course of events in the Eastern Soudan up to the middle of March 1884 has been already described.[1] Osman Digna's forces had been defeated by Sir Gerald Graham, first at El Teb on February 29, and again at Tamai on March 13. There was at one time some hope that, as a result of the latter victory, the road from Suakin to Berber would be opened without further military operations of a serious nature. It soon became apparent, however, that the effect of the victories at El Teb and

---

[1] *Vide* Chapter XXI.

Tamai had not been so great as was anticipated. The Mahdists were, indeed, discouraged, but they thought that the British troops could do no more, and that they would leave the country.

It would be necessary, therefore, to follow up the victories, at all events to the extent of making a demonstration towards Berber. On March 15, Sir Gerald Graham telegraphed to Lord Hartington that both Admiral Hewett and himself were of opinion that "an advance to Sinkat would now have a great effect, and ratify the late victories." A copy of this telegram was sent to me from Suakin. I decided to support Sir Gerald Graham's recommendation. On March 16, I telegraphed to Lord Granville: "With reference to Graham's message to the War Secretary recommending an advance on Sinkat, so far as I can judge of the situation from here, I should say it would be a wise measure. It will facilitate Chermside's negotiations with the tribes.[1] Chermside agrees in this view. It has now become of the utmost importance not only to open the Berber-Suakin route, but to come to terms with the tribes between Berber and Khartoum. If we fail in the latter point, the question will very likely arise of sending an expeditionary force to Khartoum to bring away Gordon. I do not think that he is in any immediate danger. He has provisions for six months."

On the following day (March 16), Lord Granville replied: "Graham's movement on Sinkat has been approved, but we cannot authorise the advance of any troops in the direction of Berber until we are informed of the military conditions, and are satisfied that it is necessary for Gordon's safety, and confined to that purpose. Our present

---

[1] Major (subsequently Sir Herbert) Chermside, R.E., was attached to Sir Gerald Graham's staff with the object of assisting in negotiations with the tribes.

information is that it would not be safe to send a small body of cavalry as proposed, and that it would be impossible to send a large force."

No further communication on this subject of any importance passed until March 21, on which day Lord Granville telegraphed to me that the British Government "would deprecate the despatch of an expedition against Osman Digna, with whom they would be disposed to recommend, if possible, treating on the basis of his submission, and rendering himself answerable for the safety of the Berber road and the protection of traders and other travellers." The details of the instructions to be given to Sir Gerald Graham were left to my discretion. I, therefore, telegraphed to the latter (March 21) the substance of the instructions received from Lord Granville, and added: "A wide discretion must be left to you, acting on the best local advice obtainable, as to the best method of dealing with the tribes. . . . You must judge whether it is necessary to send an expedition against Osman Digna, or whether it is possible to treat with him on the basis of submission and becoming answerable for the peace of the Berber road and the protection of traders and others."

I reported to Lord Granville the nature of the instructions which I had sent to Sir Gerald Graham, and added: "It appears to me undesirable to debar General Graham from attacking Osman Digna, if he thinks it necessary to do so in order to open up the road to Berber."

On March 22, Sir Gerald Graham replied to my telegram in the sense which I had anticipated. "It would be useless," he said, "to enter into communication with Osman Digna." I repeated this telegram to Lord Granville, and added that I was of opinion that Sir Gerald Graham "should be allowed to attack Osman Digna as he proposed."

On March 23, Lord Granville replied: "Her Majesty's Government are averse to further military operations being undertaken without any definite object; but if General Graham considers that the security of the Berber road will be thereby ensured, he is authorised to advance to Tamanib as proposed." I repeated this to Sir Gerald Graham, and in reply received the following message from Admiral Hewett: "In Graham's opinion and mine the security of the Berber road cannot be attained so long as Osman Digna remains in arms. The first object of the advance on Tamanib is, therefore, to disperse him. No further fighting is anticipated."

It will be seen from this correspondence that, whilst my opinion was veering round to the necessity of employing force to help General Gordon, the British Government, on the other hand, were daily becoming more reluctant to sanction the use of force. The truth was that, whereas the Government had but a few weeks before been sharply criticised for their delay in proceeding to the relief of Tokar, they were now being attacked for having caused the useless slaughter of a number of Dervishes. They were unwilling to yield to the pressure in the direction of vigorous action, which was now being applied from Cairo and Suakin. At the same time, they wished to do something to help General Gordon. On March 22, therefore, Lord Granville telegraphed to ask my opinion on the following points: first, whether it would be desirable to "despatch a portion of the Egyptian army to garrison Wadi Halfa in order to lend moral support to General Gordon at Khartoum"; secondly, whether some British officers "with some knowledge of Arabic and experience in dealing with natives" might not advantageously be sent to Berber, "there to await instructions from General Gordon."

I consulted Sir Frederick Stephenson, Sir
Evelyn Wood, and Colonel Watson on these.
proposals. Our joint opinion was that the despatch of a handful of fellaheen troops to Wadi
Halfa was a half measure which would be of
little use. I, therefore, telegraphed to Lord
Granville in this sense. There was more to be
said in favour of sending some officers to Berber,
but it was questionable whether they would be
able to get there. Major Kitchener and Major
Rundle were, however, directed to proceed to
Berber. By the time they got to Assouan, it
became clear that it would be imprudent to allow
them to proceed any farther. Their original
orders were, therefore, cancelled, and it was
fortunate that this was done, for, had they proceeded to Berber, they would certainly have been
made prisoners.

The more I thought over the whole matter, the
more did it seem to me, first, that it was essential
not only to open up the Suakin-Berber road, but
also to clear the road from Berber to Khartoum ;
and secondly, that this could not be accomplished
without the despatch of a British force to Berber.
I discussed with Sir Frederick Stephenson and
Sir Evelyn Wood the question of whether it
would be possible to send a British force from
Suakin to Berber. They were both of opinion
that the operation was possible, although it was
attended with risk, and although the health of the
troops would suffer from the climate. On March
24, therefore, I telegraphed to Lord Granville :
"It appears to me that, under present circumstances, General Gordon will not be able to carry
out your Lordship's instructions, although those
instructions involve the abandonment of the
Sennar garrison on the Blue Nile, and the
garrisons of Bahr-el-Ghazal and Gondokoro on

the White Nile. The question now is how to get General Gordon and Colonel Stewart away from Khartoum. In considering this question, it should be remembered that they will not willingly come back without bringing with them the garrison of Khartoum and the Government officials. I believe that the success gained by General Graham in the neighbourhood of Suakin will result in the opening of the road to Berber, but I should not think that any action he can take at or near Suakin would exert much influence over the tribes between Berber and Khartoum. Unless any unforeseen circumstance should occur to change the situation, only two solutions appear to be possible. The first is to trust General Gordon's being able to maintain himself at Khartoum till the autumn, when, by reason of the greater quantity of water, it would be less difficult to conduct operations on the Suakin-Berber road than it is at present. This he might perhaps be able to do, but it of course involves running a great risk. The only other plan is to send a portion of General Graham's army to Berber with instructions to open up communication with Khartoum. There would be very great difficulty in getting to Berber, but if the road were once open, it might be done by sending small detachments at a time. General Gordon is evidently expecting help from Suakin, and he has ordered messengers to be sent along the road from Berber to ascertain whether any English force is advancing. Under present circumstances, I think that an effort should be made to help General Gordon from Suakin, if it is at all a possible military operation. General Stephenson and Sir Evelyn Wood, whilst admitting the very great risk to the health of the troops, besides the extraordinary military risks, are of opinion that the undertaking is possible. They think that General Graham should be further consulted. We all consider that, however difficult the operations from Suakin may be, they are more practicable than any operations from Korosko and along the Nile. If anything is to be done, no time should be lost, as each week increases the difficulty as regards climate."

On March 25, Lord Granville replied : " Having regard to the dangers of the climate of the Soudan at this time of the year, as well as the extraordinary risk from a military point of view, Her Majesty's Government do not think it justifiable to send a British expedition to Berber, and they wish you to communicate this decision to General Gordon, in order that he may adopt measures in accordance therewith. Her Majesty's Government desire to leave full discretion to General Gordon to remain at Khartoum, if he thinks it necessary, or to retire by the southern or any other route which might be found available."

On the following day (March 26), I received a further telegram from Lord Granville, directing me to send the following instructions to Sir Gerald Graham : " The Government have no intention of sending British troops to Berber. The operations in which you are now engaged must be limited to the pacification of the district around Suakin, and restoring communication with Berber, if possible by other means and influence of friendly tribes. Reports of the effect of heat on the troops strengthen the desire of Government that your operations should be brought to a speedy conclusion, and preparations made for the immediate embarkation of the bulk of your force. Report when you can dispense with the services of regiments from India."

I confess that when I received these two telegrams I found it difficult to preserve the " diplo-

matic calm," which formed the subject of General
Gordon's sarcasms.[1] It was not so much that I
minded the decision that no expedition should be
sent to Berber, in so far as that decision was based
upon military grounds. The military question was
undoubtedly difficult of solution. There was
a difference of opinion amongst the military
authorities as to the practicability of opening the
road to Berber. It could, therefore, be no matter
for surprise that the Government should lean
preferentially to the side of those who deprecated
immediate action. The tone of the telegrams,
however, grated upon me. The question which I
had propounded to Lord Granville was how to
get General Gordon and Colonel Stewart away
from Khartoum. The march of events had been
rapid, and it was obvious that at this moment
the relief of General Gordon and Colonel Stewart
was the most important point at issue. On
March 25, I telegraphed to Lord Granville
that Hussein Pasha Khalifa, who commanded at
Berber, had reported that Khartoum was surrounded, and that the rebels were receiving
reinforcements. The only answer I got was that
the British Government left full discretion to
General Gordon either to remain where he was or
to retire by any route which might be found available. The Government, therefore, begged the
question. They did not appear to realise the
situation. They shut their eyes to the probability
that before long no route would be available by
which to retreat from Khartoum.

I, therefore, telegraphed to Lord Granville on
March 26: "I cannot say whether it will be
possible for me to communicate your Lordship's
message to Gordon, but in any case I cannot
reconcile myself to making the attempt to forward

[1] *Vide ante*, p. 477, note.

such a message without again addressing your
Lordship.   Let me earnestly beg Her Majesty's
Government to place themselves in the position of
Gordon and Stewart.   They have been sent on
a most difficult and dangerous mission by the
English Government.   Their proposal to send
Zobeir, which, if it had been acted on some weeks
ago, would certainly have entirely altered the
situation, was rejected.   The consequences which
they foresaw have ensued.   If they receive the
instructions contained in your Lordship's telegram
of the 25th, they cannot but understand them
as meaning that they and all with them are to be
abandoned and to receive no help from the British
Government.   Coetlogon, who is here, assures me
that so long as the rebels hold both banks of the
river above the sixth cataract, it will be quite
impossible for boats to pass.   He does not believe
that Gordon can cut his way through by land.   He
ridicules the idea of retreating with the garrison to
the Equator, and we may be sure that Gordon and
Stewart will not come away alone.   As a matter
of personal opinion, I do not believe in the
impossibility of helping Gordon, even during the
summer, if Indian troops are employed, and money
is not spared.   But if it be decided to make no
attempt to afford present help, then I would urge
that Gordon be told to try and maintain his
position during the summer, and that then, if he is
still beleaguered, an expedition will be sent as early
as possible in the autumn to relieve him.   This
would, at all events, give him some hope, and
the mere announcement of the intention of the
Government would go a long way to ensure his
safety by keeping loyal tribes who may be still
wavering.   No one can regret more than I do the
necessity of sending British or Indian troops to the
Soudan, but, having sent Gordon to Khartoum, it

appears to me that it is our bounden duty, both as a matter of humanity and policy, not to abandon him."

On March 28, Lord Granville replied: "We cannot accede to the proposals in your telegram. We have given it our most serious consideration, and, with the greatest wish to assist General Gordon, we do not see how we can alter our instructions of the 25th. Communicate them as soon as possible to General Gordon. We are not prepared to add to them until we hear what is General Gordon's actual condition and prospects as to security, and also, if possible, his plans of proceeding and his desires under present circumstances."[1]

It was evidently useless to continue the correspondence any further. I endeavoured to communicate to General Gordon the views of the British Government, as explained in Lord Granville's telegrams of the 25th and 28th of March, but I do not think that he ever received my message.

On March 27, Sir Gerald Graham telegraphed from Suakin: "I consider that my active operations are now completed and that I can at once dispense with the services of the regiments which came from India." On March 29, he was informed by the War Office that the Sinkat expedition was not to be undertaken, and that the British troops were to leave Suakin as soon as they were relieved by

---

[1] On March 29, Lord Granville wrote to me privately: "You shot a heavy cannon-ball, — your last protest as to our instructions to Gordon. Although your proposals were a complete reversal of our policy, we quite understood your feelings. We could not agree to pledge ourselves to a promise to Gordon to send a military expedition to Khartoum in the autumn. We hope that the victories of Graham may have corrected the bad effects of Baker's defeat. The military authorities assure us that, unless the garrison rebels against Gordon, the Arabs cannot take Khartoum. He is known to have six months' provisions. The only incident, as affecting the original views with which Gordon set out, and upon which we consented to send him, was the restriction upon Zobeir joining him, the objections to which were chiefly furnished by you and him."

Egyptian troops from Cairo. Shortly afterwards, the greater portion of the British garrison of Suakin was withdrawn.

Were the British Government right or wrong in refusing to send a portion of Sir Gerald Graham's force from Suakin to Berber? As in the case of the proposed employment of Zobeir Pasha, it is impossible to give more than a conjectural answer to this question. If it be admitted that the operation was practicable from a military point of view, there can scarcely be any doubt that the Government made a serious mistake. It appeared probable at the time that the decision not to send a small expeditionary force to Berber in the spring of 1884 would lead to the despatch of a larger force at a later period, and this, in fact, is what actually happened. The arguments based on the alleged necessity of obtaining "a better knowledge of General Gordon's actual position, his resources and his requirements," appeared to me at the time valueless, and I regard them in the same light on reading the correspondence over again after a lapse of many years. But it cannot on that account be stated positively that the decision of the Government was unwise. The question was wholly military. Was the operation practicable or not? On this point, the military authorities were not all of one mind. Sir Frederick Stephenson and Sir Evelyn Wood, whilst acknowledging the risks and the objections on the score of climate, thought that the operation should be undertaken. I believe that I am correct in stating that the military authorities at Suakin were less favourably disposed to undertaking the expedition than those at Cairo. I have always understood that it was not only the objections as regards the effect of the climate on the health of the British troops, but also the difficulties of providing transport sufficient even for a small force, which rendered them averse to the expedition. It is possible that they erred on the side of caution, but if they did so they can quote the high authority of Colonel Stewart to justify the advice which they gave. In the last letter which he wrote to me from Khartoum, dated March 11, Colonel Stewart said: "Notwithstanding our telegrams, I really fail to see how you can at this season of the year send an expedition from Suakin to Berber. The road is bad enough in the winter, but how any soldiers, but particularly English soldiers, could get along it in summer, I cannot conceive. I cannot picture to myself the English soldier getting over that awful plain between Obok and Berber. Also, from the time Ariab is left, there is no water. Of all animals in the world, I think the English soldier the least suited for the effort. Turks, Indians, etc., might do it, but it would be tough work." General Gordon also recognised the difficulty of employing British troops during the summer. The following entry occurs in his Journal, dated September 18, 1884: "One cannot help seeing that it is quite impossible to keep British troops after January. . . . I certainly will, with all my heart and soul, do my best, if any of Her Majesty's forces come up here, or to Berber, to send them down before January." My personal opinion at the time was that a very lightly equipped force of from 1000 to 1500 men might have been sent on camels from Suakin to Berber, and that, in spite of the risks and difficulties, the attempt should have been made. I remain of the same opinion still. On the other hand, it must be admitted that, in view of the conflicting nature of the military opinions laid before them, the Government had some fairly good grounds for rejecting the advice tendered by

Sir Frederick Stephenson, Sir Evelyn Wood, and myself. However this may be, it is certain that from the moment the proposal to make a dash to Berber with a small force was rejected as being impracticable, the despatch of a larger expedition at a later period became an almost unavoidable necessity. Some while was, however, yet to elapse before the Government fully realised the facts of the situation.

On April 8, Lord Granville telegraphed to me: "General Gordon has several times suggested a movement on Wadi Halfa which might support him by threatening an advance on Dongola; and under present circumstances at Berber, this might be found advantageous." I was instructed to consult Sir Frederick Stephenson and Sir Evelyn Wood with regard to this proposal. This matter had been already fully considered. On receipt of Lord Granville's telegram, however, a further consultation took place between Nubar Pasha, Sir Frederick Stephenson, Sir Evelyn Wood, and myself. General Stephenson thought the "step was open to great objections on account of the climate during the summer months, and he also considered it unwise to leave a detachment at so great a distance from its base." "On the whole," I telegraphed to Lord Granville on April 10, "we are disposed to think that the objections to undertaking the movement outweigh the benefits likely to accrue from it. Those benefits are of a very doubtful nature."

I am inclined to regret that I expressed an opinion adverse to this proposal, but my regret is solely based on the feeling that, situated as General Gordon then was, any suggestion emanating from him, especially if he reiterated it, should have been acted on if it was possible of execution. I did not believe at the time, and I do not believe now, that the despatch of a small body of men to Korosko or Wadi Halfa would have affected the position of General Gordon at Khartoum. When, at a later period, a British force was at Dongola, and was preparing to march on Khartoum, General Gordon wrote (November 8, 1884): "It is curious what a very little effect all our immense preparations at Dongola, etcetera, have had on the course of events; one may say that they have not had up to the present time the least."

On April 9, I received about thirty telegrams, which had been delayed in transmission, from General Gordon. They brought news from Khartoum up to April 1. In one of them he said: "I wish I could convey to you my impressions of the truly trumpery nature of this revolt, which 500 determined men could put down. Be assured that, for the present, and for two months, we are as safe here as at Cairo. I break my head over our impotence, and the more so when I feel that, once the Soudan taken, you may expect such a crop of troubles in all Moslem states. The only worry I have is that you will dawdle away your time, and do nothing till too late. If you would only put your pride in your pocket and get by good pay 3000 Turkish infantry and 1000 Turkish cavalry, the affair, including the crushing of the Mahdi, would be accomplished in four months."

General Gordon attached great importance to this proposal. He constantly alluded to the subject in his Journal. "If," he said, "the Soudan is given back to Egypt, in a couple of years we would have another Mahdi; therefore, our choice lies between Zobeir and the Turks. Now, the time has gone by when Zobeir, almost alone, would suffice. . . . Therefore, give the country to the Turks. If I was Lord Wolseley, *I would make* Her Majesty's

Government send the Turks here. . . . The Turks
are the best solution, though most expensive.
They would keep the Soudan; give them two
millions." "The more I think of it, the more the
Turk solution appears Hobson's choice. . . . I get
out of all my troubles if the Turks come, for I shunt
them on the Turks, and so do you." The Soudan
"should be handed over to the Sultan with a subsidy." "The only possible solution is the Sultan,
let the subsidy be what it may." The reasons why
General Gordon made this proposal may be gathered
from his telegrams and his Journal.

In the first place, he thought any solution was
better than allowing the country to fall into the
hands of the Mahdi. "To give up countries," he
said, "which are to some extent civilised, which, if
properly governed, are quiet and orderly, to the
Turks or to Zobeir, and to allow the Slave Trade
to flourish again in tenfold intensity, is not a very
high *rôle*, but *quoi faire?* We have not the men
to govern these lands, we cannot afford the money;
consequently, I advise what I have said. . . . It
would be nobler to keep the Soudan, but is too
much to expect our taxpayers to agree to." His
whole energy, therefore, was devoted, not so much
to evacuating the Soudan as to "smashing up" the
Mahdi. In two undated telegrams, which were
received in Cairo on September 18 and 20, 1884,
respectively, he said: "It would be the best course
to negotiate with the Porte for the despatch of
Turkish troops. . . . It is impossible to leave
Khartoum without a regular government established by some Power. . . . Perhaps the British
Government will be displeased with the advice
which I have given. The people of the Soudan
are also displeased with me on account of my
fighting against them, and on account of their not
attaining their object in following the Mahdi. I

wish for negotiations with the Sublime Porte, so that the necessary assistance may be quickly sent here, so as to render it possible to extinguish the flame of this false Mahdi before it becomes difficult."

In the second place, General Gordon was greatly irritated with the Soudanese for continuing the revolt. On April 12, 1884, he telegraphed to me : "I wonder you do not give the Soudan to the Sultan with a subsidy of £150,000 a year. He would finish the rebellion in three months, including the Mahdi. After the way these people have rejected my terms, I would be inclined to let the Turkish harrow go over them. The Sultan would need only 3000 men."[1]

These extracts are sufficient to show that General Gordon underrated the serious nature of the revolt with which he had to deal ; it was by no means a "trumpery revolt which 500 men could put down." On the contrary, from the local point of view it was a revolt of the most serious description, for the suppression of which a far larger force than that indicated by General Gordon would have been required. On the other hand, he overrated the consequences, which would ensue in Egypt and elsewhere, if the Mahdist movement were crowned with local success. He spoke of the Mahdi receiving "lots of letters from Cairo, Stamboul, and India." "What," he asked, "is to prevent the Mahdi's adherents gaining Mecca, where there are not 2000 men? Once at Mecca, we may look out for squalls in Turkey, etcetera." He spoke of the necessity of eventually "smashing up" the Mahdi if "peace were to be retained in Egypt." If the Mahdi took Khartoum he felt sure that "a rising would occur in Egypt." We now know that these fears were exaggerated. The Mahdi obtained

---

[1] I did not receive this telegram till March 26, 1890.

supreme power in the Soudan, but the effect of the rebellion was entirely local. It did not cause any trouble in other Mohammedan countries. Even at that time, it was clear that, if the Mahdists attempted the invasion of Egypt, their onward march would be arrested when once they came in contact with British troops.[1]

The reply of the British Government to General Gordon's proposal was contained in a despatch addressed to Mr. Egerton by Lord Granville on May 1 : "The employment of Turkish troops in the Soudan," Lord Granville wrote, "would be contrary to the views advocated by General Gordon on former occasions. I need not remind you that in his Proclamations issued at Berber and Khartoum, he declared that he had averted the despatch of troops by the Sultan, and had come in person to prevent further bloodshed. Moreover, such a course would involve a reversal of the original policy of Her Majesty's Government, which was to detach the Soudan from Egypt, and restore to its inhabitants their former independence. . . . It is clear . . . that General Gordon's object in asking for these troops is to effect the withdrawal of the Soudan garrisons by military expeditions, and to bring about the collapse of the Mahdi. . . . With respect to General Gordon's request for Turkish troops with a view to offensive operations, General Gordon cannot too clearly understand that these operations cannot receive the sanction of Her Majesty's

---

[1] There can be no doubt that the alleged necessity of "smashing the Mahdi" on the ground that his success in the Soudan would be productive of serious results elsewhere, exercised a powerful influence over British public opinion throughout the whole of this period. Nevertheless, the best authorities on Eastern politics were at the time well aware that these fears were groundless, or at all events much exaggerated. Thus, on March 21, 1884, Sir Alfred Lyall wrote to Mr. Henry Reeve: "The Mahdi's fortunes do not interest India. The talk in some of the papers about the necessity of smashing him in order to avert the risk of some general Mohammedan uprising is futile and imaginative."—*Memoirs of Henry Reeve*, vol. ii. p. 329.

Government, and that they are beyond the scope of his mission."

So long as General Gordon confined himself to making proposals which could, even with a certain amount of straining, be made to harmonise with the general line of policy which he had been sent to carry out, a strong moral obligation rested upon the British Government to adopt his suggestions. The proposal to hand over the Soudan to the Sultan and to utilise Turkish troops in order to crush the revolt of the Mahdi was, however, opposed both to the spirit of his instructions, and to the views which he had himself persistently advocated up to that time. From whatever point of view the question be regarded, the Government were, therefore, fully justified in exercising their own discretion as to whether so complete a change of policy as that recommended by General Gordon was either possible or desirable. It cannot be doubted that the Government exercised a wise discretion in declining to follow General Gordon's advice in this particular connection. I doubt whether the execution of the policy recommended by General Gordon was possible. I have no doubt that, supposing it to have been possible, its execution was undesirable.

I base my doubts as to the possibility of the execution of the policy on the difficulties of negotiating with the Sultan on a matter of this sort, difficulties which were exemplified when there was a question of sending Turkish troops to suppress the Arábi revolt; on the special difficulty of moving the Porte to speedy and vigorous action, such as would have been required to ensure success in this particular instance; on the impecuniosity of the Ottoman Treasury; on the impossibility of throwing the charge of the expedition on the Egyptian Treasury; and on the gravity of the rebellion, the suppression of which would have required a far larger force than General Gordon estimated.

I base my opinion on the undesirability of adopting the policy recommended by General Gordon on the fact that the occupation of the Soudan by Turkish troops would assuredly have brought in its train a continuance, and not improbably an aggravation of the misgovernment which was the primary cause of the rebellion ; and on the further fact that a Turkish occupation would not have afforded any final settlement of the Soudan question. As a choice of evils, indeed, it was preferable in the interests of England, of Egypt, of the civilised world in general and of the people of the Soudan, that the Mahdi should obtain possession of the country rather than that it should be handed over to the Sultan. Dervish rule in the Soudan was, without doubt, an evil, but even at that time it could be foreseen that the evil would in all probability only be temporary. A Turkish occupation would have been an evil of a more permanent nature. It was almost irreconcilable with the idea of future Egyptian reconquest. It would have caused endless political and financial complications. It is well, therefore, that the British Government declined to follow General Gordon's suggestions in this connection.

In the meanwhile, the situation at Khartoum was daily becoming more critical. On March 29, I received a telegram from General Gordon, dated the 17th, giving an account of an action which had been fought in the neighbourhood of Khartoum on the 16th, and in which, owing apparently to the treachery of two Pashas, who were subsequently executed, the Egyptian troops suffered a severe defeat. Shortly afterwards, a panic occurred at Berber. Every one who could get away left the place. Hussein Pasha Khalifa, who was in command at Berber, telegraphed: "The Government having abandoned us, we can only trust in God."

General Gordon had not received all the telegrams which had been sent to him from Cairo. But he was aware that the Government had negatived his proposal to employ Zobeir Pasha, and that there was no intention of sending a relief expedition from Suakin to Berber. He was greatly irritated at the rejection of these proposals. On April 7, he sent me a telegram which, Mr. Egmont Hake observes, "at once became historical." It was as follows: "As far as I can understand, the situation is this: you state your intention of not sending any relief up here or to Berber, and you refuse me Zobeir. I consider myself free to act according to circumstances. I shall hold out here as long as I can, and if I can suppress the rebellion I shall do so. If I cannot, I shall retire to the Equator, and leave you the indelible disgrace of abandoning the garrisons of Sennar, Kassala, Berber, and Dongola, with the certainty that you will eventually be forced to smash up the Mahdi under great difficulties if you would retain peace in Egypt."

The strong expressions employed in this telegram were caught up by political partisans, who dwelt with rapturous emphasis on the "indelible disgrace" which the British Government was said to have incurred. For my own part, I cannot understand how any impartial person can consider that the British Government were responsible for the difficulties which at that time beset the garrisons of Sennar, Kassala, Berber, and Dongola. Those who dwelt on the disgrace which would be incurred if the garrisons of those places fell into the hands of the Mahdi, should have had the courage of their opinions. They should have urged the only possible remedy for preventing the consummation which they deplored. That remedy was the despatch of a strong British expedition, or perhaps I should rather say, several expeditions, to the relief of the garrisons. For the most part, however, the critics shrank from adopting the logical consequences of their own criticisms.

Although the British Government were under no moral obligation to relieve the Egyptian garrisons, they were under a strong obligation to prevent General Gordon and Colonel Stewart from falling into the hands of the Mahdi. It was becoming more and more probable every day that a military expedition would have to be sent to Khartoum to bring them away. I was so impressed with the necessity for timely preparation that, on April 14, I wrote the following despatch to Lord Granville: "I wish again to draw your Lordship's attention to General Gordon's position at Khartoum. In doing so, I wish particularly to state that I have no sort of wish to urge that an expedition should be sent to relieve General Gordon, unless, after very full consideration, it would appear that no other alternative can be adopted. No one can entertain stronger objections than I do to the despatch of a force to Khartoum, but, at the same time, Lord Hartington has declared in the House of Commons that Her Majesty's Government feel that 'they are greatly responsible for General Gordon's safety,' and, even if no such declaration had been made, the fact is in itself sufficiently obvious.

"I think it my duty, therefore, to lay before your Lordship the following remarks, more with a view to showing what the actual situation is, so far as can be ascertained, than with the object of making any very definite proposals in connection with it. That situation is one of such very great difficulty that I frankly confess that I hesitate to advise very positively on it.

"Your Lordship will observe that in one of General Gordon's most recent telegrams, which are enclosed in my despatch of the 9th instant, he says that for the next two months to come, that is to say, to the end of May, he is as safe at Khartoum as at Cairo.

"I am not quite sure whether this statement is to be read as signifying that General Gordon can hold out for two months and no more. I trust this is not his meaning, for it would, I conceive, be impossible for an expedition to reach Khartoum by the end of May.

"Former telegrams had led us to suppose that General Gordon had provisions for six months, and if the Mahdi makes any advance, it is not probable that he will do so before September or October. I have asked him to explain this point more fully, but the difficulty of communicating with Khartoum is very great, and in any case a considerable time must elapse before I can get an answer.

"In the meanwhile, as it appears to me, we are in this dilemma—as a last resource the Government would, I conceive, be obliged to go to the help of General Gordon. All the authorities whom I have consulted say that, if any operations are to be undertaken along the valley of the Nile, which is by some considered the best route, no time should be lost in making preparations, so as to be ready to move directly the water rises. It may be, and I hope it will be, that General Gordon will be able to extricate himself without any expedition. In that case, the preparations will have been useless. On the other hand, unless they are undertaken now, it may be that, when the necessity for moving arises, so long a delay will ensue as to frustrate the objects of the expedition. Under these circumstances, I venture

to think that it is a question worthy of consideration whether the naval and military authorities
should not take some preliminary steps in the
way of preparing boats, etc., so as to be able to
move should the necessity arise.   It would be
better, I think, to run the risk of incurring some
unnecessary expenditure rather than to find ourselves unable to seize the opportunity of moving
when the favourable moment arrives."

1 left Cairo for England on April 21 to attend
the Conference, which was about to sit in London
to consider the financial situation of the Egyptian
Treasury.   Mr. (afterwards Sir Edwin) Egerton
was appointed to act as Agent and Consul-General
during my absence.

CHAPTER XXVII

THE RELIEF EXPEDITION

APRIL 21–OCTOBER 5, 1884

General Gordon's motives—Spirit in which the question should be approached—Did General Gordon try to carry out the policy of the Government?—The situation at Berber—Messages to General Gordon and his replies—Sir Frederick Stephenson instructed to report on the Relief Expedition—The Suakin-Berber Railway—The fall of Berber—The vote of credit—Lord Wolseley appointed to command the Nile expedition—He arrives at Wadi Halfa—Remarks on the above narrative.

BEFORE proceeding further with the narrative, it will be as well—even at the risk of repeating some remarks which have been already made—to describe the motives which, so far as can be judged, actuated General Gordon's conduct at this time. Did he make any serious effort to carry out the policy of the British and Egyptian Governments in the Soudan? Was that policy practicable? More especially, would it have been possible for him to have retreated from Khartoum without the aid of a relief expedition?

A few preliminary observations are necessary before entering upon an examination of these questions.

In the first place, it is obvious that General Gordon's conduct should be judged with the utmost generosity. I do not consider that this generosity need, or, in the interests of historical truth, should go so far as to exonerate him from blame if, on a careful examination of the evidence, it be found that blame can fairly be imputed to him. But I do hold that, looking to the very difficult situation in which he was placed, to the fact that when he arrived at Khartoum many circumstances must have been brought to his knowledge of which he was ignorant in London and in Cairo, and to the further fact that neither he nor his gallant companion are now alive to answer criticisms or to afford explanations, it will only be just to his memory to place the most favourable construction on anything he either did or said, which may appear blameworthy.

Again, looking to General Gordon's impulsive character, and to his habit of recording any stray idea which flashed through his mind, undue importance should not be attached to any chance expressions which he may have let fall. I have endeavoured to form an idea both of his motives and of the opinions which he held during the siege of Khartoum, based, not so much on any one of his utterances, as on the general tenor of his Journal, letters, and telegrams.

The action of the British Government should also be judged in a somewhat similar spirit. It is neither possible nor desirable that detailed instructions should be given to an official engaged in a difficult work such as that undertaken by General Gordon. All that the Government could do was to lay down the general policy which they wished to pursue, leaving to their subordinate a wide discretion as to the manner of its execution. In judging both of the action of the Government and of the conduct of General Gordon, regard should be had to the spirit rather than to the text of his instructions.

Did, therefore, General Gordon make any serious effort to carry out the policy of the British and Egyptian Governments in the Soudan?

There can be little doubt that when General

Gordon left Cairo he agreed in that policy. Not only did he repeatedly express his agreement in explicit terms, not only did he practically write his own instructions both in London and in Cairo, but the policy, which he was sent to carry out, was in conformity with the opinions to which he had frequently given utterance ever since his first connection with the Soudan. He was never tired of dwelling on the iniquities of Egyptian, or, as he usually called it, Turkish rule in the Soudan. He acknowledged that the country was a "useless possession." He exhorted the British Government "to leave them (the people of the Soudan) as God had placed them."[1] In fact, General Gordon persistently advocated the policy of "The Soudan for the Soudanese." But General Gordon said of himself: "No man in the world is more changeable than I am."[2] There can, in fact, be no doubt that, when he arrived at Khartoum, a complete revulsion took place in his views about the Soudan. He had seen from the first the desirability of endeavouring to provide the country with some settled form of government, and he clung to this policy long after its execution had become wholly impracticable. His first intention was to hand the country over to the local Sultans, but it soon became apparent that there were no local Sultans available who could serve as instruments in the execution of this policy. Then he proposed to set up Zobeir Pasha, and, had his proposal been promptly adopted, it is at least conceivable that the attempt to form an anti-Mahdist government in the Soudan would have been successful. But the opportunity was allowed to slip by. For reasons already narrated, the proposal to utilise Zobeir Pasha's services was rejected. From that moment, it was evident

[1] *Memorandum of January 23, 1884.*
[2] *Gordon's Letters to His Sister,* p. x.

that the Soudan must fall into the hands
of the Mahdi. This General Gordon failed to
recognise, or perhaps it would be more correct
to say that the idea of admitting the Mahdi's
supremacy was so distasteful to him that he
would not recognise the inevitable conclusion,
which could alone be drawn from a consideration
of the facts of the situation. He clung to the idea
of erecting some anti-Mahdist government in the
Soudan when, to use Lord Northbrook's metaphor,
the project had become nothing more than an
ignis fatuus. In order to accomplish this end, he
was prepared to sacrifice his most cherished convictions. Over and over again he proposed that
the Soudan should be handed over to the Turkish
administration, against whose malpractices he had
before inveighed so vigorously. He was aware
that the result would be that the people of the
Soudan would be oppressed, but he thought that
Turkish oppression was preferable to a recognition
of the Mahdi. At the same time, with characteristic inconsistency, whilst he was pressing for the
country to be handed over to the Sultan, he
admitted that it was preferable to abandon it rather
than allow it to remain "under these wretched effete
Egyptian Pashas." Whatever may have been the
defects of the Egyptian Pashas, there is no reason
to suppose that Turkish Pashas would have been
in any way superior to them. In fact, as General
Gordon well knew, the Egyptian Pashas were at
that time nearly all Turks or Circassians.

The truth is that General Gordon was above all
things a soldier, and, moreover, a very bellicose
soldier.[1] His fighting instincts were too strong to
admit of his working heartily in the interests of

[1] Sir Samuel Baker, who knew General Gordon well, said to me, some
years after the fall of Khartoum: "When I heard that Gordon was
to go to the Soudan, I knew there would be a fight."

peace. The Arabs, he said, "must have one good defeat to wipe out Hicks's disasters and *my* defeats. . . . I do not care to wait to see the Mahdi walk in on your heels into Khartoum. One cannot think that . . . it is a satisfactory termination if, after extricating the garrisons and contenting ourselves with that, we let the Mahdi come down and boast of driving us out. It is a thousand pities to give up Khartoum to the Mahdi when there is a chance of keeping it under Zobeir.[1] So long as the Mahdi is alongside, no peace is possible."

In fact, General Gordon wished to "smash up" the Mahdi. This was the keynote of all his actions in the Soudan. "If," he wrote on November 7, "Zobeir had been sent to the Soudan, we would have beaten the Mahdi without any exterior help; it is sad, when the Mahdi is moribund, that we should by evacuation of Khartoum raise him again."

As to his instructions, he threw them to the winds.[2] Both the spirit and the text of his instructions were clear. "The main end to be pursued," he was told in the letter addressed to him on January 25, 1884, "is the evacuation of the Soudan." The policy of establishing some sort of settled government in the Soudan was approved, but this, though desirable, was considered a subsidiary point. It was specifically stated that it must "be fully understood that the Egyptian troops were not to be kept in the Soudan merely with a view to consolidate the power of the new rulers of the country." When it was decided not to employ Zobeir Pasha, General Gordon should

---

[1] This was written on September 24, 1884, that is to say, several months after the Zobeir policy had been rejected by the Government, and had, in fact, become quite impracticable.

[2] On May 28, 1880, General Gordon wrote to his sister : " Having the views I hold, I could never curb myself sufficiently to remain in Her Majesty's service. Not one in ten million can agree with my motives, and it is no use expecting to change their views."—*Letters, etc.*, p. 158.

have seen that all that remained for him to do was to concentrate his efforts on evacuation. He did nothing of the sort. He thought mainly of the subsidiary portion of his instructions and neglected the main issue.

But, it may be said, even if General Gordon had abandoned the idea of establishing an anti-Mahdist government in the Soudan, he would still have been unable to carry out his instructions, for the garrisons of the Soudan were scattered, and it was impossible to save all of them. General Gordon appears to have held that it was incumbent on him to save the whole of these garrisons. "I was named," he wrote, "for EVACUATION OF SOUDAN (against which I have nothing to say), *not to run away from Khartoum and leave the garrisons elsewhere to their fate.*" He reverts to this subject over and over again in his Journal.[1] He held that it was "a palpable dishonour" to abandon the garrisons, and that "every one in the Soudan, captive or hemmed in, ought to have the option and power of retreat." On November 19, he wrote: "I declare *positively* and *once for all that I will not leave the Soudan until every one who wants to go down is given the chance to do so*, unless a government is established which relieves me of the charge; therefore, if any emissary or letter comes up here ordering me to come down, I WILL NOT OBEY IT, BUT WILL STAY HERE AND FALL WITH THE TOWN AND RUN ALL RISKS."

All that can be said about arguments of this sort is that they bring to mind General Bosquet's famous remark on the Balaklava charge: "C'est magnifique, mais ce n'est pas la guerre."[2] We

---

[1] *Journal,* pp. 56, 72, 93, 112, 113, 125, 292, 298, 305, 307.
[2] This remark is frequently attributed to Marshal Canrobert. According to Kinglake (*Invasion of the Crimea,* vol. iv. p. 269), it was made by General Bosquet to Mr. Layard in the field and at the time of the charge.

may admire, and for my own part, I do very much
admire General Gordon's personal courage, his disinterestedness, and his chivalrous feeling in favour
of the beleaguered garrisons, but admiration of
these qualities is no sufficient plea against a condemnation of his conduct on the ground that it
was quixotic. In his last letter to his sister, dated
December 14, 1884, he wrote: "I am quite happy,
thank God, and, like Lawrence, I have tried to do
my duty."[1] The phrase, which must have occurred
to many a countryman of Sir Henry Lawrence
when placed in a position of difficulty or danger, has
become historical. The words, under the circumstances in which they were first used by Sir Henry
Lawrence and afterwards repeated by General
Gordon, are particularly touching. But, after all,
when the emotions are somewhat quelled, and
the highly dramatic incidents connected with the
situation are set aside, reason demands answers
to such questions as these: What was General
Gordon's duty? Did he in reality try to do his
duty?

I am not now dealing with General Gordon's
character, which was in many respects noble, or
with his military defence of Khartoum, which was
heroic, but with the political conduct of his mission,
and from this point of view I have no hesitation in
saying that General Gordon cannot be considered
to have tried to do his duty unless a very strained
and mistaken view be taken of what his duty was.
He appears to me to have set up for himself a certain
standard of duty without any deliberate thought of
the means by which his objects were to be accomplished, or of the consequences which would probably ensue to the British Government and the
British nation from attempting to accomplish
them. As a matter of public morality, I cannot

---

[1] *Letters, etc.*, p. 290.

think that General Gordon's process of reasoning is defensible. The duty of a public servant placed in his position was to sink his personal opinions, and to consider the wishes and true interests of the Government and the nation whom he was called upon to serve. General Gordon was not sent to Khartoum with orders that he was to secure the retreat of every man, woman, and child who wished to leave the Soudan. He was sent to do the best he could to carry out the evacuation. Much was left to his own discretion. It was felt, when he left Cairo, that it would be very difficult to help the outlying garrisons, particularly those in the Bahr - el - Ghazal and Equatorial provinces. In giving General Gordon his instructions, therefore, attention was more especially drawn to the garrison and civil population of Khartoum, which were numerically larger than those situated in any other locality, and with whom it was relatively easy to establish communications. It appears to me that General Gordon's principal duty was to do his best to accomplish his difficult mission and, at the same time, to avoid all the misery, bloodshed, and waste of money, which would certainly occur if it became necessary to send a British expedition to the Soudan. The British Government were not responsible for the position in which the Soudan garrisons were placed. They might, indeed, have been made prisoners, and that was the worst that could have happened. As Lord Granville, with great good sense, wrote to me on March 14: "If Gordon can save the garrisons of Khartoum, of Berber, and of Dongola, it will be in itself a great feat. Gordon ridiculed to us the idea of the garrisons being massacred, and proved to be right as regarded Tokar." The capture of the outlying garrisons by the Mahdi would certainly have been a much less evil than the despatch of a

British expedition to relieve Khartoum. It must also be remembered that the presence of a British force at Khartoum would not have assisted the distant garrisons in the Darfour, Bahr-el-Ghazal, and Equatorial provinces. General Gordon, I conceive, would hardly have proposed to send a British expedition to those remote regions.[1]

General Gordon, however, took a different, and, as I think, a mistaken view of his duty. He wrote on October 1 : "*I think* we are bound to extricate the garrisons whatever it costs." He was aware that these were not the views of the British Government, for he added: "*they (i.e.* the Government) *do not*," but although his military training had instilled into him a certain sense of discipline, which he could not altogether shake off, he had a singular habit, when he felt that he was acting insubordinately, of discovering a number of fallacious arguments—*mentis gratissimi errores*—to still the prickings of his official conscience. In this case, he appears to have thought that his personal responsibility was covered when he suggested that, as he objected to carry out the views of the British Government, Abdul Kader Pasha should be appointed in his place, but he added: "I own the proposition I make is in some degree a trap, for I feel confident that there will be no end of trouble even in placing Abdul Kader Pasha in my place and trying to evacuate."

The truth is that General Gordon was so eager to "smash the Mahdi," and so possessed with the idea that it was the bounden duty of the Government to extricate all the garrisons, that he tried to force the hand of the Government and to oblige them to send an expedition to the Soudan. His personal

---

[1] In one passage of his Journal, however, he speaks of the desirability of sending a British force to Kordofan (p. 86). He appears to have thought that it would not be necessary " to go fifty miles beyond Khartoum."

reputation for good faith towards the people of the Soudan was involved in the despatch of a British expedition.   So early as February 27, as has been already mentioned,[1] he issued a Proclamation, in which the following words occurred : " British troops are now on their way to Khartoum."   The intention in issuing this Proclamation was, without doubt, to produce a moral effect, for he was at the time perfectly well aware that there existed no intention of sending a British force to Khartoum. But the people of that town naturally took him at his word.   They believed for a time that British troops were really coming, and when they found that none arrived, they thought that the British Government had "deserted" them,[2] the fact being that the pledge to afford military assistance had been given by General Gordon on his own responsibility without consultation of any kind with either the British Government or their representative in Cairo.

That General Gordon felt that he was under an obligation to carry out the pledges, which he had so rashly given, cannot be doubted.   On October 6, he wrote : " The appearance of one British soldier or officer here settles the question of relief *vis-à-vis* the townspeople, for then they know that I have not told them lies"; and in an undated telegram, received on September 18, 1884, he said : " Through having so often promised the people of Khartoum that assistance would come, we are now as liars in their eyes."

Obviously, the best thing General Gordon could have done, after communication with Cairo was cut off, would have been to have retreated to Berber with the Khartoum garrison, and such of the civil population as wished to leave the place.   But he does not appear to have made any serious attempt to do so, because he thought that, if he retreated, there

[1] *Vide ante*, p. 490.   [2] *Journal*, p. 307.

would be less probability of the British Government sending an expedition for the relief of the outlying garrisons. On October 5, he made the following significant entry in his Journal: "It may be argued, Why not retreat on Berber? I would rather not do that, for I would wish to show in a positive way, that I had no part or lot in the abandoning of the garrisons," etc., etc. A later entry in his Journal, dated October 29, puts the case still more clearly: "I wanted to capture Berber, which was the proper military operation to undertake. . . . Perhaps if *we* had taken Berber, Her Majesty's Government would have said that no expedition was necessary for the *relief of the garrisons*; but it would not have been correct to reason thus, for, though Berber might have been taken, we could not have garrisoned it; and it would have been a barren victory, and not have done much towards the solution of the Soudan problem, or the withdrawal of the garrisons, while it might, on the other hand, have stopped the expedition for *their relief*."[1]

I think that this was a wrong view to take. Leaving on one side any question of official subordination, and leaving aside also the waste of money, which was subsequently involved, and for the expenditure of which General Gordon was certainly in some measure responsible, I consider that it was of greater importance to the British

---

[1] Another instance of the curious arguments by which General Gordon sought to justify to himself his own conduct may here be given. On September 19 he wrote: "I think I say truly, I have never asked for a British expedition. I asked for 200 men to be sent to Berber at a time when, Graham having beaten Osman Digna, one might have supposed there was no risk for those 200 men." General Gordon, as a soldier, must have known that the British Government would never have agreed to sending so small a force as 200 men to Berber. But, in truth, General Gordon's contention that he never asked for a British expedition cannot be maintained. Not only the specific words, but the whole tenor of his Journal shows that all his actions and opinions were of a nature to force the Government into sending an expedition.

nation to have been spared the loss of such valuable public servants as General Gordon himself, Sir
Herbert Stewart, General Earle, and the many other
gallant Englishmen who fell during the subsequent
campaign in the Soudan, than to have prevented
the outlying garrisons at Sennar and elsewhere from
being taken prisoner by the Mahdi.

For these reasons I do not think that it can be
held that General Gordon made any serious effort
to carry out the main ends of British and Egyptian
policy in the Soudan. He thought more of his
personal opinions than of the interests of the State.
He did not adapt his means to his ends. He knew,
or at all events he should have known, what were
the main and what the subsidiary objects of British
policy, and he deliberately ranked the second before
the first, because his personal predilections tended
in that direction. He was left a wide discretionary
power, and he used it in a manner opposed to the
spirit, if not to the actual text, of his instructions.
However much we may admire his personal hero-
ism, the facts narrated above are, in my opinion, a
conclusive proof that a more unfortunate choice
could scarcely have been made than that of General
Gordon to carry out the policy of evacuating the
Soudan. The execution of that policy should have
been in the hands of a man who could fight if necessary, but who would devote all his efforts to turning
his mission into one of peace rather than of war; he
should have been cool, self-controlled, clear-headed,
and consistent, deliberate in the formation of his
plans after a careful study of the facts with which
he had to deal, and steadfast in their execution
when once his mind was made up. He should
have had a sufficient knowledge of English public
life to have been able to form some fairly accurate
conjecture of the motives which were likely to
guide the British Government, even if no definite

expression of opinion had been conveyed to him. General Gordon possessed none of these qualities. He was extremely pugnacious. He was hot-headed, impulsive, and swayed by his emotions. It is a true saying that " he that would govern others, first should be the master of himself." One of the leading features of General Gordon's strange character was his total absence of self-control. He was liable to fits of ungovernable and often of most unreasonable passion. He formed rapid opinions without deliberation, and rarely held to one opinion for long. His Journal, in which his thoughts from day to day are recorded, is, even in the expurgated form in which it was published, a mass of inconsistencies. He knew nothing of English public life, or, generally, of the springs of action which move governing bodies. He appears to have been devoid of the talent, so valuable to a public servant in a distant country, of transporting himself in spirit elsewhere. His imagination, indeed, ran riot, but whenever he endeavoured to picture to himself what was passing in Cairo or London, he arrived at conclusions which were not only unworthy of himself, but grotesque, as, for instance, when he likened himself to Uriah the Hittite, and insinuated that the British Government hoped that he and his companions would be killed or taken prisoners by the Mahdi. In fact, except personal courage, great fertility in military resource, a lively though sometimes ill-directed repugnance to injustice, oppression, and meanness of every description, and a considerable power of acquiring influence over those, necessarily limited in numbers, with whom he was brought in personal contact, General Gordon does not appear to have possessed any of the qualities which would have fitted him to undertake the difficult task he had in hand.

I now turn to the other questions propounded

at the beginning of this chapter. Was the execution of the policy laid down by the British Government possible? More especially, would it have
been possible for General Gordon to have retreated
from Khartoum if no expedition had been sent to
his relief?

The answer to the first question depends on the
view taken as to the scope of British policy. If it
be held, with General Gordon, that the British
Government were under an obligation to withdraw
every one who wished to leave from the most
remote provinces of the Soudan, then there can
be no hesitation in saying that the policy was impossible of execution. But, for reasons which have
been already given, I do not think that the British
Government were under any such obligation.[1] If
the garrison and civil population of Khartoum
could have been saved, a great feat would, as Lord
Granville said, have been accomplished, and, considering the extreme difficulties of the situation,
General Gordon would have done all that could
reasonably have been expected of him.

It is difficult to give a positive answer to the
question of whether General Gordon could have
retreated from Khartoum, if no expedition had
been sent to his relief. On March 27, 1884,
Colonel Coetlogon, who was then at Cairo, wrote
to me: "The White Nile to Berber is very low,
and there are only two small steamers that can
make the passage; the river begins to rise about
the middle of May. I consider that a retreat of a
force by river is now impossible, even if unopposed,
on account of the lowness of the river."

---

[1] The views of the Khedive, when General Gordon started from
Cairo, were thus stated to Baron Malortie: "I have no doubt that
Gordon Pasha will do his best to sacrifice as few as possible ; and, should
he succeed, with God's help, in accomplishing the evacuation of Khartoum and the chief posts in the Eastern Soudan, he will be entitled to
the everlasting gratitude of my people."—*Too Late*, p. 4.

Would it, however, have been possible to have effected a retreat by land?

It is almost certain that after May 26, on which day Berber fell into the hands of the Dervishes, retreat by land was impossible. When General Gordon was asked his reasons for remaining at Khartoum, he wrote in his Journal: "The *reasons* are those horribly plucky Arabs," and there cannot be any doubt that at the time he wrote these words (September 19, 1884), the explanation was sufficient.

It is, however, not so certain whether, prior to May 26, the operation might not have been undertaken with a fair prospect of success. "I wanted," General Gordon wrote, on October 29, "to capture Berber, which was the proper military operation." "Had it not been," he wrote on September 19, "for the defeat of Mehemet Ali Pasha,[1] I should have got out at least two-thirds of those at Khartoum and Sennar." On the other hand, the passage already quoted from his Journal[2] shows that he did not care for the capture of Berber as it would "not have done much towards the solution of the Soudan problem or withdrawal of the garrisons, while it might, on the other hand, have stopped the expedition for *their relief.*"

It is impossible to draw any very definite conclusions from the evidence which is available on this subject. All that can be said is that the operation of retreat would have been one of very great difficulty, but it is not certain that it would have been altogether impossible if it had been undertaken before the middle of May. It is clear, however, that inasmuch as General Gordon considered, first, that he was bound to establish some settled government at Khartoum, and secondly,

[1] This was the defeat at El-Eilafun on the Blue Nile, which took place on September 14.—Wingate, *Mahdiism, etc.*, p. 157.

[2] *Vide ante*, p. 569.

that he was under an obligation to save the garrisons of Sennar, Bahr-el-Ghazal, and the Equatorial Province, he never contemplated the possibility of withdrawing from Khartoum and leaving the other garrisons to their fate.

To resume the narrative. It has been already mentioned that by the end of March 1884, all regular communication with Khartoum was cut off. Then followed four or five months of fatal indecision. It was not till August, or even September, that it was definitely decided to send a relief expedition. I will endeavour to summarise the correspondence which passed during that period.

On April 21, Lord Granville telegraphed to Mr. Egerton that "the danger to Berber appeared to be imminent." Mr. Egerton was, therefore, requested, after consultation with the authorities at Cairo, to report "whether there was any step, by negotiation or otherwise, which could be taken at once to relieve it." Mr. Egerton replied, on April 23, to the effect that there was no possibility of effecting anything by negotiation without the employment of force, that Nubar Pasha wished to send two Egyptian battalions at once to Berber, that Sir Frederick Stephenson and Sir Evelyn Wood objected to sending the Egyptian troops by themselves, but considered that it would be possible to send an Anglo-Egyptian force to Berber either over the Korosko desert, or *viâ* Wadi Halfa and Dongola, but that, at the most favourable computation, it would take not less than eight weeks to reach Berber by the Korosko route, or sixteen weeks *viâ* Dongola. "All," Mr. Egerton said, "that can be done for the immediate safety of Berber is to give the assurance that English material aid shall be rendered as soon as possible." Lord Granville replied that the British Government could not sanction the attempt to send a British force to Berber *viâ* Korosko, neither would they allow Egyptian troops to be sent alone. The Governor of Berber was to be informed that no immediate assistance could be given to him.

On the same day (April 23), Lord Granville telegraphed to Mr. Egerton: "Gordon should be at once informed, in cypher, by several messengers at some intervals between each, through Dongola as well as Berber, or in such other way as may on the spot be deemed most prompt and certain, that he should keep us informed, to the best of his ability, not only as to immediate, but as to any prospective danger at Khartoum; that, to be prepared for any such danger, he should advise us as to the force necessary in order to secure his removal, its amount, character, route for access to Khartoum, and time of operation; that we do not propose to supply him with Turkish or other force for the purpose of undertaking military expeditions, such being beyond the scope of the commission he holds, and at variance with the pacific policy which was the purpose of his mission to the Soudan; that if with this knowledge he continues at Khartoum, he should state to us the cause and intention with which he so continues. Add expressions both of respect and gratitude for his gallant and self-sacrificing conduct, and for the good he has achieved."

Various unsuccessful efforts were made to communicate this message to General Gordon. It was not till the third week of May that a messenger was found who, it was thought, would be able to get into Khartoum. It was then (May 17) decided to make the following additions to the message:[1]

---

[1] In the interval between April 23 and May 17, Nubar Pasha and Sir Evelyn Wood asked Mr. Egerton "to request Her Majesty's Government to give their opinion as to whether or not the Moudir

"As the original plan for the evacuation of the Soudan has been dropped, and as aggressive operations cannot be undertaken with the countenance of Her Majesty's Government, General Gordon is enjoined to consider and either to report upon, or if feasible, to adopt, at the first proper moment, measures for his own removal and for that of the Egyptians at Khartoum who have suffered for him or who have served him faithfully, including their wives and children, by whatever route he may consider best, having especial regard to his own safety and that of the other British subjects.

"With regard to the Egyptians above referred to, General Gordon is authorised to make free use of money rewards or promises at his discretion. For example, he is at liberty to assign to Egyptian soldiers at Khartoum sums for themselves and for persons brought with them per head, contingent on their safe arrival at Korosko, or whatever point he may consider a place of safety; or he may employ and pay the tribes in the neighbourhood to escort them. Her Majesty's Government presume that the Soudanese at Khartoum are not in danger. In the event of General Gordon having despatched any person or agent to other points, he is authorised to spend any money required for the purpose of recalling them or securing their safety."[1]

of Dongola should be told to make the best terms he could for his safety and that of the people with him." Mr Egerton, in telegraphing this request to Lord Granville, added : "I can only explain their asking a question, which has become one of pure humanity, by their belief that, if some promise be obtained from Her Majesty's Government to send an expedition later on to relieve General Gordon, the Governor of Dongola might be enabled to offer some resistance to the stream of rebellion." This was, in effect, the same proposal which I had made in my telegram of March 26 (*vide ante*, p. 543-545). On May 13, Lord Granville replied : "Her Majesty's Government can make no promise as to future action. The Moudir should be told to make the best terms he can."

[1] General Gordon received this telegram. Allusion to it is made on pp. 39 and 59 of his Journal.

It was not till July 20 that a message was received from General Gordon, dated June 22. It was evidently not in answer to Mr. Egerton's messages. It was addressed to the Moudir of Dongola, and merely stated that Khartoum and Sennar were still holding out, and that General Gordon wished to be informed of "the place where the expedition coming from Cairo is, and the numbers coming." In forwarding this letter, the Moudir of Dongola requested to be informed of the nature of the reply which should be sent. Lord Granville, to whom the matter was referred, replied to Mr. Egerton: "Her Majesty's Government desire, in the first place, that the messages sent to General Gordon on the 23rd April and the 17th May should be repeated to him, unless you are convinced that he has already received them ; and he should further be informed that these communications will show him the interest taken by Her Majesty's Government in his safety ; that Her Majesty's Government continue to be anxious to learn from himself his views and position, so that if danger has arisen, or is likely to arise in the manner they have described, they may be in a position to take measures accordingly."

On August 17, another glimpse was obtained of what was passing at Khartoum. On that day, Mr. Egerton informed Lord Granville that the Moudir of Dongola had received a letter from General Gordon, dated July 28. This letter stated that Khartoum and Sennar were safe, and asked for information as to "the route and the numbers of the expedition coming from Cairo." By that time, preparations were being made for the despatch of a relief expedition. On August 18, Mr. Egerton asked Lord Granville whether he might inform General Gordon of the nature of these preparations. In reply, Lord Granville telegraphed : " Inform

General Gordon of the preparations for his relief
in case of need; refer him to former messages,
with directions from Her Majesty's Government
to conform to them, and ask the causes of our not
having received any reply."

On August 28, a further letter was received
from General Gordon, dated July 13, in which he
said: "We are all well and can hold out for four
months." On August 30, Mr. Egerton instructed
Colonel Kitchener in the following sense: "Tell
Gordon steamers are being passed over the Second
Cataract, and that we wish to be informed exactly,
through Dongola, when he expects to be in
difficulties as to provisions and ammunition."

It was not till the 17th, 18th, and 20th of
September that several messages were received from
General Gordon *via* Dongola, apparently in answer
to the inquiries made by the British Government.[1]
A little later (September 28) some letters were
received from General Gordon, *via* Suakin, the
latest of which was dated July 31st. The gist of
General Gordon's answer to the Government inquiries was contained in the following words:
"You ask me to state cause and intention in
staying at Khartoum knowing Government means
to abandon Soudan, and in answer I say, I stay
at Khartoum because Arabs have shut us up and
will not let us out." In a telegram to the
Khedive, General Gordon complained that the
English telegrams did not state what were the
intentions of the Government, "and only ask for
information and waste time." He insisted again
on the necessity of sending Zobeir Pasha and on
entering into negotiations with the Porte, "so as
to render it possible to extinguish the flame of
this false Mahdi before it becomes difficult." He

[1] These telegrams are given at length in *Egypt*, No. 35 of 1884,
pp. 95-99.

expressed his intention of retaking Berber, burning the town, and returning to Khartoum. "Stewart Pasha," he said, "will proceed to Dongola. Then I will send to the Equator to withdraw the people who are there. After that, it will be impossible for Mohamed Ahmed to come here, and please God, he will meet his death by the hands of the Soudanese. . . . It will be impossible to leave Khartoum without a regular government established by some Power. I will look after the troops on the Equator, Bahr-el-Ghazal, and in Darfour, although it may cost me my life. Perhaps the British Government will be displeased with the advice which I have given. The people of the Soudan are also displeased with me on account of my fighting against them, and on account of their not attaining their object in following the Mahdi."

The nature of the military preparations, which were being made whilst the correspondence summarised above was going on, must now be described.

It has been already explained that, on April 14, I urged the British Government to prepare for a relief expedition.[1] A few days earlier (April 8), Lord Wolseley addressed a Memorandum to Lord Hartington in which he discussed the composition of the force which would be required, and the route which it would be advisable to take. In this Memorandum Lord Wolseley said: "Time is the most important element in this question. . . . I recommend immediate and active preparations for operations that may be forced upon us by and by."

In consequence of these recommendations, Sir Frederick Stephenson was instructed, on April 25, to report "on the best plan of operation for the relief of Gordon, if necessary." A long interval, however, elapsed before anything was done. It

[1] *Vide ante*, pp. 556-558.

was at first intended to despatch a force from Suakin to Berber, and, on June 14, Sir Frederick Stephenson was directed to take some preliminary steps to facilitate the construction of a railway from Suakin, should one eventually become necessary. But three weeks later (July 4), it was explained that the Government had no intention of undertaking any expedition "unless it should appear to be absolutely necessary for ensuring the safe withdrawal of General Gordon from Khartoum." The Government were still waiting for General Gordon's replies to the questions which had been addressed to him. So little was known of what was going on in the Soudan that, although reports had reached Egypt of the fall of Berber, which took place on May 26, all doubts as to their truth were not removed until a month later, that is to say, on June 27.

It was not till August 8 that, a vote of credit for £300,000 having been obtained from Parliament, Lord Hartington authorised Sir Frederick Stephenson to take certain preliminary measures with a view to moving troops south of Wadi Halfa. A good deal of difference of opinion existed amongst the military authorities as to whether it would be desirable to move by Suakin, or to adopt the Nile route. Lord Wolseley preferred the latter alternative, and his view was eventually adopted by the Government.

Whilst, however, authorising these preliminary measures, the Government only did so under the following reserve: "Her Majesty's Government are not at present convinced that it will be impossible for General Gordon, acting on the instructions which he has received, to secure the withdrawal from Khartoum, either by the employment of force or of pacific means, of the Egyptian garrisons, and of such of the inhabitants as may desire to leave.

" The time, however, which has elapsed since the receipt of authentic information of General Gordon's exact position, plans, and intentions, is so long, and the state of the surrounding country, as evidenced by the impossibility of communicating with him, is so disturbed, that Her Majesty's Government are of opinion that the time has arrived when some further measure for obtaining accurate information as to his position, and if necessary, for rendering him assistance, should be adopted."

On August 26, Lord Wolseley was appointed to command the expedition. He arrived in Cairo on September 10, with Lord Northbrook[1] and myself.   On September 17, Lord Hartington, whilst complying with a demand made by Lord Wolseley for reinforcements, said : " In arriving at this decision, Her Majesty's Government desire to remind you that no decision has yet been arrived at to send any portion of the force under your command beyond Dongola. . . . You are fully aware of the views of Her Majesty's Government on this subject, and know how averse they are to undertake any warlike expedition not called for by absolute necessity."

It was not till October 8, that is to say, more than five months after communication between Cairo and Khartoum had been interrupted, that I was authorised to issue to Lord Wolseley instructions, which had been drafted in consultation between him, Lord Northbrook, and myself. The principal passage in these instructions was as follows : " The primary object of the expedition up the valley of the Nile is to bring away General Gordon and Colonel Stewart from Khartoum. When that object has been secured, no further

1 Lord Northbrook, as will be hereafter explained (see Chapter XLV.), was at the time sent on a special mission to Egypt.

offensive operations of any kind are to be undertaken.

"Although you are not precluded from advancing as far as Khartoum, should you consider such a step essential to insure the safe retreat of General Gordon and Colonel Stewart, you should bear in mind that Her Majesty's Government is desirous to limit the sphere of your military operations as much as possible. They rely on you, therefore, not to advance any farther southwards than is absolutely necessary in order to attain the primary object of the expedition. You will endeavour to place yourself in communication with General Gordon and Colonel Stewart as soon as possible."

Before these instructions were issued, Lord Wolseley had left Cairo. On October 5, he arrived at Wadi Halfa, and the Nile Campaign may be said to have definitely begun.

I now propose to make some remarks on the events narrated above.

The summer months of 1884 constitute the most gloomy period of the British connection with Egypt. It would seem, indeed, as if some spiteful fairy had presided over the deliberations of the Gladstone Government when Egyptian affairs came under consideration. Mr. Gladstone said (February 23, 1885): "The difficulties of the case have passed entirely beyond the limits of such political and military difficulties as I have known in the course of an experience of half a century." Under these circumstances, it can be no matter for surprise that mistakes were made. Subsequent events have shown that the Government were sometimes right and sometimes wrong in their decisions. In my opinion, in so far as the broad lines of their general policy are concerned, they were more right than their critics. But when it came to a question of action, they appear, whether from accident or want of foresight, to have rarely done the right thing at the right moment.

Festinare nocet, nocet et cunctatio saepe,
Tempore quaeque suo qui facit, ille sapit.

The Government were, indeed, remarkably unsuccessful in avoiding the extremes of tardiness and precipitation. If the attack on the Alexandria forts had been delayed for a day or two, reinforcements would have arrived, and the town would not have been at the mercy of Arábi's rabble. If the expedition to Tokar had arrived a day or two sooner, the Egyptian garrison would have been relieved. There can scarcely be a doubt that if the decision to send an expedition to General Gordon's relief had been taken in April or May, instead of in August, the objects of the expedition would have been attained. The main responsibility for this delay rests on Mr. Gladstone. "I want," Sir Stafford Northcote said in the House of Commons on February 23, 1885, "to see the Government a little inconsistent and to realise facts." Mr. Gladstone was slow to recognise facts when they ran counter to his wishes. The natural result ensued. The facts asserted themselves.

When a vote of censure on the conduct of the Government was moved in the House of Commons, Mr. Gladstone acknowledged that errors of judgment might have been committed. "It is not for me," he said, "to arrogate to myself or my colleagues infallibility." But Mr. Gladstone laid claim to "honesty of purpose." Every one who is impartial will readily admit this claim. The only question which admits of discussion is whether the errors of judgment, which were assuredly committed, were excusable or the reverse.

A statesman in the responsible position which Mr. Gladstone then occupied, does well to pause before he calls upon a great nation to put forth its military strength. Can, however, the lengthened pause, which Mr. Gladstone made before he decided to send an expedition to Khartoum, be justified? I will endeavour to answer this question.

Mr. Gladstone's principal reply to his critics is contained in the following words, which he used in the House of Commons on February 23, 1885: "Our contention," he said, "was that we must be convinced that an expedition for the relief of General Gordon was necessary and practicable. We had no proof, as we believed, that General Gordon was in danger within the walls of Khartoum. We believed, and I think we had reason to believe from his own expressions, that it was in the power of General Gordon to remove himself and those immediately associated with him from Khartoum by going to the south. . . . General Gordon said himself, speaking of it as a thing distinctly within his power, that he would in certain contingencies withdraw to the Equator." I proceed to analyse these remarks.

No one will be disposed to contest the statement that, before the Government decided on sending an expedition, it was incumbent on them to be convinced that the adoption of this measure was both "necessary and practicable." It only remains to be considered whether the evidence in respect to both the necessity and the practicability was not sufficient to justify action being taken before the month of August.

The practicability argument may be readily disposed of. It was conclusively answered by Lord Hartington at a later period (February 27) of the debate in which Mr. Gladstone used the words quoted above. With characteristic honesty, Lord Hartington said: "Although the difficulties of a military decision were great, and although there was a difference of opinion among military authorities, I have no hesitation in saying that the justification or, if you will, the excuse of the Government has rested mainly on the fact, which we have never attempted to conceal, that the Government were not, until a comparatively recent period, convinced of the absolute necessity of sending a military expedition to Khartoum." This frank statement, coming from the Minister who was then responsible for the administration of the War Office, effectually disposes of the argument in justification of delay based on the doubtful practicability of the military enterprise.

I turn, therefore, to the question of necessity. "We had no proof," Mr. Gladstone said, "as we believed, that General Gordon was in danger within the walls of Khartoum." The gist of the Government case is contained in these words. The same idea was embodied in all the messages, which Mr. Egerton was instructed to send to General Gordon during the summer of 1884, and which I find it difficult, even after the lapse of many years, to read without indignation. Not only does reason condemn them, but their whole tone runs, without doubt unconsciously, counter to those feelings of generous sympathy, which the position of General Gordon and his companions was so well calculated to inspire. Before General Gordon left London, I had warned the Government that, if he were sent to Khartoum, he would "undertake a service of great difficulty and danger." General Gordon, it is true, had, *more suo*, been inconsistent in his utterances on this subject. He had, in the first place, greatly underrated the difficulties of his task. So late as February 20, 1884, he had spoken of

Khartoum being "as safe as Kensington Park."
But the last messages, which he sent before
telegraphic communication between Cairo and
Khartoum was interrupted, breathed a very
different spirit. He spoke, on March 8, of "the
storm which was likely to break," of the probability of his being "hemmed in," and he added,
with something of prophetic instinct, "I feel
a conviction that I shall be caught in Khartoum." Lord Wolseley, myself, and others had
dwelt on the dangers of General Gordon's
position, and even if no such warnings had been
given, the facts spoke for themselves. General
Gordon and Colonel Stewart were beleaguered
in a remote African town by hordes of warlike
savages, who were half mad with fanaticism
and elated at their recent successes. Yet Mr.
Gladstone wanted further proof that they were in
danger. If the proofs which already existed in the
early summer of 1884 were not sufficient, one is
tempted to ask what evidence would have carried
conviction to Mr. Gladstone's mind, and the only
possible answer is that Mr. Gladstone was well-
nigh determined not to believe a fact which was,
naturally enough, most distasteful to him.[1]
General Gordon, in a passage of his Journal,
which would be humorous if it were not pathetic,
has himself described what every one of common
sense must think of Mr. Gladstone's attitude during
this period. "It is," he wrote on September 23,
"as if a man on the bank, having seen his friend in
the river already bobbed down two or three times,

---

[1] There is a close analogy between Mr. Gladstone's attitude at this
time and that of Lord Aberdeen before the Crimean War. Both practised the art of self-deception. "Almost to the last," Mr. Kinglake
says (*Invasion of the Crimea*, vol. i. p. 397), "Lord Aberdeen misguided
himself. His loathing for war took such a shape that he could not and
would not believe in it; and when at last the spectre was close upon
him, he covered his eyes and refused to see."

hails: 'I say, old fellow, let us know when we are
to throw you the life-buoy; I know you have
bobbed down two or three times, but it is a pity
to throw you the life-buoy until you are really *in
extremis*, and I want to know *exactly*, for I am a
man brought up in a school of exactitude.'"

Mr. Gladstone said that General Gordon spoke of
withdrawing to the Equator "as a thing distinctly
in his power." It is true that in two telegrams of
March 9 and of April 7, General Gordon had spoken
of the possibility of retiring towards the Equatorial
Province, but I had informed Lord Granville, on
March 26, that Colonel Coetlogon, who spoke with
authority on this subject, ridiculed the idea, and
although Colonel Stewart had said at the beginning
of April: "I am inclined to think my retreat will
be safer by the Equator," the context clearly
showed that he only used these words because he
considered retreat *viâ* Berber so difficult, unless a
British expedition were sent to open the road, that
he preferred the desperate risk of a retreat in a
southerly direction. It was, in fact, only necessary
to look at a map, to glance at the accounts given
by General Gordon himself and by Sir Samuel
Baker of the physical difficulties to be overcome in
moving up the White Nile, and to remember that
both banks of that river for a long distance above
Khartoum were in the hands of the Dervishes, to
appreciate the fact that retreat in the direction of
Gondokoro was little better than a forlorn hope.

For these reasons, the arguments adduced by
Mr. Gladstone do not appear to afford any sufficient
justification for the long delay which ensued before
it was decided to send an expedition to Khartoum.

A different class of argument may, however, be
advanced in favour of the course adopted by the
Government at this time. It may be said that
General Gordon never attempted to carry out the

policy of the Government, that he was sent to evacuate the Soudan, that he turned his peaceful mission into an endeavour to "smash the Mahdi," and that he could have retreated from Khartoum, but that he never attempted to do so. Little was said about this aspect of the question at the time, for this line of argument necessarily involved reflections on General Gordon's conduct, which, under all the circumstances of the case, would have been considered ungenerous, and which, moreover, would have produced little effect, for the public were in no humour to listen to them. General Gordon, in Mr. Gladstone's words, was considered a "hero of heroes," and, at the time, a defence based on any faults he might have committed would, for all Parliamentary purposes, have been worse than none at all. At the same time, the order of ideas embodied in these arguments did to a certain extent find expression. Whilst Sir Stafford Northcote invited the House of Commons to assert the principle that it was incumbent on England to secure "a good and stable government for those portions of the Soudan which were necessary to the security of Egypt," Mr. John Morley, in a powerful speech, moved an amendment which was hostile alike to the Government and to the Opposition. He invited the House to express its regret that "the forces of the Crown were to be employed for the overthrow of the power of the Mahdi."[1] Moreover, although Mr. Gladstone's parliamentary position obliged him to oppose Mr. Morley's amendment, it is perhaps no very far-fetched conjecture to imagine that this amendment embodied an opinion, which did not differ widely from the views which Mr. Gladstone personally entertained. Mr. Gladstone had formerly spoken of the Soudanese as a "people

---

[1] Mr. Morley's amendment was rejected by 455 to 112 votes.

rightly struggling to be free." The phrase had become historical. It was indiscreet in the mouth of an English Prime Minister, but at one time it contained a certain element of truth.[1] Moreover, I often heard at the time that Mr. Gladstone reasoned somewhat after this fashion : "The Soudanese wish to get rid of the Egyptians. The Egyptians, under pressure from England, are prepared to leave the Soudan. It is inconceivable that, if the matter were properly explained to the Mahdi, he would not agree to facilitate the peaceful retreat of the Egyptian garrisons." To the logical European mind this position appears unassailable, but Mr. Gladstone never realised the fact that he was dealing with a race of savage fanatics to whom European processes of reasoning were wholly incomprehensible. The Mahdist movement was not only a revolt against misgovernment. It was also, in the eyes of its followers, a religious movement having for its object the forced conversion of the whole world to Mahdiism. There can be little doubt that it would have been practically impossible to treat with the Mahdi on the basis of a peaceful withdrawal of the Egyptian troops.

The line of argument to which allusion is made above, would appear more worthy of attention than that actually adopted by the Government. It has been already shown that General Gordon paid little heed to his instructions, that he was consumed with a desire to "smash the Mahdi," and that the view that he was constrained to withdraw every one who wished to leave from the most distant parts of the Soudan was, to say the least, quixotic. The conclusion to be drawn from these facts is that it was a mistake to send General

---

[1] I mean that the Mahdist revolt would never have taken place if the people of the Soudan had not wished to throw off the Egyptian yoke.

Gordon to the Soudan. But do they afford any justification for the delay in preparing and in despatching the relief expedition? I cannot think that they do so. Whatever errors of judgment General Gordon may have committed, the broad facts, as they existed in the early summer of 1884, were that he was sent to Khartoum by the British Government, who never denied their responsibility for his safety, that he was beleaguered, and that he was, therefore, unable to get away. It is just possible that he could have effected his retreat if, having abandoned the southern posts, he had moved northwards with the Khartoum garrison in April or early in May. As time went on and nothing was heard of him, it became more and more clear that he either could not or would not,—probably that he could not,—move. The most indulgent critic would scarcely extend beyond June 27 the date at which the Government should have decided on the question of whether a relief expedition should or should not be despatched. On that day, the news that Berber had been captured on May 26 by the Dervishes was finally confirmed. Yet it was not till six weeks later that the Government obtained from Parliament the funds necessary to prepare for an expedition.

I began the examination of this branch of the subject by asking whether the errors of judgment committed by Mr. Gladstone's Government in the summer of 1884 were excusable. The points, which have been previously discussed, such as the tacit permission given to the Hicks expedition, the despatch of General Gordon to Khartoum, the rejection of Zobeir Pasha's services, and the refusal to make a dash to Berber in March, are questions as to which it may be said, either that the fact of any error having been committed may be contested, or that any condemnatory conclusion must in some degree be based upon an after-knowledge of events, which was not obtainable when the decisive step had to be taken.   The same cannot be said of the point now under discussion.   The facts were at the time sufficiently clear to any one who wished to understand them, and the conclusions to be drawn from them were obvious.   Those conclusions were (1) that unless a military expedition was sent to Khartoum, General Gordon and his companions must sooner or later fall into the hands of the Mahdi; and (2) that prompt action was needed, all the more so because it was only during the short period while the Nile was high that rapidity of movement was possible.   If Mr. Gladstone had said that the expenditure of blood and money which would be involved in an expedition to Khartoum was incommensurate with the objects to be attained, the argument would, in my opinion at all events, have been unworthy of the leader of a great nation, and to none of Mr. Gladstone's arguments does a censure of this description in any degree apply. Moreover, the adoption of this attitude would have probably sealed the fate of the Ministry in forty-eight hours.   But such a statement would have had the merit of being comprehensible.   The argument that no expedition was necessary because General Gordon was not proved to be in danger was so totally at variance with facts, which were patent to all the world, as to be well-nigh incomprehensible.

On these grounds, I maintain that of all the mistakes committed at this period in connection with Egyptian and Soudanese affairs, the delay in sending an expedition to the relief of Khartoum was the least excusable.[1]   The House of Commons

---

[1] Lord Northbrook wrote to me subsequently (January 13, 1886): "You gave us very distinct warnings in time that if Gordon was to be rescued an expedition would have to be sent, and no one regrets more

practically condemned the conduct of the Government. In a full House, the Government only escaped censure by a majority of 14. " If," General Gordon wrote on November 8, " it is right to send up an expedition now, why was it not right to send it up before ? " The fact that General Gordon's pathetic question admits of no satisfactory answer must for ever stand as a blot on Mr. Gladstone's political escutcheon.

than I do that the preparations were delayed from May to August." I may add that, some ten years later, I sent to Lord Northbrook a type-written copy of the portion of this work which deals with the Soudan. He wrote the following words on the margin opposite the passage to which this note is attached : "I am afraid that all this is quite true. . . . As I had the misfortune to be a member of Mr. Gladstone's Government, I have to bear the blame with the rest. But I resolved never to serve under him again ! "

APPENDIX

*Note on the Khedive's telegram to General Gordon of
September 14, 1884.*

The following entry occurs in General Gordon's Journal
(vol. ii. p. 359), dated November 25, 1884: "Tewfik, by a
telegram, cancels his Firman, which gives up the Soudan,
which I have *torn up*.

"A telegram to the Ulemas from Tewfik says: '*Baring
is coming up with Lord Wolseley.*'"

It appears from the numerous discussions which have taken
place in connection with the Gordon mission that some
misapprehension exists with regard to the circumstances
under which the telegrams to which allusion is here made
were sent. I propose, therefore, to state what actually took
place.

On September 14, 1884, the Khedive sent a telegram to
General Gordon. The full text of this telegram is given in a
note to an article written by Sir Reginald Wingate, and published in the *United Service Magazine* of July 1892. For my
present purposes the following extracts will suffice: "We
inform you now that a great change has taken place since
the time that the aforenamed (*i.e.* the British) Government advised the evacuation of the Soudan, and communication with you had been cut. . . . But the English
troops will shortly occupy Dongola, and Colonel Chermside,
the Governor of Suakin, has been ordered to communicate
with the tribes regarding Kassala; also Major Kitchener, one
of the officers of my new army, is ordered to confer at
Dongola, and we hope he will shortly be able to open communication with you. Again, it becomes necessary, under
these circumstances, to modify the Firman which we had
granted you, so that your authority will now be confined to
being Governor of the Soudan, including Khartoum, Sennar,
Berber, and their present vicinities. . . . You will also
receive the necessary instructions from the British Government, through Sir E. Baring and Lord Wolseley, who has
been made Commander-in-Chief of the English expedition,
and who is at present in Cairo."

At the same time, a telegram was sent to the Ulema of
Khartoum, urging them to do their utmost to maintain the
honour of the Government.

2 Q

So far as I am aware, no British authority was consulted before these telegrams were sent. I certainly never saw them until long after General Gordon's death. Inasmuch, however, as General Gordon could not know that the Khedive had sent the telegrams solely on his own authority, this point is of slight importance.

On receipt of the Khedive's message, General Gordon appears to have published the Proclamation given in Appendix Y to his Journal (vol. ii. p. 552). This Proclamation contains the following passage: "Formerly the Government had decided to transport the Egyptians down to Cairo and abandon the Soudan; and, in fact, some of them had been sent down during the time of Hussein Pasha Yusri, as you yourself saw. On our arrival at Khartoum, on account of pity for you, and in order not to let your country be destroyed, we communicated with the Khedive of Egypt, our Effendi, concerning the importance and inexpediency of abandoning it. Whereupon, the orders for abandoning the Soudan were cancelled."

From a perusal of these documents, it is easy to judge of what took place. On February 27, 1884, that is to say, nine days after his arrival at Khartoum, General Gordon had practically announced to the public the abandonment of the policy which he was sent to carry out. In a Proclamation issued on that day he said: "British troops are now on their way to Khartoum."[1] He had many misgivings as to the correctness of this proceeding. The Khedive's telegram of September 14, 1884, is worded in such a manner as to render it possible to misapprehend its meaning. General Gordon, therefore, readily seized the opportunity to put himself, as he thought, in the right.

A mere comparison of the dates of General Gordon's original Proclamation and of the Khedive's telegrams is sufficient to show that, as evidence as to how far General Gordon endeavoured to carry out his instructions on his arrival at Khartoum, the entry in the Journal on November 25, 1884, is valueless.

[1] *Vide ante,* p. 490.

CPSIA information can be obtained
at www.ICGtesting.com
Printed in the USA
LVHW010237230723
753131LV00005B/418